CARE STANDARDS –
A PRACTICAL GUIDE

CARE STANDARDS – A PRACTICAL GUIDE

Paul Ridout
General Editor

JORDANS
2003

Published by
Jordan Publishing Limited
21 St Thomas Street, Bristol BS1 6JS

© Jordan Publishing Limited 2003

British Library Cataloguing-in-Publication Data
A catalogue record for this book is available from the British Library

ISBN 0 85308 823 3

Typeset by Mendip Communications Ltd, Frome, Somerset
Printed by Henry Ling Limited, The Dorset Press, Dorchester, DT1 1HD, UK

FOREWORD

This book has three aims, all of which it succeeds in achieving. First, it provides a detailed commentary on the current state of the various regulatory requirements. Secondly, there are references to the many other areas of law that impact on the operation of registered care establishments and other agencies. Thirdly, explanations and examples are given of the operation of the regulatory scheme in practice. This book is designed for all those concerned with the operation of the Care Standards Act 2000 and the National Minimum Standards introduced by virtue of s 23 of that Act.

Regulation is a matter of considerable debate. No one would deny that national standards are required to ensure protection to those most vulnerable. The extent of regulation, however, has been in the past and will continue to be the focus for political debate and legal argument. The Care Standards Tribunal, as well as the courts, may well have to grapple with the sometimes conflicting policy objectives of protection and empowerment. In addition to these difficult policy issues, the Tribunal and the courts will also have to provide guidance on the meaning of key concepts such as 'fitness', 'personal care' and indeed what is a care establishment.

This book will be of immense value to those who read it. This developing area of law, perhaps more than most, requires both a detailed knowledge and appreciation of the law and a sensitivity towards its application. Those vulnerable within our community deserve nothing less.

His Honour Judge David Pearl
President
Care Standards Tribunal
June 2003

ABOUT DLA AND PRICEWATERHOUSECOOPERS

DLA is an international law firm with offices within the UK in London, Birmingham, Bradford, Edinburgh, Glasgow, Leeds, Liverpool, Manchester and Sheffield.

The DLA Healthcare team provides strategic advice and representation to the providers of health and social care throughout the UK and overseas. There are 26 members of the team, spcialising in the health and social care sector, and providing support to the industry 24 hours a day, 7 days a week. The team represents all sectors of the industry, from the very large providers with over 100 homes and thousands of beds to the single home providers with, perhaps, a dozen beds or less; from care homes for the physically infirm to private hospitals for the mentally unwell, children's homes and special schools.

DLA

In the care home sector PricewaterhouseCoopers is a leading provider of financial and commercial due diligence services to private equity houses and others, and is a major source of strategic commissioning tools to local authorities. PwC also offers guidance on operational improvement and restructuring to care home operators and other stakeholders.

PricewaterhouseCoopers

CONTRIBUTORS

Paul Ridout
Dawn Leonard
Andrew Dawson
Caroline Stockwell
Hans Scheiwiller
Susan Fanning
Lynn Davies
Marja Lasek-Martin
Phillip Boyd, Barrister-at-law
Keith Lewin
Rachel Booth
Owen Claxton
Robert Birchall, Partner, PricewaterhouseCoopers

PREFACE

Five years have passed since I wrote the Preface to *Registered Homes* (Jordans, 1998). The Registered Homes Act 1984 has been updated and replaced by the larger and much more comprehensive Care Standards Act 2000. This change was first foreshadowed by the White Paper, *Modernising Social Services*, to which I made reference in that Preface. Under that Act, new regulations, the National Care Standards Commission (NCSC), and the Care Standards Inspectorate for Wales have been established. In England, the NCSC will probably shortly be replaced by the Commission for Social Care Inspection (CSCI) and the Commission for Healthcare Audit and Inspection (CHAI).

We have had 14 months of operational experience of the CSA 2000 and this, added to the shadow period before the new regulations went live, has given some feel for the new era of regulation in health and social care.

Now is the time to produce a first successor to *Registered Homes* and hence we have prepared *Care Standards*. This time I have been joined by colleagues in the Health and Social Care Team at DLA and this has made the task easier and the product, I believe, better. I am particularly pleased that we have been joined, once again, by Philip Boyd, a Barrister who specialises in Social Security and Housing Benefit laws, and by Rob Birchell a partner at PricewaterhouseCoopers who has contributed a fascinating chapter on the vexed and, as yet, unexplained topic of financial viability.

It is possible that when we next update this work, we shall have to move into loose-leaf form. There is clearly more than sufficient material to justify such a step.

This work attempts to build upon the formula established in *Registered Homes*. We aim to guide practitioners to appropriate thoughts on the application of this new and complex legislation. In many cases we will raise rather than solve issues. That is the nature of law, so much of which has yet to be tested in any forensic arena. I hope that we may point the way and help others through the legislative regulatory minefield.

Finally, a special thanks to David Pearl for his support as we came to the end of this task and particularly for his written foreword.

Paul Ridout
DLA
Noble Street EC2V 7EE
July 2003

CONTENTS

TABLE OF CASES

References are to paragraph numbers.

TABLE OF STATUTES

References are to paragraph numbers. References in bold are to where parts of a provision are set out.

TABLE OF STATUTORY INSTRUMENTS

References are to paragraph numbers. References in bold are to where parts of a provision are set out.

TABLE OF EU AND OTHER MATERIALS

TABLE OF ABBREVIATIONS

1983 Act	Mental Health Act 1983
2000 Act	Care Standards Act 2000
2001 Act	Health and Social Care Act 2001
ACOP	approved code of practice
CHAI	Commission for Healthcare Audit and Inspection
CRB	Criminal Records Bureau
CSIW	Care Standards Inspectorate for Wales
DDA 1995	Disability Discrimination Act 1995
EHO	environmental health officer
HELA	Health and Safety Executive/Local Authority Liaison Committee
HSC	Health and Safety Commission
HSE	Health and Safety Executive
HSWA 1974	Health and Safety at Work etc Act 1974
NCSC	National Care Standards Commission
Registration Regulations 2001	National Care Standards Commission Registration Regulations 2001
ROA 1974	Rehabilitation of Offenders Act 1974
Tribunal Regulations	Protection of Children and Vulnerable Adults and Care Standards Tribunal Regulations 2002
TUPE	Transfer of Undertakings (Protection of Employees) Regulations 1981

Chapter 1

CARE HOMES AND THEIR REGULATION

1.1 INTRODUCTION

Over the past 60 years, demographic and social changes have increased both the importance and pubic awareness of establishments, agencies and business undertakings which provide support and care for people from different groups and of different ages, who are unable to care for themselves. Such establishments have developed as units operated by three distinct groups:

(a) local authorities responsible for the administration of social services or the National Health Service (NHS);

(b) voluntary organisations; and

(c) private persons or companies, often those whose vocation or qualification provided an obvious link to 'care' and who, for reasons of personal choice, operate outside what might be loosely described as the 'State sector'. Increasingly, this group has been joined by private capital-funded organisations which are involved in care as a means of investment.

The vast majority of these establishments have aimed to provide care for people, usually of advanced years, but more recently those with a variety of disabilities whose dependency on others has increased. Until the early 1970s, older or disabled persons tended to be accommodated and receive care within the family unit. Only in rare cases was the support and care of others needed.

Over the last decade there has been a steady shrinkage in the numbers of care units provided by publicly operated services, and even the NHS has reduced its provision of continuing or community care. Greater sophistication in the expectations of modern life has led to a public expectation of more transparently high professional standards within care establishments and agencies. The steady growth of those who come to the business of care purely as a financial investment has led to concerns that the quality of care may be constrained by profit margin rather than service user need. The 'pot' has been stirred by increasing pressure on finances available to public purchasers of care. Naturally enhanced standards to meet the expectations of the twenty-first century are increasingly deliverable, but at a financial cost. The normal marketplace rules would ensure that customer expectations were supplied but matched by revenue generation, which was sufficient to fund proper standards and attract investors. The dominance (in some areas almost to the point of monopsony) of public sector purchases and their aggressive determination of fees without regard to the capacity of business to deliver acceptable service within such a fee has led to a dangerous course of collision where the ability to deliver to public expectation becomes increasingly unachievable, especially for those who expect to see suitable financial returns for the necessary investment.

It is against this background that the reforming care standards legislation of 2000 and 2001 has been introduced. Within this book we will address the relevant issues that concern those who provide, use and regulate care. The picture must always be viewed in the round, because the ability to meet appropriate standards will be circumscribed by the availability of resource and the need for establishments (managed by whomsoever) to generate revenue sufficient to justify their existence by recovery of day-to-day expenditure and providing for returns, profits or surpluses. This will allow for continued reinvestment in the business and valuable return in cash or kind to those investors. Whilst there will be a difference of emphasis, the concept of the requirement for investment and for the justification for investment applies broadly to all providers, whether they be private, voluntary or public sector.

1.2   DEVELOPMENTS TO THE *BEVERIDGE REPORT* AND BEYOND

Legislation from the latter part of the Elizabethan era, culminating in the Poor Relief Act 1601, established a system through which local taxes were raised to provide relief, support and care for those who were not able to work, and facilities to improve the opportunities of re-employment for those who were able to work.

Up until the early part of the twentieth century, legislation continued to impose a legal duty on family members to support and care for the elderly, sick and needy within the family. That duty was supported by a parallel duty on local authorities to provide similar facilities.

Following the *Beveridge Report on Social Insurance and Allied Services* in 1943,[1] the Government introduced revolutionary changes to social welfare and health care provision with the NHS legislation and the National Assistance Act 1948. A cornerstone of these legislative changes was the statutory recognition that every citizen was entitled to expect free health and social welfare care. As a corollary, the legislation recognised the responsibility upon the State and local government for that support and care in the community. The legislative requirement on family members to provide for the weak and sick within their family units was effectively abolished. It took several generations to see the full effect of the release of that obligation in society as a whole. The imperative to care within the family was transformed into a moral responsibility by reducing the scope of relatives legally liable to support to husbands, wives and parents of children (ie those aged 18 or under) (National Assistance Act 1948, s 42).

The establishment of a mixed economy of care by the introduction of free health and social care for those in need tilted the development of care establishments

---

1   Cmd 6404.

towards free public sector provision and away from the private sector until the mid-1990s.

A strong, family-based society, combined with support from 'free of charge' public residential care, meant an almost non-existent market for private care needs. There was, however, a small 'cottage industry' of providers catering for those who, for reasons of social prejudice or affluence, chose to purchase care, rather than rely upon the family or the State. In such circumstances, given the small numbers of units serving a small and relatively select market, there was little need for regulation of private residential care homes, although they were regulated to a limited extent by the National Assistance Act 1948. Generally, private residential care homes were seen as small businesses requiring legal support and no different from other businesses.

The growth in expectation of publicly funded care and the increasing relevance of public bodies to be primary providers of long-term health and social care introduced a significant change.

1.3   RECENT DEVELOPMENTS

Private residential care homes now provide the vast majority of units of care for the elderly, the chronically sick, and those unable to support themselves physically. These are operated not, as before, by individuals driven by personal professional experience or vocational inclination but, increasingly, by medium-sized and large professional organisations, well capitalised and operating for profit. Groups of such homes combine together to share management services, and larger groups seek working capital arrangements, not from traditional sources such as high-street banks, but by capital-raising exercises on the public stock exchanges, the use of venture capital organisations and merchant banks and, over the final 5–7 years of the twentieth century, by asset disposal to raise cash followed by leaseback to retain operational asset use.

The growth from fringe operation, through medium to substantial cottage industry, to what has become a major sector of business has been rapid. It has brought with it an increasing need for regulation and a need for the operators of such businesses to satisfy the increasingly complex requirements on the financial, marketing and quality control aspects of their business. Legal advisers must also consider how the operation of a care business relates to the law generally and how the development of the business must comply with the developing regulatory requirements which, under current rules, underpin every business, large or small.

1.3.1   Reasons for the change

There are three main reasons for this rapid change:

(a) the increase in the number of chronically sick, long-term disabled and dependent elderly, and the increase in the proportion of older persons generally to younger working members of the population, combined with public expectation for decency of service provision for such people;

(b) the actual as opposed to philosophical break-up of traditional family life and values;
(c) the changing nature of the NHS, increasingly seen to be a provider of the relief of acute health care needs as opposed to the needs of the chronically sick. There will be continuous debate as to whether or not the NHS should be expanded to meet all needs, including those of the chronically sick. The reality is one of insufficient public resources to meet all needs, and consequent rationing. Acute health care to meet the needs of the 'working age' population is seen by government as a priority. That priority and the cost of maintaining dedicated care of the long-term chronically sick, whether elderly, mentally ill or otherwise afflicted, have led to inadequate resourcing and, in turn, inadequate accommodation, with no increase in capital contribution from the public sector to replace the hospital and social care accommodation.

Many hoped that a ground-breaking decision of the Court of Appeal in *R v North and East Devon Health Authority ex parte Coughlan*[1] had settled once and for all that the obligations of the NHS to provide health care included nursing care, in the wider sense, which was clearly established as being not merely care by nurses to support medical staff in acute hospitals but nursing care as it arose in the community and including the provision of nursing care in nursing homes (as they were known until 31 March 2002). The expectation that the Court of Appeal judgment would result in significant added financial resource from the NHS to the long-term community care business and voluntary sector was misplaced. The obligation continued to be honoured more in breach than delivery. Under the publicity banner of honouring a long-term NHS commitment to pay for nursing care for all, the Government claimed to meet the legal requirement by the introduction of the concept of a division of nursing care (nursing care by a registered nurse) in the Health and Social Care Act 2001. This was implemented with effect from the autumn of 2001 by making available fixed price contributions to fixed bands of nursing care input to residents in residential and nursing homes. This aimed to fund the part of the care which could be identified as directly attributable to a health care need, ie a nursing care need as particularised in *Coughlan* (above). These provisions will be looked at in more detail in Chapter 2, on care home operation and contract, and particularly in Chapter 3, dealing with the classification of care homes. The purpose of the policy has not been to provide additional finance for the provision of community care, but to relieve private patients (and local authority funded patients from 2003), if they so choose, from liability to pay a proportion of their fees to care home providers.

The stifled debate over the *Coughlan* decision has now been rekindled by a series of decisions by the Health Service Commissioner[2] in February 2003 explaining the need for the NHS to take *Coughlan* fully into account in assessing need to support nursing care needs in care homes and elsewhere in the community.

1   (1999) 2 CCL Rep 285.
2   20 February 2003 at HC 399 (2002–2003) *www.ombudsman.org.uk/hse/document/care03/ care03_rep.htm*.

It became widely recognised that rising numbers of elderly people and increasing life expectancy were producing a financial time bomb which, irrespective of political view, could not possibly be managed (being non-cash limited in nature) by public resources. The private sector is not ideal for the provision of general health care cover for acute health care needs. The resources and establishments required to meet a wide variety of sudden life-threatening circumstances are not compatible with running a private business which needs to operate within financial budgets and to a business plan. However, this is less of a problem in the long-term care of the chronically sick, which may include those recovering from acute medical or surgical intervention.

Accordingly, the NHS has welcomed private sector entrepreneurs into areas in which they are well suited, such as care of the chronically sick and the elderly. It is against this background that the law of regulation of such private sector operations has developed.

In the period 2000–2, this encouragement to the NHS to make use of private sector provision has been intensified by a variety of government initiatives that have not involved legislative change. From its inception, the NHS legislation has always provided power for NHS bodies to purchase required services from private and voluntary sector providers. For many years, such arrangements were made as the exception rather than the rule and generally in the context of lack of availability of cost-effective services in certain regions, particularly remote areas. All this has changed. The so-called concordat between the NHS and the private sector (negotiated between the Department of Health and the Independent Health Care Association) presented a clear policy statement from government that it proposed to make greater use of its cash resources by purchasing available resources from the private sector. In the autumn of 2001, this was followed by a reinforcing policy of 'partnership in care', which announced an increase in the use to be made of the private sector by the NHS and earmarked specific funds to be used for the purpose. At the time of writing, the policy announcements have not been matched by equal enthusiasm from NHS bodies to embrace private sector provision, at least to the extent that some private sector providers anticipated. In the budget statement in 2002, the Chancellor of the Exchequer announced considerable additional funds for support of the NHS and, the following day, the Secretary of State for Health told Parliament that in relation to the NHS plan implementation, significant portions of these extra funds would be earmarked for the use of private sector resource. The political theme was that the NHS would provide or purchase the service it needed according to quality and best value, and was not concerned with the ideological basis of whether or not the service was provided by those employed or engaged by the State. On any proper analysis this can be seen as quite distinct from any attempt to privatise the provision of health care. The commitment is to the use of resourced purchase of privately and voluntarily sourced skills, expertise and facilities. This is designed, and will lead, to larger numbers of investors and providers coming into the marketplace. They will be attracted by renewed opportunities to provide excellence in services and to use this sector as a field for the generation of surplus and profit to meet their commercial objectives and the aspirations (in the private sector) of their investors.

It is no coincidence that this move towards encouraging expansion of public sector provision to meet publicly funded need comes simultaneously with a major overhaul of the regulatory requirements for registered or licensed operations of establishments and agencies within the care sector. Greater demand leads to larger numbers of providers and prospective providers, and a greater need objectively to monitor the quality of service being provided to ensure the achievement of value for money for public purchase and, most importantly, an even and consistent quality of service to those in need – now to be known as service users.

1.4   AIMS OF THE BOOK

This book aims to bring together:

(a) a detailed commentary on the current state of the various regulatory requirements on registered care establishments and agencies;
(b) appropriate cross-references to other areas of the law which impact on the operation of registered care establishments and agencies and interrelate with the regulatory requirements;
(c) explanations and examples on the operation of the regulatory framework in practice which show the problems that have arisen and the way in which they have been solved, and which may point the way towards resolving problems that arise in the future.

However, the book does not set out to be either a definitive statement of the law as it may apply to any one situation, or an exhaustive interpretation of the relevant statutory regulations. It is principally intended to be a practitioners' handbook, giving guidance on the provisions of the law which may apply to particular circumstances, and bringing together the diverse provisions so that they may be seen as a whole, highlighting how examples in practice have been applied to the somewhat dry legislative language, and helping to solve problems which extend statutory interpretation to the limit.

Within this book we have included the complete text of the principal regulations made under the Care Standards Act 2000 and the principal and most used national minimum standards for particular establishments or agencies. Naturally, the book will comment in detail on the legal structure and basis of the national minimum standards. Since these have only recently been introduced (having effect from 1 April 2002), there is virtually no practical experience of the operation of the standards or regulations in day-to-day practice. Therefore, no attempt will be made (otherwise than by a specific example from time to time) to analyse what may be the specific meaning of every paragraph of every standard. When faced with a problem within the operation of a care establishment or agency, the provider or advising practitioner will need to look carefully at the statutory basis combined with the regulation and the impact on the statutory regulation of the relevant national minimum standard, bearing in mind the statutory limitations of application of the national minimum standards, which will be explored later in this chapter and to which reference will be made throughout this book.

It is hoped that the context of the book will identify the meaning used for particular terms on particular occasions, and the authors have endeavoured to explain the context at the outset of particular passages so as to assist the reader better.

1.5 WHAT IS A CARE ESTABLISHMENT OR AGENCY?

The essential question of what precisely is a care establishment or agency has underpinned both the need for regulation and the need for this book. The question is complex because the types of unit which are subject to regulation as care establishments or agencies under the current legislation are many and varied, and require examination of the main problems confronting the care provider.

The Care Standards Act 2000 sets out detailed definitions of the various care establishments or agencies (collectively to be known as undertakings) which are subject to regulation under the provisions of this Act. Chapter 3 of this book will be devoted exclusively to an examination of the definition in the light of past experience, combined with some reasoned anticipation of difficulties that may arise.

However, an underlying principle, to which this book will return repeatedly, is that the need for regulation is prescribed by statute. The infinite variety of circumstances which may arise in practice will inevitably mean that there are situations where an establishment or agency may qualify for one or more types of registration, or maybe no registration at all. The concept that types of business or activity must be regulated because a regulator perceives that they should be has no place in understanding the law of regulation. Regulation starts and finishes with the proper interpretation of what Parliament, through statute, has prescribed as subject to regulation, and variations or elaborations can be made only by those to whom Parliament has expressly delegated the power to fill in the details.

1.6 WHAT IS THE PURPOSE OF REGULATION?

Regulation arises out of a perceived need to control the activities of persons in their dealings with others, so as to protect those others and to ensure that society as a whole is satisfied that those in need of such protection are protected and are seen to be protected.

Whether or not there should be regulation, as a philosophical question, is beyond the scope of this book. Whether or not there should be regulation, for the purposes of this book, is a matter determined by the law. Regulation is, by its nature, geared to current circumstances, and therefore cannot arise out of the common law but only from statute. It is, accordingly, the supreme law-making body (in the case of the UK, Parliament) which will determine whether and to what extent there should be regulation.

Once Parliament has so determined, it is the purpose of the regulator to ensure that standards within the regulated activity are maintained to an appropriate level or, in many cases, to the criteria which have been prescribed either by Parliament, or experts appointed by Parliament.

1.7   REGULATION, ESTABLISHMENTS AND AGENCIES

The existence of regulation means that society, expressing its view through Parliament, has determined that there should be a degree of interference with the way in which particular members of society carry on their business or lives. In the context of this book, this involves the operation of care establishments and agencies.

The operator of a care establishment or agency, ie the provider of care, will see the regulator as a potential intruder. Disputes will frequently involve arguments that the regulator is over-intrusive, or that there is no need for interference. Whilst understandable, such arguments have no place within a system of regulation. Any change can be achieved by democratic means with a view to political change and thus change of the law. There can never be an argument justifying resistance to the actions of regulators, acting within, and in accordance with, a law in force.

It is not, however, the business of the regulator to:

(a)   operate or manage the operation of the regulated business (ie the care home) or direct the owner as to such operation; or

(b)   give detailed advice to the owner as to how the regulated business should operate.

If an owner is in need of detailed input from the regulator, or is so incapable of operating the care home business as to require his intervention in the interest of those receiving care, it is suggested that the owner is not fit to continue to carry on such a business. It must be a prerequisite of carrying on a regulated business that the owner has sufficient resources, experience, know-how and ability to conduct that business.

The regulator should appreciate that there may be many different ways of achieving the goal of acceptable standards. Those standards will at some point be defined within the regulatory legislation, either in great detail or in general terms. The powers of the regulator will be similarly prescribed. Parliament, in fixing a scheme of regulation, will have attempted to strike an appropriate balance between the need to oversee areas of concern, ie care home operation, and the need to allow private sector entrepreneurs to operate as they see fit in order to run their business successfully and profitably.

It is essential that both the regulator and the provider understand and respect the fact, nature and quality of the legal framework. Regulators will exercise their power abusively and with excessive zeal. Providers will, by accident or design, break the rules in fact and/or in spirit. Disputes will be of great importance concerning, as they do, at their centre, the lives, reputations, valuable assets, significant businesses and, most importantly, the quality of life of some of the most vulnerable and disadvantaged in society. Everybody with a legitimate interest in this area will only derive comfort and security from a fair and sensible system of law which is operated openly and subject to impartial review. A system which is manipulated by regulators so as to lead providers to lack confidence in their ability to challenge where they feel challenge is justified is as dangerous as a system, elaborate and all-consuming in principle, which is so complex and difficult to enforce that it falls into disuse. With the complexity and draconian powers of regulation set out in the Care Standards Act 2000, and its associated regulations, there are significant risks that both or either of these scenarios may be seen from time to time.

An understanding of the law, and the need for all those concerned to work within the law rather than push at its boundaries, is essential if a fair system is to be respected and used properly.

It is for that reason that a detailed knowledge of the working practice of the law is essential for all those who are concerned in the operation of care establishments and agencies at any level.

1.7.1 Scheme for regulation

In the current scheme for regulation of care homes set out in the Care Standards Act 2000 (the 2000 Act) and subordinate legislation, standards have been adopted by reference to general description rather than specific prescription.[1] This reflects the practice under the Registered Homes Act 1984 (now repealed).

In broad terms, the standards required to be met by the law are standards of adequacy, ie sufficiency and suitability, and the regulatory scheme does not yet prescribe in detail what constitutes minimum standards. This will be ascertained from an understanding of the business of the operation of care homes and from experience and practice in the field. A regulator, taking the position and expressing the view of a responsible member of society, will expect anyone running a care home to understand basic care practice and the basic requirements for operation of the home in the twenty-first century.

However, s 23 of the 2000 Act introduces a new legal concept – the national minimum standards. As yet, it is not known precisely how tribunals and courts will interpret the legal force of these standards. It is clear that no standard is a legal requirement of operation since the standards are clearly distinguished from regulations which are set out in s 22 of the 2000 Act. The standards are required to be taken into account by bodies which have to make important regulatory

---

1   Burgner, *The Regulation and Inspection of Social Services* (Department of Health, 1990), concludes that greater national benchmarking of standards is required.

decisions, ie the registration authorities, courts and tribunals. Early evidence of practice suggests that the registration authorities (the National Care Standards Commission and the Care Standards Inspectorate for Wales) will, at least for operational purposes, expect compliance with the standards, and care establishments and agencies will be measured against that compliance. More difficult is an analysis of the practice that will develop in relation to various levels of non-compliance and the extent to which compliance can be enforced given that it is not a required prescription of law. Providers and managers of care establishments and agencies are well advised to understand the standards and, to the extent that their facilities fall short of those standards, to decide whether or not this requires to be addressed, or to establish sound, professionally based arguments as to why, in particular cases, the application of the standards is unnecessary or, in some cases, inappropriate.

Major business decisions will be taken by the care home owner. The regulator cannot and should not intervene in the course of this decision-making. However, the care home owner should be aware of the scrutiny of the regulator. If the home owner's decision is so bad as to suggest that standards will fall below the prescribed level, the regulator will intervene. A prudent care home owner will ensure that he understands both the 'requirements of regulations', the applicable national minimum standards and the views of the regulator before he makes major decisions concerning, for example, the employment of senior staff.

The regulator should not seek to vet the appointment of staff (other than staff who require to be registered, for example the manager, or who may hold a position of responsibility in relation to an establishment or agency which seeks registration for the first time) or to approve major decisions. The owner may not expect detailed advice about a particular decision, but he may expect, and will no doubt receive, advice as to the general view taken by the regulator. The owner may not be bound by that view, but he will ignore it at his peril.

1.7.2   Purpose of regulation

The purpose of regulation in relation to the registration of care establishments and agencies falls into three categories:

(a) to control entry to the care home business (whether by provider or manager);
(b) to observe the conduct of that business;
(c) to determine when and how quickly a provider or manager shall be barred from the business or a particular establishment or agency closed down.

However, the purpose of regulation as set out in the law is not to substitute the regulator as the effective manager of the establishment or agency.

1.7.3   Self-regulation

The suggestion sometimes raised is that care home owners should be subject to 'self-regulation'. Good care home owners do regulate their own businesses. They visit at anti-social hours, install effective quality assurance programmes, and monitor and appraise the performance of staff and so-called 'outcomes' of the business by canvassing those in care and their relatives as to their views on the service provided. Care home owners may also devise their own methods of self-regulation or take on nationally accredited systems of regulation, such as ISO 9002. However, it is submitted that, while self-regulation or industry-organised regulation is welcome and necessary, it can never be a substitute for regulation by an external, State-controlled body.

Self-regulation may be nothing more than business common sense combined with the regulation of the marketplace. The business entrepreneur trying to ensure that he maintains and enhances his position in the marketplace will want to offer a service that satisfies existing and potential customers. Even externally accredited quality assurance schemes achieve little more than identifying whether a business has met the standards which it has set for itself. However, if regulation is determined merely by the continued willingness of an operator to be regulated, then it cannot meet the demand expressed by society, and enacted by Parliament, that there should be objective external regulation. The role of regulators of care homes is not as advisers to, or partners with, care home owners but, in a sense, as custodians of the public conscience.

Without doubt, self-regulation would remain even if statutory regulation were to be abolished.[1] However, as long as statutory regulation remains, forms of self-regulation, welcome as they are, cannot be regarded as substitutes.

1.8   HISTORY OF REGULATION

Whilst the categories of registrable establishments and agencies are many and varied, the sector is dominated by the best (known) example of the long-term care unit for older or disabled people. This has historically been underlined by an artificial distinction between personal and nursing care delivered respectively in residential care or nursing homes. Thankfully, the distinction in care homes is abolished by the 2000 Act, but differences between personal and nursing care remain. This will be developed in Chapter 3.

Regulation of nursing homes and residential care homes came together in the Registered Homes Act 1984, and the two types of home have been generally regarded as being merely different manifestations of the same idea. However, the common perception of the need for regulation of the two types of home has developed on differing scales and this can clearly be shown in an examination of the history of the regulatory statutes.

---

1   Both Burgner, ibid, and Day, Klein and Redmayne, *Why Regulate?* (The Policy Press in association with Joseph Rowntree Foundation, 1996) firmly reject self-regulation as an alternative to statutory registration and inspection.

Nursing homes	Residential care homes
Nursing Homes Registration Act 1927	National Assistance Act 1948
Public Health Act 1936 (ss 186 and 187)	
Nursing Homes Amendment Act 1963	
Nursing Homes Act 1975	
Health Services Act 1980	Residential Homes Act 1980
Health and Social Services Administration Act 1983	
Registered Homes Act 1984	Registered Homes Act 1984
Care homes	
Care Standards Act 2000	Care Standards Act 2000

Whereas society perceived the need to regulate the delivery of health care as early as 1927, residential care homes were not regulated for another 21 years and it was 53 years later before a statute, designed specifically to regulate the delivery of so-called personal or social care on a residential basis, was introduced.

1.8.1   National Assistance Act 1948

The National Assistance Act 1948 first provided for the regulation of residential accommodation for those in need, although the underlying principle of that legislation was that those in need would receive care from local authorities providing their own accommodation. By s 26 of the Act – the source of the modern community care purchasing power – local authorities were entitled to purchase private sector social care (but not health care until 1993) as an alternative to provision from within their own facilities. Now that is diminished by the *Coughlan* decision in the Court of Appeal, healthcare can only be purchased by local authorities under Part III of the 1948 Act if ancillary to the need for accommodation.[1] Certain limited offences were provided in relation to the conduct of such homes, the commission of which restricted future contracting with the local authority.

All of this was in the context of limited (as opposed to the current extensive) regulation. It was also set against a background where clients perceived that they would not purchase care themselves from a home but would receive care through provision made by the local authority, whether from its own resources or by local authority purchase from a private provider. The logic of exclusion of providers who had committed offences under the 1948 scheme is clear. Many feel that the logic of continuing that exclusion into the post-1993 'Care in the Community' scheme was not so clear. The presumption on dealing with 'combined providers' has been abolished with the repeal of the Registered

---

1   Consider also the partnering provisions for health and social services in the Health Act 1999 (in particular s 31) and the Local Government Act 2000.

Homes Act 2000, but the stigma will be retained in the discretion of the decision-maker.[1]

1.8.2 Nursing Homes Act 1975

Until 1975, regulation of privately operated health care premises was controlled by county councils and not by health care authorities, despite the fact that county councils had no function in the provision of health care. The Nursing Homes Act 1975 consolidated the existing legislation, then to be found in the appropriate sections of the Public Health Act 1936 and the amending legislation (most importantly the 1963 Act). The 1975 Act introduced the requirement that a reasonable proportion of staff in nursing homes should be qualified nurses. It also introduced the new idea that health care premises should be regulated by the Secretary of State, acting through area health authorities (as they then were[2]), so that the regulation of provision of health care in the private sector should be carried out by those responsible for providing health care in the public sector.

1.8.3 Changes of the early 1980s – a 'golden age'

The change to district health authorities in 1980 resulted in the transfer of the regulation of private health care to those new authorities, and this has been continued by retaining that function within the health purchasing unit (the health authority), now securing, as opposed to providing, health care under the National Health Service and Community Care Act 1990, as amended by the Health Authorities Act 1995 and more recently further devolved to strategic Health Authorities and Primary Care Trusts under the provisions of the NHS (Primary Care) Act 1997 and the Health Act 1999.[3]

The demographic changes discussed earlier in this chapter will be seen as resulting in the development of increasingly sophisticated legislation, throughout the 1980s, starting with the enactment of the Residential Homes Act 1980 (the first detailed regulation of residential care) and the Health Services Act 1980, which significantly advanced and refined regulation of private nursing homes.

These legislative changes were responding to demographic changes, in particular to acknowledge the notion that able family members (other than spouses or parents of young children) were no longer either legally or morally obliged to care for less able family members, with the introduction of universal entitlement to State welfare support. Many people may consider the explosion in the development and proliferation of care homes to be inextricably linked with the introduction of universal access to 100 per cent payment of care home fees by

---

1 Care Standards Act 2000, s 117(2) and Sch 6, repealing s 26(1E) of the National Assistance Act 1948.
2 Subsequently, district health authorities under the Health Services Act 1980, and now health authorities under the Health Authorities Act 1995.
3 See now, in particular, NHS (Functions of Strategic Health Authorities and Primary Care Trusts and Administrative Arrangements) (England) Regulations 2002, SI 2002/2375.

central government. Despite the removal of the legal imperative, and the erosion of the moral imperative, to care for the elderly and sick within the family, the changes could not have been implemented while traditional values prevailed and without the financial resources to meet the cost.

The introduction of support by way of social security benefit payments for residential boarders, including those in nursing homes and residential care homes, in the late 1970s, opened up an opportunity for families who were either unable to find alternative placement for dependants in need or, if able, severely financially restricted, to obtain the support needed. The potential market for the private provision of residential care was vastly increased, at a stroke.

The early 1980s were truly golden days for care home providers. The Department of Health and Social Security (as it then was) provided supplementary benefit payments to meet the full cost of residential care wherever that was supplied, and in homes selected by the patient or resident. Reimbursement of care home fees was limited to an amount which coincided with the local norm. Families released both from the legal and moral imperative of caring for the sick and needy within the domestic environment saw a true advantage, as did care home owners. The obligation, financially and physically taxing, to care for the elderly could be avoided. Personal cash resources could be released and, better still, such limited cash resources as were available to the elderly would not, subject to certain limits, be required to be employed in paying for residential care, ie benefit was not dependent on zero assets and assets were not depleted below certain levels.

The market for care homes exploded. Homes could be filled overnight at basic standards, and at fees which would show a profit and which could be adjusted on a regular basis to continue to show profits as expenditure rose with inflation and as a result of increasing demand. Clearly, this could not continue, and, on 11 April 1985, the Government effectively capped the residential care and nursing home fees which would be met by social security benefit and brought about a change of dramatic proportions in the operation of nursing and residential and nursing homes.

1.8.4   Registered Homes Act 1984

The Registered Homes Act 1984 is often described as a watershed, although, save for the introduction of the Registered Homes Tribunal and the urgent procedure for the cancellation of registration, the Act is more a consolidation of separate statutory provisions than ground-breaking legislation.

1.8.5   End of the 'golden age'

What was truly a watershed, in early 1985, and coincided with the introduction of the 1984 Act, was the combination of:

(a) greater awareness in local authority social services departments and district health authorities of the obligation to regulate, and, in consequence, the gradual development of teams which were not only required to regulate, but did regulate; and

(b) the dramatic capping of social security benefit.

Increased regulation would lead inevitably to increased costs, and capping would lead to decreased income.

The culmination of the effect of these two facts came in 1989, coinciding with the collapse of the property boom of the late 1980s. Care home owners were met with slumping capital values, and increased financial requirements derived both from expenditure required as a result of proper regulation and reductions in income as a result of capping. Within a decade, residential care homes and nursing homes had come from relative obscurity, through a 'golden age' in which they appeared to be money-printing machines, to a position where, for many, businesses were no longer viable. The change of emphasis for publicly funded patients and residents from 1 April 1993 (pursuant to the delayed introduction of the financial reforms of Part III of the National Health Services and Community Care Act 1990) completed the dramatic transformation. With those changes, apparently, although not absolutely, entitlement for all to free residential and nursing care was abolished. Entitlement was not only rationed, but rationed by a local authority. Such rationing was by reference to both individual and, possibly, local authority resources.[1] All such care and entitlement was subject to the pre-entry qualification of assessment.[2] For many, this was seen as a reversion to the pre-1948 situation where provision by the local authority had been only the final safety net, under the Poor Laws of 1927 and 1930. However, in 1993, as opposed to the period of 1601–1948, there was no legal requirement upon more able family members to provide care for their less able relatives, except upon spouses, and upon parents in relation to their children.[3]

After much deliberation, the relatively newly elected Labour Government published a White Paper entitled *Modernising Social Services* in early December 1998 (Cm 4169). This reforming White Paper set out the Government's agenda wholly to reform the regulation, but not the commissioning, of health and social care throughout the United Kingdom. The vision, which has come to pass in the Care Standards Act 2000 and its supporting regulations, was of a unified system of regulation to cover all forms of health and social care establishments and agencies (other than those operating within the NHS) with a consistency of regulator by reducing to one the number of regulators in each jurisdiction over which Parliament had authority, ie one for England and one for Wales.

---

1 Cf *R v Gloucestershire County Council and another ex parte Barry* [1997] 2 WLR 459, HL; *R v Sefton Metropolitan Borough Council ex parte Help the Aged* [1997] 4 All ER 532, CA.

2 See National Health Service and Community Care Act 1990.

3 See National Assistance Act 1948, s 42.

More controversially, the White Paper identified that the Government was determined to follow the recommendations in the *Burgner Report*,[1] which had called for national benchmarks for standards in health and social care provision. Within the White Paper, the Government announced that it had commissioned a voluntary body, the Centre for Policy on Ageing, to report on appropriate standards for services, facilities and staffing within non-NHS health and social care delivery.

In January 1999, the Centre for Policy on Ageing delivered its recommendations to the Government in a report, which has become known as *Fit for the Future*. This report, published with more unanimity than has been broadcast since the debate on subsequent consultation, was indeed followed by a period of consultation and did not result in any specific draft provisions being finally promulgated until March 2001.

In the meantime, the Care Standards Act 2000 received Royal Assent in July 2000 and has gradually been implemented from that date. Provisions relating to the reform of the regulation of childminding in day care for young children were implemented from July 2001. The provisions relating to the regulation of mainstream health and social care establishments were implemented in part from 1 January 2001 and in whole from 1 April 2002, and the provisions in relation to residential family centres and domiciliary care agencies are to be implemented on 1 April 2003.

In March 2001, the Government finalised the first of the national minimum standards for care homes for older people with a view to those standards being implemented with effect from 1 April 2002. The standards remained unchanged despite continuing discord and debate until the autumn of 2002. Following consultation and no small amount of acrimony some of the 'physical environment' standards for 'existing care homes at April 2002' were modified and the standards republished in February 2003. Whether these changes are substantial or were 'spin', given the legal status of standards, will be seen in changes in practical application. Further standards, most notably standards in relation to younger adults between the ages of 18 and 65, and independent health care standards with associated regulations were issued for consultation at the end of June 2001 and were finally promulgated between November 2001 and the end of January 2002.

The essential features of the reform of legislation may be seen as:

(a) the universal application of rules of regulation to all non-NHS health and social care establishments and agencies;
(b) a requirement for all providers of care, whether private finance, voluntary sector or public authority (other than the NHS), to be regulated to the same standard, including those establishments which have been operated by bodies previously exempt from registration, for example local authorities, Royal Charter and Act of Parliament organisations;
(c) the universal requirement for dual registration of providers and managers;

---

1   See footnote 1, at p 9 above.

(d) the establishment of single regulators for England and Wales;
(e) the establishment of national minimum standards for facilities and services in health-and-care-related industries outside the NHS to be applied as an operational benchmark in the regulatory process.

1.9 SOURCES OF LAW

1.9.1 Common law

Regulation is not known to the common law except in so far as its origins derive from the need for the Crown to regulate its subjects in all matters. However, common law principles will remain of importance in interpreting and enforcing the law of regulation as it applies to a particular area from time to time.

1.9.2 Statutes

Any regulator subordinate to Parliament must be able to point to a statutory source for the power of regulation. If no such source exists, or if the source does not permit an exercise of authority in the way or to the extent to which it purports to have been made, then, in so far as the regulator attempts to state that a rule has the force of law, it will be overturned. That does not necessarily mean that a rule that does not have the binding force of law is to be disregarded, but merely that it may not be quoted *ipso facto*, as justification for subsequent decisions.[1] By way of example, in relation to the question as to whether or not valid conditions of registration may be imposed, interpretation of the statutes shows that:

(a) in relation to residential care homes and nursing homes, conditions could not have the force of law, unless relating specifically to subject matter made the particular subject of registration by the 1984 Act;
(b) in relation to registered children's homes formerly regulated under the Children Act 1989, regulators had wide powers to impose, as conditions of registration, anything they believe to be appropriate.

1.9.3 Regulations

Chapter 2 examines the nature and powers of those involved in the regulation of care establishments and agencies. All regulation is performed by the National Care Standards Commission in England, and the Care Standards Inspectorate for Wales (the executive agency of the Welsh Assembly).

The National Care Standards Commission is a statutory body corporate established under the 2000 Act. Most importantly, the Commission is required to exercise its functions in accordance with directions given by the Secretary of State, ie it must follow orders of the Secretary of State. Furthermore, by s 6(2)(b)

---

1 Section 13(3) of the 2000 Act now provides that registration authorisation may impose no conditions, or such conditions as is considered appropriate, ie *McSweeny* is still good law, but its effect is nil since the statute now permits wide-ranging conditions.

of the 2000 Act, the Commission is required to act under the general guidance of the Secretary of State.

Serious debate may arise as to the precise definition of the guidance given and the degree of liberality of interpretation within the guidance. By its very nature, guidance will tend to be more widely drawn than directions.

The Commission is not, however, an executive agency acting in the name of and on behalf of the Secretary of State. Thus, the arguments that related to guidance from the Department of Health to health authorities under the regime regulated under Part II of the Registered Homes Act 1984 will not apply. The Commission is a free-standing statutory body corporate and, except as required to act by statute (ie s 6(2) general guidance), is not required to follow the guidance or wishes of Government, although no doubt it will take such issues seriously into account. Indeed, as will be seen in Chapter 2, the Commission has important duties and powers to advise and report to the Secretary of State about the operation of health and social care outside the NHS in England.

By contrast, in Wales, the Welsh Assembly itself is the registration authority, and the Care Standards Inspectorate for Wales is merely an agency of that registration authority. There is no need, therefore, for the provision of requirements to observe directions or general guidance from the Welsh Assembly because, unlike the National Care Standards Commission in England, it is acting as a principal regulator rather than a statutorily delegated regulator.

1.9.4   Case-law

The courts usually avoid giving guidance on general principles in particular cases because the application of legal principle will vary from one case to another. Where there is a departure, then what is said may be regarded only as being of persuasive authority. For example, in *Lyons v East Sussex County Council*,[1] the Court of Appeal was asked to give guidance on the vexed question of procedures for an application for the urgent cancellation of a registration certificate for a residential care home. Having declined to do so, the Court then expressed views about the advantages of combining an application for urgent procedure with a notice seeking cancellation by the longer and so-called 'ordinary' method. In the course of the judgment, the view was expressed that it matters not which procedure is started first. This was not germane to the dispute, and clearly *obiter dictum*. Nonetheless, where a court of authority has decided a point of law specifically germane to the determination of a particular case, that decision will be binding authority on inferior courts in accordance with the principle of judicial precedent.

1.9.5   Registered Homes Tribunal cases

Since its institution in January 1985, the Registered Homes Tribunal has heard approximately 480 cases. These make interesting, illuminating and, in some instances, amusing reading for students of the practice of the regulation of care homes. The Tribunal has now been abolished, and appeals will now be referred

---

1   (1988) 86 LGR 369.

to the Protection of Children and Vulnerable Adults and Care Standards Tribunal (CST). The decisions of the Registered Homes Tribunal will remain of interest and persuasive authority in so far as they touch upon issues similar to those canvassed before the CST.

Few of the cases that have come before tribunals have concentrated upon legal issues or issues of principle. The vast majority of such cases are exercises in the application of the principles of the law of regulation of care establishments to particular facts and circumstances, which will not be repeated here. The peculiarity of such cases to their own facts and the constitution of the tribunal in having a majority of non-legally qualified expert practitioners to determine all issues, including issues of law, means that the decisions of tribunals should be approached with caution and regarded, at the highest, as mildly persuasive. It would be dangerous to regard such decisions as being in any way binding upon future tribunals. Furthermore, the practice and procedure of care home management and operation can change and develop over the years. Tribunals must keep their thinking up to date, and it would be wholly wrong, in principle, for tribunals to regard themselves as bound by decisions on particular facts set in an historic context when considering a modern case. Circumstances can change due to the advance of technology, changes in custom and practice, changes in the availability of numbers or qualifications of particular grades of staff and, generally, in relation to what is regarded as acceptable conduct in relation to the care of the sick, the frail and the vulnerable.

Such cases are instructive for care home owners and regulators as regards the conduct of future investigations and provide a useful background to an explanation of the principles of regulation. However, in common with all trials and enquiries where particular facts are investigated, it has to be accepted that the decisions will be influenced by the impression made by the presentation of evidence and the performance of witnesses upon the individual tribunal. To seek to draw rules of principle from such circumstances is dangerous and will lead the practitioner into error.

1.9.6 Guidance

The practice of care establishment and agency regulation is fraught with difficulty, caused by the introduction of so-called guidelines, rules, 'local' regulations and 'requirements'. These are usually issued by or on behalf of bodies which appear to have the force of law, to those who are not students of the finer points of constitutional law. It is important to appreciate that such pronouncements do not have the force of law unless they can be shown to derive from statutory or delegated statutory authority.

Such guidance is issued in practice by:

(a) central government through one of the departments of State;
(b) national organisations, ie organised groupings of regulators or organised groupings of care providers;
(c) individual local regulators or local providers.

1.9.7   Departmental guidance

The Welsh Assembly is its own registration authority. Clearly, advice will be given, and policy decisions by way of direction made to the public servants who work within the Assembly, charged with the duty of performing the regulatory function in relation to health and social care and who are carrying out functions on behalf of the regulator. In so far as it conflicts with the law, or exceeds the powers granted by law to the Assembly as registration authority, such guidance will be ineffective, will not be binding upon courts or tribunals and does not have to be regarded as binding by regulated providers and managers in the field. Nonetheless, guidance needs to be considered very carefully, and challenges made only after the most astute and careful consideration. The registration authority will, of course, have given very careful consideration to the limits of its own powers before deciding to act in a particular way.

The National Care Standards Commission is autonomous, but is subject to the general guidance of the Secretary of State.[1] Such guidance will broadly fall into two areas:

(a) general guidance on interpretation of the law and the implementation of procedures for enforcement of the law;
(b) guidance as to the implementation of good care practice.

It is suggested that general guidance on interpretation of the law and procedure is nothing more than the Government's expression of its view, by way of assistance, to advise the authorities as to the way in which they go about the business of enforcing the regulatory provisions. Such guidance will be issued by seasoned and able lawyers and civil servants and, as with any guidance or advice, merits serious consideration by those who are required to act in the field. It is by no means certain, however, that such guidance will be correct, and reliance upon it can never lead to the conclusion that actions based upon it will necessarily be right. Interpretation of the law is a matter for the tribunal and, ultimately, the court. Lawyers, civil servants or others seeking to interpret without the authority to make final decisions are no more than advisers.

Certain Department of Health guidance has been shown to be wrong, and in some circumstances this has been criticised by the courts. In the late 1980s, a health circular was issued suggesting to authorities that when an owner whose registration had been cancelled sought to appeal to the tribunal, the authorities should write to the owner telling him that, in exercising the right of appeal, he was required to state briefly his reasons. Nothing could be further from the correct position. Such a prospective appellant had an appeal as a matter of right. He was not required to give reasons for exercising the appeal and, indeed, the burden of proof in establishing the reasons and justification for the decision to cancel lies upon the authority. That circular was not only misleading, but dangerously wrong. However, where the Department seeks to give guidance on general issues of care practice, and on which practices it would like to see

---

1   Care Standards Act 2000, s 6(2)(b).

encouraged, which discouraged, and which abolished, then it is submitted that the strength of the persuasive power of the circular is significantly increased.

Much assistance in this field can be drawn from a decision involving the registration of childminders.[1] This, the so-called 'right to smack' case, is very instructive on the relative force to be given by local authorities, in making pragmatic decisions on registration, to general guidance issued by the Department of Health in the *Blue Book*.[2] Wilson J said:

> 'What is abundantly clear is that the guidance in the Blue Book, whether in relation to smacking or anything else, is not intended to be applied so strictly that, if an application for registration is in conflict with part of it, there should automatically be a finding of unfitness.'

Whilst, as a matter of law, the local authority was bound to follow the guidance,[3] that guidance itself had to be construed strictly to see whether it bore the prescriptive effect contended by the local authority.

The guidance binds the Commission in the way it discharges its function, but does not bind the provider or manager. It is subject to the restrictions and limitations of the law and cannot make new law.

The guidance should itself be carefully construed to determine whether it makes the requirement suggested by or on behalf of the Commission. Two examples can be given.

In January 2002, the Minister of Health, Jacqui Smith MP, wrote to the Chairman of the National Care Standards Commission on the subject of the implementation of national minimum standards, which was clearly intended to be guidance under s 6 of the 2000 Act. The effect of the guidance was that the Commission was not to interpret the national minimum standards as requirements of existing care home owners, which it was perceived might have had an effect on destabilising the market. However, the guidance went on to suggest that the national minimum standards should be regarded, as a matter of guidance, as the standards by which applications for new registrations should be granted. Clearly, the Minister was right as to the application of the national minimum standards in relation to existing homes, but misled as to her power to suggest a different procedure for new registrations. The standards, not being requirements of care home providers or managers, cannot be made a prescriptive requirement of new applicants so as to be a requirement for registration. The 2000 Act did not so provide, and that cannot be changed by ministerial guidance to the statutory regulator.

This is reinforced by s 13 of the 2000 Act, which states that the authority must grant an application for registration if it is satisfied that the requirements of regulations under s 23 and the requirements of other enactments which are relevant have been fulfilled. The standards promulgated under s 23 of the 2000 Act cannot be construed as requirements under s 13(2) and, accordingly, the

---

1   See *London Borough of Sutton v Ann Davis* [1994] 2 WLR 721.
2   *The Children Act 1989 Guidance and Regulations*, vol 2 (HMSO, January 1995).
3   Local Authority Social Services Act 1970, s 7(1).

Minister could not give effective guidance which excluded from registration those who did not comply with the national minimum standards.

More recently, the Minister has given guidance to the National Care Standards Commission about the application of staffing levels in relation to existing registered care homes and applicants for registration of care homes under Part II of the 2000 Act. The guidance is long and complex but lacking in specific detail. It requires that in relation to new applications, the Commission must take into account the guidance on staffing establishments set out in a report made by the distinguished voluntary body, the Residential Forum, and in relation to existing establishments, the Commission must ensure that there is no regression from staffing levels required as at 1 April 2002. The Residential Forum guidance is itself complex and varied, and will have a variety of different interpretations in particular circumstances. There will be a wealth of argument as to what were required staffing levels under the previous regulatory regime, and it will certainly not be the case that staffing levels (many and varied in similar situations) across the country, derived from local health authority and social services department standard guidelines, could be interpreted to be the requirements of regulation under the Secretary of State's guidance.

The two examples above show the degree of interpretation that may arise merely where guidance is issued by the Secretary of State, let alone interpretation of the legislation and, indeed, the national minimum standards themselves.

1.9.8 National and local guidance

Local authorities, public health authorities, organisations representing regulatory authorities, and care home owners' associations frequently issue so-called 'guidelines' relating, generally, to the operation and management of care homes and to appropriate practices for health and social care. Following the implementation of the 2000 Act, this practice is likely to wane, but it will still occur. Accordingly, the principles are important. They will apply with equal force to guidance issued by the new regulators, the National Care Standards Commission and the Welsh Assembly.

From time to time, these 'guidelines' are elevated by individual practitioners to the status of binding rules and regulations. They are never so. At the highest, they represent the collected wisdom, in a particular field of practice, of those whose experience has been accumulated and which is then published for the assistance of others already in the field or who may wish to enter. The value of the guidance is dependent upon the authors' credibility, and whether or not their views coincide with generally established customs and practice throughout England and Wales.

It is not the function of regulators, local authorities or public health authorities, by the publication of guidelines or otherwise, to supplant the Secretary of State's rule-making function. Regulatory authorities may wish to influence the development of care within their jurisdiction. That aim is to be applauded. However, the authority must remember that its purpose is to regulate the establishment of care homes, and not to seek to dictate the way in which those care homes are managed.

Care home owners should resist introducing requirements which, although given as 'requirements' through guidelines, do not have the force of law unless it can be shown that they accord with nationally recognised practice, and that to operate without them would be to operate below a standard which might be regarded objectively as adequate, ie sufficient and suitable. There can be no requirement to operate within national minimum standards since the standards are not themselves required. However, care home owners should also be aware that such guidance is the accumulated wisdom of specialists in the area of care home regulation and should not be treated lightly. At the highest, the guidance may reflect modern thinking on minimum standards. At the lowest, it may represent constructive ideas about how to provide better care and better service, and how to enhance the position in the market of the particular care business. That is not to say that the absence of particular facilities indicates that a care home is unfit to operate. However, such facilities have been introduced gradually over the last 10 years, and have been seen as constructive innovations. New, purpose-built homes will rarely be without these facilities, and homes that do not provide them will compete poorly in the market.

(1) Guidance, good practice or even national minimum standards may obtain greater force in relation to the operation of a registrable care establishment or agency if, in the course of the process of registration or review or variation of registration, the registered provider or manager has agreed to abide by such provisions. Early templates of the standard application form issued by the National Care Standards Commission actually required the applicant to undertake that he would abide by national minimum standards. This is clearly not a legally justifiable requirement and the statements of some local officers of the National Care Standards Commission that they will not process applications, or may reject applications if such undertakings are not given, are clearly without substance and unlawful. Nonetheless, if the undertaking is requested and given then it may be regarded as binding, and if transgressed may justify regulatory action based on an allegation of unfitness against the registered person. It is a simple principle that if a valuable trading right is obtained by an undertaking to accept and follow certain standards of practice, then that undertaking will be expected to be observed. Those who give such undertakings must expect to be treated with a reasonable, robust regulatory hand if they do not perform, particularly if they suggest at a later stage that the standards were not binding as requirements. Given that the National Care Standards Commission is not entitled to refuse registration upon the premise that the home will not comply with national minimum standards, it will be surprising if that body seeks an undertaking for something which it cannot genuinely expect.

(2) In the changing world of purchase of community care services (since 1 April 1993), it is a commercial fact of life that local authorities and health authorities are increasingly purchasers of care services. It is inevitable that a

purchaser of care services is likely to be dissuaded from purchasing from those who do not adhere to the same standards of care as those expected by the purchaser. This is simply another example of the effect of market forces.

Regulators must be careful not to overstate requirements. The purchasing divisions of a local authority may be dissuaded from purchasing care from all available providers, if some are perceived not to meet a standard of excellence. It would be unhealthy, it is submitted, if a local authority were, in effect, to decline to purchase from a unit which was regarded as fit for registration by the registration authority. The watchword should be that, if the home is fit to be registered, it is fit to operate and thus fit to deal with any purchasers in the marketplace, including the local and public authorities. Purchasers must be free to select care services which are more attractive, but that freedom of choice should not be distorted by a misguided belief as to levels of adequacy of services or facilities. If local authority purchasers seek to contract on the basis that national minimum standards will be observed, they should be careful to ensure that their own registered establishments meet the same standards.

1.10   NATIONAL MINIMUM STANDARDS

It is convenient at this point to consider the new concept of national minimum standards in some detail. There are no similar provisions in relation to any other regulated business.

The national minimum standards are not requirements of regulation to be followed by every registered person. They are not promulgated with the force of law as enforceable codes of practice under the Health and Safety at Work etc Act 1974. The binding force of the national minimum standards must be derived from an interpretation of their statutory source.

As discussed above, registered persons must be careful to understand that they may convert the effect of the national minimum standards into requirements if, in the registration process, they undertake to abide by all or any of the standards. Questions may be raised about the morality of the National Care Standards Commission seeking such undertakings, but it is suggested that any challenge to such a requirement should be taken at the time when the requirement is made, if necessary with a challenge to the adverse regulatory actions as a result of the refusal to be bound. It is submitted that to freely undertake to be bound, and then to escape on the basis of misdirection, is risky, and to act contrary to that to which one has agreed to be bound is highly dangerous. It raises the spectre that the registered person is untrustworthy, and that is the cornerstone of an allegation of unfitness.

By way of contrast, s 22(1) of the 2000 Act provides:

> 'Regulations may impose in relation to establishments and agencies any require-
> ments which the appropriate Minister thinks fit for the purpose of this Part and may
> in particular make provision such as is mentioned in subsection (2), (7) or (8).'

Accordingly, requirements are clearly linked to regulations, and the precondition to registration is compliance with requirements under the Act.

The standards have their statutory authority in s 23(1). The appropriate minister may prepare and publish statements of national minimum standards applicable to establishments or agencies in the cases of all establishments and agencies promulgated under the 2000 Act. There is an obligation to keep standards under review, plus an obligation for consultation before introducing standards or varying standards. (The opportunities to object to non-consultation are now gone.) The importance of s 23 arises from subsection (4). The standards shall be taken into account in the making of any decision by the registration authority:

(a) in any proceedings for the making of an order under s 20 (urgent action);
(b) in any proceedings on an appeal;
(c) in any proceedings for an offence under regulations (note: not under the Act itself).

Accordingly, the standards are simply to be taken into account. They cannot be ignored. It is submitted that the correct interpretation is that the standards will be considered, and any non-compliance with the standard noted as a finding of fact. The consequence of non-compliance with the standards is then the notation that the standard has not been reached. The notation is a matter to be taken into account (together with, and balanced against, other factors) in the taking of decisions by the registration authorities, the courts or appeal tribunals.

Therefore, it is clear that non-compliance with the standards does not lead to an automatic conclusion that a decision must be made one way or another. The matter becomes one of objective discretion, taking into account all factors, including the compliance or non-compliance with the national minimum standards. In many cases, what will be taken into account is a balance of non-compliance and compliance or anticipated compliance, or indeed argument as to why compliance is inappropriate, and that the services, facilities and standards provided are right in the circumstances of the case for the needs of the particular services.

There will no doubt be much debate and many cases exploring the parameters of this provision. The regulators must regard this as highly unsatisfactory, since it leaves them, in the absence of any definite authority, with difficult judgments to make.

A combination of the reading of ss 23, 22 and 13 of the 2000 Act makes it clear that the failure of an establishment or of individuals to comply with the standards is not a matter which justifies the registration authority in refusing to comply with its duty to register if it is otherwise satisfied that requirements under the 2000 Act and other legislation will be complied with.

Again, this is contrasted with s 24 of the 2000 Act which makes it a clear and immediate criminal offence of strict liability to fail to comply with a condition of registration. This can be contrasted with the compliance or non-compliance with the national minimum standards being merely one of the many factors to be balanced in a decision. A practice is developing of seeking to require applicants for registration to accept as conditions of registration compliance with regulations and standards. This must be carefully observed as breach of a condition of registration leads to the prospect of immediate prosecution without warning, whatever may be the relevant status with the actual regulation or standards.

The position taken is now strongly supported by the first review of the *NMS for Care Homes for Older People* published in March 2003. The review is noted for its so-called retreat on environmental standards but much more important is the change to the description of the standards in the Introduction:

> 'In considering whether a care home conforms to the ... regulations, which are mandatory, the NCSC must take the standards into account. However the Commission may also take into account any other factors it considers reasonable or relevant to do so.
>
> Compliance with NMS is not itself enforceable but compliance with regulations is enforceable subject to NMS being taken into account.
>
> The Commission may conclude that a Care Home has been in breach of the regulations even though the home largely meets the standards. The Commission also has discretion to conclude that the regulations have been complied with by means other than those set out in NMS.'

This should be contrasted with the equivalent statement in the equivalent NMS published in March 2001:

> 'These standards will form the basis for judgments made by the NCSC regarding registration and the imposition of conditions of registration, variation of any conditions and enforcement of compliance with the CSA and appropriate regulations including proceedings for cancellation of registration or prosecution. The Commission will therefore consider the degree to which a regulated service complies with the standards when determining whether or not a service should be registered or have its registration cancelled or whether to take any action for breach of regulation.'

This change is said to take effect in June 2003 but that is clearly otiose and is simply a revised guidance on the law and thus of immediate effect. Further, it is suggested that this change applies by incontrovertible logic to all NMSs. It is simply a legal view of s 23 of the 2000 Act.

1.11   POLICIES

Inevitably, and correctly, registration authorities, whether exercising regulatory powers, purchasing powers or general powers in relation to the conduct of professional practice within their location, will publish and seek to implement policies. However, such policies, whether propounding guidelines or general policies on the provision of care, or the number, location or size of units of care, must not be elevated into rules of law unless there is authority in statute providing for such policies to become rules of law.

Authorities are required to register and issue a certificate of registration in relation to a care home upon being satisfied that requirements of negotiations of other relevant enactments are and will continue to be complied with. The burden of proof is therefore on the applicant, but if the burden (as statutorily limited) is discharged, their registration is compulsory.[1] However, when exercising other discretions in relation to regulation, for example the imposition of conditions of registration, the authority may take into account any matters material to the decision, including its own policies, provided it is not capricious and considers each case seriously.[2] Decisions must not be fettered or constrained by fixed policies as opposed to law.

Registration authorities should also appreciate that, whilst argument about whether or not policies may be taken into account may be interesting, it will inevitably be arcane to the layman. Whilst the decision-making power may take into account local policy, if the source of decision-making authority changes, for example to the tribunal, then it is for the tribunal or alternative decision-maker to take into account material it considers appropriate. A local policy is likely to have less effect on the tribunal than upon a registration authority, which could find that it has wasted time and money, and, indeed, may have its policy criticised if the tribunal finds that it is not justified. In *Isle of Wight County Council v Humphreys*,[3] considerable argument was deployed in trying to prevent the tribunal from considering the policy issues, particularly by the care home owner, Mr Humphreys. However, the court permitted the tribunal to consider the issue – a policy that prevented the development or extension of new care homes in the Isle of Wight beyond a fixed number. The tribunal had no difficulty in finding that it would not espouse the local authority policy and would grant Mr Humphreys the registration to which he was otherwise entitled.

Registration authorities should exercise extreme caution when basing decisions on matters of policy, and in the author's view only rarely, if ever, should a decision be based purely upon policy. Policy will rarely be enshrined in the binding rules of law, and it is the duty of the regulatory authority to implement those rules, not to advance rule-making further by attempting to give force to policies which cannot be the subject matter of law.

It may be that those who have to exercise a discretion conferred by statute will formulate policies as to how such a discretion should be exercised, but consistency and fairness will need to be shown. However, each case must be heard and no case should be determined by reference to the policy alone. In *British Oxygen Co v Minister of Technology*,[4] Lord Reid stated:

> 'There are on the one hand cases where a tribunal in the honest exercise of its discretion has adopted a policy, and, without refusing to hear an applicant, intimates to him what its policy is, and that after hearing him it will in accordance with its policy decide against him, unless there is something exceptional in his case. I think Counsel for the applicants would admit that, if the policy has been adopted for reasons which the tribunal may legitimately entertain, no objection could be taken to such a course. On the other hand there are cases where a tribunal has passed a rule, or come to a determination, not to hear any application of a particular

---

1 Registered Homes Act 1984, ss 5(2), 23(4).
2 *Isle of Wight County Council v Humphreys* [1992] COD 308, Hutchinson J.
3 [1992] COD 308.
4 [1971] AC 610.

character by whomsoever made. There is a wide distinction to be drawn between these two claims.

...

The general rule is that anyone who has to exercise a statutory discretion must not "shut his ears to an application" ...

I do not think there is any great difference between policy and a rule. There may be cases where an officer or Authority ought to listen to a substantial argument reasonably presented urging a change of policy. What the Authority must not do is to refuse to listen at all. But a Ministry or large Authority may have had to deal already with a multitude of similar applications and then they will almost certainly have evolved a policy so precise that it could well be called a rule. There can be no objection to that, provided the Authority is always willing to listen to anyone with something new to say – of course I do not mean to say that there need be an oral hearing.

...

The authority must not act capriciously but within "the rules of reason and justice, not according to private opinion ... according to law and not humour. It is to be, not arbitrary, vague and fanciful, but legal and regular." These well known words ... come from the speech of Lord Halsbury LC in *Sharpe v Wakefield* [1891] AC 173 at 179. If as appears to be the case here, the authority has determined upon a general policy they must state it publicly for the information of all concerned and must, despite their policy, apply their minds properly to the circumstances of each individual case in order to decide whether the policy should be applied in that particular case or whether there are grounds for reaching a decision at variance with the policy.'

The principal sources of the current law to be found in statute, regulations or guidance are listed below.

1.12   IMPORTANT STATUTES

(1) *Care Standards Act 2000*: this Act introduces a new code of regulatory requirements for establishments and agencies providing care outside the NHS.

(2) *Children Act 1989*: this important Act provides a unified code of the law as it relates to issues affecting children, and deals with accommodation and the care of children. Much of the Act that relates to the regulation of children's homes has been repealed and replaced by provisions of the 2000 Act, but the 1989 Act is still relevant, and contains provisions on the new registrable community homes in Parts VI and X for registering child-minding and day care services for young children (although the provisions are largely reintroduced through the reform of the 2000 Act).

(3) *Local Authority Social Services Act 1970*: this Act provides the background for the statutory provision by local authorities of social services.

(4) *Nurses, Midwives and Health Visitors Act 1979*: this Act sets out the modern code for the regulation of professionals within the nursing sector. Previous regulation was made under the Nurses Act 1957. The Act is instructive and may still be necessary for interpreting certain provisions of the Registered Homes Act 1984, despite the repeal of the Nurses Act 1957.

(5) *National Health Service Act 1977*: the 1984 Act provided for regulation of nursing homes by the Secretary of State for Health. The National Health Service Act 1977 provides for the delegation of certain of those powers, by the Secretary of State, to district health authorities, which delegation includes the function of registration, inspecting and supervising regulatory action in relation to nursing homes.

(6) *Misuse of Drugs Act 1971*: this Act contains important provisions as to the storage, recording of use and destruction of drugs which may only be obtained and used on prescription and subject to sanction. All nursing homes and residential care homes will have day-to-day regular interaction with drugs available on the prescription of registered medical practitioners. Misuse of such drugs can contravene the provisions of the Act.

(7) *Fire Precautions Act 1971*: this Act is mentioned for completeness because it does not apply to residential care homes and nursing homes save for those sections which are of general application. The Act, which provides for statutory fire certificates for certain types of buildings which may be prescribed by central government, has never been extended to health care premises in the private sector.

(8) *Protection of Children Act 1999*: this is an important act which protects children from abuse. It is the source of the power of the new tribunal for health and social care regulation (the Protection of Children and Vulnerable Adults and Care Standards Tribunal). Protection of vulnerable adults is covered by the 2000 Act and is not yet implemented.

1.13   IMPORTANT REGULATIONS

(1) *Care Homes Regulations 2001*: these Regulations relate to the operation of care homes.

(2) *Private and Voluntary Health Care (England) Regulations 2001*: the Regulations relate to the operation of independent hospitals, clinics and medical agencies in England.

(3) *Children's Homes Regulations 2001*: the Regulations relate to the operation of children's homes in England.

(4) *National Care Standards Commission (Registration) Regulations 2001*: these Regulations set out the requirements for registration of health and social care establishments and agencies in England.

(5) *National Care Standards Commission (Fees and Frequency of Inspections) Regulations 2001*: these Regulations deal with the computation of registration and annual fees in relation to the operation of health and social care establishments in England, and with the required frequency of inspection of such establishments.

(6) *Protection of Children and Vulnerable Adults and Care Standards Tribunal Regulations 2002*: these Regulations set out the procedural requirements for the conduct of appeals before the new statutory Protection of Children and Vulnerable Adults in Care Standards Tribunal.

(7) *Fostering Services Regulations 2002*: these Regulations cover private fostering.

(8) *Day Care and Child Minding (Functions of Local Authorities, Information, Advice and Training) (England) Regulations 2001*.

Chapter 2

PARTICIPANTS IN THE OPERATION OF A REGISTERED CARE HOME

2.1 INTRODUCTION

This chapter examines the participants in the operation of a registered care home, and how each interrelates with the others in their regulation.

2.2 PARTICIPANTS

The participants are as follows:

(a) *service user*: the person in receipt of care, sometimes know as the resident, patient or client;
(b) *Parliament*: as law maker;
(c) *central government*: the executive force which implements the legislation, represented ultimately by the Secretary of State for (currently) Health;
(d) *the registration authority*: the registration authority to which Parliament has delegated the day-to-day functions of effecting and overseeing regulations, currently the National Care Standards Commission and the Welsh Assembly;
(e) *provider*: the proprietor of the establishment or agency regulated by the regulatory authority upon the direction of central government in accordance with the wishes of Parliament, ie the party responsible for ensuring that the business meets the required regulatory standard. In many cases, the provider will manage the care home, but in large organisations it will delegate such functions to the manager;
(f) *manager*: the person responsible for the day-to-day operation of the care home, but who is answerable to the home owner for ensuring that the home is managed to the required regulatory standard;
(g) *responsible individual*: the person nominated by an organisation (limited company or unincorporated association other than a partnership) to supervise the management of the establishment or agency.

Each will now be considered in turn.

2.3   SERVICE USER

Modern language has determined that the recipient of a health or social care service should be described as a service user. In this book, we shall often refer to that person as 'the client'.

The service user is the most important participant in the business of care. It is the client's needs which the regulatory system is designed to protect. Whether the client is satisfied with the service or whether (since in many cases the client is not in a position to express a full and informed opinion) objective observers are satisfied that the service delivery is adequate will determine:

(a) whether the business of care in question succeeds or fails; and
(b) whether or not regulatory action is required.

Section 1(1) of the Children Act 1989 provides:

> 'Where a court determines any question with respect to:
>
> (a)   the upbringing of a child; or
> (b)   the administration of a child's property or the application of any income arising from it,
>
> the child's welfare shall be the courts' paramount consideration.'

No such provision was to be found in the Registered Homes Act 1984 in so far as it related either to the care of children or adults. Nevertheless, it is established law that the purpose of regulation is the protection of frail and vulnerable members of society.[1] This theme is now to be found in the Care Standards Act 2000 (the 2000 Act) and the regulations and natural minimum standards made in accordance with its authority. Similarly, there is no provision in the 2000 Act which mirrors s 1(1) of the Children Act 1989.

The registered person must ensure that the care home is conducted so as to promote, and make proper provision for, the health and welfare of service users, and the care and, where appropriate, treatment, education and supervision of service users. The registered person must, so far as practicable, enable service users to make decisions with respect to the care that they will receive and their health and welfare. The registered person must also take into account the wishes and feelings of the service user.

The introduction to the *National Minimum Standards for Care Homes for Older People* (March 2001) provides that:

> 'The National Minimum Standards for Care Homes for Older People focus on the achievable outcomes for service users – that is, the impact on the individual of the facilities and services of the home ... while the standards are qualitative they provide a tool for judging the quality of life of service users – they are also measurable. Regulators will look for evidence that the requirements are being met and a good quality life enjoyed by service users ... the involvement of lay assessors in inspections will help ensure a focus on the outcomes for and quality of life of service users ...'

---

1   *Lyons v East Sussex County* (1988) 86 LGR 369.

(This was not repeated in the replacement published in February (but noted March) 2003.)

> 'The following cross-cutting themes underpin the drafting of the National Minimum Standards for Care Homes for Older People ... focus on service users ... fitness for purpose ... comprehensiveness ... meeting assessed needs ... quality services ... quality workforce.'

These examples reinforce the proposition that the purpose of the law was, is and continues to be, for the purpose of protecting the vulnerable, the older and the fragile.

It is therefore a reasonable proposition that for any registration authority, tribunal, court, or indeed professional adviser determining issues relating to the regulation of registered care homes, any decision should consider, as an issue of paramount importance, the interest of service users or potential service users. This may suggest that, when in doubt, decisions should tend to favour cancellation of registration in order to protect clients where there is doubt about their welfare or safety. However, experience has shown that for frail service users, particularly older clients, moving location is traumatic and may be against their best interests unless absolutely required.

An authority considering cancellation of registration and faced with evidence which entitles it to exercise its discretion to cancel must consider the effect of the cancellation upon service users.[1] Cancellation is always discretionary. Despite the view of the Tribunal in *Zaman v Lancashire Country Council*[2] (which suggests that an authority, having found evidence to suggest that an owner or a business was unfit, was obliged to decline the registration), it is suggested that an authority must always have a true discretion in considering the option to cancel or refuse registration. Section 14 of the 2000 Act regulates the 1984 Act formula, so that the authority 'may at any time' cancel the registration.

Zaman does not sit well with the decision of the High Court in *Avon County Council v Lang*.[3] In that case, both the authority and the court were satisfied that accommodation used by an elderly woman was inadequate for general purposes. However, the woman concerned had occupied a particular room for a considerable period of time and it was not in her interest that she should be required to move. As her accommodation in that room, in effect, required that the condition limiting the number of persons accommodated remained the same, the court held that her interests overrode general policy conditions in relation to the size of rooms, ie a reduction in numbers would have caused the old lady or another service user to be moved out of the home.

The relationship of the service user with the other participants in the operation of the care home can be divided into:

(a) his or her relationship with those responsible for both the running of the home and its day-to-day operation; and

---

1   Registered Homes Act 1984, ss 10, 25, 28, 59.
2   Registered Homes Tribunal Decision No 103.
3   [1990] COD 365.

(b) his or her relationship with those responsible for the regulation of the home, namely Parliament, central government and the local authority.

2.3.1 Contractual relationship

The relationship between the client and the home provider, in the home owner's capacity as business proprietor, is the contractual relationship identifying the basis upon which the client occupies accommodation in the home.

The question of contract and the funding of registered care home placements are the subject of Chapter 11. The rights of the client and the obligations of the home owner are usually set out in a written agreement. Such agreements tend to be short and cover basic principles, with no detailed provision for service level. Much will be left to individual interpretation of appropriate standards of care, or be implied into the contract as terms that would be agreed between the parties, as a matter of commercial efficacy.

There is now a clear legal requirement for a contract. The mandatory service users' guide must include a standard form contract and terms and conditions including fee levels and terms.[1]

The advent of community care contracting via local authorities and health authorities has resulted in more detailed provisions for service level. These have developed throughout the 1990s, especially since 1 April 1993, which saw the implementation of the new 'Care in the Community' scheme.

Whether or not there should be detailed service level provision in contracts is a matter of ongoing debate. Some local authorities and associations representing particular client groups have advanced the proposition that service level needs to be defined precisely, so that clients and those representing and supporting clients can understand what is expected. In many cases, the attempt to find service levels does nothing more than reduce to writing what are basically adequate standards of care.

The difficulty for both home owner and client is that the contract of care is not a commercial contract, in the true sense of the word, but an understanding whereby one party will care for the other 24 hours a day, 7 days a week, in a domestic environment. That proposition, it is suggested, leads to the conclusion that there must be a degree of flexibility. Both parties to the contract will require flexibility if it is to work smoothly and in their mutual interest. To prescribe minimum standards for facilities is likely to be restrictive, and may be embarrassing to one party or the other. A better course is to provide detailed service guidance as to the facilities available, and provide that these facilities be available to individual clients according to need. The need for flexibility increases as the level of dependency and requirement for care increases.

The essence of a contract for care, therefore, is that the home owner is required to provide whatever care is required as and when needed. To pay too much attention to service level provisions is to confuse care homes with hotels.

---

1   Care Homes Regulations 2001, SI 2001/3965, reg 5; Private and Voluntary Health Care (England) Regulations 2001, SI 2001/3968, reg 7; *National Minimum Standards for Care Homes for Older People*, standard 2.

However, recent developments in the field have shown a move towards greater specification of care needs, and the legal requirements for detailed assessment prior to admission,[1] and the creation and implementation at all times of an up-to-date care plan,[2] make the detailed assessment and planning of service user care a legal requirement enforceable by criminal sanction. That requirement should encourage providers and service users more particularly to negotiate terms of care requirements, and it is a matter of simple annexure for these to form a part of the service user contract. A definite advantage is that such detail linked into clauses which permit the review and adjustment of fees up and down as care needs fluctuate will be of advantage to both parties and will avoid frustrating debates about the need for changes in upward movements of fees where care needs clearly demonstrate greater service requirement. This topic will be discussed in greater detail in Chapter 11.

With the passage of regulatory powers and duties to the National Care Standards Commission and the Welsh Assembly, the service users' relationships to the local authority are now limited to those of guaranteed sponsorship and the benefit of the requirement to make arrangements for residential accommodation with care.

All potential service users are entitled to have their community care needs assessed under s 47 of the National Health Service and Community Care Act 1990. As will be seen in later chapters, the reality is that for older or disabled patients there is a clear obligation on local authorities to meet the assessed needs immediately of those who qualify. The position of local authorities that their obligations are limited to financial resources or the eligibility criteria set by their policies simply does not arise once the assessed needs indicate residential care, possibly with supplements.

The service user should be aware of his or her rights to claim assessment, to enforce delivery of the assessed needs and to choose preferred accommodation – a choice which must be made when presentation is first made to the local authority for the provision of residential accommodation (in most cases during the course of the assessment process). It is important for the service user to ensure that his or her choice is effected before the local authority elects to make the choice compulsorily. Practice shows that local authorities do not draw the attention of these provisions to potential service users.

2.3.2 Relationship with registration authority

There is no direct relationship between service users and the registration authority. Service users are in fact the very purpose of the existence of regulation as implemented by the registration authority.

Service users, as a matter of law, have the right to contact and make complaints to the registration authority, but have no right to demand particular action or require that regulatory action be taken with regard to their wishes and concerns.

---

1   Care Homes Regulations 2001, reg 14.
2   Ibid, reg 15.

The service users' position is limited to notifying facts and circumstances to the registration authority, which will then take over the matter within its discretion. However, a client, and those who support him or her (whether friends, relatives or professional supporters, eg charity or social workers), will know that the continued ability of the provider to carry out his business is dependent upon continued registration. Service users will take that matter into account when deciding whether and when to raise concerns, and may wish for changes in practice rather than lose an established residential placement.

In Chapter 10, it will be seen that the registration authority has the right to interview service users, provided that they consent.[1] Service users have no corresponding right to demand an interview.

2.3.3   Problems of fees

A lack of sophistication in business methods within the care homes business and the uniformity of the weekly fee produced by capping social welfare benefit, have deflected attention from the fact that in many businesses it is regular practice that different levels of service attract different fees. With greater sophistication and more detailed contracting, fees will, inevitably, be geared to the service level provided. However, this may not always be in the interests of service users.

The provider will expect to increase charges if the level of service increases. Inevitably, this may mean that if the service user can no longer afford to pay the charges, he or she may be required to vacate the home. Services cannot be expected to be supplied free of charge, but providers would be in breach of regulatory standards if they permitted service users to stay without providing adequate care.

Furthermore, detailed service level provisions, as part of a contract, can be snares for the unwary home owner. Specific provisions as to, for example, times of day for care provision will inevitably lead to allegations of breach of contract which could disrupt the cash flow of the care homes business if used to justify withholding payment of fees.

Care home businesses are not greatly profitable. One of their advantages is the regular generation of cash, rarely affected by bad or delayed debt, so that all working capital is employed on a virtually guaranteed revolving basis. Detailed service level provisions which lead service users or their supporters to seek refunds or withhold payments would not be in the interests of service users within an establishment as a whole. The disruption to cash flow in a low margin business threatens the ability of the business to function and may lead to debt collection risk being factored into the price.

Service users are not prisoners. Their remedy, if dissatisfied, is to seek alternative accommodation or to complain, ultimately, to the registration authority, which may take action resulting in the closure of the establishment.

---

1   Care Standards Act 2000, s 31(2).

2.3.4 The 'Care in the Community' scheme

The advent of the 'Care in the Community' scheme has seen a change in contracting arrangements. Contracts are now considered to be very important. Previously, they were incidental to the acceptance of the provision of total care for a fee. Contracts made with local authorities or health authorities are contracts not *with* the service user, but *for* the service user.

In some cases, a client may be party to the contract in order to acknowledge and accept the contract, or to agree that part of the fee should be directed, as the service user's contribution, directly to the provider rather than to the local authority. However, the responsibility for payment of the fee to the provider and responsibility for the provision of the service to the local authority are obligations as between local authority and provider. The service user is incidental to the contractual agreements and many providers may expressly seek to limit the rights of service users by excluding the Contracts (Rights of Third Parties) Act 1999.

Local government, as purchaser, arranges the provision of the care service by the owner for the service user. This is a change from the previous central government-funded support of care contracts, where the service user sought care provisions, contracted provisions and claimed grant support from central government to assist with payment of fees. Such provision (via so-called preserved rights) is now completely abolished as from 1 April 2002.[1]

Even where the service user has a direct contract with the provider, he or she will not have the same power to cancel the contract or relocate. Such steps will require the intervention and support of the local authority.

A practical effect of the change is that whereas the provider, under the previous regime, had a variety of contractual relationships with every service user, it is likely that, for those homes which provide services for local authority or health authority-sponsored service users, the multiplicity of client contracts will have been replaced by one relationship with one client, ie the local authority, whether that is reflected in a block contract or a series of contracts.

Any disturbance of the contractual relationship will have a more immediate impact and the local authority will have the power of purchaser in addition to that of regulator. Service users will cease to have the power of contracting purchaser and, whilst remaining the subject of the contract of care, will be in the position of a party dependent upon a patron or sponsor. A service user's rights may or may not be spelt out in detail in the contract, but his or her power to leave the care home must be seen as diminished where his or her position is altered to sponsored client, as opposed to contracting party.

Unless the service user has effected a preferred choice of home when first seeking local authority support (under the National Assistance Act (Choice of Accommodation) Direction 1992), he or she may find it difficult to leave the home

---

1   Social security benefits, eg income support, disability living allowance, remain but the specific residential boarder supplement is no longer available.

selected by the local authority. It is uncertain whether the right to accommodation is lost, and certainly whether a choice could be effected subsequently.[1]

2.3.5   Relationship with registered manager

Prior to the implementation of the 2000 Act, the day-to-day manager of the home (if different from the provider) would have enjoyed a relationship with the service user, in legal terms, effectively through his employment by the provider. The requirement in the 2000 Act that each home has a manager who is registered (where the provider is not an individual or individuals who conduct the day-to-day management of the home) means that there will be a direct relationship between the service user and the registered manager. The registered provider and the registered manager are described together in the legislation as 'registered person'. Wherever the registered person is outlined in regulations or in national minimum standards as having obligations, then the manager has an individual and personally accountable responsibility to ensure the delivery of the standard to the benefit of the service user. Even where the manager does not have a professionally regulated accountability to the service user, the manager will have personal accountability for proper delivery of facilities and services and may be held accountable to the point of having his registration cancelled if he fails to perform those obligations.

2.3.6   Relationship with local authority

The service user's relationship with the local authority, as a purchaser, is one of the benefits of the exercise of the power (sometimes duty) of the authority to provide accommodation.[2] The matter is now circumscribed by law and details are set out in the Care Homes Regulations 2001 and the various national minimum standards. Quotations are given from the national minimum standards for older people, but, for other establishments, similar provisions are contained in the relevant regulations and national minimum standards.

Regulation 22 of the Care Homes Regulations 2001 sets out in detail a requirement for a complaints procedure which is to be appropriate to the needs of service users. All complaints are to be fully investigated, and reports must be made within 28 days. All service users must have copies of the complaints procedure in such a form as they are capable of understanding. Complaints procedures must contain details of the name, address and contact arrangements for the National Care Standards Commission, so as to enable complaints to be made directly should the client be dissatisfied.

Summaries of the provisions are required to be kept within the establishment's statement of purpose and further summaries are required to be within the service user guide, provided as required by reg 5 of the Care Homes Regulations 2001 to every service user.

---

1   See the National Assistance Act 1948, ss 21–26; National Health Service and Community Care Act 1990, s 47.

2   See the National Assistance Act 1948, s 21, as amended by the National Health Service and Community Care Act 1990.

Standard 16 of the *National Minimum Standards for Care Homes for Older People* makes it a standard (which barely adds to the statutory requirements) that there is 'a simple, clear and accessible complaints procedure which includes the stages and timescales for the process'. Standard 16 does little more than repeat what is contained in the Regulations. This may be because the Regulations were drafted after the promulgation of these particular standards.

Standard 22, which is formulated for younger adults, significantly advances and enlarges the outline standards set out in the *National Minimum Standards for Care Homes for Older People* and shows how the thought process of refining and developing the standards has progressed – notably in the requirement for the registered manager and staff to listen to and act on the views and concerns of service users and with an express requirement that service users should be assured that they will not be victimised for making complaints.

2.3.7   Complaints procedure

As a matter of good practice, over the years, every provider has been required to publish a complaints procedure. This should provide for the effective referral by the client of complaints to objective parties. In large homes, complaints should be referred in the first instance to the home manager and thereafter to the owner. Many homes arrange for outside counsellors to be available to investigate complaints and report to the owners on their substance, and any action which may be required. Ultimately, service users know that they may complain to the registration authority.

The principle of 'whole service' purchase extends even to circumstances where, under the National Assistance Act (Choice of Accommodation) Direction 1992, local authorities are required to purchase preferred accommodation supported by a third-party contribution to defray the difference between the care home fees and the amount which the local authority would normally expect to pay. Surprisingly, the third-party contribution is not a matter of direct contract between the third party and the care home, but rather a contract between the purchasing local authority and the third party. Whilst in practice the contribution may be paid directly, default by the third party will expose the local authority to liability even where it does not recover from the third party. This would explain why many local authorities seek to restrict the ability of care homes to seek third-party contributions.

The current position of local authorities is to undertake a properly managed system of credit risk and credit control, and to accept third-party contribution arrangements only where they are satisfied about the credit risk involved in accepting the extra charge.

In relation to NHS contracts, the position is now clear. Section 23 of the National Health Service Act 1977 authorises NHS bodies to purchase services from private or voluntary providers. No one may be charged directly or indirectly for the provision of an NHS service, nor for the provision of an NHS service to a third party. Accordingly, if the whole of the service is required by the NHS patient, the NHS must provide in full. The provisions of the Department of

Health guide to charging for residential accommodation[1] make it clear that the provision by local authorities is to be for the whole of the required service.

The concept of a top-up as being the difference between the price properly payable by the local authority or NHS body and that charged by the private sector does not arise, and is illegal in civil law (and possibly in criminal law).[2] The only legitimate reason for a legal payment additional to the charge paid by the local government or NHS body is where it is legitimately identified and used to pay for services or goods in addition to the service specification paid by the public body.

Accordingly, as a result both of law and practice, the relationship between clients and the regulatory authority leaves open clear lines of communication for clients to communicate their concerns directly to the regulatory authority, and thus to involve the regulatory authority in quality-control issues.

2.3.8   Relationship with Parliament and central government

The client will have a relationship with Parliament or central government only to the extent that opinion as to the effectiveness of the operation of the regulatory scheme may prompt amendment of executive regulations and directions made by central government, and thus changes to the regulatory framework as prescribed by Parliament.

2.4   PARLIAMENT

Parliament creates, repeals and amends the law of regulation by statute. Furthermore, powers will be circumscribed by the wording of statutes or by appropriately passed subordinate legislation. Accordingly, while regulators appear to those they are required to regulate, or even to those for whose protection the regulation is designed, to be powerful in themselves, their power is always limited and circumscribed.

Having observed that Parliament can appoint the makers and implementers of regulations, it is important to remember that a delegate cannot sub-delegate his authority unless specifically authorised or required to do so.[3] The maxim *Delegatus delegare non potest* applies. The principle is that an agent cannot sub-delegate his appointment, except to the extent that he is authorised so to do by his principal. This is a general principle of English law and applies to the field of public administration in the same way that it applies to private sector agency law.

Parliament cannot be involved in monitoring good practice in the operation of care homes, nor can the Secretary of State be responsible for day-to-day

---

1   *Charging for Residential Accommodation Guidance* (DoH).
2   To receive on demand payment which is not due may be seen as theft or obtaining property by deception contrary to the Theft Act 1968.
3   See, eg, National Health Service Act 1977, ss 13, 14 and also the NHS administration regulations.

decisions. Accordingly, the 2000 Act places these responsibilities with the National Care Standards Commission for England and the Welsh Assembly for Wales. Parliament has set out the rules and established the regulation. More detailed requirements and standards are to be outlined by the Secretary of State. Parliament has described and limited the functions and powers of its obligations.

2.4.1 Relationship with other participants

(1) *The client*: Parliament's relationship with service users is indirect. Parliament reacts to changes of demand from service users and concerns expressed by or on behalf of service users by adjusting the statutory framework of regulation.

(2) *Central government*: the link between statute passed by Parliament and central government is the crucial link of authority for any action to implement or enforce the regulatory requirements.

(3) *Local government*: local government, including the NHS, derives its authority to provide and purchase health and social care service from legislation enacted by Parliament, which will expressly permit and restrict such powers. Action outside these powers will be illegal and in itself of no effect.

(4) *Provider/manager*: there is no direct relationship between Parliament and a provider or manager. The position is similar to the position of the service user. Parliament, in providing the framework of regulation, takes account of the perceptions of society as to the need for regulation, guided by evidence on the conduct of providers and the need to ensure a plentiful supply of care homes, in order to enable those in need and able to purchase to choose appropriate care.

2.5 CENTRAL GOVERNMENT

The function of central government is to act as an executive to implement the requirements of statute enacted by Parliament. Most legislation will be introduced at the behest of the government of the day which will be seeking powers to implement policies it has formulated, thus seeking the seal of legal approval before taking steps to implement changes in policy.

The function of central government, through the Secretary of State, is to generate a detailed framework of regulation to expand upon the basic framework created by statute. Its aim is to ensure that the rules so promulgated are enforced by the bodies identified and authorised by Parliament (ie under the 2000 Act, the National Care Standards Commission and the Welsh Assembly), which are sufficiently able and well resourced to ensure that the law is observed and enforced.

Central government and practitioners advising in the care business need to look to statutes to identify the regulation-making power of the Secretary of State. A variety of Secretaries of State may make regulations in relation to care. Principally, this is likely to be done by the Secretary of State for Health, or possibly the Secretary of State for the Environment, but other Secretaries of State also have this power.

When construing regulations, those responsible must also ensure that the regulations are actually within the limits prescribed by the relevant statute and are not made unreasonably, taking into account the power granted and the mischief against which the regulations are aimed. It will be only in rare cases, however, that the exercise of power granted by Parliament to the Secretary of State will be said to be unreasonable.

Whether or not regulations are *ultra vires* (either because they go beyond the powers granted or because they are unreasonable) is a matter to be considered by a court or tribunal. Tribunals, however, should make decisions as to the unreasonableness or legality of regulations only to the extent that such a decision is required to determine the issue before it.[1]

The Secretary of State has power to make regulations under ss 3, 11, 12, 14–16, 22, 25, 31, 34, 35, 45, 51 and 118 of the 2000 Act, without being exhaustive.

In order to judge the validity and applicability of regulations, the statutory authority should always be the first reference source.

The Secretary of State sets the rules by which the registrative authorities are required to operate. Parliament has also provided for the Secretary of State to direct and give binding general guidance to the registration authority in England. In addition, the registration authority:

(a) must keep the Secretary of State informed about the availability of provision and quality of services;
(b) must encourage improvement of quality in services;
(c) must make information about services available to the public;
(d) must give specific advice to the Secretary of State when requested;
(e) may at any time give advice concerning changes required to improve services or other matters.

In due course it will no doubt be interesting to see the extent to which the Secretary of State feels bound to implement such advice and the extent to which the Commission as regulator will seek to force the Secretary of State's hand. They are both public bodies required to act reasonably and rationally.

2.5.1 Funding

The issue of funding in this context is the function of central government in providing funds for the purchase of care by those in need, who are unable to meet the financial requirements of the care home from their own resources. The history of the development of care homes, as has been seen, is closely identified with the debate as to whether or not funds for the purchase of health care and

---

1   See *Chief Adjudication Officer v Foster* [1993] 1 All ER 705, HL; see also *Boddington v British Transport Police* [1999] 2 AC 143, HL.

social welfare should come exclusively from private individuals, from central government, or from local government. Central government is required to ensure that, for every citizen, there is promoted a health care service provided free.[1] Local government has traditionally been charged with providing residential accommodation and other welfare services for those in need within its area, to the extent that such services do not amount to health care requirements.[2] The power to provide residential accommodation has been made an obligation where central government so directs. Such powers and obligations have, since their inception, included the power to purchase services from the private sector where these are not available from public sector resources.[3] This power was extended so that local authorities may purchase health care services with effect from 1 April 1993.[4]

Prior to 1 April 1993 and thereafter up to 1 April 2002, in respect of those who were entitled to and in receipt of residential and nursing care home care prior to that date, central government made available means-tested grants for those in need of care. Budgets were not in any way cash or resource limited. The amount of grants, whilst unlimited when first conceived, were cash limited (from April 1985) to a statutory maximum, adjusted from time to time to take account of inflation.

Limited cash expenditure in the support of care home placement was effected by switching the obligation from one of central government to citizens in need, to an obligation on the part of local government to citizens who are assessed by local government as being in need. This remains the case, notwithstanding the availability of means-tested and non-means-tested welfare benefits to the sick, disabled and needy, which continue beyond 1 April 1993 for those who are not assessed by a local authority as being in need or who do not seek such assessment.

All central government funding for any client (even those placed prior to 1 April 1993) has now been withdrawn. All publicly funded provision is now made either through local authorities or through the NHS. No NHS patient has a right to claim individual care or treatment. The details of funding care home placement of registered homes will be discussed in greater depth in Chapter 11.

Central government has two distinct roles:

(a) determining the detail of regulation;
(b) providing funds to support the provision of care to individuals, by funding or providing facilities for raising revenue for those who are responsible for such care.

---

1   See the National Health Service Act 1977, s 1.
2   See, eg, the National Assistance Act 1948, Pt III, and the Chronically Sick and Disabled Persons Act 1970.
3   See, eg, the National Assistance Act 1948, s 26.
4   See amendments to the National Assistance Act 1948, Pt III, s 21 by the National Health Service and Community Care Act 1990. But *Coughlan*'s case limits this increase in powers only to the extent that the nursing care services are ancillary to the need for residential accommodation.

2.5.2   Relationship with clients

The relationship between client and central government is remote but experience as to the conduct of care homes shows that criticism, whether negative or positive, of the operation of care homes will filter through to central government and, to that extent, the service user will have an indirect influence upon the way in which central government exercises its role in promulgating regulations.

Further, the increasing or decreasing needs of service users for funds to meet their care requirements means that they are ultimately dependent on central government to provide sufficient funds. Since clients are also voters, shortfalls in funds could be reflected in the ballot box, with adverse consequences for central government.

2.5.3   Relationship with local authorities

Local government is not entitled to look to central government for funds specifically to support the provision of care purchased by local government. Subject to specific exceptions (eg the special transitional grant made by central government to local government to assist with the transfer of responsibility for residential community care, and a further grant to support the abolition of the 'preserved' rights to social security benefits with effect from 1 April 2002), local government must look to its own resources to meet its obligations as a purchaser and provider. Those resources may be acquired by local revenue-raising powers or general grants from central government. Central government will inevitably frustrate local government by simultaneously expecting the delivery of required services and capping revenue-raising powers.

Where local government decides to purchase care, it should be aware of the extent of its powers, and the limitation on those powers imposed by Parliament or central government. There is always the vexed question as to whether or not a purchasing power includes a power to pay part of monies incurred by clients. The better view is that local authorities seek reimbursement from clients, but do not seek to pay, by way of 'top up', a shortfall in fees left after the main portion has been discharged by the client or third parties.

2.5.4   Relationship with care home owners and managers

The relationship between central government and care home owners/managers is remote. Central government sets the framework and, to a certain extent, provides funds available for the purchase of services, reacting to the demands of society by amending the regulatory regime. Having created the general regulation scheme, as permitted by Parliament, central government is not directly responsible or accountable to home owners, nor are home owners entitled to leapfrog registration authorities and deal directly with central government, otherwise than by way of political lobbying.

2.6 REGISTRATION AUTHORITY

2.6.1 National Care Standards Commission/Welsh Assembly/ Care Standards Inspectorate for Wales

The registration authority is the statutorily created body responsible for regulation of health and social services. The prior jurisdiction of health authorities and social services departments of local authorities was abolished with the repeal of the Registered Homes Act 1984. Two registration authorities (the National Care Standards Commission (NCSC) and the Welsh Assembly) have been established as the relevant registration authorities for their jurisdiction under s 5 of the 2000 Act. The Welsh Assembly needed no further establishment.

Section 6 of the 2000 Act establishes the NCSC as a body corporate. The NCSC clearly has the responsibilities (and may exercise the powers) identified in the 2000 Act, particularly Part II. The Commission is a free-standing body but it must act:

(a) in accordance with directions from the Secretary of State; and
(b) under guidance from the Secretary of State.

The provisions have been explored in earlier sections of this book.

The establishment of the Commission is set out in Sch 1 to the 2000 Act. Section 7 sets out general duties of the Commission, and s 8 sets out general functions of the Assembly. The general functions of the Assembly are necessarily limited because the more detailed provisions in relation to the promotion and improvement of health care by changes in legal regulation are, of course, a matter for the Assembly itself under the legislation devolving certain administration of public powers to it. That legislation is no part of the remit of this book.

The general duties of the NCSC were set out earlier in this chapter. The Commission's duties are extensively wider than simply implementing the role of registration authority. The positive duty to provide information on the availability and quality of services means that the Secretary of State cannot avoid accepting responsibility for failings within the system which may be capable of being addressed by legislative change or government funding. It will be interesting to see the extent to which the Commission adds pressure to the debate on the suggestion that additional public funds are required to fund local authorities to purchase proper levels of community care.

The duty to encourage the improvement in the quality of services is widely drawn and difficult to limit, but the requirement to make information about services under Part II of the 2000 Act available to the public is interesting. It would appear that if members of the public require information that should be within the possession of the Commission, the Commission will have to make that information available or explain its absence. There may be some debate as to whether the duty to make information available is a duty in relation to all information or a duty in relation to such information as the Commission may think it appropriate to release.

Most interesting is the power of the Commission to give (unsolicited) advice to the Secretary of State on changes which should be made to improve the quality of community care services and other issues. It will be interesting to see the extent to which the Commission is prepared to press its advice if it is ignored by the Secretary of State, and how the Secretary of State would react (possibly in a public administrative law challenge) if he declines to take steps, within his power, to follow the advice of the Commission. One can conceive of situations where it would be wholly irrational for the Secretary of State to fail to heed the advice of his own appointed Commission possessed of the right information to inform appropriate policy decisions.

2.6.2   Relationship with the service user

There is no direct relationship between the registration authority and the service user. However, the purpose of establishing the registration authority is to act as a public protector of the rights of the service user. As has already been identified, the new statutorily binding requirements for the establishment of complaints procedures require that they be set out in the service user guides and include details of the address and contact numbers for the NCSC and the Welsh Assembly. These provisions create a clear link of invitation to service users to take up issues directly with the regulator. Service users will not be able to direct or order the registration authority on the extent to which it investigates, but are clearly actively encouraged to discuss with the registration authority concerns or expressions of satisfaction.

Within the powers of inspection set out in ss 31 and 32 of the 2000 Act, the registration authority is given specific power to interview service users with their consent. Such interviews are already commonplace in the course of regulatory intervention, and the statutory provision is more addressed to ensuring that the provider and manager of a care establishment understand that there is a clear right (which should not be obstructed) of interview for a client. The registration authority must appreciate the limitations and understand that it cannot force interviews where interviews are not wanted. Also, the limitation of consent suggests that there is no power to interview the incapacitated service user. Providers and managers will risk the criminal sanction of a prosecution for obstruction if they seek in any way to prevent the registration authority from interviewing or to discourage service users from willingly participating in interviews.

However, there is a tension between the 2000 Act, the Police and Criminal Evidence Act 1984 and the Human Rights Act 1998. If a criminal offence is suspected, a 'caution' must be given to the suspect. Failure will prevent the prosecutor from relying on the caution in criminal proceedings, but *not* in civil proceedings. A caution will probably justify a refusal to participate in the interview.

2.6.3   Relationship with Parliament

The registration authority owes its creation (in the case of the Commission) and its powers (in the case of the Welsh Assembly) to Parliament. This link is continued and reversed through the Secretary of State for Health in the case of the Commission through its duties to advise and report upon the state of community care services and its power to make unsolicited advice.

The Welsh Assembly is, to a limited extent, its own law maker in the field of community care, and thus registration authority and devolved parliamentary assembly are one and the same.

2.6.4   Relationship with central government

To the extent that central government reflects the machine of government operating out of Westminster in relation to England, it has no application whatsoever to the Welsh Assembly as registration authority in Wales. To the extent that central government embraces the powers devolved to the Welsh Assembly, the registration authority and the Assembly are one and the same.

In relation to the NCSC in England, the Commission is subject to direction and general guidance of central government under s 6 of the 2000 Act. The relationship is symbiotic in the combination of duties and power imposed upon and granted to the Commission under s 7 of the 2000 Act, and through its establishment as the registration authority for non-NHS health and social care services, with extensive duties under Part II of the Act.

2.6.5   Relationship with local government and NHS bodies

Registration authorities have no relationship with NHS bodies since NHS-operated facilities are outside the remit of the NCSC and, indeed, effectively the Care Standards Inspectorate for Wales, although NHS facilities within Wales will be managed through the Welsh Assembly as a direct manager carrying out a separate function from its function as registration authority.

The position with local government is different. Prior to the implementation of the 2000 Act, local government (and certain other public authority operators) carried on what are recognised as care establishments and agencies without any requirement for registration, or in some cases being exempt from registration. Those exclusions and exemptions have been repealed and not replaced within the 2000 legislation. The registration authority's relationship to the local authority as a provider of health and social care services outside the NHS is exactly the same as the relationship that the registration authority has to any other provider of health and social care services required to be regulated under the 2000 Act. There are no apparent distinctions or reliefs for local government as a provider of care.

Local government must be aware that care commissioned or provided by it will be subject to scrutiny by an independent registration authority in the same way that any other provision is scrutinised. The matter will be addressed in detail in Chapter 3 in an analysis of the registrable care establishments and agencies, but where local government has commissioned care so as to access government-funded benefits, such as housing benefits which are excluded from registrable care, the schemes may need to be reviewed. The political status quo whereby the Commissioner (the Director of Social Services) was able to determine eligibility or requirements for registration will no longer apply when regulation is conducted by a body separate from the commissioner. This will remove what has become, in many ways, a complex and embarrassing conflict of interests which may not always have worked to the benefit of service users.

2.6.6   Relationship with providers and managers

The whole detail of this book centres upon this relationship. The registration authority is the regulatory body controlling, through the application of regulations and the interpretation of standards, the way in which both the registered provider and the registered manager (many times combined as the registered person for a registered care establishment and agencies) operate. The registration authority will control the gateway to registered or licensed activity, monitor activity following registration, and be the controlling agency in seeking to remove from the licensed or regulated activity those considered inappropriate to be there (subject to the appeal jurisdiction of the Care Standards Tribunal).

2.7   LOCAL GOVERNMENT

In considering the position of local government, it is appropriate to begin by looking at organs of local government which may be concerned with the delivery of care. These are:

(a) social services authorities (in the appropriate context this will mean county councils or unitary authorities, metropolitan borough councils and London boroughs);
(b) health authorities;
(c) NHS trusts and Primary Care Trusts.

2.7.1   Social services authorities

Social services authorities have roles as purchasers of care supplied within care homes and, since 1 April 1993, nursing homes (all care is included if incidental to the local authority's duty to provide residential accommodation). However, specialised medical, health or nursing care is beyond the power of the local authority.[1]

2.7.2   Health authorities/Primary Care Trusts (NHS bodies)

NHS bodies have the function, in the context of registered care establishments and agencies, on behalf of the Secretary of State, to commission (ie purchase) care for those in need within their jurisdiction. Accordingly, to the extent that NHS facilities may not be available to the health authority, it may purchase health care from private sector providers operating registered care homes.

With the abolition of health authorities and the creation of strategic health authorities, the actual purchasing function will increasingly be provided by

---

1   *R v North and East Devon Health Authority ex parte Coughlan* (1998) 2 CCL Rep 285.

primary care trusts and even care trusts jointly exercising local government and NHS powers.

2.7.3   NHS trusts

NHS trusts were created (under the National Health Service and Community Care Act 1990), in broad terms, to own or provide hospital buildings and facilities and manage services conducted from such buildings and facilities. More recently, this power has been widened to the provision of goods and services for the purposes of the NHS under s 13 of the Health Act 1999 amending s 5 of the National Health Service and Community Care Act 1990. As such, they are described as the *providers* of services, as opposed to the *purchasers* of service. NHS trusts are not concerned with the regulation of registered care homes, or the purchase of care for patients. As part of their own diversification of service, they may seek to make available facilities equivalent to registered care home facilities or to purchase, in order to enhance their own facilities, registered care home placements to fulfil the requirements of purchasers attracted to the service of the trust. In addition, NHS trusts, organised to provide community services, may see the need to purchase, in block or individually, nursing home placements, to fulfil the requirements of their own private or NHS purchasers for care needs.

A care home owner dealing with an NHS trust will make arrangements for the provision of a facility for the trust, rather than the provision of care for an individual.

2.8   PRIMARY CARE TRUSTS

Primary care trusts came into existence as a result of the complex development of legislation passing from the National Health Service Primary Care Act 1997 through the Health Act 1999, and more recently the Health and Social Care Act 2001. A detailed consideration of the powers, duties and legislative origins of NHS bodies is beyond the scope of this book.

Increasingly, the provision of community care services (seen in the context of primary care services) will be either provided or purchased by the bodies known as primary care trusts. These are NHS bodies set up with centrally or regionally controlled budgets to control the delivery of primary care in particular areas. The trusts will deliver what is currently known as community nursing services and will purchase various forms of NHS-required care, for example:

- intermediate care for those requiring an approximately 6-week bridge between acute NHS care and a full-time placement in another establishment or preferably within the community;
- continuing care for those who have a need without foreseeable end for long-term care in the community;
- the management and supervision of the provision of free nursing care by a registered nurse delivered in accordance with the Health and Social Care Act 2001.

Providers contracting with primary care trusts will be contracting directly with the purchaser of services or, in some limited cases, contracting to provide facilities to the trust as a provider of services to some other NHS body. Primary care trusts will exercise no regulatory role save for the regulation that arises out of drafting, implementing and enforcing standards through negotiation of contracts for services with providers of regulated establishments and agencies to the extent that those establishments and agencies are not directly managed and provided by the NHS.

2.8.1   Social services authorities and NHS bodies as purchasers

Local authorities have the function of purchasing care. Whether such care can be purchased and whether contracts for purchase are valid, once again, requires an analysis of whether the ability to purchase is within the powers of the authority. The ability must be seen to be within the powers of the authority, not merely as a matter of principle, but in the individual case. If the exercise of the power to purchase goes beyond the purchase of care for an individual, but involves a block contract over a period of time, it needs to be shown that the authority not only had the power to purchase, but also exercised that power taking into account all relevant circumstances. The contract must be *intra vires*, and the actual contract must have been concluded only after due consideration, taking into account all relevant matters, and leaving aside irrelevant matters.

Social services authorities have powers and obligations to provide and purchase care pursuant to the National Assistance Act 1948, Part III. Health authorities have powers and obligations to make arrangements with third parties for the provision of health care services pursuant to s 23 of the National Health Service Act 1977.

The widening of social services authorities' powers to purchase health care, with effect from 1 April 1993, and the consequent implications of government policy that residential care home and nursing home placement should be purchased through the local authority (whether or not health care), has led to consideration of whether potential or existing arrangements for the purchase of health care from the private sector by health authorities are or remain valid.

2.8.2   Social service authorities and NHS bodies as providers

Although the House of Lords decided in *R v Wandsworth London Borough Council ex parte Beckwith*[1] that there was no requirement for local authorities to retain any directly managed provision, many social service authorities continue to provide directly managed residential and non-residential services.

The simple implementation from 1 April 2002 under the 2000 Act that local authorities are regulated in exactly the same way in relation to the provision of care establishments and care agencies will mean that they must deliver standards to the same objective level as that required of the private and voluntary sectors, or face the ignominy of being required to invest further funds to improve or close services. Local authorities will face the full rigour of regulation and may expect,

---

1   [1996] 1 WLR 60, HL.

in the case of poor practice, to find themselves prosecuted. Officers and elected members of social service authorities who are directly responsible for mis-performance in regulated care establishments and agencies may be personally prosecuted.

The Court of Appeal has recently decided in *R (Heather) v Leonard Cheshire Foundation*[1] that private and voluntary providers contracting with the local authorities, who provide residential accommodation with care, are not providing public services so as to make those provider agencies public bodies for the purpose of s 6 of the Human Rights Act 1998 (implemented in the United Kingdom with effect from 2 October 2000). We await to see whether there will be further appeals in relation to that issue to the House of Lords or possibly to the European Court of Human Rights in Strasbourg. However, it is difficult to see how a regulated local authority provider (as opposed to a voluntary or private provider) of such accommodation of care with service would not be subject to the full obligation to meet citizens' expectations under the European Convention on Human Rights.

Local authorities could face an interesting dilemma, in cases of directly managed care homes with residents of many years' standing, when confronted either by a requirement to improve services or proceedings to close registrable establishments. A decision to close might be met with a challenge from long-term residents that this shows insufficient respect for the residents' family lives, as enshrined (subject to certain protections) within Art 8 of the Convention.

There will be many difficult issues and hard choices for local authorities in their new role as providers of care establishments and agencies subject to external and enforceable regulation. If local authorities lawfully continue to provide care establishments and agencies, they must have sought registration for those establishments and agencies and the associated managers prior to the date appointed under the 2000 Act, which will in general be 1 April 2002. This factor, combined with the clear rule that local authorities may not make arrangements for the provision of accommodation under the National Assistance Act 1948 other than in care homes which are registered under the 2000 Act, may lead to difficulties for authorities which continue to provide services either without being registered, following the cancellation of registration, or possibly having failed to make appropriate applications in time. The wide-ranging supplementary powers conferred by the Local Government Act 2000 (increasingly viewed as a power of first resort) may bring some assistance and comfort to individual dilemmas.

2.8.3 Relationship with NHS bodies

(1) *Service users*: the public body will now relate to service users as the body which has either acquired or accepted responsibility for making or arranging the provision and delivery of accommodation and care services. Service users will have rights against local authorities under the National Assistance Act 1948 and the National Health Service and Community Care

---

1   [2002] EWCA Civ 366, (2002) *The Times*, April 8.

Act 1990. Service users will have no direct personal enforceable rights as against NHS bodies other than to expect that these bodies will make available to them, upon the same terms and within the same time frames as others, such facilities as the bodies perceive to be required, and such services as they perceive are required to meet needs in their areas of authority. An important distinction between local government and the NHS is the existence of directly enforceable personal rights against local government. However, the Human Rights Act 1998 and the NHS administration regulations (particularly at para 3) may well give some scope for claims to personal entitlement.

(2) *Parliament*: neither local authorities nor NHS bodies have any relationship with Parliament save for Parliament being the creator of the rights and obligations by statute within which they function.

(3) *Central government*: local authorities are required to deliver social services in accordance with their statutory powers and in accordance with the general guidance of the Secretary of State (being the principal representa-tive of central government).[1] NHS bodies are required to act upon the direction of the Secretary of State representing central government and to act in accordance with guidance issued by the Secretary of State which falls short of a direction. Thus, both local authorities and NHS bodies may expect to be the subject of binding directions or guidance which require them to exercise their powers (now limited to the provision or com-missioning of health and social care) in a way required by government or for particular citizens identified by government on particular bases. Neither local government nor NHS bodies can look for specific assistance on a case-by-case basis to support the provision of health and social care as required by central government, but will receive annual lump-sum grants to support (in the case of local authorities, their own revenue-raising abilities) the obligations expected of them by law and government direction.

(4) *Registration authority*: local government, as provider of registrable care establishments and care agencies, will be a registrable person required to comply with the terms of the 2000 Act, subordinate and complementary legislation in exactly the same way as any other provider of health and social care. NHS bodies have no relationship with the registration authorities since NHS services are outside the remit of the registration authorities.

(5) *Other care providers*: local authorities have no relationship with other care providers, except that, to the extent that they deliver their duties and powers to commission arrangements for residential accommodation and care from registrable establishments and agencies, they will have a contractual relationship. Similar provisions apply to NHS bodies.

(6) *Managers of care home establishments and agencies*: neither local govern-ment nor NHS bodies will have any direct relationship with care establishment or agency managers. The contracting relationship will be

---

1   Local Authority Social Services Act 1970, s 7(1).

with the providers, and the obligations of the care establishment and agency managers will be owed to the registration authority.

2.8.4 Care establishment or agency provider

The provider is the person who carries on the business of the establishment or agency which provides care for those in need, ie the service users.

2.8.5 Problems of definition

The legislation (the Registered Homes Act 1984 and the Children Act 1989 gave little assistance in determining what is meant by 'carrying on'. No further assistance is given by the 2000 Act. It is submitted that the term carries with it the usual meaning ascribed in law, namely that it indicates that the person is entitled to ownership and profit and is expected to bear losses. In so far as the business undertakes responsibility, the person 'carrying on' the business is the one who undertakes responsibility for its liabilities. The person carrying on the business is also clearly the person responsible to the regulators for compliance with regulatory requirements as provider.

The person carrying on the business is registered. He or she is the person who, on loss of registration, will therefore lose the business. It is submitted that the person carrying on the business is the business owner, as opposed to the person having day-to-day management of the business.

'Carry on' is defined in the *Concise Oxford Dictionary* (1991 edn) (as a second meaning) as 'engage in business'. How much activity may be needed to constitute 'carrying on' will be a matter of fact and degree in each case. Some managers may leave such a degree of control that they should (if individuals) properly be registered as providers and not managers. Care establishments and agencies must be managed by individuals, ie the provider must be an individual or partnership or must appoint an individual to be manager.[1]

In relation to limited liability partnerships,[2] it is suggested that the person is the partnership organisation itself. Similar principles apply to other 'partnerships' as a partnership is an unincorporated body.[3] Some may argue that a partnership requires registration of each partner (but what is the position with limited partners, who have no conduct of the business?). It has not been the practice under the Registered Homes Act 1984 to require each partner to be registered as a condition of admission to the partnership.

2.8.6 Registration

Registration is required of any person carrying on or managing a care establishment or agency.[4]

---

1   Care Standards Act 2000, s 12(3); Care Homes Regulations 2001, SI 2001/3965, regs 8–10.
2   Ie registered as a separate body under the Limited Liability Partnerships Act 2000.
3   See Interpretation Act 1978.
4   Care Standards Act 2000, s 11.

2.8.7   Duties

The care home provider owes duties:

(a) to service users, to provide a sufficient and adequate standard of care according to their needs, in so far as commitments are made over and above adequate standards as defined by the registration authority in accordance with contractual commitments asked and given, including ensuring that the home complies with the regulatory requirements of regulations;
(b) to the registration authority, to comply with the requirements of regulations.

The consequences of breach of these duties are, however, different. Breach of duty to a client (or an extended client if the contract is made with a local authority acting as a purchaser) will give rise to financial consequences, including those arising out of termination of contract. Breach of an obligation to the registration authority may lead, ultimately, to the loss of registration and thus, in effect, the loss of the licence (registration) to carry on the business.

2.8.8   Rights

The care home provider also enjoys certain rights. To be a care home owner, the provider must have secured acceptance as being fit to operate a care home, in accordance with the standards of the registration authority. That acceptance is signified in the certificate of registration granted pursuant to s 13 of the 2000 Act. Armed with the certificate of registration, the provider is entitled to trade, to 'carry on' the business of running the home. He has thus been admitted to a privileged sector entitled to carry on a regulated business, and this will give him the advantage of a marketplace in which only those who have been objectively tested and have reached a satisfactory standard are permitted to carry on the business.

The process of regulation must be seen against the background that admission to the right to trade is a privilege not accorded to all and, accordingly, is subject to review and cancellation, should standards anticipated at the time of registration not be maintained.

If the provider is required to appoint a manager,[1] the right to trade, but more probably the registration itself, will not become effective unless and until that manager is registered.[2] What happens in the case of the departure of a registered manager before the appointment of a replacement is an open question. This will be discussed in Chapter 3. On the face of it, the establishment will be trading unlawfully at the whim and mercy of the registration authority. That is hardly a comfort to a would-be investor. However, the non-appointment of a manager carries no minimal sanction so that the heavy legal penalties may fall on a person who manages without being registered.

---

1   See the Care Homes Regulations 2001, reg 8.
2   Care Standards Act 2000, s 11.

2.8.9 Relationship with service users

The provider is in a direct relationship with the service user. In traditional care home management, the service user is the customer of the provider. Their relationship is defined by contract, usually supplemented by a review as to the supply of adequate and proper standards of care, from time to time. In the modern 'community care' context, the relationship, often described as one of service performance, may be created in contract, but may be one limited to an obligation on the part of the owner to supply services to a standard agreement with a third party, ie the local authority or other sponsor. It is suggested that this relationship is nothing more than an extension of the former relationship where relatives contracted as sponsors for the person in care so that the person in care was not a contracting party, but was entitled to receive the benefit of the contract negotiated and maintained on his or her behalf by a third party.

2.8.10 Relationship with Parliament

The provider is in no direct relationship with Parliament, but his or her ability to carry on the business is circumscribed by changes in the regulatory structure specified by statutes enacted or amended from time to time by Parliament.

2.8.11 Relationship with central government

The provider is not in direct relationship with central government but, in so far as central government, through the Secretary of State, reviews and amends the detailed provisions of regulation, which impact upon the direct operation of care homes or particular classes of care homes, then the home owner operates subject to a licence subject to the changing rules of regulation or deregulation as decided by central government in accordance with the brief outlined by Parliament. If the rules are changed (by proper process) the home owner cannot complain, even if his interests are seriously adversely affected. He may, however, test the validity of the process. If it is defective, the change will be of no effect. Government is constrained to legislate in accordance with the provisions of the Human Rights Act 1998.

2.8.12 Relationship with local government and NHS bodies

The provider is in direct relationship with local government as a supplier of services to local government acting as a purchaser. The owner will be in a contractual relationship with the local authority or NHS body as with any other client/customer. The practical differences are:

(a) greater comfort on credit risk; and
(b) the need to ensure that the local authority has acted within its powers. The downside may be an inability to demand or negotiate adequate fee levels.

2.9   THE MANAGER

Whatever may be his or her relationship with other participants in the operation of a care home business, it is submitted that the manager will always be the employee or agent of the provider. He or she may have a position of independence or individual responsibility, but his or her relationship with the care home owner will be circumscribed by a contract requiring him or her to provide services (ie an independent contractor) or a contract of service, making him or her the employee of the provider.

The manager, as will be seen in Chapter 3, must be registered with the registration authority. The provider's relationship with the manager will be one of control in relation to the proper conduct of care home business. However, with the universal requirement for managers to register and accept direct criminal accountability for the operation of the establishment, the ability of providers to control, and the wisdom of the managers in accepting control, should be tempered.

Conflict may arise if the care home owner requires the manager to operate in such a way as is outside proper standards of care or in breach of conditions of registration, or in circumstances that may put his registration in jeopardy. It is submitted that because of the relationship between owner and manager, any conflict will usually only be resolved by the manager's resigning from his appointment. The care home owner, being the business proprietor, is entitled to expect compliance with instructions. The manager may be entitled to claim damages for breach of contract, or (if employed) constructive dismissal, as being unfair and/or wrongful.

To require a care home manager to act in such a way as to contravene rules of good practice, conditions of registration or to endanger his own certificate of registration must surely be seen as conduct entitling the manager to determine his contract by way of fundamental breach, so as to entitle determination of a contract for services, or such as to amount to constructive dismissal from a contract of employment, ie in either case a breach going to the root of the agreement. For a manager to continue to act in contravention of rules of good practice is highly dangerous. His personal registration will be at risk, and a cancelled registration could leave his professional career in ruins.

2.9.1   Who is the manager?

'Manager' of a care establishment or agency may have a number of meanings. 'Manager' may be a term of art used to describe a person responsible for the whole of the operation of a care home, or one or more divisions of the care home business. A manager will operate either under a contract for service or a contract of service and will, in effect, be the employee or agent of the care home providers.

Managers may be individuals or limited companies. Frequently, care home owners who lack the ability, knowledge or time to conduct the business will appoint managers to have control of the business on a day-to-day basis, reporting regularly to their principals. A manager is required particularly where the provider is not an individual. The manager must be an individual. 'Individual' is not defined in the 2000 Act, but the common understanding is that it means a human being.

Managers who have complete control of a care establishment or agency may seek to be registered as providers. This may, in some limited cases, avoid double registration, but, in such circumstances, the manager/provider will be carrying on the business, and the 'owner' will be limited to investors' rights.

From a regulatory point of view, a manager who is registered must accept that loss of registration for failure to meet standards will mean his or her (and the owner) acquiring a reputation for providing inadequate service.

A manager who is not carrying on the business, but who obtains registration, should be careful to establish that he or she has sufficient means, at all times, properly to fulfil the obligations of management, supported by an appropriate contract of indemnity for business liability.

Managers should proceed with care. Registration cannot be resigned and may only be cancelled voluntarily with difficulty;[1] it can never be surrendered once adverse regulatory action has been started and, once adopted, it may carry tremendous risk. This is all the more so where managers conduct business providing management services to several owners of a number of centres. The essence of such arrangements is that the business risk is taken by the business owner and the executive function is carried out by the manager. This executive function cannot be carried out without sufficient resources, and the manager needs to know that he or she can resign if resources are withheld or are not available to meet proper standards. Some national minimum standards, notably the *National Minimum Standards for Care Homes for Older People*, suggest that a manager must be limited to one establishment. Be that as it may, the practical requirements of registration mean that it will be increasingly rare for a sensible manager to be willing to accept responsibility for more than one establishment or agency.

2.9.2 What is a manager?

No definition was provided in the Registered Homes Act 1984, and none is proffered by the 2000 Act. It is submitted that a manager is a person who is vested with power to direct and control the business on a day-to-day basis, making all decisions which may be relevant to day-to-day control of the business, as opposed to medium or long-term strategic development of the business. The manager may or may not be synonymous with the person in charge of care.

If the above definition is correct, the manager will assume business control. He or she may be a skilled and experienced carer or nurse, although it may not be necessary that he or she is so in every case. If such skills and experience are not present, the manager must procure for his or her principal such skills by appointing suitably qualified and experienced persons to deliver and manage

---

1   See s 15 of the 2000 Act and para 15 of the Registration Regulations.

care, subject to his or her direction and control as a business manager. The *National Minimum Standards for Care Homes for Older People* suggest that where nursing care is provided, the manager must be a registered nurse.

In exactly the same way, a business owner who lacks experience or skill in the particular field of care must either acquire those skills, dispose of the business, or appoint sufficiently experienced and qualified staff to supply the care skills needed.

Whatever may be the precisely correct interpretation of the relationship between the national minimum standards, the regulations and the 2000 Act, any sensible interpretation (and indeed common sense itself) suggests that, whether in the position of registered manager, provider or in a senior position, controlled by the provider but free to exercise independent professional judgment, a manager must be someone of sufficient skill and experience to deliver the care required and to secure the outcomes for service users necessary for proper management and conduct of the care establishment or agency.

Irrespective of national minimum standards, it is clear that proper delivery of the requirements set out in the regulations will require the appointment in some role (usually as provider or registrable manager) of people who have the relevant experience and qualifications to fulfil the role.

Owners and managers must appreciate that, if the person in charge of care in residential or registered children's homes is not a business proprietor or appointed manager, his or her replacement is vital to the continued operation of the home. The absence of such a person in charge of care will inevitably lead to consideration of whether the registration should be cancelled and, in appropriate circumstances (ie if no experienced carer or nurse is available), may lead to the conclusion that there will be a serious risk to life, health or well-being, entitling the registration authority to apply for urgent cancellation.

Cancellation does not necessarily carry with it the stigma of bad behaviour, but simply the recognition of an inability to carry on the business in a proper way or, in the case of urgent cancellation, without what is perceived objectively as a serious risk to clients' health and safety.

2.9.3   Duties and rights

The duties and rights of the care home manager will be circumscribed, in the contract of employment or appointment, by the business owner. A care home manager who holds professional responsibilities will owe duties in respect of conduct of management and discharge of duties at a professional level to the relevant professional body (eg the Nursing and Midwifery Council, if he or she is a nurse), as well as to the business owner under the appointment or contract of employment. If the two come into conflict, a manager must appreciate that his or her own status will be affected unless he or she procures proper performance of adequate standards by the business owner or, as previously suggested, he or she resigns. This, of course, applies only in extreme cases.

The manager will not be directly responsible or accountable to clients, except in so far as his or her own acts or omissions in the discharge or non-discharge of his or her duties impact directly upon clients, or he or she holds him or herself out to be a principal. The care home owner will be vicariously responsible for employees and, possibly in some cases, those appointed as managers pursuant to an appointment to perform services.

2.9.4   Relationship with other parties

The care home manager has no direct relationship with Parliament or central government, except in so far as enactments and regulations may impact upon the owner's ability and obligation to provide what is seen, in contemporary terms, to be an adequate service for clients in a care home.

The manager has a clear direct relationship with the registration authority. The clear requirement for registration of the manager of every care establishment and agency means that the regulations and applicable national minimum standards require commitments by the registered manager and the registered manager, who must fulfil those commitments irrespective of the availability of means and resources from the provider. In many cases, failure to meet those obligations will lead not only to the risk of cancellation of registration, with its obvious adverse impact on the manager's future career, but also criminal prosecution. The difficulties caused in the relationship between provider and manager where the manager, who is registered, departs from his or her position prior to the appointment of a substitute manager who is also registered, will be considered in Chapter 3.

2.9.5   Responsible individual

The Care Homes Regulations 2001 introduce the new concept of account-ability. Regulation 2 provides that an organisation is a body corporate or an unincorporated association other than a partnership. Regulation 7 provides that a person shall not carry on a care home unless he or she is fit to do so, and (in reg 7(2)(c)) that a person is not fit to carry on a care home unless the person as an organisation and the organisation:

> 'has given notice to the commission of the name, address and position of the organisation of an individual (in these regulations referred to as the "responsible individual") who is a director, manager, secretary or other officer of the organisation and is responsible for supervising the management of the care home; and (2) that individual satisfies the requirements set out in paragraph 3.'

Those requirements will be considered in Chapter 3.

The clear provision is that legal bodies, which do not carry personal accountability for the individual business owners, must 'pierce the corporate veil' by appointing an individual who will accept personal accountability for supervising management. This is a real responsibility of regulatory account-ability. Regulation 10(2) of the Regulations provides that the responsible individual shall undertake training to ensure that he or she has the experience and skills necessary for carrying on the care home.

Section 42(3) of the 2000 Act introduces the usual extension of criminal liability to individuals when offences have been committed by a body corporate. Where offences are committed with consent or connivance, or are attributable to the neglect, of directors, managers or secretaries of body corporates, they are also guilty of an offence, together with the body corporate itself. In the vast majority of prosecutions it is almost inconceivable that the responsible individual would not find themselves subject to prosecution alongside the company. That seems to be the inevitable conclusion of accepting appointment as responsible individual.

The responsible individual, whilst required to sign application forms for new registrations, is not subject to vetting and approval by the registration authority, but will be expected to be accountable for day-to-day operations.

The law provides no prescription as to the maximum number of establishments or agencies in respect of which an individual can be nominated as responsible individual. However, the individual should determine how may homes he or she can accept within his or her personal responsibility for supervision of management in order that he or she is able to fulfil the obligations on behalf of the registered provider, and also ensure that neither the provider nor him or herself is exposed to the risk of criminal prosecution or other regulatory action. It is submitted that the number of establishments or agencies that can be so supervised in management will be limited geographically, and probably limited in number to not more than eight or 10. Ultimately, the matter will be determined in the evidence on the quality of management supervision. Senior managers who are persuaded by boards of directors to accept too many nominations may well find themselves uncomfortably positioned when they are required abruptly and immediately to explain the steps they have taken to supervise management in establishments or agencies that have revealed faults or failings.

It has been suggested that the liability of responsible individuals to prosecution was limited by the removal of inclusive words from reg 43 of the Care Homes Regulations 2001. That would not be correct. The removal of the words was to avoid duplication with the provisions of s 30 of the 2000 Act, which clearly extend to offences under Part II of the Act, or any regulations made under it.

A care home manager has no direct relationship with local authorities, except to the limited extent that he or she may be required to be registered. A manager will, in addition to registration responsibilities, have professional responsibilities (if he or she is a member of a recognised profession) for conduct towards clients in the performance of his duties as manager of the care home.

Managers in control of care homes on a day-to-day basis (and indeed nominated responsible individuals) are in an invidious position, particularly now that they are required to be registered. They should understand the capacity and financial strength of the business owner who appoints them, and recognise that their ability to supply a proper service is entirely circumscribed by the means and resources of their appointer or employer. Their ability to provide proper service and to maintain their own professional reputation is entirely in the hands of others.

Chapter 3

ESTABLISHMENTS AND AGENCIES

3.1 INTRODUCTION

The guiding principle of the Care Standards Act 2000 (the 2000 Act) is to establish a universal system of regulation for activities identified by the Act as requiring regulation. Those activities are differentiated as between 'establishments' and 'agencies'. In broad terms, establishments are activities which are conducted from identifiable premises. Agencies are activities which are provided to service users by businesses which are available to visit the service users in their own premises (usually premises that will be described as their own home) or possibly away from premises.

Each category of establishment and agency is supported by separate regulations and national minimum standards with which registered persons will need to be familiarised. In relation to each establishment and agency, both the provider and the manager are required to be registered (unless the provider is also the manager). Where the provider is an organisation (see Chapter 2), a responsible individual must be nominated and registered.

The whole context of the legislation is that an 'individual' (where that expression is used) must be an individual human being, rather than simply an individual person which might incorporate a limited company.[1] It will be interesting to see whether attempts will be made to justify registration or nomination of limited companies as individuals. It is submitted that such a course would be contrary to the spirit of the legislation and thus likely to fail on a straightforward purposive interpretation.

3.1.1 The basic rule

Section 11 of the 2000 Act lays down the basic rule for registration, and is central to the scheme of the Act. Contravention of s 11 constitutes a criminal offence, and repeated or serious contravention may result in imprisonment. The section provides as follows:

'(1) Any person who carries on or manages an establishment or agency of any description without being registered under this Part in respect of it (as an establishment or, as the case may be, agency of that description) shall be guilty of an offence.'

---

1   See Interpretation Act 1978.

No statutory definition is given either of 'carries on' or 'manages', which issues have been canvassed in Chapter 2.

It is submitted that it may be relatively easy to identify a person as carrying on an establishment or agency. Whether or not a person is *managing* an establishment or agency may be more difficult in the absence of case-law. Identifying the manager and establishing that he or she is actually managing may be easy to ascertain in relation to a small care home. However, this may be more difficult where there exist different establishments or agencies, or establishments or agencies which are provided as part of a group activity by a supervising limited company, or a major voluntary organisation. Furthermore, business may identify as managers people who manage specific aspects of business activities. The statutory requirement (which will be construed strictly as it contains a criminal sanction) is in relation to management of the establishment or agency. Therefore, it is submitted that management responsibilities for less than the whole of the establishment or agency may not trigger the requirement for registration.

Section 11(2) sensibly provides that agencies which have several branches must register each branch. However, experience has shown that there are a number of situations where an establishment is taken to embrace a number of buildings, units or activities, rather than being assessed on a building-by-building basis. If activities within more than one unit of activity can be described on the facts as a single establishment, then one registration would seem to follow. This will be of particular importance to businesses which, in the best interests of their service users, provide services in a number of units, often widely geographically spread. The units are brought under single control by way of management, and thus may be seen as either a group of separate establishments or a single establishment. A group of separate establishments might endanger or pose the risk of destruction of the business as a whole if each unit is to operate independently with the separate providers and managers separately accountable, thus breaking the chain of disciplinary management control from the centre. In the past, when smaller units were exempt from registration, regulators adopted the single-establishment rule to endeavour to bring within the remit of regulation those who sought to avoid regulation by dealing through separate units. Careful attention must be given to this problem, particularly where the homes are operated by an organisation and where that fact will trigger the requirement to nominate a responsible individual and secure the appointment of a manager.

In broad outline, the requirements for a manager's appointment are as follows.

(a) The provider is an organisation or partnership and either is not fit to manage a care home or is not or does not intend to be in full, day-to-day charge of the home.

(b) Given that the manager must be an individual (a human being), most organisations cannot fulfil the requirements, which would exclude the obligation to appoint a manager and, accordingly, managers will be appointed.

(c) Given the various draftings of the national minimum standards, there will be variable expectations as to the appointment of separate managers for separate establishments. *The National Minimum Standards for Care Homes for Older People* suggest that there should be one manager for each establishment. Similar provisions do not occur in other areas, notably care homes for younger adults between 18 and 65 years old. If a group of units registers separately, and there is thus a need for separate registration of managers, the substrata of the business will be at significant risk. In those circumstances, it may be difficult to find sufficient managers who meet the appropriate tests of fitness, and those individuals may not be prepared to accept the responsibility of accountability.

The issue of geographical diversity of establishments was raised (albeit not directly in point) in the Court of Appeal decision in *Harrison v Cornwall County Council*.[1] In that case, the establishment consisted of a major mansion house with separate lodge buildings. There was little difficulty in recognising that the mansion house and the lodge buildings were one establishment. However, the operations also extended to another building used as a 'holiday respite unit', which was hundreds of miles away. The Court of Appeal recognised that such premises could, in appropriate circumstances, be regarded as a part of a single establishment.

3.1.2 The basic rule is absolute

The major problem with the 2000 Act lurks in the absolute nature of the provisions of s 11(1) ('any person who carries on or manages ... shall be guilty of an offence'). There is no provision for transitional protection during a change in accountable responsibilities. This will be routine and standard in relation to changes in the person carrying on the establishment or agency. However, changes in manager are an issue of which we have little or no experience. Although registration of managers was apparently required under the Registered Homes Act 1984, the matter was open to such uncertainty that little issue was taken over additional time lapses between managers. Section 11 of the 2000 Act, on the other hand, is abundantly clear. A person who takes on the role of management without being registered commits a criminal offence. However, what happens when a registered manager departs before his or her replacement has been appointed, or has been appointed but not registered? What professionally competent manager would take on the role of management unless and until he or she is appropriately registered? The NCSC has suggested unofficially that such circumstances will not cause a problem in practical terms, provided that applications are being appropriately processed. That is hardly a comfort. It means that the security of a business is hostage to the whims of individual officers of the Commission.

It is clear that there will be situations where providers and managers are forced to commit breaches of the requirement of s 11, unless they close the establishment or agency and cease business until the new application process has been completed (eg death or sudden dismissal or resignation of manager).

---

1   90 LGR 81.

Providers must therefore establish banks of competent staff who are capable of being upgraded to registered managers to suit the needs of the business. Individual registered managers should be expected to sign contracts of employment that will provide for substantial periods of notice so as to ensure that the provider will have sufficient time to recruit, appoint and register a replacement manager before the resigning manager departs. However, significant difficulties will arise in circumstances where the acting manager dies, becomes disabled or is dismissed for misconduct, ie continuation of the business may be unlawful in the intervening period.

A practice could develop where independent contractor, pre-qualified managers can take up locum positions to meet the problem.

3.1.3   The scope of 'establishments' and 'agencies'

The scope of 'establishments' and 'agencies' is limited by s 4(8) and (9) of the 2000 Act. Establishments are, exclusively:

- children's homes;
- independent hospitals;
- independent hospitals in which treatment or nursing is provided for persons liable to be detained under the Mental Health Act 1983;
- independent clinics;
- care homes;
- residential family centres.

Agencies are:

- independent medical agencies;
- domiciliary care agencies;
- nursing agencies;
- fostering agencies;
- voluntary adoption agencies.

Without statutory extension, there is no possibility that a business which does not fulfil the appropriate constitutional requirements of any of the above establishments or agencies can be treated as a registrable establishment or agency.

3.1.4   Can the categories of establishment or agency be extended?

Section 42 of the 2000 Act provides that the Secretary of State may make regulations to extend the categories of person who can be registered under the Act. Under s 42(2), these categories are limited to:

(a) local authorities providing services in the exercise of their social service functions; and
(b) persons who provide services which are similar to services which:
  (i) may or must be so provided by local authorities; or

(ii) may or must be provided by health authorities, special health authorities, NHS trusts or primary care trusts.

Section 42(3) and (4) include agencies which are not currently registrable but which provide services for the purposes set out in s 42(2). All of this is mystifying. On the face of it, one might take the view that this provision is delaying the extension of the legislation to local authorities. However, that is plainly not the case. Section 42 is supplementary to the exhaustive provisions in Part I of the 2000 Act. If a provider or manager comes within the provisions of Part I of the 2000 Act then it/he or she is already registrable. Since there is no exception for local authorities from liability for registration as providers or managers of establishments or agencies, s 42 is not, clearly, addressing that issue. The point appears to be that local authorities and other persons may carry out activities which are not registrable as an establishment or agency. To the extent that those activities are activities which may or must be provided by local authorities under their social service function powers, then the Secretary of State may extend registration requirements in due course by separate regulations. To put some 'flesh' onto this arcane point, the first and most obvious example is day care services provided by local authorities or others which are not currently registrable. Government interpretation is that accommodation within the definition of a care home means overnight accommodation. Whatever arguments might be addressed if government and the NCSC continue to consider that interpretation to be correct, there will be no pressure for the registration of day care centres unless and until the Secretary of State seeks to embrace such establishments within the remit of registration.

In addition, Part VI of the 2000 Act amends the 1989 Act by inserting new provisions in relation to the registration of childminders and those who provide day care for young children. Those provisions are subject to separate regulation. The registration authority is Her Majesty's Chief Inspector of Schools, in England, and the National Assembly for Wales, in Wales, and the scheme of regulation (as previously with the 1989 Act) is separate and distinct.

3.1.5 Definitions

Having identified the principles and the basic legal definitions of establishments and agencies, this chapter will now consider in detail the statutory definitions of each of the statutorily prescribed establishments and agencies, and the revised definition for childminding and day care. The chapter will then consider the individual registration requirements in respect of each establishment and agency in relation to both the provider and the manager and, where appropriate, the nomination of the responsible individual, tracking the requirements to the provisions of the regulations applicable to each of the separate establishments and agencies. It is important for the reader to appreciate clearly at the outset that every one of the establishments and agencies previously registrable has been abolished. Legal precedent, reasoning and understanding in relation to previously registrable establishments and agencies may be helpful for interpreting the new provisions, particularly where those provisions mirror the former provisions. However, the starting point must be the consideration of the definitions under the 2000 Act, and the previous reasoning applies only where there is genuine reason to anticipate that the drafting mirrors or closely follows that which preceded the 2000 Act.

For the sake of convenience, the order in which the establishments or agencies are considered will follow the order set out in the 2000 Act.

In addressing each establishment or agency, the analysis will consider the statutory provision, provisions for exemption or further definition set out in the appropriate regulations, and material derived from the appropriate national minimum standards which may help to clarify ambiguities within the statutory or regulatory drafting.

3.2   CHILDREN'S HOMES

Definition: 'An establishment is a Children's Home ... if it provides care and accommodation wholly or mainly for children.'[1]

3.2.1   'Care and accommodation'

Neither 'care' nor 'accommodation' are statutorily defined. However, care is not nursing care or personal care as in a care home (see s 3 of the 2000 Act) and thus, if possible, must be taken to be more generic than either of those two. It is submitted that 'care' is an almost redundant word given the age and vulnerability of children. If children are accommodated then it must be inevitable that those responsible for the accommodation will be conducting activities which must embrace the widest notion of care.

'Accommodation', although capable of including accommodation provided without overnight accommodation, is interpreted by the Department of Health and the NCSC as embracing overnight accommodation, so that day care centres for children would not be covered. However, it is open to argument that accommodation includes day accommodation. Those in doubt should seek written confirmation from the Commission or the Welsh Assembly that their day care facilities for children do not, in the opinion of the registration authority, qualify for registration.[2]

3.2.2   'Wholly or mainly for children'

A child is defined as a person under the age of 18 years (thus mirroring the definition in the Children Act 1989). The term 'mainly' is interesting. It clearly embraces, in appropriate circumstances, a situation where young people who are not children might be accommodated with care in a unit also occupied by children. The 18-year-old cut-off point has been inappropriate and negative in a number of specific circumstances.

---

1   Section 1(2) of the 2000 Act.
2   Day care for children under the age of 8 years, and for disabled children under 15 years, is defined by Part VI of the 2000 Act.

Providers should note that they will need to satisfy the registration authority that the unit is properly described as a children's home. Providers should also bear in mind that the definition of care home does not prevent a care home from accommodating children and registration as a care home does not prevent an establishment from also being registrable as a children's home.

It may be possible and appropriate (and very possibly necessary) for a unit providing for a variety of young people to be registered both as a children's home and a care home, but this presents an interesting conundrum. There is no restriction upon an establishment being a children's home if it is also a care home, but if an establishment is registered as a children's home then it is not a care home.

It is not inconceivable to contemplate two or more establishments co-existing within the same overlapping physical environments.

The logical conclusion would seem to be that registration as a children's home would include registration as a care home. However, this creates a problem for care homes which seek to be registered to provide personal or nursing care for children. The definition of children's home may indeed effectively require a care home in such circumstances to register as a children's home, which makes the care home registration redundant.

No doubt this problem will be addressed in practice. There will be cases where it is appropriate for children to be accommodated in a setting which is properly registered as a care home for younger adults, and that much is recognised extensively both within the care home regulations and national minimum standards for care homes.

3.2.3　Exemptions

In addition to the above debate, there are a number of exemptions or partial exemptions. Section 1(3) of the 2000 Act provides that:

> 'an establishment is not a children's home merely because a child is cared for and accommodated there by a parent or a relative of his or by a foster parent.'

This sensible exclusion prevents every domestic household with an appropriate family unit being registrable as a children's home. However, the exclusion is not absolute. It clearly anticipates that there will be children's homes (which may not be residential family centres – see below) which are properly registrable as such even where the children are cared for and accommodated there by parents, relatives or foster parents. 'Parents' include those who have parental responsibility for children (see s 121 of the 2000 Act). 'Parental responsibility' and 'relative' have the same wide meanings as set out in the Children Act 1989.

Foster parents are specifically defined for the purpose of s 1 by s 1(7) of the 2000 Act. They include the following alternatives:

(a) local authority foster parents;

(b) foster parents with whom the child has been placed by a voluntary organisation under the Children Act 1989.

(c) foster parents who foster a child privately, and fostering a child privately has the same meaning as in the 1989 Act.

'Foster parent' is defined by reg 2 of the Fostering Services Regulations 2002 and includes a person who is not a foster parent but with whom a child is placed by a local authority where immediate placement is required. This is a wide and specialist subject, but, in essence, foster parents, for the purposes of the Regulations, are persons identified and deemed to be suitable to look after children in a foster placement situation as a result of the checks carried out by the provider and manager of the fostering agency. (No attempt is made to address the more difficult generic issue as to what is a 'foster parent'.)

3.2.4   Further general exemptions

For the sake of completeness, an establishment is not a children's home if it is:

(a) a health service hospital;
(b) an independent hospital;
(c) an independent clinic;
(d) a residential family centre.

These definitions will be explored below.

3.2.5   Regulatory exemptions

The Children's Homes Regulations 2001 provide for exceptions from the requirement to register. To a certain extent these mirror and extend the exemptions from registration which have long been established in the Children Act 1989. They are as follows.

(1) An institution within the further education sector as defined by s 91(3) of the Further and Higher Education Act 1992 is not required to register. The rationale is that such institutions are separately regulated.

(2) An establishment providing accommodation for children for less than 28 days in any 12-month period in relation to any one child for the purposes of holiday or recreational sporting, cultural or education activities is similarly not required to register. It should be noted that this exemption does not apply where the children:[1]
(i)   are or have been ill;
(ii) have or have had a mental disorder;
(iii) are disabled or infirm;
(iv) are or have been dependent on alcohol or drugs.

This exemption thus applies only to fit and healthy children who are not disabled, and thus may be considered by some to be discriminatory given the inevitability that many children who visit such holiday centres are likely

---

1   See s 32 of the 2000 Act; applied by reg 32 of the Children's Homes Regulations 2001.

to qualify within the disqualifying parameters of the legislation. It should be noted that the qualifying provisions for these exemptions are strict. Each child must be considered separately, and the period in which the children reside at the establishment must be less than 28 days in any 12-month period, ie the maximum period of accommodation is 27 days, or 3 weeks and 6 days. This is cumulative and not on a visit-by-visit basis. Children may not return to the same centre within the same year.

(3) Premises at which a person provides day care[1] for less than 28 days in any 12-month period are not required to register. Similar observations apply as in relation to holiday accommodation, and the exemption is not available in relation to sick and disabled children. It is difficult to envisage a unit which might meet this exemption – possibly a nursery which provides occasional respite care for working parents – but 27 days a year for a particular child, and for the establishment to cater only for such children, seems an artificial business restriction. Oddly, in calculating the 28 days' day care, no account is taken of any 24-hour period during which at least 9 hours is spent by the child in the care of the parent or relative and day care is not provided during that time (ie care by someone other than the parent or relative). The period of 24 hours is not defined as having a start or finish time. It is suggested that this is nothing more than a piece of statutory draftsmanship to ensure that operations that are generally day care or childminding operations are not caught by dual requirements to register as children's homes. If a child spends less than 9 hours with his or her parents, it might sensibly be argued that they are being cared for elsewhere, or indeed that the care is provided in a children's home rather than in a day care setting regulated by OFSTED.

(4) A school is not a children's home, and is not therefore required to register, unless it complies with the requirements set out in s 1(6) of the 2000 Act that, either in a period of 2 years prior to the moment of determination accommodation was provided for children at the school or under arrangements made by the proprietor of the school for more than 295 days, or that it is intended to provide accommodation under such circumstances for more than 295 days a year. The law has been extended to cover accommodation arrangements made by the school, and is not restricted to accommodation at the school itself. Further, the counter-exemption in relation to special schools approved by the Secretary of State under the Education Act 1996 is removed. Residential special schools are registrable as children's homes, where pupils are accommodated for longer than the prescribed limits. The previous limits on the number of children accommodated have been removed. The term 'children' should, it is submitted, be interpreted to include one child and this is reinforced in relation to the alternative, there being evidence of intention to provide long-term accommodation, the obligation to register does not arise unless at least one child is so accommodated for the relevant number of days. It is submitted that such interpretation should bring the school within the children's home

---

1   As defined by the Children Act 1989, as amended by the 2000 Act.

registration requirements where one child is accommodated with the intention that that accommodation will be for more than 295 days even if 295 days has not yet expired. This could then be distinguished from the historic view which looked back over each of the previous 2 years.

(5) An establishment which provides accommodation for children over the age of 16 years: (a) to enable them to undergo training and apprenticeship, (b) for the purposes of a holiday, or (c) for recreational sporting, cultural and educational purposes are not required to register. The exclusion for sick and disabled children identified above applies equally to this exemption. The exemption clearly embraces the concept that young people who are almost adults may not need the same degree of intrusive protection as younger children. Interestingly, the previous exemption for football club academies is removed and the replacement appears to be the above provision.

(6) Approved bail hostels and approved probation hostels are not required to register.

(7) Institutions provided for young offenders by virtue of s 43(1) of the Prison Act 1952 are not required to register.

3.3   PRIVATE FOSTERING

The nature of private fostering has never been satisfactorily defined in legislation. It may be said that everyone knows the nature of fostering when it is observed. Clearly, fostering is identifiable where fostering arrangements are made by local authorities or voluntary organisations. However, in private fostering (still regulated under the Children Act 1989) the distinction between providing care and accommodation, on the one hand, and fostering, on the other, may be difficult to discern as a matter of practice. The previous restriction which prevented homes accommodating three or fewer children from being registered has not been retained. Many considered that the exclusion from regulation of small homes was a deliberate ploy to avoid the confusion between private fostering and registered children's homes.

People of good faith who care for and accommodate children in their own homes or accommodation procured from others will correctly say that they do not require to be registered as a children's home because they are foster parents. The difficulty, however, is that that they will be providing exactly the same services as those who operate a small, registrable children's home.

Private foster parents must notify their activities to the local authority and must not be disqualified from caring for children under the Disqualification from Caring for Children (England) Regulations 2002.[1] However, exclusion from the need for regulation means that, in effect, small family-style units caring for children will continue not to require registration, unless the registration authority seek to categorise such establishments as children's homes.

---

1   SI 2002/635.

3.4 HOSPITALS

Section 2 of the Care Standards Act 2000 (the 2000 Act) brings within the scope of registration specifically a variety of health care units which are drawn together under the generic title 'hospital'.

Immediately excluded from the ambit of regulations are health service hospitals which have the meaning given to that expression in the National Health Service Act 1977, ie (i) any institution for the reception and treatment of persons suffering from illness, (ii) any maternity home, and (iii) any institution for the reception and treatment of persons during convalescence or persons requiring rehabilitation operated by the NHS (author's paraphrase in part from s 128 of the National Health Service Act 1977). Accordingly, the theme is re-enforced that the NHS (a publicly capitalised managed and maintained service) is outside the remit of regulation.

Under Part II of the Registered Homes Act 1984 a wide variety of health care establishments were registrable as nursing homes or mental nursing homes. The historic redundancy of that expression applying to a wide variety of health care units which would not fit the public perception of a care home has led to the sensible introduction of separate regulation for independent health care units which will generally be recognised as hospitals.

Inevitably, there are still units which are registrable as hospitals which will not appear in the public eye as representing typical 'hospitals'. Equally, there are considerable difficulties about the classification and categorisation of premises that provide for service users that have mental health needs. There may be a significant number of cases where it is necessary to secure dual registration both as an independent hospital and as a care home (if that is possible).

Whereas in many definitions of establishment it is clear that the establishment is registrable only if it provides overnight care, such restrictions do not apply to independent hospitals where the eligibility for registration is determined by the nature of the service provided, irrespective of whether or not the service involves overnight accommodation. However, the position appears to remain that the former requirement to register day centres providing nursing care appears to have been abolished and not replaced either within the definition of care home (under s 3 of the 2000 Act) or within the definition of independent hospitals.

3.5 DEFINITION OF HOSPITAL

To be a hospital, an establishment must fall into one of three categories:

(a) it must provide medical or psychiatric treatment for illness or mental disorder or palliative care;
(b) it must provide listed services;
(c) it must provide treatment and/or nursing for persons liable to be detained under the Mental Health Act 1983.

3.5.1 Medical or psychiatric treatment

Section 2(3)(a)(i) of the 2000 Act states:

'The main purpose of which is to provide medical or psychiatric treatment for illness or mental disorder or palliative care.'

Section 121 of the 2000 Act states that 'medical' includes 'surgical', and 'illness' includes 'injury'. 'Psychiatric' is not defined.

'Mental disorder' means mental illness, arrested or incomplete development of mind, psychopathic disorder and any other disorder or disability of mind (ie a repetition of the definition in the Registered Homes Act 1984, paraphrasing the detailed definition set out in the Mental Health Act 1983).

'Palliative care' is not defined.

'Main purpose' may be important if the prescribed treatment is not "main purpose", thus registration as a hospital will not be required or possible.

'Treatment' is defined by the Private and Voluntary Health Care (England) Regulations 2001 as including palliative care and nursing, and listed services within the meaning of the 2000 Act.

Regulation 3(3) of the Private and Voluntary Health Care (England) Regulations 2001 specifically exempts certain establishments from registration, as follows:

(a) establishment which provides no overnight beds (it should be noted that this exclusion does not apply to hospitals which provide palliative care);
(b) an establishment which is a service hospital within the meaning of the Armed Forces Act 1981;
(c) an establishment which is or forms part of a prison, remand centre, young offender institution or secure training centre within the meaning of the Prison Act 1952.

(1) Independent clinics as defined by the regulations

This is identified clearly to avoid dual registration of similar provisions. It is an open question whether the provision of listed services to private patients might require registration as a hospital since the legislation speaks merely of listed services to 'a' patient, not to patients receiving general medical or personal medical services under the NHS. This would not be wholly anomalous because the general scheme is to recognise that where medical practitioners are operating within the NHS scheme, it is not thought appropriate for them also to be regulated under the 2000 Act. If the establishment is not an 'independent clinic' it may well be an independent hospital, if it otherwise meets the criteria for hospital registration.

An establishment, the sole or main purpose of which is the provision by a general medical practitioner of general medical services, or personal medical services, is not a hospital simply because the general practitioner provides listed services (see below) from such an establishment. This slightly arcane provision would seem simply to ensure that NHS services are not required to be regulated where they are carried out by medical general practitioners from premises which do not fit within the definition of a health service hospital. Such general practitioners are usually private practitioners who have contracts to provide such services to the NHS.

(2)   The patient's private residence where the patient is the only person to receive the treatment

(3)   Sports grounds and gymnasia where health professionals provide treatment to persons taking part in sporting activities and events

'Health professional' is not defined, but it is suggested that it may be taken to be the same as health care professionals defined as persons registered as professions to which s 60(2) of the Health Act 1999 applies or who are clinical psychologists or child psychotherapists.[1]

(4)   A surgery or consulting room not being part of a hospital, where a medical practitioner provides medical services solely under arrangements made on behalf of the patients by their employer or another person

Exclusion as to 'part of a hospital' is clearly to reflect that if part of a hospital regulation would be required in any event.

Neither 'surgery' nor 'consulting room' is defined.

Medical practitioners are registered medical practitioners, ie under the Medical Act 1983. The provision clearly purports to exclude from regulation those establishments where the patients (service users) are introduced to the doctor through a third party, ie their employer or someone else. The clear intent of the exclusion is to avoid registration of occupational health schemes run by responsible employers, but the addition of the words 'or another person' clearly embraces a situation where the referral of the patients to the doctor for the consultation or other service is channelled through a third party rather than the patients selecting the doctor themselves.

A variety of businesses who sell goods and services with the backup of medical consultation to the service purchaser are thus apparently excluded from regulation. The rationale would appear to be that the regulation is aimed at doctors practising medicine on their own account, rather than doctors who are employed or engaged by others to provide specific consultancy or other services to those introduced by the doctors' principal.

3.5.2   Listed services

An establishment is registrable, unless excepted from registration, if it provides any listed services whether or not other services are provided. Listed services are:

(a)   medical treatment under anaesthesia or sedation;
(b)   dental treatment under general anaesthesia;
(c)   obstetric services and, in connection with childbirth, medical services;
(d)   termination of pregnancies;

---

1   Private and Voluntary Health Care (England) Regulations 2001, SI 2001/3968, reg 2.

(e) cosmetic surgery;

(f) treatment using prescribed techniques or prescribed technology;

(g) haemodialysis or peritoneal dialysis;

(h) endoscopy;

(i) hypoberic oxygen therapy, being the administration of pure oxygen through a mask to a patient who is in a sealed chamber which is gradually pressurised with compressed air, except where the uses as given to the appropriate provisions of the Diving at Work Regulations 1997 or the Work In Compressed Air Regulations 1996 or otherwise for treatment of workers in connection with the work which they perform;

(j) in vitro fertilisation techniques being treatment services for which a licence may be granted under para 1 of Sch 2 to the Human Fertilisation and Embryology Act 1990.

(1) Cosmetic surgery

Regulation 3(4) of the Private and Voluntary Health Care (England) Regulations 2001 excludes from cosmetic surgery:

(a) ear and body piercing;

(b) tatooing;

(c) the subcutaneous injection of a substance or substances into the skin for cosmetic purposes;

(d) the removal of hair roots or small blemishes on the skin by the application of heat using an electric current, ie electrolysis.

Generally, the above exclusions prevent registration of minor beauty treatments within the context of independent hospitals.

(2) Treatment using prescribed techniques or prescribed technology

Prescribed techniques and prescribed technology are identified in reg 3(1) of the Private and Voluntary Health Care (England) Regulations 2001, and include:

(a) a class 3B or class 4 laser product as defined in Part 1 of the British Standard EN60825;

(b) an intense light, being broadband, non-coherent light filtered to produce a specified range of wave-length, delivered to the body with the aim of using thermal, mechanical or chemical damage to structures such as hair follicles and skin blemishes while sparing surrounding tissues.

No attempt will be made to analyse this specialist definition. This does, however, reinforce and retain the Department of Health's determination that the use of lasers (and now intense light equipment) for minor cosmetic processes should be subject to regulation by the registration authority as an independent hospital subject to various exclusions (see below). To this extent many establishments which might not strike the public as being independent hospitals will be required to be regulated as such and entitled to use the description, assuming that they achieve regulation.

The exclusions set out in reg 3(2) of the Private and Voluntary Health Care (England) Regulations 2001 are:

–   treatment for the relief of muscular and joint pain using an infrared heat treatment lamp;
–   treatment using a class 3B laser where such treatment is carried out by, or under the supervision of, a health care professional.

The definition of 'health care professional' has already been identified. However, much of the use of class 3B lasers is actually carried out in establishments where training may be conducted by health care professionals or other skilled laser users, but the actual use of the equipment will be carried out by those who, whilst skilled, do not possess a professional qualification within one of the professions identified in the Health Act 1999. The words 'under the supervision of' will be insufficient to exclude regulation establishments where lasers are used following training but no health care professional is in attendance. A long line of case-law establishes that the words 'under the supervision of' require that the supervisor should be present in the room where the unqualified person is conducting the particular activity. For example, in the classic case an assistant in a pharmacy dispensary is not acting 'under the supervision of' the pharmacist where the pharmacist is in a different part of the building and is not present when the assistant is dispensing products, albeit exactly in accordance with the pharmacist's instructions.

Accordingly, this exclusion will only apply where the health care professional is in attendance during the course of the treatment.

In relation to the use of class 3B and 4 lasers and intense light sources, reg 42 of the Private and Voluntary Health Care (England) Regulations 2001 is important. This applies when the establishment is registered as an independent hospital. Therefore, the provision will apply where the establishment is not exempt from registration because the class 3B laser is operated by or under the supervision of a health care professional. Regulation 42 expressly envisages that the equipment be used otherwise than by or under the supervision of a health care professional, and sets rules which will apply to the establishment. Some establishments may find it more appropriate to be regulated as an independent hospital than employ the necessary number of health care professionals to avoid regulation. This was, no doubt, the intention of the draftsman.

Class 3 or 4 lasers may not be used (reg 42(1)) unless:

'The hospital has in place a professional protocol drawn up by a trained and experienced medical practitioner or dentist from the relevant discipline in accordance with which treatment is to be provided and is so provided.'

Regulation 42(2) provides that the laser or intense light source must only be used by a person who has:

'Undertaken appropriate training and has demonstrated an understanding of:

(a)   the correct use of the equipment in question;
(b)   the risks associated with using a laser or intense light source;
(c)   its biological environmental effects;

    (d)   precautions to be taken before and during use of a laser or intense light source; and

    (e)   action to be taken in the event of accident, emergency or other adverse accident.'

Registrable establishments are thus entitled to use non-health care professionals provided they have had comprehensive and detailed training, and it is demonstrated that they have understood the training.

'Training' is merely described as 'appropriate', and such a general word clearly leaves the registered person to justify to the registration authority that the training is appropriate to ensure that the users of the equipment demonstrate the necessary skills to comply with reg 42(2).

3.5.3   Treatment and/or nursing for persons liable to be detained under the Mental Health Act 1983

Establishments which provide treatment and/or nursing for persons liable to be detained under the Mental Health Act 1983 (the 1983 Act) must be registered as independent hospitals. The definition of 'treatment' in the Private and Voluntary Health Care (England) Regulations 2001 is unhelpful, and no definition is given of 'nursing'. However, if an establishment is or expects to receive persons liable to be detained under the 1983 Act, it must be registered as an independent hospital.

It is interesting that the the draftsman sought to re-use the description 'liable to be detained', which is found in the 1983 Act as justifying compulsory powers of detention and administration of medication. If a patient is liable to be detained, he may be detained by the appropriate hospital following appropriate consideration. It is thus surprising that the definition does not seek to identify those who are detained, as opposed to those who are liable to be detained.

In practice, it may be that only those who are liable to be detained and who are detained will be admitted into such establishments. However, theoretically it is at least possible that a patient could be liable to be detained (coming within the permitted circumstances in the 1983 Act) but is not detained, but remains so liable for a future occasion. What is clear is that a number of patients with significant psychiatric difficulties will not be liable to be detained.

If the establishment has a purpose which is mainly to provide medical or psychiatric treatment, it will have been registered as an independent hospital in any event. However, many care homes are specifically established to provide personal and nursing care for those with mental health or mental disorder needs, and there will clearly be difficulties in establishing whether such homes should be registrable as care homes or independent hospitals or, in some cases, may be required to be dually registered.

Specifically, s 2(6) of the 2000 Act excludes from persons liable to be detained those who have been detained but are absent from their hospital in pursuance of leave granted under s 17 of the 1983 Act.

Therefore, as is very often the case, establishments that receive detained patients on leave which may be nursing care homes, non-nursing care homes or other establishments, will not have to register as independent hospitals just because they take patients who are on leave from detention.

Providers and managers will have to make conscious decisions on whether or not they wish their activities to include the reception of detained patients. An establishment for the reception of detained patients will not usually be an establishment that would be recognised as a medium-secure or secure unit, or a special hospital such as Broadmoor, Rampton and Ashworth. Detained patients may be mixed with non-detained patients in a voluntary environment; the purpose of the detention order having passed or the urgency having diminished. Review of the detained status may still suggest that retention of detained status is appropriate.

Registration as a care home does not preclude registration as a hospital. Instead, as with children's homes, care homes are not care homes if they are hospitals and are registered as such. This may cause difficulty for an establishment which primarily presents as a care home, but wishes to take patients who are liable to be detained, ie who in practice are detained. Under the Registered Homes Act 1984 such an establishment would have been registered as a mental nursing home and would have added to its registration capacity the entitlement to take patients liable to be detained under the 1983 Act.

Any service users formerly in mental nursing homes are supported by arrangements made by the local authority under the National Assistance Act 1948, as amended. Prior to 1 April 2002, such placements were clearly permissible, the establishment being registered under Part II of the Registered Homes Act 1984.

Section 116 of, and Sch 4 to, the 2000 Act provide that the limitation of arrangements for the provision of accommodation for persons in need of nursing or personal care is restricted to accommodation provided in a care home as defined in the 2000 Act, and that the providers of the home are registered under the 2000 Act. Accordingly, an establishment which is not registered as a care home may not be able to enter into contracts with local authorities through arrangements to provide accommodation in care for persons in need. Persons in need of care in a care home may include those who have or have had a mental disorder (s 3(2) of the 2000 Act). It is far from clear that it would be unlawful for a local authority to place persons in need of accommodation with care in an independent hospital, but the point must arise that potentially such a placement is unlawful. If that were the case, the alternatives for patients and local authorities would be severely curtailed (the Local Government Act 2000 may provide a solution to the lacuna in powers).

Those seeking to register or continue the registration of establishments caring for persons with past or present mental disorders must consider very carefully whether they wish to accommodate patients liable to be detained under the 1983 Act. Unless they are able to persuade the registration authority to register the establishment both as a care home and as a hospital (which will be difficult given the exclusion from the care home definition of hospitals) the facility to take patients liable to be detained may, in fact, severely limit the options for some providers of mental disorder care. One effect may be that those who are liable to be detained are not able to be accommodated in care homes except where they are accommodated pursuant to leave under s 17 of the 1983 Act.

The effect of the implementation of the 2000 Act has clearly been to abolish the establishment formerly known as the mental nursing home more effectively than the abolition of other establishments.

The provisions of the national minimum standards for independent health care establishments are considerably more flexible in relation to the provision of services and facilities within a physical environment than are the standards in relation to the establishment of care homes for various different types of service users.

3.6   INDEPENDENT MEDICAL CLINIC

Section 2(4) of the 2000 Act defines such an independent medical clinic as an establishment:

> 'of a prescribed kind (not being a hospital) in which services are provided by medical practitioners (whether or not any services are also provided for the purposes of the establishment elsewhere), the regulation of independent clinics is thus considered optional by Parliament for no such clinics are established unless regulations are made prescribing a particular description.'

Independent clinics are not registrable in respect of premises which are registrable as an independent hospital. The only statutory limitation is that services are provided by medical practitioners.

Independent medical clinics have been prescribed by the Private and Voluntary Health Care (England) Regulations 2001, and are defined by reg 4(2) as:

(a)   walk-in centres;
(b)   surgeries or consulting rooms for private medical practitioners.

3.6.1   Walk-in centres

Walk-in centres (which are not defined) are registrable where:

> 'one or more medical practitioners provide services of a kind which, if provided in pursuance of the NHS Act would be provided as general medical services under Part 2 of that Act.'

Section 1(4) of the 2000 Act provides that establishments cannot be prescribed for regulation as independent clinics if provided by medical practitioners in pursuance of NHS legislation. Accordingly, a walk-in clinic will be exclusively for patients who purchase medical services privately and will exclude centres where any of the patients are NHS patients.

It is important to note that many medical practitioners deliberately provide services only to private patients and not to NHS patients. The inclusion of NHS patients within a practice triggers the application of the provisions of the National Health Service Act 1977, which makes it unlawful to receive payments of premiums in relation to the goodwill of the business in an NHS practice, however that goodwill is generated. Accordingly, the inclusion of a few NHS patients within the practice may have significant effects well beyond the perceived adverse implications of the need for registration.

It is unlawful to sell the goodwill of a medical practice which has provided general or personal medical services under the Act except in very limited circumstances (s 54 of the National Health Service Act 1977 and further Sch 10 which goes to some length to treat as sales various types of practice-related transaction).

Given that it is inevitable that a significant number of patients will 'walk into' such centres, it is suggested that the identification of walk-in centres adds nothing to the definition, but that the requirement for registration identifies group practices of general medical practitioners, that practise in a way being similar to those who provide their services to the NHS.

3.6.2 Surgeries and consulting rooms

Surgeries and consulting rooms are registrable under the following circumstances. The establishment must be a surgery or consulting room:

> 'in which a medical practitioner who provides no services in respect of the NHS Act provides medical services of any kind (including psychiatric treatment) otherwise than under arrangements made on behalf of the patients by their employer or another person.'

There is specific provision that where the same premises are used at different times by different practitioners, each practitioner must register as an establishment.

The critical exclusion is that if a practitioner conducts any NHS practice, he or she is not required to register the establishment under the 2000 Act. Practitioners must remember the risks of destroying the value of goodwill of established practices if they seek to add NHS patients to their list. However, the exception is not (as in s 1(4) of the 2000 Act) limited to patients who visit the establishment, but rather to the services provided by the practitioner generally. Thus, if the medical practitioner provides services to the NHS away from and separate from his or her private consulting room or surgery then his or her independent private consulting room will not be registrable under the 2000 Act.

Similarly to the exclusion from registration as an independent hospital, where the patients are referred to the doctor by the patients' employer or another person, then again, the establishment is not registrable. This clearly excludes occupational health provision, but equally, any provision where the patients are referred to the medical practitioner by another person.

It seems that this provision is aimed solely at regulating private practice medical doctors to whom patients self-refer or probably by referral from another source as opposed to a direct contractual commitment (eg employment) to another source.

This may be the basis for advice from the Department of Health and the National Care Standards Commission (NCSC) that practitioners who enjoy private consulting room facilities in registrable independent hospitals are not separately registrable. On a strict reading of the 2000 Act that advice would seem to be misguided unless it proceeds on the basis that use of consulting rooms in a hospital will mean that only patients referred through the hospital will be seen and advised. In practice, many private practitioners actually use rooms to see patients who attend upon them as a result of a direct introduction. Those who wish to be secure in their position may seek to make negotiations with their host hospitals to ensure that all patients are at least referred through the hospital, so that their introduction can be said to be made 'by another person'.

Some private medical practitioners consider that the requirements for the application for registration are unnecessarily burdensome given the simple nature of their practices. However, they will be expected to comply with the full requirements of the National Care Standards Commission (Registration) Regulations 2001 even though their practices are small and in no way similar to the substantial businesses registrable as independent hospitals and care homes.

If such medical practitioners wish to avoid registration, they must consider seeking NHS appointments or ensuring that their patients are all referred through another person with whom they have a clear contractual obligation to advise and/or treat the patient.

Some instructive information is set out in the Independent Healthcare National Minimum Standards, which explain the rationale behind independent clinics, as follows:

> 'Exclusively private medical practitioners and private walk-in medical centres will be brought within regulation for the first time. Exclusively private medical practitioners include a range of doctors such as private GPs, consultants and psychiatrists who fall outside the NHS clinical governance framework.'

It is therefore essential that such practitioners are regulated to ensure that they deliver quality care to their patients.

Regulation does not extend to private medical practitioners to whom the general public does not have access, for example, doctors whose work solely comprises the provision of occupational health services for employees of an organisation, or who solely provide services for insurance companies or government departments.

> 'Many of the elements necessary to provide quality assurance in a private medical practitioner's premises or in a private walk-in medical centre are already covered in the core standards, these additional service specific standards build on the core standards to reflect the nature of the provision of treatment in such premises such as consultations, health assessments, screening and vaccinations.'

This introductory note to the specific standards for private doctors[1] (an unusual explanation in terms of the national minimum standards) is not a statement of

---

1   Ie in the *National Minimum Standards for Independent Healthcare*.

law, but does reflect the Government's understanding of the interpretation it wishes to place upon the legislation, and, it is submitted, supports the interpretation set out above.

3.7 INDEPENDENT MEDICAL AGENCIES

Section 1(5) of the 2000 Act defines an independent medical agency as an undertaking (not being an independent clinic) which consists of or includes the provision of services by medical practitioners.

Services provided in an independent clinic or pursuant to the National Health Service Act 1977 are excluded:

> 'Furthermore, paragraph 5 of the Private and Voluntary Healthcare (England) Regulations 2001 excludes medical services provided solely under arrangements made on behalf of patients by their employer or another person.'

It will be seen, therefore, that exactly the same exemption is provided for as in relation to independent hospitals or independent clinics.

Although the concept of agency is that the services are provided away from a fixed establishment operated by the provider, the statutory definition of independent medical agency could embrace operators of an independent clinic if the additional exclusion had not been added, since the definition in no way identifies that the undertaking is only registrable if it is not linked to an establishment. Accordingly, in the absence of express exception, if an establishment were to be exempted from registration as an independent hospital or clinic it would be registrable as an independent medical agency unless also exempted from those provisions.

3.8 INDEPENDENT HEALTH CARE NATIONAL MINIMUM STANDARDS

The national minimum standards for independent health care must cover a wide variety of registrable establishments and agencies. These standards are less prescriptive generally than the other national minimum standards.

Unusually, the standards are divided. They contain a section of core standards, which apply to every independent hospital, clinic or medical agency, and then separate service-specific standards, which apply to the particular type of hospital, clinic or agency concerned.

Those who seek or are required to obtain registration under s 2 of the 2000 Act must ensure that they are registered correctly to provide services at an establishment or through an agency which is identified appropriate to the service-specific standards so as to ensure that they are not required to provide services which are inappropriate to their intent.

3.9   CARE HOMES

Care homes are defined by s 3 of the 2000 Act. The definitions are superficially simple. They bring together those establishments which were previously known under the Registered Homes Act 1984 as residential care homes and nursing homes, and mental nursing homes. Readers should refer back to the discussion above as to the registration requirements, and opportunities for hospitals providing treatment or nursing for those liable to be detained under the Mental Health Act 1983.

The core definition of a care home is set out in s 3(1) of the 2000 Act:

> 'For the purposes of this Act an establishment is a care home if it provides accommodation together with nursing or personal care for any of the following persons.'

The detailed analysis of this definition will be addressed later.

Eligible persons are:

(a)   persons who are or have been ill;
(b)   persons who have or have had a mental disorder;
(c)   persons who are disabled or infirm;
(d)   persons who are or have been dependent on alcohol or drugs.

It is striking that there is no reference to age within the definitions, ie accommodation and care for those who are simply old is no longer regulated; but one must question how many older people who need care will not be covered by the eligibility criteria set out above.

The generic definitions in s 121 of the 2000 Act are that: illness includes injury; mental disorder means mental illness, arrested or incomplete development or mind, psychopathic disorder, and any other disorder or disability of mind, ie the definitions from the Registered Homes Act 1984 and the Mental Health Act 1983 are retained.

Section 121(2) of the 2000 Act provides that a person is disabled if:

(a)   his sight, hearing or speech is substantially impaired;
(b)   he has a mental disorder; or
(c)   he is physically substantially disabled by any illness or any impairment present since birth or otherwise.

An adult is mentally impaired if he or she is in a state of arrested or incomplete development of mind (including a significant impairment of intelligence and social functioning).

It is thus clear that eligibility for accommodation within a care home is swept broadly over exactly every generic category of person who might reasonably be expected to be within a care home other than children who have no care needs, other than those arising out of the fact of their childhood. This issue has already been discussed in this chapter in those paragraphs addressing children's homes (see para **3.2**).

3.9.1 Exceptions

Establishments are not care homes if they are hospitals, independent clinics or children's homes. Under the Care Homes Regulations 2001, further exceptions from establishments being care homes are:

(a) a health service hospital at which nursing is provided;
(b) an establishment which provides accommodation together with nursing and is vested in the Secretary of State or in an NHS trust;
(c) a university;
(d) an institution within the further education sector as defined in s 91(3) of the Further and Higher Education Act 1992;
(e) a school.

Universities include university colleges, colleges or institutions in the nature of colleges of a university.

Institutions within the further education sector are expressly removed from the exception if they provide accommodation with nursing and personal care for any person, and the number of persons for whom such nursing or personal care is provided exceed 10 per cent of the number of students in the institution.

3.9.2 Accommodation

The Department of Health and the NCSC take the view that 'accommodation' means overnight accommodation, and thus the establishments registrable are those which provide overnight accommodation. Despite arguments to the contrary, the reality is that day care only centres, whether for personal or nursing care, will not be expected to be registered. Those in doubt should seek specific confirmation from the NCSC.

Those who provide day care facilities in relation to overnight accommodation facilities should beware. The day care facilities may or may not be separate from the overnight facilities. If the day care facilities are embraced by and are part of the establishment which is registrable as a care home then the whole establishment is registrable, and the impact of the day care services on facilities, staffing, operations, etc will be an integral part of the observation and monitoring of the establishment as a registrable care home.

3.9.3 Nursing or personal care

Establishments are registrable as care homes where they provide solely personal care or solely nursing care, or where they provide a combination of the two. The concept of dual registration (as previously known under the Registered Homes Act 1984) has thus ceased to exist.

A care home may now provide personal or nursing care, or both.

In the process of registration or the transfer of registration from the Registered Homes Act 1984 to Part II of the 2000 Act, the National Care Standards Commission (Registration) Regulations 2001 provide for identification of categories of care homes for registration. These include:

(a) care home only (PC);
(b) care home with nursing (N);
(c) care home providing adult placement (AP);
(d) care home not providing medicines or medical treatment (NM).

The identification of a care home with nursing makes it clear that if a care home is registered to provide nursing, it may provide the full range of care services, and the concept that a nursing home (as registered under the Registered Homes Act 1984) cannot provide personal care is no longer valid. Therefore, the concept of unlawful provision of nursing care within a residential care home (a thorn in the flesh of many regulators and operators under the Registered Homes Act 1984) has ceased to exist.

A care home which is registered for personal care only may not provide nursing care. A care home which is registered to provide for nursing may provide the full range of personal or nursing care as patients require, provided that it has the appropriate facilities in place.[1]

3.9.4 Nursing care

Nursing care is not defined in the 2000 Act. Regulation 18(8) of the Care Homes Regulations 2001 provides that:

> '... where the care home provides nursing to service users and provides, whether or not in connection with nursing, medicines or medical treatment to service users, the registered persons will ensure that at all times a suitably qualified registered nurse is working at the care home.'

The precise meaning of reg 18(3) is explored in Chapter 6. However, it is clear that if nursing is provided, specialised staff will be required. It is thus surprising that nursing is not defined in the legislation.

Providers and managers may seek to set their own definitions of nursing (to fill the void left by the legislation) with the opportunity granted by the issue of the required statement of purpose as to services, facilities and operations at the care home. A definition set out within the statement of purpose may help tailor the staffing levels and impact upon the meaning of reg 18(3).

Even though there is no definition of nursing care, the Health and Social Care Act 2001, s 49 gives a definition of nursing care by a registered nurse. The purpose of this definition is to identify nursing care for which the Government will make payment through the NHS under the new so-called 'free nursing care scheme'. Section 49(1) of the 2001 Act states:

> 'Nothing in the enactments relating to the provision of community care services should authorise or require a local authority, in or in connection with the provision of any such services to:
>
> (a) provide for any person; or
> (b) arrange for any person to be provided with nursing care by a registered nurse.'

---

1   See National Care Standards Commission (Registration) Regulations 2001, reg 8, Sch 1.

It should be noted that there is no such restriction on the provision of nursing care per se, but only on nursing care by a registered nurse.

Section 49(2) states:

> 'In this section, nursing care by a registered nurse means any services provided by a registered nurse and involving:
>
> (a) the provision of care; or
> (b) the planning, supervision or delegation of the provision of care
>
> other than any services which, having regard to their nature in the circumstances in which they are provided, do not need to be provided by a registered nurse.'

Nursing care by a registered nurse excludes tasks which do not require to be carried out by a registered nurse.

Local authorities are only restricted from purchasing the health care element of nursing care, ie services that can be provided only by a registered nurse, and are not otherwise restricted. The Government's own guidance in relation to the implementation of the free nursing care scheme makes it clear that establishments may provide nursing care which is not 'nursing care by a registered nurse'.[1] Accordingly, the definition of nursing care in s 3(1) of the 2000 Act is clearly not restricted to nursing care by a registered nurse, but is wider. Providers and managers should take particular care with their contracts. The aim must be to ensure that nursing care and nursing care by a registered nurse are provided separately. Providers and managers may also wish to ensure through their statement of purpose that the difference between nursing care and nursing care by a registered nurse is defined. The statement of purpose could identify nursing care, for the purposes of a particular establishment, as nursing care by a registered nurse alone. This would limit the number of nurses required to provide that specific nursing care. However, if an establishment identifies nursing care for its purposes as being nursing care by a registered nurse, it would probably be appropriate to interpret the Care Homes Regulations 2001 for that establishment as the requirement for nursing care being limited to the requirements for registered nurse intervention. The establishment would need to ensure that its general care services, not within its interpretation of nursing care, were carried out satisfactorily and monitored by appropriate professionals (who would probably be registered nurses in any event). The issue would then be the adequacy of general staffing to meet the assessed needs of service users, rather than a prescriptive need to employ registered nurses simply because a more wide definition of nursing care was applied. The statement of purpose can be used to assist in formulating the operational policy of the home so as to manage expectation on levels of facilities, staffing and service provision.

With effect from 1 April 2003, free nursing care will be available for local authority funded service users. Readers are referred to Chapter 11 for more detailed guidance.

---

1 *Guidance on Free Nursing Care* HSC 2001/17, LAC 2001/26, 25 September 2001.

3.9.5   Personal care

No issue is more fraught with difficulty than the definition of 'personal care'. Section 121(3) of the 2000 Act provides that 'personal care' does not include any prescribed activity. Section 121(9) provides that an establishment is not a care home for the purposes of the Act unless the care which it provides includes assistance with bodily functions where such assistance is required. This provision merely reinstates the current law because this definition (under the 2000 Act, excluding from definition of a care home an establishment which fails to provide certain activities) is nothing more than the reinstatement of the definition of 'personal care' established in s 20 of the Registered Homes Act 1984 and considered by the Court of Appeal in *Harrison v Cornwall County Council*.

The debate in *Harrison* centred upon whether personal care was restricted to assistance with bodily functions. Kennedy J (as he then was) at first instance held that the definition was so restricted. The Court of Appeal, by a majority, held that that was wrong. The words 'where required' governed the interpretation of the whole clause so that assistance with bodily functions was a constituent element of personal care where it was required; but where such care was not required, it did not follow that the care provided did not come within the definition of personal care.

The circumstances in *Harrison* suggested that the service users concerned in the debate were in receipt of only emotional counselling and not assistance with bodily functions. Reading the case, some may question whether the assumptions about the care needs of the particular individuals were correct. Nonetheless, the context of the case makes it clear that personal care as defined in the Registered Homes Act 1984 (and now repeated in the 2000 Act) is wider than 'assistance with bodily functions' because of the inclusion of the words 'where required'. The Government deliberately inserted these provisions and thus must be deemed to have stood by the *Harrison* definition. In fact, the then Minister, John Hutton MP, in debate in the House of Commons, specifically referred to the *Harrison* case when introducing s 121 by way of an amendment.[1]

The Court of Appeal in *Harrison* had decided unanimously that whatever might be the specific interpretation of s 20 of the Registered Homes Act 1984, the application of the definition of 'personal care' to the activities of a particular care home or the needs of particular service users should be viewed in the round over a long period of time. Judgments should not be made on a day-to-day basis, but rather the fact that some service users might have such needs at certain times but not at others, for example if they are afflicted by temporary infections, should be taken into account.

Accordingly, it is clear that the definition of 'personal care' which, when combined with accommodation, triggers the need for registration of an establishment under the 2000 Act as a care home, is very broadly based.

---

1   In this case, the minister's statement must be an aid to construction of the statutory provision under the principles of *Pepper v Hart*.

However, there may be significant difficulties in this area. Some service users with a variety of needs have been accommodated in so-called sheltered housing or extra care units (sometimes as a result of collaborative working between local authorities and housing associations). Registrability of establishments under the Registered Homes Act 1984 excluded entitlement to housing benefit. At the time of writing, the exclusion does not appear to have been extended by replacement to establishments registered under the 2000 Act. The author considers this to be an oversight, which will surely be corrected if service users seek to make housing benefit claims. As such, if premises are registrable, a significant income stream may be lost. These issues have been avoided, as a matter of former practice, where regulation and commissioning were carried out by the same department of the same local authority. Effectively, officials were able to make their own value judgments about whether or not care was personal care. It is submitted that artificial distinctions between 'personal care', 'sheltered care', 'extra care', and 'support' as opposed to 'care', are hopelessly ineffective given the lack of precise limitation on the definition of 'personal care' previously established, and now confirmed in the 2000 Act.

Such problems have been heightened because those who are encouraged to provide so-called supported living schemes have also been encouraged to seek increased financial grants available from public sector bodies, for example the Housing Corporation, by combining accommodation and support/care. Such combination may have the effect of putting at risk some of the funding streams from publicly available benefits, such as housing benefit. The solution is to ensure complete and transparent separation between accommodation provision and care provision, in which event the accommodation provider is not registrable, and the care provision will be registrable, if at all, through the registration of the care service providers as domiciliary care agencies.

Some will no doubt argue that the Government should seek to define 'personal care' more precisely so as to avoid these difficulties. However, there are substantial objections to this potential route. A definition of 'personal care' which restricts it to assistance with bodily functions would take outwith the remit of regulation providers who provide care for those who do not need assistance with bodily functions, ie a very large number of people with care needs in the mental health sector. Furthermore, personal care is central to the definition of domiciliary care agency, which means that the provision of personal care for persons in their own homes who are unable to care for themselves without assistance because of illness, infirmity or disability, is registrable. The restriction of personal care to assistance with bodily functions would take out of the regulatory requirement many personal care support services for persons who need care, support and assistance in the wider context.

A more effective answer may be to readdress the restriction on availability of housing benefit for those who live in forms of regulated residential care.

3.10 RESIDENTIAL FAMILY CENTRES

Under s 4(2) of the 2000 Act, regulation of residential family centres is required if the following elements are present:

(a) accommodation is provided for children and their parents;

(b) the parents' capacity to respond to their children's welfare is monitored or assessed; and

(c) the parents are given such advice, guidance or counselling as is considered necessary.

'Parents' include persons who are looking after children. The essential ingredient appears to be that children and parents are accommodated together, and that the parents can be supported and receive guidance and skills required to bring up their children.

Regulation of residential family centres will commence from 1 April 2003.

3.11   DOMICILIARY CARE AGENCIES

Prior to the implementation of the 2000 Act, agencies which provided nursing services were regulated under the Nursing Agencies Act 1957. Agencies which supplied care workers who were not qualified as nurses were not regulated.

With effect from 1 April 2003 domiciliary care agencies will now be registrable. A 'domiciliary care agency' is defined by s 4(3) of the 2000 Act as:

> 'An undertaking which consists of or includes arranging the provision of personal care in their own homes for persons who by reason of illness, infirmity or disability are unable to provide it for themselves without assistance.'

The requirement for registration arises where the service users are unable to provide personal care for themselves without assistance, and that lack of ability arises out of illness, infirmity or disability.

'Illness' and 'disability' are defined in s 121 of the 2000 Act. The legislation is drafted loosely. The words 'in their own homes' have effectively no meaning. No definition is given of home, or ownership of or association with a home. It is submitted that 'home' means the place where a person has his or her normal dwelling place from time to time, so that service users may be in their own homes if in other forms of regulated care.

The Government has suggested that the definition of 'own home' is limited to people who own a freehold or have the benefit of a protected leasehold which gives them some security of tenure and occupation. Those whose occupation is limited by licence are not 'in their own homes'. It is submitted that this cannot be right since persons may be receiving accommodation with personal or nursing care so as to be in a care home even though the rights of occupation include greater protection which may extend to certain forms of protected tenancy.

The requirement for regulation of an establishment as a care home is the combination of accommodation with care, and is not limited by the quality of ownership or the protected rights of occupation. Indeed, many argue that residents of care homes should have greater rights to protection than those provided by the normal revocable licence under which most residents occupy care homes.

Little further assistance is to be gleaned from the Domiciliary Care Agencies Regulations 2002[1] and the national minimum standards, which are to take effect on 1 April 2003.

3.12 FOSTERING AGENCIES

Fostering agencies are defined by s 4(4) of the 2000 Act and are:

(a) undertakings which consist of or include discharging functions of local authorities in connection with the placing of children with foster parents; or

(b) voluntary organisations which place children with foster parents under s 59(1) of the Children Act 1989.

The Fostering Services Regulations 2002 do not provide for any exceptions (as envisaged by s 4(6) of the 2000 Act).

The definition of 'foster parent' in s 1(7) of the 2000 Act is limited to use in relation to s 1, ie the definition of children's homes. As such, the definitions and provisions of the Fostering Services Regulations 2002 should be read carefully in any circumstances in cases involving these particular provisions.

3.13 NURSES AGENCIES

Section 4(5) of the 2000 Act defines nurses agencies as follows:

(a) employment agencies or employment businesses (as defined in the Employment Agencies Act 1973);[2]

(b) consists of or includes supplying registered nurses, registered midwifes or registered health visitors; or

(c) provides services for the purpose of supplying registered nurses, registered midwives or registered health visitors.

In essence, business can comprise the direct introduction of a nurse worker to the service user, or assisting the service user in finding and employing a nurse worker. In either case it would appear that the requirement for registration applies to those who supply registered nurses to provide nursing care to service users wherever those service users may be.

Some suggest that 'home nursing' is now unregulated. The basis for this assertion is unclear, particularly if the service user is introduced to the nurse through an intermediary. Further, if the nurse provides 'personal care' the need for domiciliary care agency registration may arise.

---

1   See SI 2002/3214.

2   As defined in the Employment Agencies Act 1973; but no business which is an employment business should be taken to be an employment agency: see s 121 of the 2000 Act).

3.14 VOLUNTARY ADOPTION AGENCIES

Voluntary adoption agencies are adoption societies as defined in the Adoption Act 1976.

3.15 CHILDMINDING AND DAY CARE

The regulatory provisions affecting childminding and day care have been redrafted in the 2000 Act. The Children Act 1989 contains provisions regulating childminding and day care in Part X. The provisions of Part X begin with revised definitions and exemptions from registration for childminding and day care, and set out the identity of the registration authority and the requirements for registration.

3.15.1 Requirements for registration

The distinctions between childminding and day care are important. Childminders are generally individuals who are not involved in commerce or business, but who simply look after the children of others.

Day care is a significant and substantial commercial business.

Section 79D(1) of the Children Act 1989 provides that no person shall act as a childminder in England or in Wales unless registered by the appropriate registration authority. A registration authority may serve a notice of enforcement which, by s 79D(3), takes effect for one year, and the effect of which is to warn an unregistered childminder of his or her transgression. Continuing to act as a childminder after service of an enforcement notice is an offence under s 79D(4).

By contrast, under s 79D(5) no person in England and Wales may provide day care on any premises unless registered, and contravention without reasonable excuse constitutes an offence. Offences are punishable by fines.

Neither offence is constituted unless it is shown to have been committed without reasonable excuse. The burden of proof to the criminal standard (beyond reasonable doubt) lies with the prosecutor, who must establish a lack of reasonable excuse.

3.15.2 What is childminding?

Section 79A(2) defines childminding as:

> 'looking after one or more children under the age of 8 on domestic premises for reward.'

There are a number of exceptions. The following people are not required to register as childminders:

(a) parents or relatives of a child;

(b) those who have parental responsibility for a child;

(c) local authority foster parents in relation to a child;

(d) foster parents with whom a child has been placed by a voluntary organisation;

(e) private foster parents.

Where an individual looks after the child of one family, and in addition looks after another child for different parents, and the work is conducted either in the home of the first parents or wholly or mainly in the two homes, this does not constitute childminding. The exception enables a full or part-time nanny to service two families without requiring to be registered.

Under s 79A(8) childminders are not required to register if they do not work between 2 am and 6 pm, ie a 16-hour period; it therefore seems that babysitting between 6 pm and 2 am is excluded. The restriction does not apply to day care.

A person does not act as a childminder if the period of time during one day in which he or she looks after children does not exceed 2 hours. The previous ambiguity has been corrected, so that it is 2 hours looking after children generally, rather than 2 hours in relation to a specific child. The same exemption applies to day care.

'Domestic premises' are defined by s 79B(6) as premises wholly or mainly used as a private dwelling, and any area or any vehicle, including gardens or parks and the carrying of children in motor vehicles.

3.15.3 What is day care?

Section 79A(6) defines day care as:

> 'care provided at any time for children under the age of 8 on premises other than domestic premises.'

A day carer must spend more than 2 hours per day looking after children.

The exemptions discussed in para **3.15.2** for parents, those with parental responsibility, foster parents and nannies do not apply.

The requirement for regulation of day care is directly concerned with the registration of commercial businesses providing professional day care, ie the so-called day nurseries.

3.16 REGISTRATION REQUIREMENTS

3.16.1 Introduction

The following discussion will centre on the requirements in relation to individual establishments and agencies for the registration of providers, managers and responsible individuals. The discussion will follow the order of registrable establishments and agencies set out earlier in this chapter and, to the extent that provisions are identical, will not be repeated.

3.16.2   Children's homes

The appropriate provisions are regs 6–9 of the Children's Homes Regulations 2001.

(1)   *Fitness of registered provider*

Regulation 6 of the Children's Homes Regulations 2001 provides that a person shall not carry on a children's home unless he or she is fit to do so. The requirements of fitness are set out in reg 6(3) and are:

(a)   integrity and good character;
(b)   physical and mental fitness to carry on the home.

The information set out in Sch 2 to the Regulations must be provided, and is as follows:

(a)   proof of identity;
(b)   criminal record certificate;
(c)   two written references;
(d)   verification as to reason for termination of previous employment;
(e)   documentary evidence of qualifications;
(f)   full employment history.

These requirements must be fulfilled by the following persons:

(a)   where an individual carries on a home alone, that individual;
(b)   where an individual carries on a home in partnership with others, that individual and each partner;
(c)   where in a partnership carries on a home, each of the partners;
(d)   where an organisation carries on a home, the responsible individual.

An 'organisation' is a body corporate or an unincorporated association other than a partnership, ie all bodies other than individuals or partnerships.

(2)   *Appointment of a manager*

An appointment of a manager is required by reg 7 of the Children's Homes Regulations 2001 where there is no registered manager and the provider is an organisation or a partnership and is not fit to manage the home or does not intend to take full day-to-day charge of the home. An organisation clearly cannot take full day-to-day charge of the children's home and, accordingly, in the case of an organisation, the requirement for appointment of a manager is absolute. However, it has not been provided that failure to appoint a manager is capable of becoming a criminal offence. The offence is for the manager to manage unregistered.

Fitness of a manager
In addition to the criteria for fitness of the provider and the responsible individual in the case of an organisation, a manager must demonstrate (under reg 8 of the Children's Homes Regulations 2001) that:

'having regard to the size of the children's home, it's statement of purpose and the number and needs (including any needs arising from any disability) of the children accommodated there, he has qualifications, skills and experience necessary for managing the home.'

(3) Wales

Identical provisions apply in Wales.

3.16.3   Independent hospitals, clinics and medical agencies

The provisions in relation to independent hospitals, clinics and medical agencies are set out in regs 10–13 of the Private and Voluntary Health Care (England) Regulations 2001. The provisions for registration of providers, managers and the nomination of responsible individuals are exactly the same as for children's homes.

(1) Care homes

The provisions in relation to care homes are set out in regs 7–10 of the Care Homes Regulations 2001. The provisions are identical to the provisions set out in relation to the children's homes and the Children's Homes Regulations 2001.

(2) Wales

The provisions in relation to Wales introduced by the Care Homes (Wales) Regulations 2002 are identical to the provisions in relation to England in the Care Homes Regulations 2001.

Chapter 4

APPLICATIONS FOR REGISTRATION

4.1   INTRODUCTION

This chapter examines the process whereby the applicant for registration secures a certificate of registration The participants involved will be the prospective care home owner (or, in certain circumstances, the care home owner already registered) and the appropriate regulatory authority. The application process will be discussed in relation to:

(a)   care establishments and agencies; and
(b)   childminding and day care.

The discussion involves:

(a)   identifying the nature of the application, and whether registration is a matter of right, subject to statutory restriction, or a matter within the discretion of the regulatory authority;
(b)   where the authority is bound to grant registration, the grounds upon which registration may be refused;
(c)   where the authority is not bound to grant registration, the matters which it may take into consideration;
(d)   the material an authority is entitled to receive in the course of an application;
(e)   the material an authority may reasonably require in order to enable it to decide whether or not it will exercise any discretion as may exist.

Whatever may be the position as to the authority's duty or discretion to register, no duty or obligation falls upon the authority until the applicant has made an application and, with that application, supplied at least such information as is required by statute or regulation. Without a properly completed application, there is no application and the duty to register does not arise. Thus, the efficiency and speed of the process whereby an application will be considered are in the hands of the applicant.

Accordingly, two items are required:

(a)   a formal application; and
(b)   the information required to be provided by regulations controlling registration.

That required information can be found in relation to care establishments and agencies, in Schs 1–6 to the National Care Standards Commission (Registration)

Regulations 2001[1] (the Registration Regulations), and the Child Minding and Day Care (Applications for Registration) (England) Regulations 2001.[2]

4.2   THE REGISTRATION REGULATIONS

Schedules 1 and 2 to the Registration Regulations are generic, ie they apply to every application for each establishment or agency. Schedule 1 sets out the information for anyone proposing to carry on an establishment or agency, and Sch 2 sets out the documents which are to be supplied. Schedule 3 sets out the information and documents required to be supplied by an applicant to be registered as manager of an establishment or agency.

Schedules 4–6 are particular to specific types of establishment or agency. Schedule 4 deals with care homes, Sch 5 with children's homes and Sch 6 with independent hospitals, independent clinics or independent medical agencies.

Regulation 3, sub-paras 1–4 of the Registration Regulations establish the obligation to supply the minimum information in relation to the various different types of application. The primary source for the obligation to supply the information is contained in s 12(2) of the Care Standards Act 2000 (the 2000 Act), which requires information prescribed by the Regulations, and any other information which the Commission reasonably requires the applicant to give.

4.3   FEES

Under s 12(2) of the 2000 Act, the application should be accompanied by the prescribed fee. Registrations are not transferable. Every application is an original application and a prescribed fee will be payable. The fee may vary as between situations where the application is for the first registration of a home and where the application is for variation of an existing registration.

The current fees are prescribed by Part 2 of the National Care Standards Commission (Fees and Frequency of Inspections) Regulations 2001 for England, and the Registration of Social Care and Independent Health (Fees) (Wales) Regulations 2002[3] for Wales. The fees payable are broadly the same whether the home is in England or Wales.

No distinction is now drawn between an application for transfer of ownership and an application for first registration.

---

1   SI 2001/3969.
2   SI 2001/1829.
3   SI 2002/921 (W109).

The fee payable by a person *carrying on* the establishment or agency is £1,100; the fee payable by a person *managing* the establishment or agency is £300. In relation to small establishments or adult placement homes, those fees are reduced to £300 and nil, respectively (£150 for small establishments and adult placement homes in Wales).

Managers of existing establishments or agencies who were not required to be registered as managers before the coming into effect of the appropriate provisions of the 2000 Act and associated regulations, and those whose registrations transferred, were entitled to relief from payment of fees.

In the case of variation of registration, the fees are £550 in respect of a registered provider, and £300 in respect of a registered manager. In relation to small establishments or adult placement homes, those fees are reduced to £300 and nil, respectively.

A minor variation (ie one which involves no material alteration in the register) incurs a fee of £50.

4.3.1 Annual fees

An annual fee is payable in respect of each registration, as follows:

(a) care homes: £150 plus £50 for each approved place above three;
(b) children's homes: £500 plus £50 for each approved place above three;
(c) fostering agencies: £1,000;
(d) hospices: £150 plus £50 for each approved place above three;
(e) acute or mental health hospitals: £2,500 plus £100 for each approved place from four to 29, and £50 for each additional approved place;
(f) hospitals using prescribed techniques: £750 plus £100 for each approved place from four to 29, and £50 for each additional approved place;
(g) hospitals providing listed services: £1,000 plus £100 for each approved place from four to 29, and £50 for each additional approved place;
(h) independent clinics or independent medical agencies: £1,000;
(i) residential family centres: £400 plus £50 for each approved place above three;
(j) domiciliary care agencies: £750;
(k) nursing agencies: £500;
(l) boarding schools and further education colleges: £250 plus £15 for each approved place from four to 29, and £7.50 for each additional approved place;
(m) residential special schools: £400 and £40 for each approved place from four to 29, and £20 for each additional approved place;
(n) local authority fostering services: £1,000.

For adult placement homes or care homes which are small establishments, the annual fee is £100. In the case of care homes, the flat initial fee is set out above. In relation to small agencies, the fee is reduced by 50 per cent. Where an independent hospital falls into one or more categories (which will be frequent), the highest flat fee quoted above applies.

It should be noted that the fees apply to *all* applicants on *each* occasion an application is made. The fee is payable on delivery of the application and is then the property of the registration authority, ie the National Care Standards Commission (NCSC). No refunds are payable in respect of aborted applications.

Annual fees are payable as a matter of statutory obligation and are therefore payable on time, whether or not a demand is delivered. The first annual fee for a new registration is payable on the grant of registration, ie the application fee is for the process of the application and the annual fee is paid in respect of the service in inspecting and regulating registered premises. In broad terms, annual fees are payable on the anniversary of the fees payable under the Registered Homes Act 1984 or the Children Act 1989 or, in the case of new registrations, on the date when the new provider (even of transfer of an existing establishment) is registered by issue of certificate. In the case of existing providers, annual fees are payable on 1 April 2003.

4.4 THE APPLICATION FORM

The application must be on a form in the style and format prescribed by the NCSC. The content of the form must be studied carefully.

The Registration Regulations require the use of a prescribed form, but that does not entitle the registration authority to seek further information other than the prescribed information set out in the Regulations. In previous application forms, applicants were required to promise to comply with the national minimum standards in respect of their establishment or agency. This was an unlawful request, notwithstanding that it was pressed urgently and ferociously by a number of locality managers and inspectors. This has now been changed.

Applicants and their advisers should study the Schedules to the Registration Regulations and application form carefully, and determine for themselves whether the questions posed seek the prescribed information or other information. If the information is prescribed, it must be supplied.

Regulation 9(1) of the Registration Regulations requires production of a cashflow forecast. However, no such requirement appears in the Regulations. A cashflow forecast is a complex document. It may be very useful in relation to a new business, but will have little meaning in relation to a business which is being acquired. Further, in some simple businesses, production of a cashflow forecast may be onerous and will in any event be dangerous, given that inspectors who are not skilled in financial matters may regard the forecast as a promise of performance and allege bad faith or incompetence if the cashflow forecast is not met. This is an example where the applicant should think carefully as to whether or not he or she are prepared to supply information which is not prescribed.[1]

---

1 See, eg, *Simon and Chin v Merton and Sutton Health Authority* Registered Homes Tribunal Decision No 136.

Regulation 3(6) of the Registration Regulations mirrors s 12(2)(b) of the 2000 Act. An applicant is required to supply other information and documents that the NCSC reasonably requires. The position is thus clear. For matters which are not prescribed, the Commission may not insist upon such material as a condition of the application unless the requirement is reasonable. The Commission has argued that its additional requirements to the application form are all justified, since in respect of every application for every establishment or agency under every circumstance without deliberate consideration of the matter, it will reasonably require such information. With respect to the NCSC, such a submission must be flawed, and the writers would suggest this to be patent nonsense.

Whether the test of reasonableness is subjective on the part of the Commission, or objective in the eyes of an observer, one thing is clear: for the requirement to be reasonable it must be reasonable in relation to the particular application. It is submitted that the Commission must consider in relation to each application what, if any, further information it requires and then determine whether that information is reasonable in the particular circumstances. In the example of the cashflow forecast above, it is easy to see that in some cases such a requirement would be reasonable, whilst in others it would be onerous and overbearing.

The NCSC will undoubtedly endeavour to short-circuit the delivery of its obligations. Naturally, multiple similar tasks devolved through line-account-able management to remote locations suggest that it is sensible to try to standardise as much as possible. It is submitted that such standardisation is inappropriate and unlawful in so far as the Commission seeks either to fetter its discretions in relation to individual applications, or unilaterally and innovatively to invent developments in the law beyond the powers given to it by the Secretary of State through the Registration Regulations.

The style and format of the application form must be used, but care must be taken to check whether there is genuine justification, by way of prescription or reasonableness, for requirements that are made. Similar provisions will apply to subsequent requests for further information.

The NCSC will no doubt be urged and advised to argue that it can demand absolutely anything in relation to any application. It is submitted that that would be wrong. There must be a decision. Either in relation to the surplus material required on the application form, or subsequent information, the minimum process required should be:

(a) that the Commission identify and pronounce a reason; and
(b) that that reason be then shown to be objectively reasonable.

To apply a subjective test to the Commission's reasoning process would be to negative the protective drafting. The Commission might have all kinds of reasons which seem subjectively reasonable, but the reason should be objectively reasonable to the reasonable observer to the process, ie that observer should say, 'Yes I would like to know that about this application as it would help me to decide its outcome'.

4.4.1   Accompanying documents

The application form must be accompanied by a statement of purpose, and much of the other documentation and information is likely to be embraced within the statement of purpose. The statement of purpose will be considered briefly below (see para **4.12.1**), and in detail in Chapter 6.

(1)   Birth certificates

It is a curiously European, and particularly British, concept that births should be registered. In many parts of the world there is no tradition of certification of birth. Given the wide cultural and ethnic diversity now prevailing in England and Wales, the simple requirement to supply a birth certificate, therefore, may cause difficulties. It is suggested that suitable alternative identification should suffice, and that rather than taking a technical view (given that this is an important application to establish licences affecting the right to earn a livelihood), this provision should be interpreted so as to require alternative evidence which suitably satisfies a commencement to identification.

(2)   Medical certificates

A certificate of physical and mental fitness will be required to carry on or manage the establishment or agency, or in the alternative a statement by the applicant as to physical and mental health. It will be unusual for an applicant not to be able to procure a report from his or her own medical practitioner. It is submitted that only in the rarest of cases would it be appropriate for the NCSC to look behind the report and certificate of the medical practitioner. However, the Commission will certainly be entitled to challenge robustly and cynically the suggestion that a report cannot be obtained.

Applicants who self-certify health must remember that the provision of false information in relation to the application is a criminal offence under s 27 of the 2000 Act. Given that power, and the clear drafting of the Regulations, it would be inappropriate for the Commission to seek any other form of physical or mental certification in the absence of cogent evidence to suggest non-compliance.

(3)   Criminal record certificates

Criminal record certificates are required under the Police Act 1997 in respect of the applicants to be registered, the provider and registered manager, and the responsible individual. In due course, criminal record certificates will be required of everyone working at the home.

The Criminal Records Bureau (CRB) is now up and running, although it has had, and continues to have, teething problems.

The law is clear. All applicants and responsible individuals must produce a criminal record certificate. A simple certificate is required of anyone who will merely have contact with service users. An enhanced certificate is required of anyone who will be involved in the day-to-day care and management of service users. These are simple paraphrases of the differences. In most care establishments and agencies (and in particular care homes, children's homes and mental health hospitals) it will be very difficult for anyone to argue that they are not required to hold an enhanced criminal record certificate. The broad difference is that an enhanced certificate will include not only information on convictions or other statutorily recordable evidence of transgression, but also so-called soft information, ie police cautions, warnings and possibly evidence about police suspicions which have not culminated in conviction, whether by way of acquittal or non-prosecution. Clearly, the latter gives rise to serious concerns about the rights of the individual. For the purpose of the application for registration, however, it must be produced.

Regulators will no doubt seek to standardise reasons for refusal to register by reference to the existence of certain criminal or soft information. However, there is no justification for the proposition that the disclosure of a criminal record automatically disqualifies an applicant from registration. Everything will depend upon the particular facts. Clearly, in the vast majority of cases, recent convictions for dishonesty or violence are likely to be a strong sign that the registration should not be accepted or that the worker should not be employed or retained. For existing workers, greater difficulties will arise.

However, in many other cases, the simple proposition that a conviction disqualifies will be erroneous. The simple link to disqualification would be wrong in any event, but in other cases, genuine judgment will have to be shown, taking into account the history and age of the applicant, the nature of the offence, and the nature of the care home, before a satisfactory decision is reached.

(4) Accounts

Company applicants must produce copies of their last two annual accounts. Companies cannot be registered managers. Registered managers must be individuals. Annual accounts of holding companies must be produced. In each case, two are required (it will be noted that the standard application form requires three – another example of the NCSC having little regard to its statutory limitation). Only the two last annual accounts must be produced.

(5) Bank references

A bank reference as to the applicant's financial standing must be produced. Experience would suggest that a bank reference is not likely to be particularly illuminating.

(6) Insurance certificates

Certificates of insurance against liabilities for death, injury, public liability or damage or loss must be produced. In a number of cases, for example in children's homes and homes for adults with learning disabilities and challenging behaviour, insurers are becoming more and more reluctant to take risks. If this continues, the absence of insurance may become a disqualifying precondition for registration. However, this would probably only be the case if insurance was statutorily required, for example employers' liability insurance. If it is not statutorily required, then, again, a value judgment should be made, for example in the case of local authorities or voluntary organisations registered as Industrial and Provident Societies.

4.5   IS REGISTRATION MANDATORY OR DISCRETIONARY?

Much debate raged on this issue under the Registered Homes Act 1984 and the Children Act 1989. The position is now identical in relation to all applications. The matter is set out in s 13(2) of the 2000 Act, which applies only where an application has been made. An application is not made until submitted in the correct form, with the correct fee and containing the prescribed information. Section 13(2) states:

> 'If the registration authority is satisfied that –
>
> (a)   the requirements of regulations under section 22; and
> (b)   the requirements of any other enactment which appears to the registration authority to be relevant,
>
> are being and will continue to be complied with (so far as applicable) in relation to the establishment or agency, it shall grant the application, otherwise it shall refuse it.'

There are a number of distinctions from the jurisprudence established under the 1984 and 1989 Acts. We start from the proposition that nothing is required of the registration authority until there is an application. The registration authority continues to be obliged to grant the application, provided that it is satisfied as to compliance and continued compliance with the requirements of regulations under s 22 and any other relevant enactment, ie the obligation arises upon satisfaction only, rather than simply upon receipt, of the application, subject to discretions to refuse (see ss 9 and 23 of the Registered Homes Act 1984).

Accordingly, it is clear that compliance with national minimum standards is not a precondition to registration and that the NCSC cannot require evidence of current compliance or future compliance with national minimum standards as reason to be dissatisfied with an application. To justify its refusal to register, the NCSC must identify the standard linked to the requirements of the regulations, and be prepared to argue that the evidential material not only suggests non-compliance with the standard, but that that non-compliance leads incontrovertibly to breach of the requirement in the regulations, ie in most cases that the circumstances will constitute the commission of an offence under the regulations if registration is granted.

4.5.1   Duty to refuse

Once all material is before it, the NCSC must make a decision to refuse or grant the application. If the Commission is not satisfied as to the necessary compliance, it must mandatorily refuse the application. This will be welcomed by those who have been frustrated by previous registration authorities which delayed the application process even though all matters were before them, simply by stating that concerns remained and they were not ready to grant the application. These new provisions will make it much easier for an applicant to force the Commission's hand by proceedings for judicial review to deliver its decision. This is important because in an obdurate and difficult case, an applicant may wish to appeal to the Care Standards Tribunal, without delay.

This issue will be discussed below in consideration of the burden of proof, but it is clear, as intended by Parliament and outlined in the Department of Health notes to understanding the 2000 Act, that the burden of proof is in fact shifted from the Registered Homes Act 1984 provision to that equivalent to the Children Act 1989, ie that the applicant must prove to the Commission that the requirements are and will be complied with, and only upon that having been proved does the obligation to grant arise or, in the absence of such proof, that the obligation to refuse similarly arises.

Although the burden of proof is shifted clearly to the applicant, it is suggested that these changes substantially delimit the ability of the Commission to prevaricate. There remains the practical, financial and commercial difficulty associated with taking legal action to force the Commission to carry out its legal obligations. In an appropriate case, however, that delay might be compensated at least in relation to the costs of the application.

It should also be remembered that registration remains 'of an individual in respect of an establishment or agency'. The application is likely to fail if the availability of the establishment or premises ceases. This reflects the developed position under the 1984 and the 1989 Acts. In circumstances where the opportunity to register an establishment is lost through unlawful prevarication in the registration process, there will be a clear breach of statutory duty by the registration authority. It remains to be seen whether courts will find that statutory duty as one which was intended to be protected by a private right to claim damages on breach. There are already some signs, following the Human Rights Act 1998, that judges are more willing to construe such provisions favourably for applicants from the private sector, rather than simply adopting the argument on grounds of public policy that regulators must never be put in jeopardy in the way in which they carry out their day-to-day duties.

There are undoubtedly powerful reasons why registration should not be effected lightly with the consequence that vulnerable people are in the care of inappropriate persons, but equally there are cogent reasons why those who are able and willing to provide valuable service to those in need should not have their aspirations frustrated without compensation by maladministration of the regulation process.

The cases of *Douce and Another v North Staffordshire County Council*[1] and *Welton v North Cornwall District Council*[2] arose out of facts which preceded implementation of the Human Rights Act 1998. The claimants in *Douce* alleged

1   [2002] EWCA Civ 506.
2   [1997] 1 WLR 570.

large losses caused by the rigorous and literal application of a staffing policy (not a condition of registration). The court refused to strike out the claim as showing no cause of action. In *Welton*, an environmental health officer had required costly improvements to be made to a private hotel, when such were clearly beyond his authority. His employer was obliged to compensate the cost even though the underlying business was enhanced.

Loss caused by failure to process applications may well attract similar claims.

4.6 APPLICATIONS FOR CHILDMINDERS AND PROVISION OF DAY CARE

The process of application for childminders and the provision of day care is covered by the Child Minding and Day Care (Applications for Registration) (England) (Regulations) 2001. The requirements are relatively simple. All applicants are required to include in their applications information about matters specified in the Schedule. Provision of this information is mandatory, and is as follows:

(a) date of birth (or date of incorporation, if a company);

(b) full names and former names extending to the full names of membership of a partnership committee or corporate or incorporate body, dates of birth and full names and former names for all relevant people. This extension to committees, and the legal issues that arise, reflect the frequent practice of small ad hoc play groups in residential areas throughout the country where it has been difficult for regulators to identify exactly who is responsible for day-to-day management of what is registrable as a day centre for child care and was so registrable under previous legislation;

(c) addresses of the premises which are to be used by the applicant and all the persons involved in companies, committees, partnerships and corporate or incorporate bodies concerned with the provision of the care;

(d) whether or not the premises are domestic premises, ie whether this is childminding or professional day care;

(e) in the case of day care, a complete description of the facilities and resources available;

(f) whether the applicant wishes to register as a childminder or a provider of day care;

(g) relevant experience of the applicant and persons in charge, including experience of caring for elderly or disabled people. The relevance of similar experience, references (good or adverse) or other experience by and of the applicant will be relevant in considering their suitability to mind or care for children;

(h) the number and ages of children for whom the applicant and persons in charge are responsible (other than those in their care as a childminder or day carer) whilst the childminding or day care is in process, ie whether the applicant or persons in charge have sufficient time given the responsibility to their own children;

(i) any relevant qualifications of the applicant or persons in charge, including details of study courses, degrees and the nature of qualification;

(j)   full details of the employment history of the applicant and all persons in charge and, where there are gaps in employment history, a full explanation for each gap;

(k)   names and addresses of two referees;

(l)   name and address of the GP of the applicant and the proposed persons in charge and full details of their current medical difficulties (if any), hospital admissions within the previous 2 years, and serious illnesses within the previous 5 years;

(m)   for childminders, the name, date of birth and address of anyone who will be looking after children on the premises (although in many cases this would require registration of the childminder if not the applicant) and details of other people living at or employed on the premises;

(n)   for day care, the name, date of birth and address of anyone who will be looking after children on the premises. There will clearly be an expectation that carers will be separate from the registered person and anyone else living or working on the premises, other than people whose work is not carried out on those parts of the premises where children are looked after, or who do not work at the premises when the children are present;

(o)   in relation to such identified people, full details of any criminal convictions, including the date of the offence, the nature of the offence, the place where the offence occurred, the court of conviction and the penalty imposed;

(p)   similarly in relation to people on the premises used for childminding or day care, details of their medical practitioner, current medical difficulties (if any), hospitalisation within the previous 2 years or serious illness within the previous 5 years.

The requirements are very clear and robust. The provisions mean that anyone seeking registration either as a childminder or as day carer will need to identify all those who are at or near the premises and likely to come into contact with the children in any way at all, ensure that they have full information about those persons, and that those persons' details are checked at the CRB. There will inevitably be a reduction in the number of people who wish to pursue these applications because of the intrusion to the privacy of friends, relatives and other third parties associated with the premises, particularly in the case of childminders. Such restrictions are inevitable in light of the clear purpose of the Regulations, which is to make it very transparent that all those close to or associated with looking after children in any form of professional or quasi-professional way should be subject to the full vetting procedures of child protection systems.

In conclusion, regulators must be careful to heed the following good practice:

(a)   ensure that it is in receipt of a proper application;

(b)   consider carefully what additional information or documentation is required;

(c)   be satisfied that there are reasons for requiring additional implementation, information or documentation, and be ready to articulate such reasons so that the justification can be seen;

(d) apply the exercises in (b) and (c) above to information requested on the application form (but not supplied), which is not actually prescribed by the Schedules to the Registration Regulations;

(e) evaluate all the information, documents and interviews and then make the decision to grant or refuse rapidly.

In adopting this process, a regulator must take great care never simply to state that its decision is based on non-compliance with national minimum standards. As has already been argued in this book, national minimum standards are clearly only to be taken into account. The registration authority should, therefore:

(a) identify non-compliance with the national minimum standard;

(b) decide whether the matter is of any consequence;

(c) take it into account, in the sense of deciding whether or not the evidence of non-compliance is sufficient to sustain at least as to 51 per cent (and perhaps a higher proportion), that registration would immediately lead to the prospect of a successful prosecution for breach of the Regulations based upon the evidence of non-compliance.

Unless all the above categories have been satisfied, a regulator would be erring in law in declining registration simply by reference to national minimum standards, and in any event would be acting completely unlawfully by simplistic reliance on non-compliance with national minimum standards as opposed to reasoned reliance identifying the evidence to justify the refusal.

4.7   OTHER CONSIDERATIONS

4.7.1   Convictions

Applicants must supply full details of convictions treated as spent under the Rehabilitation of Offenders Act 1974 if so required (see reg 4 of the Registration Regulations). This adds little more than emphasis to the existing position under the Rehabilitation of Offenders Act 1974 (Exceptions) Order 1975.[1]

4.7.2   Changes in applicants' details

Somewhat obviously, reg 6 of the Registration Regulations requires that the NCSC be informed of important changes in relation to the applicant, members of partnerships or directors, managers, secretaries or responsible persons within the management of companies. Since staff are employed to work at the establishment or prospective establishment, criminal record certificates (usually enhanced certificates) must be supplied.

4.8   INTERVIEW

The Registration Regulations (reg 5) require that the responsible person attend for interview. 'Responsible person' means the registered provider or the

---

1   SI 1975/1023.

registered manager and, thus, it is submitted, by analogy the prospective registered provider or manager. In the case of an organisation, the company will be represented by the responsible individual.

Strong indications from the NCSC are that it regards the interview as wholly private and confidential. No policy has yet been formulated. However, the Commission is showing an absolute reluctance to the point of refusal to arrange or permit for the arrangement of any contemporary recording of the interview. This is surprising and very worrying.

In justifying its stance, the Commission has argued that the interview is akin to a job interview. It is no such thing. The interview is an important part of the process of licensing by registration of an important source of income. It carries with it a right to be registered under certain circumstances, as identified above (and a right of appeal). Neither of such rights exists in relation to the supposed analogy of employment.

The interviewee is not likely to be able to make his or her own notes. There will inevitably be substantial disagreements both about the questions posed and the answers given. In many cases, this may be in good faith on both sides. There may have been a rapid interchange of views about a particular subject. To suggest that one of the interviewing panel can be trusted to write an objective and fair summary of the outcome of such an exchange is to avoid reality.

The absence of contemporary records will make it almost impossible for those seeking to advise upon or judge the circumstances of the interview in any sensible way. The reality may be that evidence of what occurred at the interview or substantial parts of the interview may never be penetrable.

If the onus of proof were upon the registration authority at a subsequent appeal hearing then, frustrating as this would be, it would be the registration authority which would be unable to sustain its case by discharging the burden of proof. However, with the onus of proof clearly to satisfy the tribunal that the NCSC should have been satisfied, absence of critical evidence on critical issues at interview may mean that the tribunal is not able properly to determine the appeal other than by conducting the interview itself or by remitting the matter back to the Commission with directions for future conduct. Costs orders against the Commission are hardly a remedy where a home has been lost, with no prospect of re-opening.

It would be a bold tribunal that would embark on the interview process itself. How would this be conducted? Would the tribunal take on an inquisitorial role, like a coroner (for which there is no provision in its regulations) and, if not, how would examination-in-chief and cross-examination be ordered? It is submitted that no tribunal would want to usurp the position of the original decision-maker in this way, since in effect the decision would then be without appeal, save on a point of law, possibly as to perversity. The purpose of the appeal must surely be to judge the reasons of the original decision-maker, albeit at a re-hearing and not simply upon a review. There can be no doubt that this issue will be tested by litigation at some stage.

In the meantime, applicants are urged to take whatever steps they can to persuade the Commission officers to permit contemporary recording or shorthand writing. In the absence of such arrangements, applicants should do what they can to make contemporary notes of important points. The interview notes will probably never be seen except in the case of a refusal to register, and objection to the content of the notes many weeks or months after the interview will be impossible and would certainly strain credibility.

This is a disastrous position to be taken by the Commission at this early stage, and will undoubtedly cause significant difficulties.

Given the difficulties in obtaining a real remedy by way of appeal in the absence of proper contemporary evidence, there may be room to challenge the Commission's decision in an individual case by reference to those parts of the European Convention on Human Rights, and particularly Art 6, which has been enacted into English law by the Human Rights Act 1998. A simplistic answer would be to say that there is no deprivation of rights by failing to provide a proper legal redress since there is legal redress to the tribunal. However, for the reasons that have been advanced above, if the tribunal is left in the impossible situation that it cannot do justice between the parties because of the absence of appropriate information without itself becoming an original decision-maker, it may be that it will, inevitably and repeatedly, allow appeals without an endorsement for registration. In those circumstances, there is a very real risk of loss of legal rights without proper legal protection. It would be the Commission, not the tribunal, which was acting unlawfully, ie by manipulating the legal process so as to disable the tribunal and frustrate the applicant's legitimate expectation of legal redress.

On an appeal against a decision of the registration authority, the tribunal may confirm the decision, or direct that it shall not have effect. In practice, under the Registered Homes Act 1984, the conclusion that a decision to refuse should not have effect has, in practice, led to the grant of registration, but that was in a situation where there was no obligation to refuse where a lack of satisfaction was established. It does not follow inevitably that a decision that the refusal to register shall not have effect leads to the proposition that the registration shall be granted. The tribunal might take the view that the refusal is unjustified but it has insufficient material to recommend the grant of registration, and thus a circle might be perpetuated (see s 21(3) of the 2000 Act).

4.9 CONDITIONS OF REGISTRATION

The law in relation to conditions of registration has been completely changed so as to accord essentially with that previously applicable under the Children Act 1989, and not the provision under the Registered Homes Act 1984.

The principle, as enunciated in the well-known case of *Warwickshire County Council v McSweeny*,[1] was that conditions which operated to derogate from

---

1   (1998) December 8, unreported.

the entitlement to the grant of registration could not be imposed unless there was provision for such conditions in the legislation. There was very limited provision to that effect within the 1984 Act.

However, s 13(3) of the 2000 Act provides that an application may be granted either unconditionally or subject to such conditions as the registration authority thinks fit. Interestingly, there are no mandatory conditions of registration, even as to numbers of service users who may be accommodated.

Breach of the conditions of registration will amount to a criminal offence. Section 24 of the 2000 Act provides that:

> 'If a person registered in respect of an establishment or agency fails without reasonable excuse to comply with any condition for the time being in force by virtue of this part in respect of the establishment or agency he shall be guilty of an offence and liable on summary conviction to a fine not exceeding level five on the standard scale' (ie magistrates' court, and currently a £5,000 fine).

The position is mitigated from the previous legislation in that the absence of reasonable excuse must be shown, and criminal jurisprudence would suggest that the absence of reasonable excuse must be proved by the prosecution to the criminal standard. In practice that should be achieved easily unless the bare circumstances of reasonable excuse have been raised by the prospective defendant so that the prosecution must negative the reasonableness of the excuse in order to succeed. The element of absolute strict liability is thereby mitigated.

However, the immediacy of the offence committed by breach of the conditions without reasonable excuse is in contrast to the offences of failing to comply with the regulations. In general terms, such offences are only committed after the standard warning notice identifying breach, regulation, substance of breach and remedy with time for remedy has been served and ignored. Accordingly, conditions of registration are very important rules.

There are no constraints, save for the normal constraints of public administrative law, upon the Commission in imposing conditions. The authority can take into account any relevant material (which would include the national minimum standards, although, it is submitted, not a bare statement that it is a condition of registration that the national minimum standards should be met) or any other material which was relevant and appropriate in the circumstances.[1]

If conditions are agreed, which will speed registration, there will be no avenue to challenge those conditions at a later date, even where the imposition of the condition makes the business difficult to establish or sustain. As with conditions in other regulatory areas, for example town and country planning, applicants should be very clear that any conditions that they propose to accept are matters with which they can comply 24 hours a day, 7 days a week.

---

1   See *Isle of Wight County Council v Humphreys* [1992] COD 308.

In imposing conditions, the registration authority must act reasonably. A number of suggestions are as follows:

(a) conditions should be simple in their drafting;
(b) that which is required and in respect of which failure will lead to breach should be obvious for all to see;
(c) conditions should be relevant to the particular type of establishment or agency being registered;
(d) most importantly, the conditions should not be a matter of standard practice but should be crafted to the particular application;
(e) substance and drafting should limit, where possible, extensive opportunities for 'reasonable excuse pleas', ie the meaning must be simple and clear.

Whilst there is no reason for the NCSC not to take into account its own policy guidance as a starting point in determining conditions of registration, it is submitted that conditions not accepted which are established as a matter of standard policy are likely to face greater scrutiny in any subsequent appeal tribunal.[1]

Regulators who seek to impose or achieve by agreement conditions which do not meet the tests set out above may face difficulties in any prosecution, since there is no valid condition (this being a criminal prosecution) which leads to an offence, which must be clearly understandable to the citizen and subsequent courts.

Following the decision in *Boddington v British Transport Police*, the law has clearly permitted challenge to the legality of local lawmakers' rules (if appropriate) by way of defence to prosecution.

4.10 BURDEN OF PROOF

The issue of the burden of proof has caused some difficulties in appeals heard by the Registered Homes Tribunal. This issue is central to the conduct of any judicial or quasi-judicial proceedings. Such proceedings are concerned with determining disputes over fact and law by adversarial procedures. The principle is that any proposed activity which is to the disadvantage of a person should be justified by the proposer, ie he who advances the claim must prove it. Such proceedings are to be contrasted with public enquiries, the rationale of which is to establish the truth about an issue without, as a part of that procedure, purporting to determine issues affecting individuals. Identifying issues to be proved and by whom they must be proved is crucial.

Since all decisions are taken by the registration authority, it is convenient if the authority is placed in a position of having to prove facts to justify its decision. However, mere convenience does not settle the matter. Where jurisdiction is conferred by a statute, that statute will indicate where the burden of proof lies, ie

---

1   In *Isle of Wight County Council*, ibid, the offending condition was one which restricted the creation of new establishments to a particular size as a matter of demographic policy, as opposed to issues that related to the application or the establishment itself.

balancing, by statutory drafting, the interests of owners who wish to conduct business, and residents who are vulnerable and in need of the protection of the law.

In terms of residential care and nursing homes, the burden of proof previously clearly lay with the authority and this became accepted as practice in the tribunal. In the *Hett* case the tribunal seems simply to have decided, perhaps by way of assumption, that the same position should apply to children's homes. In *Bryn Alyn Community* more powerful submissions were made, and the tribunal appears to have been persuaded, correctly in the author's view, that the burden of proof lay upon the appellant. If Parliament has decided that people who wish to run children's homes should face greater registration difficulties than those who apply to register residential care and nursing homes, it is not for the tribunal to change the law. This, of course, is now redundant, but puts into an historic context the changes effected by the 2000 Act.

It is accepted that the authority must give reasons for refusal, but those reasons do not limit the tribunal's jurisdiction, and may, in general terms, for example, be that it is not satisfied that the appellant should be registered. At most, identification of areas where there was a failure so to satisfy the authority might be indicated. If the appellant fails to satisfy the tribunal that he should be registered, the authority need not call on the evidence.

In *Bryn Alyn* the tribunal sought to distinguish the legal and evidential burden of proof so as to suggest that the burden could switch between the parties during the course of proceedings. This is to confuse a rule of law with practice. Evidence, once adduced, may be seen to have discharged the burden of proof, unless rebutted. This cannot dilute or dispel the rules as to the party upon whom the legal burden lies throughout the case:

> '. . . the legal burden is the burden of proof which remains constant throughout the trial; it is the burden of establishing the facts and contingents which will support a party's case . . .'[1]

Accordingly, appellants had to prove their whole case for registration of children's homes to the extent that issues were not conceded by the authority. It may be that, whilst individual matters were satisfactory, the picture presented as a whole was not sufficiently satisfactory so as to justify registration.

The question as to whether the evidential burden should lie with the authority, where it relies upon evidence of past performance to justify refusal, should be approached with caution. In *Berry and Berry v Calderdale Metropolitan Borough Council*,[2] the tribunal approached the issue pragmatically, the authority voluntarily accepting the burden of proof with the appellant's consent (for technical reasons the case was really a cancellation case).

This debate is of direct relevance to considering applications under the 2000 Act in relation to all establishments and agencies. The burden of proof clearly lies upon the appellant, who must satisfy the registration authority that it does and

---

1   See *Halsbury's Laws of England*, Vol 17: Evidence (4th edn), p 11, paras 13 *et seq.*
2   Registered Homes Tribunal Decision No 321.

will comply with the appropriate requirements. On appeal, the appellant must satisfy the tribunal that it does or will comply with the requirements.

The same principles may arise as under previous legislation. No doubt the NCSC will have to identify any other enactments which it considers to be relevant, and may have to justify that position, but it will be for the appellant to satisfy the tribunal that it will comply with the requirements and/or the s 22 regulations, and the Commission may take the position argued in relation to children's homes under the Children Act 1989, that it is not satisfied that the appellant would continue to comply with the requirements of particular regulations.

This will create difficulties for appellants in lengthy preparation for tribunals where the issues are not really known, and may cause considerable difficulties where the issues are unclear or the evidence is weak. Under the previous jurisdiction of the Registered Homes Tribunal, the failure to discharge the burden of proof meant that the registration authority lost. Failure to discharge the burden of proof under the 2000 Act will mean that the appellant will lose. Much of this is mitigated by the different material which has to be considered in determining satisfaction, and in the detailed rules for the conduct of the Care Standards Tribunal as set out in the Protection of Children and Vulnerable Adults and Care Standards Tribunal Regulations 2002.

The principal regulations with which compliance will have to be satisfied are the Care Homes Regulations 2001, the Private and Voluntary Healthcare (England) Regulations 2001 and the Children's Homes Regulations 2001, as they may apply to particular establishments. (Very broadly, similar regulations have been promulgated by the Welsh Assembly imposing for Wales regulations with the same titles *mutatis mutandis*, and very similar content.)

4.11   THE REGISTRATION PROCESS

The registration process is important both for the registration authority and for the applicant, ie the prospective home owner or manager. The applicant should not place too much reliance on any supposed entitlement to registration, particularly as this has now been diminished by the partial reversal of the burden of proof. The registration authority should not shrink from carrying out its duties correctly in the process of ascertaining whether or not it is satisfied as to current and future compliance with requirements.

The conduct of a home owner is one of the vital ingredients in establishing fitness to operate. The applicant's conduct during the registration process is therefore a good pointer as to how he or she will conduct him or herself as a registered owner.

An applicant who prepares his or her application swiftly and efficiently, supplying all relevant information, with explanations for omissions, and approaches the process in a professional and polite manner, is likely to be a good home owner. An applicant who muddles the application, fails to understand questions, dodges difficult areas, withholds information from the authority, delays, complains about the authority's delay when the circumstances are within his or her control and generally presents an unprofessional image is likely to be unsuitable for the rigours of operating a regulated care business. Authorities should not shrink from refusing to register persons who present themselves in a negative way, nor from seeking to cancel the registration of persons who, despite producing technically efficient homes, conduct themselves in relation to the authority, their staff, clients or those with whom they have to do business in a way that is less than professional or satisfactory given the intimate nature of the business of operating a registered care home. The registration process is a golden opportunity for the authority to judge objectively and fairly whether the applicant is suitable to operate a care home. If in doubt, there is a clear obligation to refuse registration. The applicant will then have a right of appeal to the Care Standards Tribunal. The authority should, however, ensure that it acts on the basis of reasoned judgment based upon evidence and not prejudice.

In the course of operating a registered care home, the registration authority will be entitled to inspect information about the business during the course of the inspection process. The authority must be able to rely upon the owner as a person of integrity, whose work can be trusted and accepted.

Any action which is seen to mislead the authority will be regarded seriously. Tribunals tend to regard such behaviour as very serious. Non-disclosure will be regarded more seriously in many cases than that which has been concealed.

In *Alaton v Wandsworth Health Authority*, one of the applicants was found to have failed to disclose a criminal conviction which his wife had received. The offence, whilst appearing serious, itself does not seem to have impressed the tribunal as being a crucial reason in upholding a decision to refuse a registration. What was overwhelming was the applicant's failure to disclose something which was not necessarily serious. The tribunal took the view that if the applicant failed to disclose such a matter, the authority could not trust him to disclose more important matters whilst operating a regulated care home.

This position has now been re-emphasised. Section 27 of the 2000 Act makes it an offence to make false statements in applications. The switch in the burden of proof means that the applicant has the burden of satisfaction as to the issues of disclosure and fitness. Doubt will lead to dissatisfaction which now leads to an obligation to refuse.

4.12 CARE HOMES REGULATIONS 2001

An applicant for registration, or variation of existing registration, must satisfy the requirements of the Care Homes Regulations 2001, together with their regulations, the Private and Voluntary Health Care (England) Regulations 2001 and Children's Homes Regulations 2001.

---

1   Registered Homes Tribunal Decision No 159.

In particular, applicants must consider:

(a) the statement of purpose;
(b) the service user guide;
(c) the fitness of the provider, manager and responsible individuals (where applicable);
(d) the health and welfare of service users;
(e) the assessment of service users;
(f) the service users plan;
(g) facilities and services;
(h) records;
(i) staffing and fitness of workers;
(j) complaints;
(k) fitness of premises;
(l) its financial position.

This is a simplistic but very useful checklist (which can be supplemented by more detailed reading of the Regulations). The structure is the same for Private and Voluntary Health Care and Children's Homes.

If the above matters are addressed in a satisfactory way, it is likely that the regulator will be satisfied that there will be compliance with the regulations, for that compliance will also have complied with the regulatory process required of the Registration Regulations.

When considering the breadth and extent of the issues covered by these topics, and by the many subsidiary or less important topics within the Regulations, the burden of satisfaction with compliance with the Regulations becomes very clear. Indeed, the applicant will have to satisfy the Commission, and, in an appropriate case, the tribunal, about every material aspect of how the home will operate once the certificate is issued.

4.12.1 Statement of purpose

The statement of purpose will be considered in more detail in Chapter 6. The statement is a new requirement for care homes and independent hospitals, but is built upon the same construct as applies to children's homes registrable under the Children Act 1989.

The statement of purpose embraces, but goes well beyond, the formalised but short statement of aims and objectives relevant to residential care homes. It is not a simple philosophical statement as to ethos, and it is most definitely not a marketing tool. It is, in effect, a constitution for the establishment or agency concerned, and its requirement is backed by criminal sanction.

In effect, the statement must detail the policies and procedures in relation to every aspect of the operation of the care home or other establishment or agency.

Time and time again throughout the Regulations, standards, facilities, staffing and operations are required to comply with the statement of purpose. Great care must be taken to establish a statement of purpose 'owned' by the registered person, the registered manager, the responsible individual and all effective and senior controlling staff. The statement is a working document, which must satisfy the regulators as to the adequacy of the operation, but it must not set unrealistic targets. The target of the statement of purpose will be the benchmark for the standard expected for regulatory compliance, with prosecution for non-compliance.

Standard forms are not acceptable. Appropriate professional advice must be taken on the preparation of the document. A false start could be fatal to an application for registration because it would demonstrate a lack of professionalism, knowledge and capability.

4.12.2 Service user guide

The service user guide, also known as the patient's guide in private and voluntary health care, and the children's guide in children's homes, is a statutory requirement backed by criminal sanction. It must contain a summary of the statement of purpose, but it is recommended that the whole statement of purpose be included. The statement of purpose is so important that any summary to such an important person as a service user may deflect the substance. In any event, a summary should direct the reader or the reader's supporters and advisors to study the statement of purpose.

The service user guide must also contain the terms and conditions of the accommodation and the standard form of contract. Amendments (subject to consultation at the time of writing) will require that the amount of the fees identifies sums payable in respect of accommodation, personal care and nursing care. The Regulations are somewhat opaquely drafted. The difficulty is that care homes do not provide services broken down into specific price heads. A correct reading of the proposed regulations suggests that a statement that accommodation and personal and nursing care are provided within a single price, and that the price is inclusive of all those services without payment for any extras, save those that may be identified at the time of making the contract, will comply with the proposed regulations.

The guide must also contain the most recent inspection report, a summary of the complaints procedure and the address and telephone number of the NCSC.

The guide is much more than a brochure to promote the establishment. It is an extended contractual statement both to those who pay for, and those who receive, the service. Even where the contractual party is not the service user, the guide will operate as an enforceable legally representative statement to the service user of the standards they (and those who are paying for them) may expect. There should be a clear link to the contractual documentation which allocates risk, apportions responsibility and limits liability.

4.12.3 Assessment

It goes without saying that every responsible provider and manager will want to assess the needs of a client before admission to an establishment or agency. Hitherto such has been regarded as good practice. However, in relation to care homes and children's homes, this is now an obligation enforceable by criminal sanction.

Under reg 14 of the Care Homes Regulations 2001, it is an offence to provide accommodation to a service user without such an assessment. Regulation 14(1) states that:

> 'The registered person shall not provide accommodation to a service user at the care home unless, so far as it shall have been practicable to do so –
>
> (a)   the needs of the service user have been assessed by a suitably qualified or suitably trained person;
> (b)   the registered person has obtained copy of the assessment;
> (c)   there has been appropriate consultation regarding the assessment with the service user or a representative of the service user; and
> (d)   the registered person has confirmed in writing to the service user that having regard to the assessment, the care home is suitable for the purpose of meeting the service user's needs in respect of his health and welfare.'

The statement of purpose, as an integral part of the application for registration, will need to set out the detailed processes for assessment and admission and the substantial obligation to identify needs, resolve that such needs can be met by the establishment, and formally confirm to the service user that the needs will be met.

Admitting clients in the hope that their needs will be within the range met by the establishment is no longer good practice. It will be an offence not to have a care plan. If risks are taken and disasters occur, there may be very grave consequences.

Within the application for registration, the full policy and procedure for determining such a process must be identified.

4.12.4   Service user plan

The application for registration will need to detail the approach to service user care planning. This will involve a review of the service user's needs and revision of the plan so as to meet moving needs from time to time.

Of course, if the service user's needs can no longer be met in the establishment then discharge of the service user from the establishment must be arranged. That will be enforceable to the criminal standard despite the very obvious practical difficulties, particularly where clients are publicly funded.

The care planning process must be transparent from the application. Both in assessment and care planning, impracticability to carry out consultations and assessments is a defence, but it is clear that the circumstances in which a trained professional will find it impractical to assess and plan for the needs of a person before admission will be rare. Those who seek to justify emergency admissions will be informed either that there should be specific emergency admission procedures or that, if in doubt, the impracticability did not justify the admission and the admission should have been declined.

It is not an offence to admit without the existence of a service user plan. However, it is an offence, in respect of any person actually accommodated in the home, not to have a service user plan in place. Thus, the very clear implication is that, in all but the most exceptional circumstances, the plan must be set before admission, or else the offence of non-compliance with the Regulations will arise at the moment of admission.

4.12.5 Private and voluntary health care

The rigidity of assessment and care planning is mitigated in the case of private and voluntary health care. No doubt this is the case because admissions to private and voluntary health care establishments will be conducted under the control of a medical practitioner. Here we are dealing with specialised acute health or mental health services. Within such a setting, there is no requirement for a pre-admission assessment.

Treatment must be provided in accordance with the statement of purpose and, so as to ensure that treatment and services meet patients' individual needs, must reflect public researched evidence and guidance from appropriate professional and expert bodies as to good practice and, where necessary, by means of appropriate equipment.[1] In other words, the obligation is generic, rather than converted into specific obligations in relation to specific care.

The obligations of review of quality of treatment and services are provided by reg 17 of the Private and Voluntary Healthcare (England) Regulations 2001. These Regulations again are generic. The obligation is 'to introduce and maintain a system of reviewing at appropriate intervals the quality of treatment and other services provided in or for the purposes of the establishment'. Clearly, Parliament felt that the presence of control over admission and care planning in the hands of established medical practitioners regulated through the General Medical Council justified the lesser obligation on an establishment to manage admission and care planning. In reality, operators of a health care establishment are not in any position to control admission decisions, which are made by the medical practitioners who enjoy practising privileges, ie self-employed professionals who are permitted to use facilities at the hospital and introduce their patients for treatment provided by it. The distinction between these establishments and care homes or children's homes is important.

4.12.6 Staffing and fitness at work

The application form and the statement of purpose must set out details of the staffing provided and demonstrate the fitness of staff, and indeed all workers, to meet the needs of service users accommodated within the establishment. Such statement will, even in the absence of a staffing condition, set a benchmark which can be enforced to the criminal standard after appropriate notice.[2]

However, the statement gives sensible applicants and registered proprietors the opportunity to describe and circumscribe their staffing policy by reference to the practical realities of shortage of staff in a location, staff absences due to sickness or accident, or other aspects of life which make it difficult to manage a labour

---

1   Private and Voluntary Health Care (England) Regulations 2001, SI 2001/3968, reg 15.
2   Care Homes Regulations 2001, regs 8, 43.

force to perfection. A properly crafted staffing policy within and appended to a statement will provide protection from prosecution at least for non-compliance with the statement where day-to-day problems arise. Of course, the practical reality of shortages will be reviewed against the context of the statement of purpose, but at least there is an opportunity for openness about the reality of staff problems. It is submitted that with a properly crafted statement of purpose providing for staff shortfalls from time to time, and for sensible reasons, it would be difficult for a prosecuting regulator to justify inadequacy of staff, simply by reference to explicable absences on an irregular basis.

Workers cannot not be employed unless they are fit to work at the care home. Fitness will be addressed below. Again, as with the Registered Homes Act 1984, there is no attempt to define what is fit, but assistance is given in reg 19(5) of the Care Homes Regulations 2001 and reg 19(2) of the Private and Voluntary Health Care (England) Regulations 2001 as to persons not fit to work within a care home or a private and voluntary health care establishment.

The statutory guidance on fitness to work is hardly illuminating. A person is not fit unless.

(a) he or she is of integrity and good character;
(b) he or she has suitable qualifications, skills and experience;
(c) he or she is physically and mentally fit for the purposes of the work he or she is to perform; and
(d) suitable Criminal Record Bureau certificates have been made available, and the information is both full and satisfactory.

A simple glance through those criteria discloses that they will pose more questions than they will provide answers. They do provide benchmarks largely based upon the jurisprudence of the former Registered Homes Tribunal, and the Care Standards Tribunal no doubt will identify similar matters in determining how to establish fitness.

Criteria for qualification, skill, experience, integrity and good character can usefully be worked into the recruitment policy sections of the statement of purpose and the application for registration. The more that this is identified in advance, the less difficulty there will be in processing the application. Applicants are urged and encouraged to get this information in place, rather than have it dictated to them by the registration authority during the process. There is a danger in allowing the registration authority to write the statement of purpose during the application process, which could suggest to the regulator unfitness of the applicant through lack of knowledge, but may also result in a less workable plan for the applicant.

4.12.7 Premises

The application and statement of purpose must describe the premises and identify them in such a way so as to show that they are suitable for the purpose of achieving the aims and objectives of the home, and are appropriate to the needs of the service users.

4.12.8 Financial position

The financial position of the applicant is of vital importance to the application for registration. As a minimum expectation, the applicant must demonstrate that he or she will, and will continue to, comply with the requirements of Regulations. Regulation 25 of the Care Homes Regulations 2001 and reg 27 of the Private and Voluntary Healthcare (England) Regulations 2001 provide that the registered provider 'shall carry on the establishment or agency in such manner as is likely to ensure that the establishment or agency would be financially viable for the purpose of achieving the aims and objectives set out in the Statement of Purpose'.

Chapter 15 deals extensively with the issue of financial viability.

Regulation 25(2)(c) of the Care Homes Regulations 2001 requires information to be provided on financing and financial resources for care homes, and the same obligation is reflected in reg 27(3)(b) of the Private and Voluntary Healthcare (England) Regulations 2001.

This does not justify any demand for a cashflow forecast, but it will concentrate the mind of the applicant on how to satisfy the NCSC with sufficient information about financing and financial resources to show that this business will run as a going concern.

Additional requirements in relation to finance are:

(a) annual accounts;
(b) bank reference;
(c) equivalent information for associated companies;
(d) certificates of insurance.

Failing to meet the obligations of operating so as to be financially viable is a criminal offence, subject to sufficient and adequate warning. In practice, evidence of financial viability may be difficult to address within the short timescale which may be entirely proper for a registration authority if the safety and security of service users are placed in jeopardy.

Furthermore, reg 13 of the Registration Regulations imposes an obligation on registered persons (ie both provider and the individual manager) to notify the Commission if they suspect that the business is, or will within 6 months cease to be, financially viable. There is no criminal sanction for non-notification, but such notification would certainly minimise the risk of future prosecution, or mitigate any penalty imposed.

4.13   FIT, UNFIT OR SUITABLE

Issues relating to the grounds for refusal of registration are bedevilled by the words 'fit', 'suitable' and 'appropriate'. Is the applicant a fit person or not a fit person? Are the premises fit or unfit? Are staffing levels fit or unfit? When considering what is meant by the term 'fit', the first point to note is that under the

Registered Homes Act 1984 neither an authority nor a tribunal was ever required to decide who or what was fit. What had to be established was unfitness.

Every case will depend upon its individual circumstances and therefore attempts at exhaustive definitions are redundant. An attempt to define an unfit person is a useless exercise. The question will always be whether a person or situation is unfit when judged against the particular facts of the case.

The matter is different under the Care Homes Regulations 2001 and associated regulations. The *Oxford English Dictionary* defines 'fit', 'appropriate' and 'suitable' as synonyms.

The test for registration, and thus maintenance of registration, is compliance with the prescribed requirements. The requirements are, in essence, that persons shall not carry out functions unless they are fit to do so. Unfitness is defined by generic terms, ie lack of integrity and good character, physical and mental unfitness, less than full and satisfactory information on criminal records. Attention should be paid by way of example to reg 7 of the Care Homes Regulations 2001, which states that:

'(1)   A person shall not carry on a care home unless he is fit to do so.

(2)   A person is not to fit to carry on a care home unless the person:

(a)   is an individual who carries on the care home:

(i)   otherwise than in partnership with others and he satisfies the requirements set out in paragraph 3 ...

(3)   The requirements are that:

(a)   he is of integrity and good character; and

(b)   he is physically and mentally fit to carry on the care homes; and

(c)   full and satisfactory information is available in relation to him [in relation to criminal record information].'

The applicant for registration must therefore demonstrate his or her fitness to the satisfaction of the NCSC or tribunal, and a clue as to what is considered unfit in certain circumstances is given by sub-para (3). That is by no means exclusive. The burden remains on the applicant to satisfy the Commission that he or she is and will be fit. As with cases under the Registered Homes Act 1984, this is impossible to predict in advance.

A distinguished expert in the English language, when asked to define a teapot, stated that he found the task difficult, but that he knew a teapot when he saw one. The tribunal, when offering indications for criteria of fitness, recognised that it was probably easier to recognise the quality of fitness than to attempt to define it.[1] It is submitted that attempts to provide exhaustive definitions of fitness should be abandoned in favour of the 'teapot' approach.

---

1   Registered Homes Tribunal Decision No 76, *Eleanor Azzopardi v London Borough of Havering*.

Time may be spent identifying qualities such as 'trust', 'integrity', 'uprightness', 'honour' and 'truthfulness', as the tribunal has attempted.[1] The problem that seems to have arisen is the pejorative tone with which some have attempted to interpret the concept of fitness. The *Concise Oxford Dictionary* (1991 edition) defines 'fit' as:

(a)   well adapted or suited;
(b)   qualified, competent;
(c)   in a suitable condition;
(d)   good enough;
(e)   in good health or athletic condition;
(f)   proper, becoming, right.

It is suggested that a simple approach is the correct approach. In essence, 'fit' equals 'suitable'. If 'fit' is synonymous with 'suitable', all that the regulator or tribunal is asked to decide is whether the applicant, the premises or the staffing, whatever issue may be at stake, is suitable for the purpose in hand.

'Suitability', which is less pejorative than 'fitness', simplifies the task. The tribunal approved this approach in *Oldfield v Stockport Health Commission*.[2]

Indeed, if some circumstances associated with an application for registration of a regulated care home suggest 'unsuitability', no one would argue against a refusal of registration. Similarly, tests of unreasonableness, impropriety and undesirability are, essentially, objective tests of suitability for the conduct of the care home business.

It is assumed that those responsible for making decisions about registration, whether officers or members of a public authority or members of the panel constituted for a Care Standards Tribunal, have knowledge and experience relevant to considering issues on the regulation of care homes. Such persons can be relied upon to use their common sense and experience to make sensible decisions on suitability (including unreasonableness, impropriety and undesirability).

It is unsatisfactory that lawyers or others should seek to limit words which are in themselves limitless. The categories of fitness, suitability or propriety should never be closed, and will certainly change as society evolves, and develops its attitudes to regulated care. More sophisticated facilities, greater training for staff and greater opportunity for qualification for those who aspire to operate care home businesses will all mean that what is considered suitable or fit today, may be considered unsuitable or unfit tomorrow.

4.14 CRITERIA FOR REFUSAL OF REGISTRATION

This may now be stated simply. If the applicant fails to satisfy the Commission that he does and will comply with the prescribed requirements then his

1   Registered Homes Tribunal Decision No 76, *Eleanor Azzopardi v London Borough of Havering*.
2   Registered Homes Tribunal Decision No 289.

application must be refused. The criteria may be widely based on any matters arising out of the Regulations, but more particularly the Care Homes Regulations 2001, the Private and Voluntary Health Care (England) Regulations 2001 and the Children's Homes Regulations 2001.

4.15   RE-REGISTRATION

Each change of ownership will require a new application. Each new owner will have to satisfy the Commission, or on appeal the tribunal, as to current and future compliance with the prescribed requirements.

Given the structure of the Registered Homes Act 1984 and the jurisprudence which developed, it was relatively easy to suggest that if an establishment was satisfactory today, it should be satisfactory tomorrow, subject to the fitness of the incoming applicant. The situation now is different. The incoming applicant will have to deal with the issues of fitness, but will also have to deal with current and future compliance with the prescribed requirements. That will mean demonstrating that he will continue or possibly improve compliance in day-to-day operations. With the requirement for positive proof to the satisfaction of the Commission, as opposed to the Commission having to rely upon negative evidence, the political reality of applications disputes has changed dramatically.

Vendors and purchasers should no longer assume, to the extent that they ever did, that transfers of ownership will proceed simply with applications for registration. The Commission, if addressing its task properly, will look critically at the incoming applicant in the context of its knowledge of the existing home and its view on the ability of that applicant to continue the operation.

4.16   OTHER ISSUES TO BE TAKEN INTO ACCOUNT BY THE AUTHORITY

There can be no limit on the material an authority may consider appropriate to examine, in relation to an application for registration. Many authorities take the view that, whilst their powers may be limited, there is no reason why they should not probe extensively and request information. When resistance is encountered, the reasons for that resistance will be analysed.

In one case that went to the local ombudsman, authorities were criticised for requesting medical reports on directors of a company who would not be concerned in the day-to-day management of a company. Officious concern over long-spent criminal convictions might be an example of irrelevant material, but the authority will be attempting to establish this information, first, to assist it in performing its duty of registration and, secondly, to enable it to take a proper view of any material that may be relevant to that duty or, if appropriate, in exercising a discretion to refuse registration.

There follows a list of issues which, in the author's experience, may arise and be of importance.

4.16.1 Applicant's aspirations

One of the most important questions to ask an applicant is why he or she wants to become registered to operate a care home. Motives in applying for a care home registration may be very important. His or her answer will be illuminating and, whilst it may not be determinative of the issue, an applicant who expresses interest and concern for care of vulnerable groups, but shows a lack of knowledge, experience or aptitude for coping with the problems required in caring for or supporting those in need may not succeed in acquiring registration.

Similarly, if an applicant indicates that his or her primary consideration in operating a care home is making a profit, this may serve as a warning to the registration authority.

4.16.2 Applicant's experience

Many of the matters upon which the applicant is required to supply information will relate to his or her experience in life. Authorities should be astute to explore and investigate the full extent of an applicant's experience. This may be less important for directors of limited companies who will not themselves have day-to-day control of the management of the business.

4.16.3 Applicant's business capabilities

The operation of a regulated care home is a business. In the past, it may have been seen as a vocation, and the relatively easy availability of public grants to support clients meant that applicants needed to concentrate less on standard business acumen skills. With the change in community care implemented from 1 April 1993, if those distinctions were ever valid, then their justification will be seen to be diminishing.

Applicants should be questioned about their policy in relation to marketing, their understanding of the needs of client groups for care and the anticipated requirements of the growing business.

4.17 ROLE OF THE APPLICANT

Applicants must now appreciate that the path to registration is more arduous. The role of the applicant must be seen as one of attempting to assist the authority to discharge its duty with maximum speed and minimum inconvenience.

The applicant should not approach registration on a confrontational basis. The more confrontation, the more likely that doubts will be raised as to their character, and thus their ability to carry on a home. Good relationships with the authority are vital. Registered owners often find themselves subject to proposed cancellations as a result of their inability or unwillingness properly to co-operate with the regulatory authority in the regulatory process.

Sensible applicants will prepare their application having taken advice on the law, Regulations and practice. They will complete an application form, incorporating all the information required by the Regulations, and such further information as they consider to be helpful to the authority in assisting it in making a decision.

Applicants should remember that their conduct in the course of an application will be one of the yardsticks by which the authority judges personality, character and business ability. That in itself, rather than detailed responses to requests for information, may have a significant effect upon the authority's judgment on issues such as fitness.

Applicants should be sufficiently experienced to know where the application will meet difficulties. Applicants should be aware of national practice and of the authority's locally established view of practice, even where that may differ from the applicants' views or from established national views.

4.18   ROLE OF THE AUTHORITY

The authority is the appointee of Parliament under guidance and direction to process the application for registration on a local basis. It is not an adviser to the applicant in relation to the application, and should avoid appearing to give guidance and support to an application.

Some applications may take months or years. Principles of policy and practice may change. An authority exposes itself to risk if it indicates that it will grant registration in respect of certain facilities, only for the applicant to find expectation dashed because policies or practices have changed.

An authority which encourages an applicant to refurbish, develop or construct a home to a certain standard, only to refuse to register it subsequently because of changes in practice, may be exposed to an action for damages based on the tort of negligent misstatement. However, such an action may be difficult. Authorities will not usually be exposed to liability in tort if the registration process is conducted in accordance with legal limits, but if the officer embarks on a course outside the limited role of regulator and creates a special relationship upon which the applicant relies, cost and expense wrongly incurred as a result of such reliance may found a claim for damages for which the authority is vicariously liable. Such a situation often arises where applicants, architects or other professional advisers seek an authority's approval for particular plans and specifications.

Surprisingly, in 2001, a court refused to strike out a claim for damages based upon oppressive and (so it was said) unlawful demands for staffing levels, said to be in excess of those required by the home. There being no allegation of bad faith or improper motive, the authority would have been surprised to see the case continue when the allegation was of officious and over-zealous regulation to protect service users, rather than an abuse of powers or actions driven by inadmissible motive, ie malfeasance in public office.

If courts continue to be prepared to investigate the facts in order to ascertain allegations of inappropriate regulation, then that will apply equally to the conduct of applications for registration, as well as to the conduct of inspection and monitoring of homes after registration.[1]

No home is fit for registration until it is built, furnished, commissioned and staffed. Any indication of approval should be made clearly on the basis that plans are considered appropriate for registration in accordance with current law and practice and the current policy of the particular authority, but that they are subject to review when the home is inspected subsequently to construction but prior to registration.

Some authorities have developed a stamp for plans in terms similar to the following:

> 'Approved in principle, but subject to reconsideration and final approval on final inspection for registration after the buildings and facilities shown in these plans and/or specifications have been constructed, furnished and commissioned.'

In the registration process, the regulator or authority's position is to wait, question and review. The authority is not an initiator of action. It is for the applicant to get its material in order and to bring the application to the authority in a form which is sufficiently full to enable the authority to make a decision.

It is not for the authority to tell the applicant where there are gaps in information. Naturally, the authority will wish to be helpful, but an authority should not be required to spend considerable time endeavouring to educate each applicant into how an application should be presented. Failure to present an application in an appropriate form may be indicative of lack of fitness or suitability to be registered. It is for the applicant to satisfy the Commission.

The Commission is required to make a decision only once all information is available and the unit is ready to operate. If the Commission is pressed to make decisions earlier, inevitably some information will be unavailable, or buildings or facilities will be incomplete. Injudicious pressure from applicants for early determination of registration applications can only lead to disappointment when the applications are rejected. Once rejected, the applicant's opportunities are for appeal to the Care Standards Tribunal or, if that time is lost, for reapplication.

There may be some room for manoeuvre by using the new and wide-ranging powers to modify and/or improve conditions of registration (see s 13(3) of the 2000 Act). A condition which suspends the ability to operate an establishment or agency may entirely properly permit registration subject to condition, so as to guarantee operational ability after the condition has been fulfilled.

4.19 VARIATION OF REGISTRATION CONDITIONS

Variation of registration means variations of the conditions attached to registration, from time to time.

---

1 See *Douce and Another v North Staffordshire County Council* [2002] EWCA Civ 506.

The 2000 Act provides that the Commission may at any time vary or remove conditions, or impose additional conditions. Section 14(1)(a) of the 2000 Act provides that the registered person may apply to the registration authority for variation or removal of any condition for the time being in force.

There is no provision for the registered person to seek the imposition of new conditions, presumably because it is thought unlikely that anyone would wish to open up new avenues for potential criminal responsibility.

An appeal lies to the Care Standards Tribunal against any decision of the registration authority under Part II of the 2000 Act. Accordingly, the anomaly that arose under the Registered Homes Act 1984, whereby there was no provision for an appeal against a refusal of an application for variation or removal of a condition, may now have been removed. This is a very important development. However, the right of appeal will only be against the decision of the Commission. There is no obligation to grant or refuse the application for variation and, in the absence of a decision, once again it may be that no appeal will be permitted.

In the absence of agreement with the previous regulators, the only way to force the issue on registration, variation or change was through an application for re-registration. This caused difficulties. An application for re-registration entitled the registration authority to reconsider the registration as a whole, rather than focusing on the issues germane to the variation.

Now a registered person may make application for variation and invite the Commission and the tribunal on appeal to concentrate simply on the variation issue. Of course that will be taken in the context of the home as a whole; if the variation does not take into account the remedy of perceived defects in the existing home, or if the condition as amended would adversely affect the operation of the home and the interests of service users within the home, that may be a good reason for refusing the application. What the Commission cannot do is reject the application, confident that there is no jurisdiction for appeal, and force an application for re-registration or its abandonment to a position which may, in effect, be dictated by the regulator, as was the position with the previous authorities.

The Commission may decline to consider the application and argue that no appeal right exists. However, it is arguable that this would not be rational or reasonable in accordance with the European Convention on Human Rights, and particularly Art 6. It is submitted that this could be applied to require a decision of the Commission. Once there is a decision, the right of appeal arises. Alternatively, it might be argued by the Commission that the decision not to consider the application was a 'decision' in itself.

In consequence, the line of authority stemming from *Coombes and Coombes v Hertfordshire County Council*[1] is no longer of firm application.

The right to appeal is clearly to be discerned from s 15 of the 2000 Act, which states that:

---

1   (1991) 89 LGR 774.

'(1) A person registered under this Part may apply to the registration authority

(a) for the variation or removal of any condition for the time being in force in relation to the registration ...;

...

(3) An application under subsection (1) shall be made in such manner and state such particulars as may be prescribed and, if made under paragraph (a) of that subsection, shall be accompanied by a fee of such amount as may be prescribed.

(4) If the registration authority decides to grant an application under subsection (1)(a) it shall serve notice in writing of its decision on the applicant (stating, where applicable, the condition as varied) and issue a new certificate of registration.'

It follows that if the application is not granted, the only conclusion is that it has been refused. If delayed, administrative law procedures would provide a remedy to force a decision.

The decision is clearly a decision under Part II of the 2000 Act. Under s 21, an appeal against a decision of the registration authority lies to the Care Standards Tribunal. Again, the difficulty arises that in deciding to overturn a decision to refuse variation or removal of a condition, the tribunal's jurisdiction is limited by s 21(4) to determining that the decision in relation to the variation shall cease to have effect. The tribunal does not have power expressly to order the variation requested, but does have an overriding power to vary or impose new conditions in any circumstances.

In practical circumstances, even where the tribunal declines to make a positive order, the application will almost certainly be renewed and, if rejected again, will be likely to be subject, absent a genuine remedy with the Care Standards Tribunal, to administrative law review in the High Court.

One suspects that in practice the Commission will bow to an adverse decision not to uphold its decisions on variation refusal.

4.19.1 Distinction between application and cancellation or variation

The procedure for application is remarkably similar to procedures for variation and cancellation. The only significant difference is that cancellation or variation can only be instigated by the authority. Application can only, obviously, be instigated by an applicant, ie the prospective owner. The appeal, however, is always against the decision of the Commission, so that the appeal is triggered by the decision of the authority.

4.20 THE DECISION PROCESS

The procedure for a decision by the authority follows a common form whether the issue is an application for registration, variation of registration, a proposal to vary conditions of registration, or a proposal to cancel registration (in the latter case, save where the cancellation is taken via the emergency route). In the case of a provider's application for variation, the procedure will pass directly from adverse decision to appeal. The representation process is not available.

The procedure is to be found in ss 17, 18 and 19 of the 2000 Act. The common procedure follows this form:

(a) notice of proposal;
(b) an opportunity for representations from the owner;
(c) a decision by the authority.

4.20.1   Notice of proposal

Section 17(2) and (3) of the 2000 Act applies to applications for registration (see s 17(1)). It does not apply to other regulatory actions.

In relation to an application for registration, the notice must be in writing and must:

(a) indicate that the application is granted as requested, or is granted subject only to agreed conditions (in these cases no further formality to the notice is required for obvious reasons); or
(b) give notice that the authority proposes to refuse the application; or
(c) give notice that the authority proposes to grant the application subject to conditions which are not agreed.

Most importantly, the notice must give reasons for the proposal where there is no agreement (s 17(6)).

The notice must also (s 18(1)) state, in the case of a non-agreed notice, that within 28 days of service, a person may make written representations to the Commission concerning any matter which he or she wishes to dispute.

4.20.2   Need to give reasons

Much debate has centred upon the need to give reasons. The authors are of the opinion that an authority proposing a course of action should be in a position to give its reasons and the evidence which sustains those reasons at the time the notice of proposal is issued.

Submissions to tribunals that authorities are bound by the evidence supporting reasons presented with the initial proposal for refusal of registration, or indeed cancellation, have not met with success. Tribunals favour the view that, whilst a registered care home remains in operation, the Commission has the opportunity to supplement, expand and develop reasons, and to rely upon matters that have come to light after the service of the initial proposal.

However, it makes sense that, where reasons are known, these should be identified in the fullest and most particularised detail at the first opportunity for formal communication with the applicant. The reasons should be supported by the evidence upon which the Commission relies. It will not be possible to keep such evidence secret indefinitely. Production of further evidence will, in accordance with the rules of natural justice, delay the opportunity to make the decision.

Further, the authority will then be ready for the subsequent procedures. The applicant will know the position. The tribunal and, indeed, members of the authority, before the tribunal, will have knowledge of the issues from an early stage, and have greater confidence in the approach of the authority's officers.

Where information is to hand and evidence has been gathered, there can be no justification whatsoever for not making it available. This is a matter of principle in accordance with the rules of natural justice, or possibly simply a matter of common sense. Many tribunal hearings and disputes have collapsed because authorities have provided minimal reasons at the outset, only fleshing these out with detail and serving supporting evidence days before a substantial tribunal hearing.

Very often, appellants to tribunal hearings decide to withdraw their appeals when they see the strength of the evidence. It is likely that they would have withdrawn earlier had they known the full extent of the case. They would certainly have received advice from their lawyers and been in a better position to judge their own actions.

In addition, since the introduction of the Human Rights Act 1998, it may be that Art 6 of the European Convention on Human Rights is engaged. First, it could be argued that a person's rights are infringed because the process is begun without a proper explanation of the reasons which substantiate the case against him. It would be correctly counter-argued that nothing is lost at this stage because full disclosure of reasons is eventually required in any case at the appeal to the Care Standards Tribunal, supported by the detailed procedural requirements of the Protection of Children and Vulnerable Adults and Care Standards Tribunal Regulations 2002. However, given the enormity of the decision, particularly with the relatively modest opportunity for representations to be made, thus enabling a proposal to be converted into a decision very quickly (as opposed to the procedure under the Registered Homes Act 1984), it may be argued that the position of the applicant/appellant is irreversibly damaged (even on an application appeal as opposed to a cancellation appeal) by the taking of the decision where reasons have not been appropriately articulated, and the opportunity to avoid the final decision-making process is not made available fairly. Time will tell how these contrasting positions are adopted. It is to be hoped that the Commission will avoid the difficulty by making sure that the notice of proposal contains sufficient information for the applicant to understand the position, and for him or her to make effective representations in writing within the limited period allowed. Indeed, if there is not such particularity, it may well be that the notice itself will be challenged in the administrative court with more success than such proposals were challenged in cases proceeding under the 1984 Act. The paucity of information in a notice of proposal is to be criticised. However, such criticism may not be as cogent as it would have been under the 1984 Act. If the application was a matter of entitlement subject to the establishment of grounds which permitted the discretion to refuse to arise, then reasons were critically important. In a case where the substance of the procedure has changed and the applicant has to satisfy the Commission as to current and future compliance with the requirements, it may be easier for the Commission to justify a simple statement of non-satisfaction. No doubt, the tribunal would find that unhelpful and the applicant/appellant would find the matter very difficult to address by way of representations in writing prior to the final decision. It is to be hoped that the Commission will identify broad areas, at least, where they are not satisfied, but, given the statutory structure and the switching of the burden of proof, it may be hard for appellants to justify that simple, bald statements are insufficient to trigger a proposal process.

4.20.3   Representations

The applicant for registration must have an opportunity to make representations as to matters which he or she wishes to dispute in relation to a proposal to refuse.

As already indicated, s 18(1) of the 2000 Act requires that the notice of proposal should identify the right to make written representations within 28 days of service of the notice. The previous law merely required an indication of intention to make representations, and then allowed an unlimited period for representations to be made either in writing or orally.

Perhaps because of the specialist nature of the Commission, and certainly because delay in the process (a particular annoyance in relation to cancellation or adverse variation cases for the regulator), that procedure is now repealed.

The applicant may only make representations in writing, which must be made within 28 days. This emphasises the need for the proposals to be understandable, at least to the extent of addressing those issues where dissatisfaction has arisen.

The registration authority may not determine the proposal until:

–   written representations have been served;
–   the applicant has notified that he or she does not intend to make representations; or
–   the 28-day period has elapsed.

Applicants need to be very alert to making their representations very quickly. Twenty-eight days is not long, and certainly if there is to be a challenge to the validity of the notice for inadequate reasons, that needs to be formulated in an application for permission for judicial review within days, rather than weeks.

The Commission, for its part, should know exactly why it is making the proposal, and there can be no excuse for not providing sufficient information to enable the applicant to form a view about the merits of further representations and possible appeals, and to formulate his or her response on disputed matters.

The shortening of the period, and the removal of the opportunity for oral representations, should speed up the process and concentrate minds.

4.20.4   The decision

Once representations have been received, the authority must make a decision, considering the issues that arise on the proposal, and those that are answered by the representations. Its decision will be issued and notified even if it is a decision to grant registration upon conditions agreed or imposed.

If the decision is to grant registration on agreed terms, it will take immediate effect. If the decision is other than to grant on agreed conditions, ie to refuse, or to grant subject to conditions which are the subject of contention, the decision will not take effect until:

(a)   the date on which the appellant notifies the Commission that there will be no appeal;
(b)   the twenty-ninth day after the decision of the authority; or
(c)   immediately after the abandonment or determination of the appeal.

The appeal is determined by the issue of a decision in writing by the tribunal. It is not likely that such a decision will be issued earlier than 6 months from the date of the authority's decision, and is more likely to be 9 months or even one year. The home may not be operated until the conditions have been accepted or the appeal abandoned.

The notice of the decision must give details of the right of appeal conferred by s 21 of the 2000 Act. The notice should identify the right of appeal and indicate that it shall be notified within 28 days from the date of the decision.

Twenty-eight days from the decision and details of the decision made, ie refusal or the conditions to which the application is granted or the conditions varied, removed or imposed (given the wide ability to impose wide-ranging conditions), it is very possible the removal of a condition might be to the disadvantage of a registered person or applicant.

The appeal process is now significantly different. The Commission will have to identify the process on the notice of decision. Application to appeal is made to the secretary of the Care Standards Tribunal using an appropriate form (currently form B1). The form must include:

(a)   the appellant's name and identification details;
(b)   the name and address of the persons representing the appellant;
(c)   address for service of documents;
(d)   telephone numbers, etc;
(e)   the nature of the appeal, for example refusal of registration or imposition of conditions of registration;
(f)   a short statement of grounds of appeal; and
(g)   the signature of the appellant/applicant rather than a professional adviser or other representative.

The address of the Care Standards Tribunal is 18 Pocock Street, London SE1 0BW. The Commission should include this information, other relevant addresses, B1 forms and further relevant information in a note sent with the notice of decision, so that there can be no doubt that the prospective appellant is fully informed within the relatively short 28-day period of appeal.

The wording of s 21(2) is clear:

> 'No appeal against a decision … may be brought by a person more than 28 days after service on him of notice of the decision or order' [ie a correct notice incorporating all the appeal information].

These explicit words, it is submitted, leave no room for any form of application for an appeal out of time. The words limit the statutory jurisdiction of the Care Standards Tribunal.

4.20.5 Decision to grant registration subject to conditions

Where the decision is to grant registration subject to conditions which are not agreed, an anomaly exists. Many prospective appellants would be prepared to observe the conditions pending appeal. This situation will often arise because conflicts will be on matters of principle, rather than issues of fact. However, the procedure does not permit for registration to be granted with the conditions binding pending a decision of appeal. An applicant must therefore decide:

(a) to accept the conditions, in which case they are binding and not subject to further appeal; or

(b) to fight the appeal and take the consequence of delay.

It is doubtful that a grant of registration upon an undertaking to observe conditions of registration pending appeal is valid.

The result of such an undertaking is not easy to determine. If the tribunal accepts jurisdiction, it may be argued that registration has been effected without conditions in force, and that the authority is required to serve notice to propose to vary conditions or impose additional conditions. However, it is arguable that the registration is a nullity, since, without the condition, the authority would not, in any event, have granted registration.

Such difficult issues obstruct the common-sense approach of operating a care home, subject to the disputed condition, pending registration. This difficulty is as follows:

(a) there is no power to accept conditions conditionally;

(b) accordingly, if conditions are accepted, the issues are complete and there is no jurisdiction for the tribunal;

(c) if the conditional acceptance of conditions is invalid as a matter of law, then the consent does not take effect and the registration has not been correctly effected, as the decision of the authority cannot take effect;

(d) accordingly, the operation of the care home is unlawful and unregistered.

It has been suggested that it would be appropriate to accept the conditions and then, by agreement, to lodge a 'paper' application for re-registration which enables the issue to be argued. This can only work by agreement. Difficulties remain even then. The tribunal will view a home operating as suggested by the authority. Will it readily sanction a reduction in facilities? How will the tribunal view an applicant's accepting conditions on the one hand, and challenging those same conditions on another? In any event, if the home operates in compliance with the conditions, it may be difficult to show that a lower standard is adequate.

4.20.6   Registration made with invalid conditions

The effect of a registration purporting to be made with invalid conditions raises an interesting debate, which will depend for its results on the facts of each particular case as to whether the illegality of the conditions vitiates the whole decision or permits the decision to stand, with the offending conditions being excised.

The argument proceeds in this way.

(1) An authority is only entitled to make a decision within its powers.
(2) A decision *ultra vires* is void, ie of no effect.
(3) If an authority makes a decision subject to invalid conditions, consideration must be given as to whether the whole decision is invalid, or simply the conditions.
(4) To decide this, the court will look to see if the authority would have made the decision at all if it had known that the conditions were invalid.
(5) Only if satisfied that the decision would have been made, irrespective of the offending conditions, may the decision stand.

These arguments, which did not surface very frequently under the 1984 Act, are even less likely to do so under the 2000 Act. The ability to impose wide-ranging conditions shuts down the opportunities for argument that the condition is invalid. That argument may still arise where a condition is imposed which is simply not comprehensible when properly interpreted by the parties or the tribunal. However, such conditions are more easily excisable from the whole of the decision, and it is unlikely that such a condition (by its very poor drafting) will be seen to have been so central to the grant of registration that the whole registration will be seen as a nullity.

In practice, the matter is likely to be addressed under s 21(5) of the 2000 Act, since the tribunal would no doubt use its power, which arises upon any appeal, to vary conditions for the time being in force and to direct that other conditions shall have effect, as it thinks fit. It seems likely that a tribunal faced with an incomprehensible condition which was central to the very registration itself would invite submissions and redraft the condition, rather than exercising the alternative option (and direct that the decision ceased to have effect as a whole).

Chapter 5

THE PHYSICAL ENVIRONMENT

5.1 INTRODUCTION

The physical environment, size, design and the philosophy of care at an establishment are said to be 'interwoven'.[1] The layout, condition and facilities at an establishment will have a considerable impact on the service and standard of care which the persons accommodated will receive. The new legislation and associated Regulations[2] go a long way to ensure that the premises and facilities are appropriate to meet the assessed needs of service users. In this chapter we will consider the structure and regulatory context of the law in relation to the physical environment under the Care Standards Act 2000 (the 2000 Act), Regulations and associated standards.

The 2000 Act creates a broad range of regulation-making powers covering matters such as facilities, premises and the physical environment of establishments providing care services. The legislation[3] is far reaching and covers establishments such as children's and nursing homes, through to private and voluntary health care services (including private hospitals, clinics and private primary care premises) and care homes.

Section 22 of the Act provides the Secretary of State with power to make regulations in respect of both 'the fitness of premises' and 'the facilities and services provided'. Furthermore, s 23 of the Act grants the Secretary of State the additional power to publish statements of national minimum standards which outline the requirements necessary to demonstrate compliance and which must be taken into account by the regulatory authority when making its decisions. However, they are not themselves legally enforceable.

It is important to consider the national minimum standards in the context of current government health care policy and also in terms of the sociological and philosophical thinking behind modern care practice. In this chapter, we will examine the principles that are common to all the physical environment standards and consider how the standards are used to determine whether the establishment in question is able to meet the needs and secure the welfare of the people who live there.

---

1   *National Minimum Standards Care Homes for Older People*, Ch 5, p 25 (amended March 2003 – in force June 2003).
2   See Care Homes Regulations 2001, Children's Homes Regulations 2001, Private and Voluntary Health Care (England) Regulations 2001.
3   See Care Standards Act 2000, ss 1, 2, 3.

5.1.1 Structure and regulatory context of the law

The relationship between the Act, Regulations and national minimum standards is worthy of clarification and can be simply explained as a three-tier process:

– the Act sets the framework for the rules;
– the Regulations set the rules;[1]
– the national minimum standards set the standards by which compliance with the rules will be judged.[2]

5.2 ARE THE REGULATIONS MANDATORY OR DISCRETIONARY?

The Regulations are mandatory. The Act gives the Secretary of State the power to dictate that failure to comply with any Regulation as specified therein will be an offence.[3] Furthermore, each set of statutory requirements details those Regulations with which non-compliance constitutes a prosecutable offence.[4] Persons who are found guilty of an offence are liable to a fine upon conviction. The decision to exercise one's discretion in relation to the non-compliance of specific Regulations is likely to result in enforcement action.

5.3 ARE THE NATIONAL MINIMUM STANDARDS MANDATORY OR DISCRETIONARY?

Compliance with the national minimum standards is not enforceable, but compliance with the Regulations is enforceable subject to the national minimum standards being taken into account. There is no legal requirement to comply with the standards as such.

The national minimum standards are used by the regulatory authority as a basis for registration and inspection and are likely to be applied in full. It is intended that they should form the basis upon which the regulatory authority determines whether the establishment is able to meet the needs and serve the welfare of the people accommodated.

All newly registered services must comply with the national minimum standards in order to obtain registration in the first instance. It is important to appreciate the breadth of the standards concerned. The legislator has initiated a different set of stated requirements in respect of each type of establishment and the service user group catered for. Unlike the Regulations, whilst the national minimum standards are not legally binding, the manner in which the legislation is

---

1   See Care Standards Act 2000, s 22.
2   Ibid, s 23.
3   Ibid, s 25(1) – 'A person guilty of an offence under the Regulations shall be liable on summary conviction to a fine not exceeding level 4 on the Standard scale', s 25(2).
4   See Care Homes Regulations 2001, reg 43.

structured has made the distinction between the two practically negligible in parts.

Further, the national minimum standards are intended to form the basis for the exercise of discretion and judgments[1] made by the regulatory authority when considering such matters as variation or imposition of conditions in respect of registration, proceedings for cancellation of registration and compliance with the Act and associated Regulations.

5.4   THE REGULATIONS – THE REQUIREMENTS

The substantial contexts of all the different Regulations and standards are numerous. However, the content of the Regulations can be broken down into those standards that relate to 'premises', 'accommodation' and 'facilities'.

The Regulations require that the premises are:

–   fit to be used;
–   suitable for the purpose of achieving the aims and objectives set out in the establishment's statement of purpose; and
–   located in an area appropriate to meet the needs of service users.

Whether premises can be said to be 'fit' for use is a question that has troubled registration and inspection authorities for many years. The two key points to note are that:

–   the concept of 'fitness' is not capable of definition. Each particular set of circumstances will turn on its own facts;
–   the National Care Standards Commission (NCSC) and the Care Standards Tribunal are only required to determine what is not fit, not what is. It is suggested that the diagnosis of what is 'fit' is something that can only be recognised from an examination of particular facts using the experience and expertise of the decision-maker.

In previous editions of this book, the writer[2] has suggested that the word 'fit' can be defined as 'suitable'. To this effect, the question that the regulator or tribunal must ask is whether the premises are suitable for the purpose of achieving the aims and objectives as set out in the establishment's statement of purpose. The Care Homes Regulations 2001 and the Children's Homes Regulations 2001 identify the following as essential requirements.

---

1   See Care Standards Act 2000, s 23(4).
2   Paul Ridout, *Registered Homes. A Legal Handbook* (Jordans, 1998) at p 162.

5.4.1   Premises[1,2]

The essential requirements of premises are as follows:

- The premises should be of sound construction and kept in a good state of repair.

- The physical design and layout of the premises and the size and layout of rooms used by service users must be suitable for their needs.

- All parts of the establishment must be kept clean and reasonably decorated.

- The external grounds must be suitable for, and safe for use by, service users, and appropriately maintained.

- The ventilation, heating and lighting must be suitable for service users and must be provided in all parts of the premises used by service users.

- The registered provider must consult with the authority responsible for environmental health and the fire authority for the area in which the establishment is situated.

5.4.2   Accommodation[3,4]

The essential requirements of accommodation are as follows:

- Adequate private and communal accommodation must be provided for service users.

- There should be adequate sitting, recreational and dining space provided separately from the service user's personal accommodation.

- The communal space provided for service users should be suitable for the provision of social, cultural and religious activities appropriate to the circumstances of service users.

5.4.3   Facilities[5,6]

The facilities that must be provided are as follows:

- Service users must be provided with suitable facilities in which to meet visitors in communal accommodation, and in private accommodation which is separate from the service users' own private rooms.

- There must be sufficient numbers of lavatories, wash-basins, baths and showers fitted with a hot and cold water supply provided at appropriate places in the premises.

---

1   See Care Homes Regulations 2001, reg 23.
2   See Children's Homes Regulations 2001, reg 31.
3   See Care Homes Regulations 2001, reg 23.
4   See Children's Homes Regulations 2001, reg 31.
5   See Care Homes Regulations 2001, reg 16.
6   See Children's Homes Regulations 2001, regs 15, 18, 31.

In addition to the above requirements, the Children's Homes Regulations 2001 require that children must be provided with sleeping accommodation that is suitable to meet their needs.[1] In particular, the requirement is that no child shares a bedroom with an adult (except in the case of siblings), a child who is of the opposite sex or a child of a significantly different age.[2] The draftsperson has sensibly dictated the requirements in respect of sleeping arrangements within the Regulations (rather than including these particular criteria within the national minimal standards) so that it disposes of any uncertainty as to what may or may not be appropriate.

To strengthen the regulatory requirements in respect of the physical environment,[3] the Regulations compel the registered provider to include in its statement of purpose[4,5] a statement as to the facilities, services and accommodation provided. This document can be utilised as a performance benchmark which creates certainty as to the organisational structure and services on offer. The statement of purpose is a legal document, and provides an additional standard by which the home can be measured. The Regulations place the burden on the registered provider to make clear in its statement of purpose the 'people' for whom the home is intended, which places the onus on the registered provider to ensure that the physical environment is compatible with their assessed needs. The Regulations, of course, detail the requirements in relation to both the facilities to be provided and the fitness of the premises. However, failure to comply with a statement of purpose is, in itself, an offence which is punishable by way of a fine. Alongside this exists the requirement that the registered provider[6] must[7] file a copy of the statement of purpose with the NCSC, which must also be notified of any revisions to the document within 28 days of the amendment.[8] The legislator's use of the statement of purpose in this way is interesting, in that it operates to increase the onus of the obligation on the registered provider by requiring it to state in what ways the physical environment and facilities are appropriate to meet the needs of those accommodated.

5.5 NATIONAL MINIMUM STANDARDS

The national minimum standards are intended to build upon the underlying principles of the 2000 Act and ensure that a coherent and national approach is adopted by the regulatory authority responsible for the regulation of such services. Section 23(4) of the Act requires that the national minimum standards are to be taken into account by the NCSC in decision-taking:

---

1   Children's Homes Regulations 2001, reg 31(8)(a).
2   Ibid, reg 31(9).
3   See also Private and Voluntary Health Care (England) Regulations 2001, reg 25.
4   Care Homes Regulations 2001, reg 4, Sch 1.
5   Children's Homes Regulations 2001, reg 4, Sch 1.
6   Care Homes Regulations 2001, reg 4(2).
7   Children's Homes Regulations 2001, reg 4(2).
8   Also see Private and Voluntary Health Care (England) Regulations 2001, reg 8.

– in urgent applications for closure;
– in appeals;
– in prosecutions.

The detail in respect of what is required in relation to the physical environment in establishments is contained in the national minimum standards. The overriding principle is that the standards are intended, first, to empower the service user and, secondly, to focus on achievable outcomes which are expected to contribute to the quality of life of the service user. For the first time, the legislator has taken steps to recognise the unique and complex needs of each type of service user group and implement standards in respect of the many groups catered for. When fully implemented, there will be 12 sets of standards which will detail (where applicable) the physical environment standards in respect of each establishment and its service user group, ranging from those accommodated in care homes and boarding schools, to those in residential family centres.

The *National Minimum Standards for Care Homes for Older People* and those in respect of *Care Homes for Younger Adults*[1] became effective on 1 April 2002. It was intended that the physical environment standards would apply in full to all applications for first time registration. However, for homes which had been subject to registration prior to 1 April 2002 the standards provided operators with a period of time in which to act in order to secure compliance with the standards. These standards related to matters which affected the structure and fabric of the premises. It soon became apparent that many service providers would have to invest a great deal of time and money if they were to successfully comply with the requirements as stated.

The care sector reacted vociferously to the national minimum standards requirements. It was alleged that the standards were to blame for home closures, because some service providers could not afford to undertake the work required to comply with the new 'higher' standards. Social commentators have noted that the real issue behind the closures was less to do with 'room sizes' than with inadequate government funding for residential care.[2] The case of 108-year-old Alice Knight,[3] who went on hunger strike following the closure of her residential home in Norwich, forced the issue into the public domain. The home where Alice Knight had lived for 6 years was alleged to have closed down because the service provider could not afford to pay for the work needed to comply with the new standards. In a bid to respond to what was perceived by many as a sector in crisis, the Government took steps to revise those standards[4] which it believed presented 'the most demanding requirements in terms of changes to the fabric of the existing care homes and their associated cost'.[5]

---

1   Amended February 2003 – referred to as *National Minimum Standards for Care Homes for Adults (18–65) and Supplementary Standards for Care Homes Accommodating Young People Aged 16 and 17* (in force June 2003).
2   John Carvel Social affairs editor, *The Guardian* – Tuesday 20 August 2002.
3   Ibid.
4   *Care Homes For Older People and Younger Adults*. Proposed Amended Environmental Standards Consultation Document, August 2002 (Department of Health).
5   Ibid, p 1 at para 3.

The Government published a consultation document which proposed amendments to certain environmental standards to care homes. The intention was to remove the term 'existing' from the original standards and replace it with the word 'pre-existing'.[1] This meant that care homes which existed before 1 April 2002, but which had not been subject to registration under the Registered Homes Act 1984, would not be treated as 'first time registrations'. The higher standards would apply to entirely new provisions only. This would include a new provision in an old building which was not used as a care home on 31 March 2002. Existing care homes which may previously have been exempt,[2] ie Royal Charter and local authority homes, would not be treated as first time registrations. The standards proposed for amendment were as follows:

Care homes for older people	*Care homes for younger adults*
20.1/20.4: communal space	24.2: living space
21.3: assisted baths	24.9: wheelchair access
22.2: passenger lifts	25.3: single rooms
22.5: doorways	25.5: shared bedrooms
23.2/23.4: single room floor space	27.2/27.4: toilets and bathrooms
23.11: single rooms	28.2: shared space

The consultation document provided that such care homes would be expected to spell out in their statement of purpose and service user guide the details of individual accommodations and communal space provided at the home.

After a period of consultation the government published the revised *National Minimum Standards for Care Homes for Older People* and those in respect of *Care Homes for Adults (18–65)*. The move was seen by some as an attempt by government to backtrack on the legislative requirements in order to obscure the real issue of governmental funding of residential care.[3] The truth is that the Care Standards Act 2000 and associated Regulations had not been the subject of revision and as such the core legislative requirements remained unchanged. It is intended that the regulatory authority will note in its inspection report the extent to which the home complies with the standards. The inspection report is then, of course, made available to the service users and the general public.[4]

5.5.1 The underlying principles of the physical environment national minimum standards

It is important to appreciate that the national minimum standards are not only intended to fix premises with particular physical requirements, but also have

---

1 Ibid, p 3 at para 13.
2 Ibid, p 3 at para 14.
3 The regulatory body responsible for registration and inspection of care homes was quick to respond: 'the Government has not relaxed or changed the Care Homes Regulations 2001. These regulations make providers legally responsible for ensuring that their residents are protected from abuse, receive good care in a safe and reasonable environment and that care is given by staff who are trained and competent to deliver it. They must provide services and premises which match the home's stated purpose' (Anne Parker, Chair, National Care Standards Commission, Press Release 18 February 2003).
4 See Care Standards Act 2000, s 32(5)–(7).

specific underlying principles which are intended to underpin the sociological and philosophical thinking of modern care practice. The main principles are:

- fitness for purpose;
- quality of life;
- assessed needs;
- quality services, facilities and equipment;
- living space;
- health and safety.

(1)   Fitness for purpose

The financial resources of service users or their sponsors will greatly influence the quality, standard and choice of accommodation available to them. This is particularly so in the case of the elderly whose income may be limited to state benefits or the statutory pension. Elderly women particularly are likely to have limited income and few assets or investments. The fees levied in the private care home sector will ultimately dictate both the quality of service provided and the physical environment of the care home itself.

The regulatory powers provided by the Act are designed to ensure that the establishment premises are 'fit for their purpose'; this is without reference to the cost of the service or environment provided. This is the overriding principle that the regulator will seek to apply when assessing against the standards whether or not the physical environment at the establishment is capable of meeting its stated objective. The 'fitness or otherwise' of the premises must be considered by having proper regard to an establishment's statement of purpose and the needs of persons accommodated.

(2)   Quality of life

Each standard focuses on an achievable objective and is intended to bring about and secure a positive outcome for the service user. The standards are intended to 'empower' service users. The document *Modernising Social Services*[1] called for standards to focus on the key areas that most affected the quality of care that service users received. In applying this objective, the regulators are expected to measure the premises against the standards to assess whether the service users' physical environment is consistent with the principles of self-determination, privacy and dignity. The Care Homes Regulations 2001 specifically require the registered provider to detail the arrangements made to respect service user privacy and dignity within its statement of purpose.[2]

What does or does not define 'quality of life' is a subjective matter and one which is often the subject of debate. It is accepted, however, that a life of quality will include the freedom to make autonomous decisions. Difficulties arise where for some reason a person's capacity is impaired. The responsible health care professional will ensure that an assessment of a service user's capacity is

---

1   *Modernising Social Services* (Department of Health, 1998), at para 4.48.
2   Care Homes Regulations 2001, reg 4(1)(c), Sch 1.

properly conducted and, where possible, take steps to give effect to those decisions that affect the service user's choice of lifestyle and environment. However, for reasons of infirmity, age or disability, people are extremely vulnerable and often have little control over their environment. The physical environment standards go a long way towards securing those requirements which are said to be intrinsic to a person's mental and physical well-being. The underlying principle acknowledges the fact that the environment within which care is delivered will greatly influence the quality of care received.

(3) Assessed needs

The physical environment must be compatible with the service users' assessed needs. Where service users, who by reason of infirmity, illness or disability, spend long periods of time within the confines of one building, it is paramount that their environment is appropriate to meet their particular lifestyle and needs.

The underlying principles of the national minimum standards go a long way towards ensuring that service users have the necessary access to facilities in an environment which is respectful of their privacy and suitable to their require- ments. Service users' requirements must be kept under constant review and the onus is on the registered provider to ensure that the layout of both private and communal space at the establishment continues to match any revised requirements.

(4) Quality services, facilities and equipment

There is no doubt that standards are intended to provide a greater assurance of quality services. Like many other service industries, the care sector has become service user 'focused'. As such, service users are not expected to accept a 'make do' response from service providers. Documented quality standards and quality procedures will play a much greater part in the delivery of care services from now on. It is clear that compliance with national minimum standards in many respects can only be evidenced by accurate record-keeping and controlled documentation procedures on the part of the registered provider.

The national minimum standards demand a commitment to continuous improvement and sustained maintenance in respect of accommodation and facilities, which, where appropriate, include the provision of suitable specialist adaptions and equipment for persons with disabilities. In particular, the standards require clear programmes and documented procedures in respect of matters such as maintenance, risk assessments and hygiene. All these require- ments link back to the overriding principle that the physical environment should be suitable for the people who live there. This includes taking proper account of any element of 'risk' to which the service users may be exposed in the delivery of that service.

(5) Living space

Whilst some of the standards prescribe the minimum room sizes in terms of measurable floor space,[1] it is essential that the standards are read as a whole. The underlying principle is that a service user's own room accommodates his or her personal possessions, is sufficient to meet his or her assessed needs and offers appropriate privacy.

The living space requirements are intended to provide people with sufficient space in which to live their lives. In 1998, it was established that in England alone, approximately 270,000 people over the age of 65 years were living in residential accommodation, with a further 159,600 living in nursing homes. Increased longevity means that the numbers of people accommodated will continue to rise. The national minimum standards place the onus firmly on the service provider to ensure that every service user has a 'minimum' area in respect of their private and communal occupation of the premise. These standards are intended to ensure that the physical environment in terms of space or overcrowding is not able to undermine or impact the mental, emotional or physical health of those accommodated.

(6) Health and safety

As both a provider of services and an employer, the registered person is subject to many and different statutory requirements in relation to health, safety and hygiene. These range from the statutory and common law requirements in respect of the workplace,[2] to those in respect of service users under the national minimum standards.[3] Duties may extend to the public at large, as well as to service users and employees, and many statutes which are intended to protect health and safety give rise to criminal liability for certain acts or omissions.

The national minimum standards underpin the statutory requirements and regulations by providing statements of best practice where appropriate and give clear direction as to what is required.[4] The requirements in respect of health and safety will be greatly influenced by the assessed needs and vulnerabilities of the service user group accommodated. The layout of the building and the physical environment must be compatible with the delivery of care and must not operate to undermine the principles of self-determination or expose service users to risk of injury. This is particularly pertinent in respect of care to those with physical disability and/or sensory impairment.

The draftsperson has acknowledged the vulnerability of persons placed, for whatever reason, in the care of others, and has taken steps to place the onus to

---

1   See para 5.5 (above).
2   Health and Safety at Work etc Act 1974, Management of Health and Safety at Work Regulations 1999, Workplace (Health, Safety and Welfare) Regulations 1992.
3   See *National Minimum Standards for Care Homes for Older People*, Standard 38.4 (amended March 2003 – in force June 2003).
4   *National Minimum Standards for Care Homes for Adults (18–65)*, Standard 24.11 '... the premises meet the requirements of the local Fire Service and Environmental Health Department, Health and Safety and Building Regulations and from 1 April 2004 the Disability Discrimination Act 1995 part 3' (in force June 2003).

secure their health, welfare and safety firmly on the provider by clearly defining and reiterating the standards by which the service provider will be assessed.

5.5.2 Specific standards

The physical environment requirement in respect of each set of standards can, for convenience, be grouped together in the following general categories:

- the premises;
- the accommodation;
- shared space; and
- lavatories and washing facilities.

It is not practical or advisable to detail each of these standards here. It is, however, possible to consider some of the standards in a broader context. Such an approach provides an insight into the operation of the generic underlying principles of the standards as they attach to each service user group.

(1) National Minimum Standards for Care Homes for Older People[1]

In the absence of a stated guidance, it is, by implication only, that the national minimum standards in respect of care homes for older people apply to persons over the age of 65 years.

Older people will often have very special requirements, which may be due to physical and emotional frailty or physical impairment brought about by the condition of old age. Where such needs are prevalent, the design and layout of the home will be crucial. The structure of the home must be compatible not only with the needs of the visually and physically impaired, but also to support the emotional requirements of those accommodated. It must be remembered that service users may have different priorities and needs. Some may prefer to be supported in a domestic family-type environment; others may wish to exercise a greater degree of control over their lives and seek to retain their independence. These considerations will be reflected in their choice of environment and the delivery of care.

The standards require that premises and grounds are accessible, well maintained, safe and attractive,[2] with service user access to safe communal facilities both indoor and out. Indoor communal areas must be sufficient in size and location to allow for a variety of social,[3] cultural and religious activities and give suitable access for those with poor mobility. The standards require providers to give proper consideration to the nature and quality of furnishings[4] and lighting, all of which must be suitable to meet the needs of service users with impaired

---

1   Amended March 2003. In force June 2003.
2   *National Minimum Standards for Care Homes for Older People*, Standard 19.3.
3   Ibid, Standard 20.2.
4   Ibid, Standard 24.2.

physical and sensory cognitive impairments. The registered provider must ensure that a proper assessment of the premises and facilities is undertaken by a suitably qualified person, to ensure that any aids and adaptions[1] provided are suitable to meet the assessed needs of service users. Facilities must include sufficient and suitable lavatories and washing facilities[2] having regard to the number of people accommodated.

The standards dictate that service users have adequate private space that is suitably and comfortably furnished with sufficient space to store personal possessions and maintain privacy. Having regard to the potential physical vulnerability of those accommodated, the standards require that special attention must be given to the maintenance of hygiene and cleanliness[3] to prevent the spread of infection and disease.

(2)   National Minimum Standards for Children's Homes

The 2000 Act replaced the provisions in the Children Act 1989 which dealt with the regulation of voluntary and registered children's homes. Section 2 of the Act defines a children's home as 'an establishment which provides care and accommodation wholly or mainly for children'.

Of all the categories of service users discussed, those under the age of majority are likely to be regarded as the most vulnerable. The physical environment requirements in respect of the operation of children's homes clearly reflect the current philosophical thinking in relation to modern care practice and in particular methods of behaviour control and protection of children.

The standards require that the location of the home is in keeping with its purpose and function.[4] The design and size of the establishment must be suitable to meet the needs of the children it accommodates, which first and foremost must provide security[5] for the children accommodated without hindering individual development. Special attention[6] must be given to the physical restriction of a child's normal movement within the building, and the arrangements that secure privacy and promote childhood independence.

The standards provide for arrangements in respect of washing and bathing facilities with particular attention given to a child's sleeping arrangements[7] and private accommodation areas. Facilities must also be provided which promote a child's education and allow for private study. Continuity in respect of the delivery of care to children is crucial, and the provider is required to demonstrate that proper consideration has been given to health and safety, and to

---

1   *National Minimum Standards for Care Homes for Older People*, Standard 22.
2   Ibid, Standard 21.
3   Ibid, Standard 26.
4   *National Minimum Standards for Children's Homes*, Standard 23.
5   Ibid, Standard 23.9.
6   Ibid, Standard 23.5
7   Ibid, Standard 24.16–24.19.

contingency[1] responses in respect of foreseeable crises, such as a sudden reduction in staffing levels, childhood illness, control, and serious allegations which undermine a child's safety and protection.

(3)   National Minimum Standards for Boarding Schools

Prior to regulation by the NCSC, independent boarding schools had always been regulated and inspected by local social services and were assessed against local welfare standards. This often created discrepancies in the standards applied and, consequently, the service delivered. Some local authorities were said to marginalise the inspection of independent boarding schools. Consequently, there was concern that there was little guarantee that the health and welfare of the children living in such settings were safeguarded. The Commission is approved under s 87 of the Children Act 1989 to carry out inspections of independent boarding schools. The standards are intended to ensure that a minimum level of care is provided to the children accommodated by the private education sector. Boarding schools which accommodate any child for more than 295[2] days a year are required to register with the Commission as children's homes. Such schools are subject to the *National Minimum Standards for Children's Homes*, rather than the boarding school standards.

The standards require that boarding houses (including dormitories and communal areas) should be appropriately lit, heated,[3] ventilated and furnished, all of which must also be readily accessible to disabled pupils. Particular attention is given to pupils' sleeping accommodation[4] – with appropriate divisions made in respect of the age and gender of the children accommodated. Attention must also given to a child's storage and space, furnishings and changing facilities. There must be adequate toilet, bathing and private facilities.[5] The registered provider is required to ensure that arrangements are made to protect pupils from safety hazards,[6] with safe recreational areas provided both indoors and out.

(4)   National Minimum Standards for Residential Special Schools

These standards are designed to be used in respect of any school providing accommodation for a child which is either:

(a)   a special school in accordance with ss 337 and 347(1) of the Education Act 1996; or
(b)   an independent school, not falling within (a) above, which, as its sole or main purpose, is the provision of places with the consent of the Secretary of State for pupils with special needs or who are in public care.

---

1   *National Minimum Standards for Children's Homes*, Standard 26.4.
2   Care Standards Act 2000, s 1(6)(b).
3   *National Minimum Standards for Boarding Schools*, Standard 40.
4   Ibid, Standard 42.
5   Ibid, Standards 44 and 45.
6   Ibid, Standard 47.

A school is a special school if it is specially organised to make special educational provision for pupils with special education needs.[1]

It is important to appreciate that there will be many different reasons why children are accommodated at residential special schools. The needs of such children can often be far reaching and complex in nature. It is therefore crucial that the design, layout and location of the premises are compatible with the assessed needs of the children.

The standards give careful regard to the function and purpose of the school, and detail extensive requirements[2] in respect of access, use of aids, adaptions and modifications,[3] and storage at the premises. The interior and exterior of the school must be in a good state of repair, and be properly lit, heated and adequately ventilated. There are detailed requirements in relation to sleeping accommodation[4] arrangements, in respect both of the structure of the sleeping accommodation and the number of children who may be accommodated therein. As one would expect, there are detailed standards with respect to the provision of baths, showers, lavatories[5] and changing facilities, and all facilities must take into account a child's need for privacy, dignity and safety. Having regard to the complex needs of these children, positive steps must be taken by the registered provider to secure their health, safety,[6] welfare and security.

(5) National Minimum Standards for Care Homes for Adults (18–65)[7]

These standards apply to all homes which provide accommodation and nursing or personal care for adults aged 18–65[8] years who may have physical or sensory disability, HIV, autism, mental health, alcohol or substance misuse, and complex multiple disabilities. The broad scope of this set of standards acknowledges the complexity of the conditions these young adults may have. It is paramount that the living environment is reflective of the person accommodated, particularly his or her lifestyle. The standards state that the key requirement is 'that a service user's own room accommodates their possessions, enables them to pursue their chosen interests and activities and offers sufficient privacy'.[9] The standards reflect the age of the group accommodated and, in

1   Education Act 1996, s 337 'Special Educational Needs' are provided in respect of a child who has a learning difficulty which calls for special educational provision (s 785) cross ref s 785(3) as per the meaning of 'special educational provision'.
2   *National Minimum Standards for Residential Special Schools*, Standard 23.
3   Ibid, Standard 23.2.
4   Ibid, Standard 24.5
5   Ibid, Standard 25.
6   Ibid, Standard 26.
7   The Standards previously referred to as the *National Minimum Standards for Care Homes for Younger Adults* were subject to amendment in February 2003 (see para 5.5). The new *National Minimum Standards for Care Homes for Adults (18–65)* and the supplementary *National Minimum Standards for Care Homes Accommodating Young People Aged 16 and 17* are due to come into force in June 2003.
8   *National Minimum Standards for Care Homes for Adults (18–65)*, p 9.
9   Ibid, p 42.

particular, are more prescriptive and less paternalistic than some of their counterparts for other service user groups.

In general terms, the standards require that premises are suitable for the stated purpose, and are safe, well maintained[1] and amenable to all service users. The registered person must ensure that any environmental adaptions[2] and disability equipment are sufficient to meet the stated purpose of the home and that there are sufficient communal areas for shared activity and private[3] use. Premises must have rigorous[4] systems in place with respect to cleanliness and hygiene to control the spread of infection.

(6) National Minimum Standards for Adult Placements

An adult placement is an arrangement whereby persons over the age of 18 years are able to live a domestic life as part of the adult placements family.[5] The domestic setting referred to is not intended for more than three persons. These standards are therefore separated from the standards in respect of younger adults to reflect the very distinct nature of the placement. The key requirements relate to the accessibility and location of the premises.[6] They must be suitable for a service user's individual needs, with special provisions relating to the use of aids, adaptions and mobility.[7] The standards require that the premises present as a homely, comfortable and safe environment.[8] Furnishings must be of good quality and a service user's private space must be appropriate to meet his or her needs including, where appropriate, more complex nursing needs.

---

1   *National Minimum Standards for Care Homes for Adults (18–65)*, Standard 24.
2   Ibid, Standard 29.
3   Ibid, Standard 28.
4   Ibid, Standard 30.
5   *National Minimum Standards for Adult Placements*, Introduction, p 75.
6   Ibid, Standard 23.
7   Ibid, Standard 25.
8   Ibid, Standard 23.

Chapter 6

CARRYING ON A CARE ESTABLISHMENT OR AGENCY

6.1 INTRODUCTION

This chapter addresses the day-to-day operations of the establishment or agency. It will review the individual positions and interrelation of the registered provider and the registered manager and, where the registered provider is an organisation, the responsible individual. The chapter will also address the relationship between these three key position-holders, the registration authority (National Care Standards Commission (NCSC), Care Standards Inspectorate for Wales (CSIW)) and service users.

6.2 REGISTERED PROVIDER

The registered provider is the person registered to carry on the establishment or agency. That person may be an individual, a partnership or a company. The registered provider is directly responsible to the regulator, ie the NCSC, for the full operation of the care establishment or agency. That responsibility cannot be shirked, delegated or avoided. The Commission will look to the registered provider for full compliance with all the registration obligations. The appointment and registration of a manager will not devolve any degree of responsibility from the registered provider. It will add an accountable person.

The appointment of the registered manager will be critical for the registered provider. Each will have a separate accountability to the Commission. If the establishment or agency is to work properly, the provider and the manager must work together. They must be bound by an appropriate contract, but, more importantly, their relationship must be seamless. Where cracks in that relationship arise, the efficient operation of the establishment or agency will suffer, and that in itself may lead to a perception on the part of the Commission that the establishment and its individual registered persons are not fit to continue to operate because of their inability to work together in the interests of service users.

The Care Standards Act 2000 (the 2000 Act) does not define carrying on an establishment or agency. Some might say the term is obvious, but there will be some difficulties at the margins. The best equivalent is to consider the registered provider as the owner of the business, or, if not the owner, the person who has effective final say over all the day-to-day decisions in the business, and who is thus the employer, in the widest sense, of the registered manager. The registered provider is the person who is accountable for the operation of the business. In an appropriate case, he or she may have neither ownership of the business assets nor the goodwill, but will be answerable to no one else in relation to day-to-day conduct.

It would be foolish for a registered provider to seek such a position without understanding in depth the requirements of the business. The Commission will identify such inadequacy in the pre-registration process and may well decline to register such a person, if he or she shows lack of aptitude or understanding. There should never be a case of a registered provider learning on the job. In a registered care home business, a registered provider is taking on responsibility for some of the most frail and vulnerable members of society.

6.3   REGISTERED MANAGER

In many cases, the registered provider will be required to appoint a manager. Where appointed, a manager must be an individual (s 12(3) of the 2000 Act). That manager must be separately registered (ss 11 and 12).

There is no definition of manager, but this is taken, without debate or exception, to mean the individual who will have day-to-day control of the management of the home.

A registered manager must be appointed and registered (before he or she can manage the home) in all cases except where the registered provider is an individual or partnership who or which is fit to manage the care home but does not intend to be in full-time, day-to-day charge of the care home, or where the organisation can never be in full-time, day-to-day charge of the care home. This is taken as the logical conclusion of the requirement for a manager to be an individual and the obvious conclusion that the individual tasks to be conducted in relation to day-to-day management have to be conducted by a human being, rather than an amorphous corporate entity.

This leads to the anomaly that an appointed manager cannot manage lawfully until registered. There is no answer to this lacuna. The manager cannot and should not take up management responsibilities until registration has been achieved. A practical solution must be found to resolve this dilemma. The Commission has stated informally that it recognises the dilemma and will not take steps to prosecute either provider or manager, provided the registration process is proceeding as it would wish. This is deeply unsatisfactory for both provider and manager since it leaves the legality of their operation and the security of the business at the whim of the Commission. That, however, is the law, and it must be so recognised. To that extent, during a period of change, the Commission has control over the business. Care should be taken because the Commission may seek to exploit that position in its demand for conditions of registration, both in relation to variation of existing registration conditions or new conditions.

The manager cannot hide behind the registered provider. The manager is separately fully accountable to the Commission as regulator for the day-to-day management of the home and for compliance with the vast majority of regulatory requirements relating to its day-to-day operation. The manager will have his or her registration challenged and possibly cancelled or subjected to adverse condition if he or she performs badly in the view of the Commission. He or she will have separate routes of appeal, but unless he or she has appropriate indemnities and protections from his or her employer, those routes will be for him or her to pursue in his or her own time and at his or her own expense.

No doubt the vast majority of registered providers will provide wholesome financial and moral support for their managers. Those advising must be careful of the conflict of interest. A registered manager should not necessarily assume, nor should his or her advisers, that he or she must blindly accept the instructions of the registered provider. The purpose of dual registration is that there should be protection for the vulnerable in this double accountability.

The question sometimes arises as to whether or not a person may be registered manager of more than one establishment. There is no rule of law that prevents more than one appointment for one individual. The matter is one of interpretation of the facts, coupled with a large slice of common sense. The individual will know whether his or her capacity extends properly to fulfilling the regulatory accountable duties of registered manager in relation to more than one establishment or agency. In many cases, where establishments are close together and may be relatively small, there will be a serious issue as to whether or not the establishment is really several establishments or one linked by common management. The question will be one of fact to determine whether the particular individual can, or indeed is, properly discharging the functions of manager in relation to the various 'units', to use a neutral word. Managers should be slow to accept extended responsibility, since they will be held accountable to the full regulatory level in respect of all of those establishments they manage.

The registered manager will have full accountability for all the service users in all the establishments of which he or she is registered manager. The manager will thus be exposed to almost the whole of the adverse risk of day-to-day operation of the home and will rightly expect a contract which reflects the acceptance of those risks. A registered provider would be well advised to enter into a contract of employment with the manager which rewards those risks with commensurate benefits and, in turn, asks of the manager commensurate commitments.

6.3.1 Manager's contract

The relationship between registered provider and registered manager is critical. The establishment or agency cannot lawfully continue and in practice cannot continue for a significant period of time, unless the relationship operates seamlessly.

The contract will need to address plainly the responsibility to the employer (registered provider) from the manager for the manager to perform and discharge all those functions of regulation that relate to day-to-day operations. The manager, for his or her part, will wish to ensure that he or she has cash and non-cash resources available to him or her without superior veto, so that he or she is able to perform those functions.

When appointing a manager, the registered provider must ensure that he or she has exactly those management characteristics and capabilities which are expected by the regulator. The registered provider in fact will be the first-step regulator of the registered manager. The success of the establishment or agency will very much depend upon the capabilities and commitment of the manager. The registered provider will necessarily expect the manager to stay with the establishment or agency, and a period of notice to terminate employment well beyond that expected of ordinary employees is indicated. Senior employees in commerce and industry regularly accept notice periods of as much as 12 months, and it is submitted that such a period is appropriate for the appointment of registered manager. This shows commitment and protects the registered provider against the illegality of operation and exposure to the Commission.

Given the expectation for such a notice period, and given the acceptance by the registered manager of regulatory accountability, it is not unreasonable that the registered manager should share in the success of the business by way of bonus or profit share. That will be a matter for individual negotiation, but such points of principle mark out the territory which is likely to establish a good working relationship between provider and manager. That, in turn, will create a seamless relationship and earn the respect of the Commission.

6.4   RESPONSIBLE INDIVIDUAL

An individual registered person is the responsible individual. The law does not state as much, but that follows inevitably from the absence of anyone else to fulfil that position.

Where the registered provider is a company or partnership, in every case in relation to a company and in relation to those cases where the partners by themselves or one of their number do not take day-to-day charge of the establishment or agency, there must be an appointed responsible individual. There is no such person as the 'responsible person'. That is a misnomer which has crept from previous law through an inaccurate application form issued by the Commission into shorthand parlance in operation. Legally, the term is 'responsible individual'.

Where the registered provider is not required to take or does not take day-to-day charge of the business, it must appoint a responsible individual. That responsible individual must be a fit person (see Chapter 4).

The appointment of the responsible individual is not subject to any control by the Commission. However, the identity of the responsible individual, whoever he or she may be, and his or her replacement from time to time, must be notified in writing to the Commission.[1]

Clearly the requirement for the responsible individual to be a fit person requires the registered provider to be satisfied that that individual is fit for the role to which he or she is appointed.

The role, as identified in the relevant Regulations, is to take responsibility for supervising the management of the home, ie the responsible individual is the link between the registered provider and the registered manager. Once again, there is no limit on the number of appointments a person may take as responsible individual, as a matter of prescribed law. However, it is clear that an individual cannot accept an unlimited number of appointments since he or she would be unable to function effectively as a manager. As with other decisions, and particularly the number of establishments within the control of a registered manager, it is really for the registered provider and the responsible individual sensibly to determine how many establishments may come within the management of one individual. It is submitted that this should be no more than 10, and, in some cases, a much smaller number.

The Commission will look to the responsible individual for explanations and accountability in relation to day-to-day issues. It will expect that individual to know the details of how the establishment works. It will not expect the individual to know exactly what has happened in a particular incident on a particular day, but the individual will be expected to be aware of that incident, and to be able to speak to the Commission after a proper (albeit short) period for investigation. The Commission will expect the individual to know how the policies and procedures work, and to be in close touch with the day-to-day management so as to be able properly to report to the registered provider and Commission on the state of operation. This makes it clear that the individual must not be responsible for an excessive number of establishments over which he or she cannot exercise proper control.

The responsible individual will be required to visit each establishment at least once a month for the purpose of a formal and detailed review of the premises.[2] At such visits, the responsible individual will be required to interview service users and their representatives and employees, inspect the premises and prepare a written report. It is submitted that in reality the responsible individual should visit at least once a week so as to be in a position to properly respond to issues of accountability and so as to ease the process, which is relatively onerous, of the monthly inspection and report. Such inspection visits should take one whole day, and this in itself sets a limit for the number of establishments within the potential supervisory responsibility of one individual.

---

1   Care Homes Regulations 2001, SI 2001/3965, reg 7(2)(c); Private and Voluntary Health
    Care (England) Regulations 2001, SI 2001/3968, reg 10(2)(c); Children's Homes
    Regulations 2001, SI 2001/3967, reg 6(2)(c).
2   Care Homes Regulations 2001, reg 26; Children's Homes Regulations 2001, reg 33; Private
    and Voluntary Health Care (England) Regulations 2001, reg 26.

6.5   CRIMINAL ACCOUNTABILITY

Each registered person, ie provider and manager, is fully accountable from a regulatory point of view, to the criminal standard, for performance of the statutory obligations. Furthermore, where an offence is committed by a body corporate (under s 30 of the 2000 Act) other individuals within the organisation may be criminally accountable. Directors, managers, secretaries or others who purport to act in that capacity who have consented to, connived at or have been negligent in respect of incidents are personally accountable. This also extends to officers and members of local authorities where local authorities are registered.

It is clear that the legislation intends that the responsible individual shall be in a position where he or she takes criminal accountability for breaches of the law. The innate position of the responsible individual is such that it would be virtually impossible for him or her to argue that he or she had neither consented to, connived at nor been negligent in respect of such breaches. His or her role in supervising the management must mean that he or she knew or ought to have known of such activities. An exception might be where something contrary to policy happened out of context with no precedent. However, experience in the operation of care homes shows that such circumstances are rare. Having said all that, such breaches are, in practice, unlikely to lead to a prosecution. Prosecutions usually arise out of desperation and as a last resort because of a continued failure to address structural deficiencies, rather than as an isolated incidence of bad behaviour or bad luck, which can generally be addressed by individual circumstances and a correction in policies and procedures.

Each registered person, registered manager and responsible individual should expect full accountability to the criminal standard for breaches of the law. For that reason again, the person appointed responsible individual should ensure that he or she is fulfilling his or her functions of supervision of management correctly. To take a risk is pure folly.

6.6   NOTIFICATION OF ABSENCE

The registered persons are very important people. Their absence from the establishment is a matter of significance. Where the provider is an individual or in any other case the manager, a proposal for absence for more than 28 days continuously must be notified to the Commission. Except in cases of emergency, that notice must be given not later than one month before the absence commences.

The notice must tell the Commission:[1]

–   how long the person will be absent;
–   the reason for absence;
–   the arrangements for running the care home during absence;

---

1   For further details, see Care Homes Regulations 2001, reg 38; Private and Voluntary Health Care (England) Regulations 2001, reg 29; and Children's Homes Regulations 2001, reg 37, which are written in similar terms.

- the names, addresses and qualifications of those responsible for running the home during absence; and
- in the case of the registered manager, arrangements for appointing a substitute.

These arrangements include all absences and will apply when the registered manager departs employment for whatever reason.

In such circumstances, the registered provider will be in breach during the period of non-appointment of a manager, and indeed during the period in which that manager is unable to take up the appointment because to do so would constitute a breach of law. The appointed manager cannot, of course, take up, without breach of law, the position of management without registration.

In these dire circumstances, individuals not in day-to-day charge and partners, none of whom are in day-to-day charge, will have to return to the business, and companies will have to take greater interest in the business through the responsible individual.

6.7 APPOINTMENT OF LIQUIDATORS

Disruption of business may arise through insolvency or insolvency law appointments. Such appointments will need to be considered carefully as to their legal status. It is beyond the remit of this book to consider insolvency appointments in detail. However, some insolvency appointments will constitute a complete divesting of the registered provider of ownership and control to the trustee in bankruptcy or liquidator, and others will preserve the legal status of the registered provider through the fiction that the insolvency practitioner is acting as agent of the registered provider, which usually means that the registered provider is the borrower from a financial institution.

If, in law, the registered provider has been permanently separated from the premises, the registration will cease to have effect, and the insolvency practitioner will not be able to operate the care establishment or agency unless he or she is registered. Acting in any other way would constitute a criminal offence.

It is thus important for the insolvency practitioner to take careful advice and to be sure, if that is his or her wish, that any operation of the home, however short, does not constitute a criminal offence.

Regulation 31 of the Care Homes Regulations 2001 requires a practitioner:

- to notify the Commission of his or her appointment forthwith;
- to appoint a manager to take full-time charge where there is no registered manager (and, of course, that manager will have to be registered before he or she can take up that appointment);
- before the end of 28 days, to notify the Commission as to intentions for future operation (which is an anomoly since future operation will not be possible unless there has been a form of registration).

The creation of the position of administrative receiver under the Insolvency Act 1986 created the most usual agency appointment – directly intended to enable a business to be preserved. This appointment is likely to be largely superseded by administrative appointments under the Enterprise Act 2000 which is in the process of coming into force. Such an administrator is considered to be the agent of the company but administration is not directly recognised by the 2000 Act.

Similar provisions apply to children's homes and private and voluntary health care establishments.[1]

6.8 OPERATING STRUCTURE OF THE ESTABLISHMENT OR AGENCY

The 2000 Act and its associated Regulations create, for the first time, a legal requirement for a formal structure to the operation of establishments and agencies. Such a structure is intended to formalise the pathway to care delivery and to enable external inspection more easily to identify the constitution which the establishment or agency has set for itself to monitor and regulate the quality of service that it delivers in accordance with the philosophical basis upon which the business operates.

This structure will centre upon three vital and dynamic documents:

(a) the statement of purpose in relation to the operation of the establishment or agency;
(b) the individual assessment of need for each service user;
(c) the service user plan for each service user.

Each of these structural documents is required to be in existence at all times as a matter of regulation to criminal standard, and is required to be reviewed and updated dynamically in accordance with day-to-day change. They are also the documents to which inspectors will look to inform their visual and auditory inspection of the home.

6.9 STATEMENT OF PURPOSE

The statement of purpose is critical to each establishment or agency. Its existence is a statutory requirement.[2]

For convenience, commentary will proceed on the basis of the requirements for care homes, which are the same for these purposes for other establishments.

The statement will set out every material particular of the operation of the care home so that the reader can discover exactly how the registered proprietor has

---

1   Children's Homes Regulations 2001, reg 39; Private and Voluntary Health Care (England) Regulations 2001, reg 41.
2   Care Homes Regulations 2001, reg 4, Sch 1; Children's Homes Regulations 2001, reg 4, Sch 1; Private and Voluntary Health Care (England) Regulations 2001, reg 6, Sch 1.

decided the care home should function and operate, and how those functions will be delivered, so as to ensure a satisfactory service to service users.

This document should be used on a day-to-day basis by the manager and staff at the care home. Every manager and all senior staff should know the terms of the statement of purpose and know how it operates so that they can apply it in a particular situation.

In operating the care home in accordance with the statement of purpose, provider, manager, responsible individual and senior staff should appreciate that the statement will outline the benchmark to which the home should be operating for the basis of regulatory accountability. It will be this statement against which the home will be judged as a first instance. If the statement is inadequate, failure to meet its terms will be a criminal offence in many cases. Its drafting must be carefully addressed and should be conservative. It is vital that all senior management understand and own the document, since they will be held accountable. The excuse of lack of knowledge will sound bad for the organisation and protests of impossibility will be dismissed.

In effect, the statement of purpose is set beside the Regulations applicable to the establishment so that it will inform the reader that the establishment knows of the requirement and describes how it will be addressed.

6.9.1 Aims and objectives

Operators of former residential care homes will be accustomed to a requirement for the establishment to have aims and objectives. Historically, this was a battered and little-seen piece of paper held somewhere in the proprietor's office, speaking in altruistic terms of philosophy and aspiration. The presence of such a document was mandatory. Enforcement by reference to such a document did not enter the thoughts of even the most rigorous regulator. The statement of purpose, however, presents both risk and opportunity.

The risk is clear. Over-expansive statements of expectations of patients and aspirations for care workers will cause trouble if there is an inability to meet the set objectives.

The opportunity is equally clear. The establishment is able, by thoughtful drafting, to map out its purpose and function and to set realistic objectives for its workers and for service users who seek its care. Careful drafting may indeed be a defensive shield against regulation in times of crisis and difficulty. The aims and objectives will be a useful bulwark to which to return to show how the home has presented itself.

The risk posed by over-marketeering should be balanced by sensible and realistic objective establishment. It is suggested that the aims and objectives should be:

-   specific;
-   measurable; and
-   attainable.

If that formula, borrowed from modern employment performance appraisal manuals, is followed, the aims and objectives may be useful rather than dangerous.

In drafting the statement of purpose, managers and senior staff must be involved to the point of ownership, and there should be a healthy debate as to purpose and achievability so as to present a robust and dynamic business which knows where it is going and how it will achieve its aims.

6.9.2   Facilities and services

The statement of purpose must describe all the available facilities and services. In effect, the drafting will have to address every item appearing within reg 16 of the Care Homes Regulations 2001.

A sensible course is to take reg 16, use it as a checklist and ensure that the statement of purpose addresses correctly, specifically and measurably how the establishment will address each issue.

The questions of opportunity and risk need to be considered at each turn of the drafting.

An over-ambitious statement aimed at promoting establishment will risk the day of accountability when there is a failure, perhaps a persistent failure, to set out what has been described.

The opportunity is to show the business as thoughtful and careful in the preparation of its structures and to protect from risk by conservatively assessing the availability of services and facilities and ensuring that what is described is something which the provider and manager feel sure can be delivered on a day-to-day basis.

The opportunities include the opportunities to protect the business from claims and risks.

The following examples are given as to issues that could be covered in the statement of purpose. These are not exclusive, but should trigger thoughts on a home-by-home basis as to what is appropriate.

(1)   *Telephone and facsimile facilities for management* – the extent to which these facilities will be available to service users can be outlined and how this may facilitate ready communication with those who need to contact the home.

(2)   *Telephone facilities for service users, private use* – the method of charging service users for telephone supplies and internet use can be addressed.

(3)   *Furniture, bedding, curtains and floor coverings* – the differences or distinctions from national minimum standards can be specified and justified. The opportunity for bringing in personal belongings and furniture can be addressed, as can a sensible policy to protect from the risk of allegations relating to loss and value.

(4) *Permission for own furniture and belongings* – the risks arising from fire and theft can be specified.

(5) *Laundry* – a charging regime can be set out, and risks arising from allergies can be identified. Labelling and loss policies can also be addressed.

(6) *Self-laundry* – if permitted at all, the obvious risks to service users can be limited or constrained by policy, for example with permission of the home manager.

(7) *Kitchen equipment, crockery, etc* – special equipment for special dietary needs, the philosophy of the home, and health and safety policies can be addressed.

(8) *Self-food preparation* – as with laundry, the matter can be constrained by reference to permission from staff, the limitations on choice and the availability of particular types of foods, and the need for mutual respect in community living.

(9) *Suitable, wholesome and nutritious food* – special diets and religious diets may be addressed. Here, the home could protect itself from the advances of some enthusiastic regulators by specifying the exact limit of choice of foods and what facilities will be made available for individual choice, including notice periods and charging mechanism for extras.

(10) *Hygiene arrangements* – the difference between routine and emergency maintenance and cleaning, and the regularity of domestic cleaning can be specified. If it is difficult to have domestics at all times or on particular days of the week, and this position can be made clear in the statement.

(11) *Eradication of offensive odours* – odours, of course, may be a feature in the short term. This can be addressed as a matter of principle. Expectations can be managed and, as with hygiene, routine and emergency maintenance can be addressed.

(12) *Safekeeping of valuables* – in conjunction with business insurers, the limitations of liability which the home will accept can be set out clearly, ie where a home will expect valuables to be placed, the variable limitations on liability dependent upon whether the rules are maintained or broken, and in certain circumstances an indication of which valuables will not be accepted within the home or when no liability will be accepted.

(13) *Social interests and external engagement in community activities* – the ethos of the home, the arrangements which the home would endeavour to make as a matter of course and the facility for making special arrangements can be set out, together with a clear policy as to charging for extra facilities. There may be opportunities to indicate a clear ethos to favour a particular religious or cultural background. Whilst endeavours may be made to meet individual requirements, there must be an acceptance of the overall needs of community. If special facilities are required then extra charges may be made, particularly where individual transport or escort arrangements need to be made.

(14) *Recreation, fitness and training* – facilities that will be made available as a matter of course can be identified. For example, the home may have a gymnasium or swimming pool, or particular arrangements with community facilities. However, the policy of what may be expected, what is available by way of special arrangement and whether these facilities will be included in the home's fees, should be set out.

(15) *Religious services* – clearly there is a need to meet expectations for religious worship. As a matter of practice, many homes have a strong denominational basis. Some have none at all. Geographical location will limit the availabilities of certain faith worship opportunities. For some religious worshippers the ethos of the home may be inappropriate, whilst meeting the particular religious needs of others may be extremely difficult and expensive. The availability and charging mechanism can be addressed in the statement.

(16) *Drink, including alcoholic drink* – for those homes that make alcohol available, the rules and times of serving and the rules as to keeping alcoholic drinks within personal accommodation can be specified. Alternatively, if alcohol consumption is considered inappropriate, this can be made clear in the statement.

In general terms, the statement of purpose is an opportunity to set the ethos and management methodology of the home. It is also an opportunity to avoid the whims of individual regulators who may seek to assert that individual choices and unusual activities must be the subject of provision within standard fees. In addition, the statement provides an opportunity to manage the risks of an individual disrupting the ethos of the home, the intrusion of the politically correct, as some would describe them, and generally to show what may be expected of service delivery from context to context.

6.9.3   Statutory information

Statutory information is contained in Sch 1 to the Care Homes Regulations. In short, the statutory information to be supplied by the home in its statement of purpose is as follows:

– the names, addresses, qualifications and experience of the registered provider and registered manager;
– the number, qualifications and experience of staff working at the home.

The home should describe, through reference to its operational policies, the type of staff who will be engaged, what experience they have and how that experience may vary (perhaps in reflection of the available labour market). The home can also indicate that there will be work sharing, work experience for teenagers, recent school-leavers, young people, older people, those with qualifications and/or experience, and those without. Grounds for defences to regulatory criticism can be laid, by showing how it is intended to mix and match staff to meet changing circumstances, including those created by demographical or local commercial difficulties.

(1)   Organisational structure of the home

The so-called 'organogram' should show how the lines of accountability within the home operate, and how staff at all levels may refer complaints or criticisms, or seek guidance and support if they are unsure about their terms and conditions of work or the acceptability of practices within the home. This document can work closely into a Public Interest Disclosure policy (the so-called 'whistle-blowing' policy), with which every home should be established.

(2)   Age range, sex and needs of service users

The home should specify its policy on the type of patients available for admission, based upon the service user categories and subject to individual pre-admission assessment and care planning. The home can demonstrate exactly who it will propose to admit and how it may require removal or discharge if assessed needs move outside the range of needs which the home is intended to meet. The home can protect itself against the inevitable risks associated with change of needs in service users.

(3)   Nursing

No definition of nursing is given. The provider and manager should establish in the statement of purpose their understanding of nursing, differentiate nursing from nursing care by a registered nurse, and address the extent to which nursing may be provided by external sources, from agencies or from the community nursing service, and where the home sees the demarcation between personal care and nursing. Whilst this may not be determinative, it will be of major influence in disputes over whether the home is providing nursing.

Where nursing is provided, or where medicines or medical treatment are provided with or without nurses, a qualified nurse is required permanently to be present at the care home. Careful drafting of the home's understanding of what is and what is not nursing will assist in determining whether this very expensive provision applies to the particular care home.

The home can establish relevant levels of expected qualified nursing and when nurses should be described as working at the home.

(4)   Admission policy, including emergency admissions

Admission and discharge are two of the most important events in the accommodation cycle of a service user in the establishment. They will also be areas most fraught with difficulty. A clear admissions policy will be required by the regulator, but as a working tool it is vital for staff (who may not be the most senior staff) who deal with the pressures associated with admission from day to day. A clear and workable admissions policy will protect the home from the most damaging risks, including mistaken admission of those who are not really within the home's capacity to care for.

(5) Arrangements for social activities and hobbies

This overlaps with the facilities and services described above.

(6) Arrangements for consultation with service users on operational matters

The home should indicate in the statement of purpose, where this is appropriate, that there will be little or no consultation. There is also, more realistically, an opportunity for the home to indicate the extent to which the consultative process will be expected to change and where the ultimate decision lies. The creation of residents' meetings and the paying of lip service to consultation exercises may raise service users' expectations about their influence which are impractical or which are not intended.

(7) Fire precautions

Fire policies should be specified and dovetailed to the age, range and needs of service users who are accommodated. The home could also indicate the limitations on choice of accommodation within the home, and specific limitations on the home's ability to retain certain service users if their dependencies increase.

(8) Contact with service users, friends, relatives, etc

The statement of purpose should identify visiting times, booking arrangements for the availability of private rooms, rules relating to the conduct of visits and the ultimate control of visits by the registered manager. Children and pets may or may not be welcome.

(9) Complaints

A complaints procedure is a statutory requirement. The statement should explain the difference between complaints and suggestions, and the way in which complaints can be directed, perhaps by reference to the organisational structure set out in the organogram described at (1) above.

(10) Review of care plan

The statement should explain the care plan, identify key workers, identify those within the organisational structure to whom reference can be made, and set expectations for review, subject to emergency.

(11) Size of room

Where rooms are undersized by reference to national minimum standards, the statement should explain the reasons for this, which can then be taken into account by a regulator when he or she is considering non-compliance with the standards. The statement should explain how some undersized or strangely shaped rooms, or rooms located with difficulties of access, may be restricted to use by service users of different needs and dependencies from those who may be accommodated in more standard accommodation.

(12)   Therapeutic techniques

The statement should set out special therapeutic techniques which are available and whether additional therapies are available at additional cost.

(13)   Privacy and dignity

The issue of service users' privacy and dignity causes as much difficulty and misunderstanding as any aspect of care home management. The statement should therefore identify the home's understanding of such issues and set out in detail its policies, which may extend to the use and circulation of confidential information. It would be useful to address the nature of confidential information and its confidentiality to the individual service user. The statement should identify those with whom it will share confidential information as a matter of routine, and those with whom it will not, and identify the ultimate decision-maker as the registered manager.

Relatives or friends of a service user may demand access to information which is confidential to the service user. The home will have to decide whether it is in the service user's interest that that information be imparted and this will be governed by the wishes of the service user, provided they are of full capacity. Many service users may not have the capacity to make an informed choice, in which case it may be appropriate to supply the information to certain close contacts but not to others. A policy that protects the registered manager's position and justifies control can be conveniently identified in the statement of purpose.

6.9.4   General points

The statement of purpose is a document whereby any deviations or failings of standards required by the national minimum standards can be acknowledged and supported. The home should, in general terms, either put in place a long-term action plan to address the situation, or may, in appropriate circumstances (particularly where change is not possible in the physical environment), advocate by operational policies why it is acceptable or even desirable that such changes exist. Such arguments will be much more persuasive if they are addressed through the home's operational policies, as identified in the statement of purpose from the outset.

6.10   PRIVATE AND VOLUNTARY HEALTH CARE

Statutory requirements under the Private and Voluntary Health Care (England) Regulations 2001 are much more limited in relation to independent hospitals, clinics and medical agencies than for care homes and children's homes. The statement of purpose must identify the number, relevant qualifications and experience of the staff working *in* the establishment. This can be contrasted with the similar provision in relation to care homes, where the staff are described as working *at* the establishment. It is submitted that working *at* the establishment embraces anyone who has working contact with the establishment. Working *in* the establishment suggests a direct relationship of employment or engagement in the independent hospital or other facility, rather than mere contact by visiting to provide professional services independently to service users. The word 'staff' is uniformly used, but in the context of either working *at* or working *in* the establishment, a clear distinction can be seen.

This reinforces the view that registered providers of care homes and children's homes must have more careful regard for, and control over, those who visit the home to support service users, whereas in the independent hospital context it is recognised that those who visit may themselves be subject to external regulation, and by their professional qualification and relationship with the service users are outwith the remit for control of the registered provider and thus outwith the control of the regulator.

6.11   ASSESSMENT OF CARE

An assessment of care must be set out in the statement of purpose and in the application for registration. The assessment is a requirement peculiar to care homes. It is not required for children's homes or independent hospitals. In relation to children's homes, this is because placements are usually made in close association with local authorities or other public bodies. Nonetheless, the requirement for preparation of a plan before or as soon as possible after placement suggests a process similar to an assessment of need and, as with the service user care plan in care homes, the requirement for the existence of the plan at or shortly after admission to the children's home suggests that an assessment should be carried out before a child is accepted into the home.

In relation to independent hospitals registered under the Private and Voluntary Health Care (England) Regulations 2001, the absence of requirement of an assessment reflects the nature of circumstances in which service users visit an independent hospital or like establishment and the strong likelihood that admissions are under the control of a private medical practitioner not subject to control by the NCSC. The regulatory requirements of control of an independent hospital appear to relate to the conduct of the establishment rather than control of individual patient treatment or care. An independent hospital is inspected and regulated by reference to its institutional policies and procedures without direct and individual regulatory accountability in respect of individual service user care.

The requirements of the assessment are as follows.

– The assessment of the service user's needs must be by a suitably qualified or suitably trained person. It is not clear whether that person must be employed or engaged by the care home, but the subsequent requirement suggests that it would be unwise for any registered person of a care home to rely upon assessment conducted by a third party.

- The registered person must have a copy of the assessment. This indicates clearly that the assessment should be in written form.

- There must be appropriate consultation with the service user and his or her representatives.

- The registered person must provide confirmation to the service user that the home meets the service user's need, as identified in the assessment. This means that the registered person should not rely upon an assessment that has not been conducted by persons within his or her control in the establishment. Third parties will not know the precise nature of the available facilities and the flexibility of those facilities to meet individual needs. Only somebody intimately involved in the operation of the care home will be able to give the registered person satisfactory confirmation that needs will be met.

Under reg 14 of the Care Homes Regulations 2001, it is a criminal offence for a registered person to accommodate a service user at a care home without an assessment, *unless it is impractical to do so*. It is submitted that the impracticality defence will only be available on very rare occasions. If impractical, the simple answer is not to admit until the assessment can be conducted. Impracticability will probably only relate to homes which specifically expect to admit in emergencies, and which will have identified their emergency procedures and the minimum information they will require about the client before triggering the emergencies procedures. This will be set out in the home's admission policy and identified in its statement of purpose. It is submitted, therefore, that there will be virtually no cases where, absent a policy for emergency admission, it is sustainable that it was impractical to carry out a pre-admission assessment.

It is also a requirement, subject to criminal sanction, to keep all assessments under review and to revise assessments where necessary. This clearly indicates a review of the assessment process and a renewal of the confirmation that individual service user needs can continue to be met by the care home. The regularity of review should be identified in the statement of purpose, and its consequences should be addressed within the accommodation and service agreement. If the registered person is unable to renew the confirmation as to availability of service, the contract must allow for speedy discharge.

6.12 CARE/PLACEMENT PLANS

Under reg 15 of the Care Homes Regulations 2001, service user plans are a requirement of continued accommodation and care for a service user in a care home. In relation to children's homes, the provision of a child's placement plan before or as soon as possible after admission is a requirement subsequent again to criminal sanction (reg 12 of the Children's Homes Regulations 2001).

In the case of the care home, the service user plan will clearly work with the assessment. It is suggested that the two will become indistinguishable so that the review of the assessment in effect becomes a review of the service user care plan as required by reg 15(2) of the Care Homes Regulations 2001.

No such provisions are required for independent hospitals or similar establishments or agencies under the Private and Voluntary Health Care (England) Regulations 2001.

In the care home, as with assessments, the following are relevant.

- The service user plan must be made available to the service user. This clearly indicates a written document.

- The plan must be kept under review. This clearly indicates a dynamic document prepared in a way which allows for additions and amendments so that the history of care can be reviewed by an inspecting regulator.

- The plan must be prepared and reviewed in consultation with service users and representatives.

- Revisions to the plan should be notified to service users.

Any review of the service user plan which identifies needs that cannot be met will mean that the registered person will be unable to confirm in writing the continued ability to meet the assessment of need, so that in this way the plan and the assessment merge.

On the related issue of confidentiality, the registered person and manager will be strongly influenced in decisions on the sharing of confidential information by the identities of those family members or representatives with whom they can consult and with whom they share the reviews of the assessments and care plans. Confidentiality is breached where the conscience of the confidant is touched by the sharing of the information externally. Clearly, there would be no such breach where information is being shared with those who are an integral part of care assessment and planning.

In relation to children's homes, the child's placement plan, to be prepared as soon as practicable after admission, must address:

- day-to-day issues of care and welfare;
- arrangements for health care and education;
- arrangements for contact with parents, relatives and friends.

The plan must be reviewed regularly and regard must be had to the child's age and understanding in taking his or her views into account.

The plan must be consistent with the care plan established by the placing authority and made on the basis that information will be shared with the child's placing authority, with regular mutual attendance at meetings by representatives of the children's home and the local authority. This reinforces the practical reality that placements in children's homes are virtually exclusively made as a result of arrangements by local authorities in accordance with the appropriate provisions of the Children Act 1989. This also explains the absence of a criminal sanction or requirement of assessment prior to admission to a children's home. Interestingly, there is a requirement for a full assessment where a child is admitted into a care home, as opposed to a children's home, where this is required because the child's needs extend to considerable physical care and attention as opposed to pastoral educative and life-skill training care.

6.13   HEALTH CARE AND WELFARE

The conduct of establishments and agencies is inextricably concerned with control over health and welfare of service users. The various regulations provide, in generic terms, provisions to protect the overall quality of care and treatment in such establishments. The drafting is necessarily generic, since it is impossible to identify specific circumstances which will be relevant to particular risks. The provisions re-emphasise the need to address many issues within the constitutional statement of purpose and to reflect those constitutional bound-aries in every assessment or care planning exercise.

6.13.1   Care homes

In the conduct of a care home, the registered persons are required to ensure that arrangements are made:

-   to promote and make proper provision for health and welfare of service users;
-   to make proper provision for care, treatment, education and supervision of service users;
-   to enable service users to participate in decisions relating to health and welfare;
-   in taking such decisions, to ascertain and take account of the wishes and feelings of service users so far as practicable;
-   to conduct the home with respect to privacy and dignity;
-   to conduct the home with due regard to sex, religious persuasion, racial origin and cultural and linguistic background and disability.

The final requirement emphasises the need to address the facilities for different types of service users within the statement of purpose. Issues of language and disability may be critical in determining admission and care arrangements. Difficulties will arise if the absence of such facilities is not documented within the statement of purpose and possibly does not emerge from the assessment and care planning process until some time after admission. Registered persons may have to meet needs in the short-to-medium-term for which they have no capacity, and thus may have to use existing financial resources, with no opportunity to charge extra sums. Local authority placement teams are notoriously unwilling to increase fees as a result of change in circumstances. It simply does not suit their budgets.

Registered persons are also required:

-   to conduct the home so as to maintain good, personal and professional relations between provider and manager, and service users and staff;
-   to conduct the home so as to maintain good, personal and professional relationships between staff and service users.

These generic terms are set out within reg 12 of the Care Homes Regulations 2001. In addition, under reg 13, registered persons are required to make certain specific arrangements. Service users must be registered with a general practitioner of their choice. Allocation to the home's GP will not suffice. The statement of purpose may need to address the availability of GPs and the limitations on choice (particularly in outlying rural areas).

Service users are also entitled to receive treatment and advice from appropriate health care professionals. The extent to which such treatment and advice will be charged as an extra service to users must be specified in the statement of purpose. Significant losses may arise if this is not addressed. This will be particularly important where service users are placed by local authorities, since the local authority will be unwilling to underwrite provision of care otherwise than through the NHS, which is free of charge. Non-availability of NHS service is never an excuse for non-provision in a care home where needs are identified.

Registered persons are also required:

– to make arrangements for recording, handling, safekeeping, safe adminis-tration and disposal of medicines;
– to make suitable arrangements to prevent infection, toxic conditions and spread of infection in the home;
– to ensure that all parts of the home are free from hazards;
– to ensure that activities are free from risks so far as reasonably practicable;
– to identify and eliminate unnecessary health and safety risks;
– to make arrangements for training of staff in first-aid;
– to make arrangements for safe systems of moving and handling;
– to make arrangements for training staff in prevention of harm and abuse to service users;
– to ensure that no service users are subjected to physical restraint save where that is the only practical means of protection, and in exceptional circumstances.

The very clear double standard for restrictions on physical restraint should be noted. There will clearly be no tolerance in viewing compliance with this provision for a regime which uses physical restraint on a regular basis. Physical restraint must be exceptional, and then only where it is the only means of protection. The issue of potential need for restraint is critical during the assessment, care planning process and review. If patients need persistent restraint, it is unlikely that they are appropriately placed within any care home. All occasions of physical restraint must be recorded, including details of the restraint.

Many of these issues are obvious. They are routine, and were routine in the operation of care establishments before the coming into force of the 2000 Act. However, two very important points must be noted:

(a) compliance is enforceable even to the criminal standard;
(b) the requirement for compliance falls upon both registered provider and registered manager and, by obvious extension, in the case of the registered provider, which is an organisation, onto the responsible individual.

Under reg 43(2) of the Care Homes Regulations 2001, prosecution may only follow an appropriate warning but the terms of the warning may be simple and clear and the time-limits for compliance short.

6.13.2 Private and voluntary health care

Regulation 15 of the Private and Voluntary Health Care (England) Regulations 2001 provides that treatment and service for individual patients must meet the following standards:

- they should meet individual needs;
- they should reflect published research evidence and guidance issued by expert bodies as to good practice;
- they should be provided by appropriate equipment.

Within the context of an independent hospital there will always be tension between the duties and responsibilities of the controlling medical practitioner and those of the hospital provider. Clearly, the obligations of the provider will be delimited by the interaction of the medical practitioner to the extent that that medical practitioner is directly involved in patient treatment.

It is submitted that the registered provider should rely upon the medical practitioner's assessment of resources meeting individual needs, and that practitioners will use procedures in accordance with research evidence and guidance, unless it appears to the provider that there is significant and creditably challenged objections to the course being followed.

The provider should also be able to rely upon the professional expertise of visiting and privileged medical practitioners, who are themselves subject to separate and individual regulation of professional accountability to the General Medical Council under s 31 of the Medical Act 1983.

In addition, registered persons in respect of an independent hospital must ensure that:

- all equipment used is suitable for the purpose and maintained in good working order;
- where reusable medical devices are used these are subject to appropriate cleaning, disinfection, inspection, packaging sterilisation, transportation and storage;
- there are appropriate procedures to ensure safe decontamination of reusable medical devices;
- suitable arrangements are made for ordering, recording, handling, safe-keeping, safe administration and disposal of medicines;
- suitable arrangements are made to minimise the risk of infection, toxic conditions and spread of infection; and
- where food is made available for service users it is adequate in amount, provided at appropriate intervals and is wholesome, nutritious and suitable to need.

It is suggested in this last regard that the aspirations of most private independent hospitals will far exceed the minimum requirement in relation to food.

The purpose of reg 15 of the Private and Voluntary Health Care (England) Regulations 2001 is to identify the regulatory obligation of the registered persons to provide safe services and facilities within a safe system of operation in accordance with proper policies and procedures, rather than to be responsible (as with care homes or children's homes) for all the treatment directly provided to the patient. Clearly, treatment provided by an independent hospital through its own directly controlled staff will be regulated in a way similar to care homes and children's homes, but the care and treatment provided through external consultants (comparable to the general medical practitioner in the care home or children's home) is beyond the control of the registered person of the independent hospital and thus beyond the regulatory control of the NCSC. The Commission does not, it is submitted, have power to regulate the activities of medical practitioners introducing patients to, and treating those patients within, an independent hospital.

In addition, the registered person of an independent hospital must address care and welfare issues. The patient must be enabled to make decisions about the way in which he or she receives care and about his or her welfare. This suggests that the independent hospital's registered person and manager should address the way in which patients are informed about, and consent to, their treatment. There is a clear overlap here between the obligations of the registered persons and the professional duty of the medical practitioners in treatment. This overlap should be addressed in the hospital's statement of purpose so as to ensure a safe and correct procedure for allocating the responsibility for ensuring appropriate consent to treatment.

The registered person must ensure that patients control their own money, or that where patient monies are controlled by the hospital, appropriate accounting procedures are in place. This will be of limited practical interest in most private independent hospitals in the acute sector, but obviously has important principles of application in relation to hospitals that deal with longer-term care and patients of limited capacity, for example mental health institutions.

Patients' wishes and feelings must be taken into account in determining the manner and style of their care and the services provided to them.

The establishment must be conducted so as to respect the privacy and dignity of patients having regard to their sex, religious and spiritual needs, racial origin and cultural and linguistic backgrounds. Of paramount importance is the identification, where appropriate, of the policies and ethos of the home in relation to such matters through its statement of purpose.

The establishment must be conducted on the basis of good personal relationships between registered provider and registered manager, and between each of those persons and the patients and staff.

Under reg 17 of the Private and Voluntary Health Care (England) Regulations 2001, independent hospitals must introduce and maintain systems of review of the quality of treatment and services within the establishment, and must provide for consultations with patients and representatives. Any report of any review must be supplied to the NCSC and made available to patients.

6.13.3 Children's homes

Regulation 11 of the Children's Homes Regulations 2001 sets the generic background to the regulatory requirements for protecting the welfare of children.

The registered person must ensure that the home is conducted so as to:

- promote and make provision for the welfare of the children; and
- make proper provision for the care, education, supervision and treatment of the children.

The registered person must make arrangements to ensure:

- that the privacy and dignity of children are protected; and
- that the home is conducted with regard to the sex, religious persuasion, racial origin and cultural and linguistic background and disability of children accommodated.

These are common features of care establishment and agency regulation. Equally, they should be set out in the statement of purpose, drafted in an appropriate context for children, bearing in mind the general guidance issued above in relation to care homes, and linked to powerful and transparent operational policies.

The placement and care of children are, in this context, commissioned and paid for by local authorities.

Regulations 13–24 of the Children's Homes Regulations 2001 set out a wealth of technical operational detail in relation to the welfare of children, and are as follows:

- reg 13 – food;
- reg 14 – clothing, pocket money and personal necessities;
- reg 15 – content and access to communications;
- reg 16 – child protection arrangements;
- reg 17 – behaviour, management, discipline and treatment;
- reg 18 – education, employment and leisure activity;
- reg 19 – religious observance;
- reg 20 – health needs;
- reg 21 – medicines;
- reg 22 – surveillance;
- reg 23 – hazards and safety;
- reg 24 – complaints and representations.

In the context of children's homes there is detailed regulatory requirement reflecting the general perception within the public of the need clearly and carefully to protect children from abuse, neglect and mistreatment. Registered persons should remember that compliance with all these requirements is enforced to the criminal standard of regulatory compliance. The registered person is strongly advised to ensure that members of his or her staff include a compliance team working exclusively to ensure that the registered person and manager are appropriately supported, and that staff are aware of the need for total compliance with a wealth of regulatory detail which needs to be kept under review on a regular basis.

Compliance with regulations within a children's home, more than any other home, must be observed and monitored on a day-to-day basis.

6.14   STAFFING

No question will be more important in the day-to-day conduct of a care home than maintaining the appropriate staffing levels. Not surprisingly, the matter is constrained by regulation. In addition to general regulation, this issue is likely to be the subject of specific conditions in the home itself, breach of which will give rise to strict liability criminal offences.

What follows is secondary to any obligations which may be imposed by specific staffing conditions imposed by the care establishment or agency itself.

Breach of staffing regulatory requirements, as set out below, will only occur following service of the appropriate warning notice, typically under reg 43 of the Care Homes Regulations 2001.

6.14.1   Care homes

Regulation 18(1) of the Care Homes Regulations 2001 states that:

'The registered person shall having regard to the size of the care home and the Statement of Purpose and the number and needs of service users –

(a)   Ensure that at all times suitably qualified competent and experienced persons are working at the care home in such numbers as are appropriate for the health and welfare of service users.

(b)   Ensure that the employment of any persons on a temporary basis at the care home will not prevent service users from receiving such continuity of care as is reasonable to meet their needs.

(c)   Ensure that the persons employed by the registered person to work at the care home receive:

(i)   training appropriate to the work they are to perform; and
(ii)   suitable assistance, including time off for the purpose of obtaining further qualifications appropriate to such work.'

This presents a number of important issues. Staff must be geared to the statement of purpose, thus linking the statement of purpose and the staffing establishment. Staff must also be varied in accordance with numbers and needs of service users.

Therefore the argument that staff must be maintained to the level which assumes the home to be full is no longer compliant (if it ever was) with statutory regulations. Staff numbers will change according to numbers and needs of service users.

Staffing levels are linked to the generic provisions to provide for health and welfare of service users. The term 'employment' includes engagement by an agency.

Temporary workers can only be employed so as not to disrupt care programmes. It is submitted that 'temporary' does not relate to the nature of the employment, ie by direct employment, agency employment or self-employed engagement, but rather to the permanence of the relationship between the staff and the patients or service users in care. In that way, 'temporary' can relate to the employment of new staff or the engagement of inexperienced workers or, more obviously, to the engagement by one route or another of cover to fill shortages. The purpose of the express legislation is, however, confusing. The very fact of a shortage which leads to the necessity for temporary workers will inevitably mean that service users are at some risk because the permanence of the establishment will have been disrupted.

There is a clear obligation enforceable to the criminal standard to provide paid training with time off for all staff. This will add significantly to the cost burden of homes. It is likely that the provisions in relation to training apply also to the responsible individual employed by an organisation. Regulation 18(2) ensures that the registered person must provide appropriate supervision and that, of course, includes supervision and training for the responsible individual supervising management.

6.14.2 Nursing

Under reg 18(3) of the Care Homes Regulations 2001, where nursing is provided, medicines or medical treatment are provided by the care home to the service users, then suitably qualified registered nurses must be working at the care home at all times. A number of difficult issues arise, as follows.

Nursing is nowhere defined – readers are referred to the discussion in relation to definitions of nursing to be incorporated within the statement of purpose. The reference to the provision of medicines and medical treatment is oblique. Virtually every care home administers medicines to service users. Provision of medical treatment will be more clearly indicated by the presence of medical practitioners. It is submitted that what is intended here is not a situation where the care home acts as an agent to introduce medical treatments through the patient's own medical practitioner, or administers medicines dispensed on the prescription of the medical practitioner by the local NHS service, but rather where the care home has its own retained medical practitioners or own stocks of medicines which, through appropriate medical prescription, are administered without NHS or other external intervention. In other words, reg 18(3) applies only to those very limited number of care homes which have their own dispensing pharmacies, and employ doctors who provide a full health care service, rather than merely supporting health care provided externally, usually through the NHS.

Fulfilling either of the conditions triggers a very expensive requirement to have qualified registered nurses working at the care home at all times. None of this is appropriately defined. The statement of purpose will identify the nature of the qualified registered nurses, but what is meant by 'working at' the care home? Does this mean engaged in patient or service user care 24 hours a day, or does it mean engaged upon the permanent establishment of the home, or available to the home as and when required? The expression 'at all times' is straightforward, but is clearly defined by the context of the appropriate interpretation of 'working at'.

Given that there is no definition of nursing, and given that the Government has drawn distinctions between nursing and nursing care by a registered nurse,[1] there is clear statutory recognition that nursing will not always be delivered by registered nurses or in a way that is required to be delivered by registered nurses. However, if the care delivered can properly be described as nursing, registered nurses will be required to be working at the care home at all times. This justifies the assertion that the statement of purpose should set out clearly what the care home considers to be nursing, and what it does not. It is strongly suggested that the term 'nursing' in this context should be equated with the definition of nursing care by a registered nurse, as set out in s 49(2) of the 2001 Act. It is submitted that, if by legal interpretation and proper construction of the purpose of the statement of purpose, 'working at the care home at all times' is interpreted to mean 'available to the care home at all times', the need for a registered nurse to be on duty from time to time will be determined by the needs of the service users in care from time to time.

6.14.3   Statutory guidance on staffing levels

There is little current guidance on the level of staffing. Staffing is individual to particular homes, and the numbers and needs of service users – exactly as reflected in the Regulations.

The *National Minimum Standards for Care Homes for Older People* make provision for the staff complement within standard 37. This refers to guidance issued by the Secretary of State, which is in somewhat woolly terms. This guidance is contained in a letter from the Secretary of State for Health to the Chairman of the NCSC dated January 2003 and refers to academic statistical research on staffing carried out by a body known as the Residential Forum.

In essence, the guidance indicates that the problem is difficult and that further guidance will be forthcoming in due course. It states:

(1)   that staffing levels should not be allowed to regress below those set prior to 1 April 2002 by the previous registration authorities; and
(2)   that in relation to new registration, staffing levels should be set by reference to the statistical methodology and working tool established by the Residential Forum.

All of this is set against the context that the Secretary of State does not wish the Commission to cause additional burdens for care home proprietors. Given that operational use of the Residential Forum tool in many cases reduces staffing levels to below those sought to be imposed by registration authorities prior to

---

1   See s 49(2) of the Health and Social Care Act 2001, and attendant NHS guidance.

1 April 2002, the guidance is muddled. Furthermore, the close interpretation of the Residential Forum tool makes it difficult to see how it provides an absolute statistical answer in every case. In practice there has been little obvious use of the Residential Forum tool by regulations.

Given the inconsistency of the Secretary of State's guidance and the difficulties in achieving accurate results from application of the Residential Forum tool, particularly where that suggests staffing levels lower than those which may have been in place by informal arrangement or disputed demand prior to 1 April 2002, it is suggested that the guidance and the Residential Forum tool are by no means an exclusive method of calculating staffing levels, and if the Commission seeks to rely upon those to justify a prosecution, it may not succeed unless the evidence establishes clear failures on any ground to meet the requirements of reg 18.

6.14.4   Fitness of workers

Regulation 19 of the Care Homes Regulations 2001 makes it a criminal offence to employ persons unless they are fit to work at the care home and that statutory minimum information has been supplied and, where that includes references, that the registered person is satisfied as to the authenticity of the references.

Readers are referred to the detailed discussion of 'fitness' in Chapter 4.

The onus is clearly on the registered provider and registered manager (who must allocate risk between themselves) to be satisfied as to fitness. The position is no longer that the Commission must prove unfitness to establish regulatory complaint. The Commission, in carrying out its duties, and with evidence which suggests inadequacy of service, may call upon the registered person to justify his or her views as to the fitness of persons working at the home.

Unfitness includes certain matters identified in reg 19(5) of the Regulations. However, that is not exclusive and the categories of unfitness are broadly based on the following:

- lack of integrity or good character;
- lack of suitable qualifications, skills or experience;
- insufficiency of physical or mental fitness;
- insufficiency of full and satisfactory information as to criminal records.

It is submitted that whilst the presence of criminal record information does not exclude a worker from being fit, the registered person should consider very carefully whether to employ a person notwithstanding evidence of, in particular, serious and recurrent criminal convictions.

6.14.5   Criminal Records Bureau

The Criminal Records Bureau (CRB), which has its origins in the Police Act 1997, is an executive agency of the Home Office and a public–private partnership between Her Majesty's Government and Capita plc.

Since 1 April 2002, the CRB has undertaken all searches in respect of a person's criminal record in England and Wales. These searches are called 'disclosures'. The primary sources of data upon which the contents of disclosures are based are the police forces of England and Wales (note that Scotland is not included), the Police National Computer and information maintained by the Department of Health and the Department for Education and Skills.

Whether a disclosure is needed in a given context will largely be a matter governed by regulations issued by the relevant Secretary of State. However, as a rule of thumb, anyone who comes into contact with children and/or vulnerable adults in a professional capacity, whether paid or otherwise, must have been subject to checks and the relevant disclosure notice obtained.

However, the Domiciliary Care Agencies Regulations 2002 (whilst repeating the need for providers and managers to be CRB checked) do not extend such a requirement to employed domiciliary care workers.

There are three levels of disclosure:

(a) *basic disclosure*, which is intended to be primarily available for recruitment purposes (not specifically for those involved with children or vulnerable adults) and will show only current convictions;

(b) *standard disclosure*, which is available for anyone involved in working with children or vulnerable adults and any occupation or profession specified in the exceptions order in the Rehabilitation of Offenders Act 1974. Standard disclosures will show both current and spent convictions, together with cautions, reprimands and warnings held on the Police National Computer. Additionally, if the post involves working with children, lists held by both the Department of Health and the Department for Education and Skills will also be checked for relevant information;

(c) *enhanced disclosure*, which is the highest level of checking available for anyone regularly involved in caring for, training, supervising or being in sole charge of children or vulnerable adults. An enhanced disclosure will contain the same information as a standard disclosure but will, in addition, include 'soft intelligence', which, although there has been no formal action taken by the police, may be relevant.

Clearly, over the course of time, Government must hope and expect that in continuing to drive up standards generally, and, amongst the workforce in particular, it becomes an automatic part of the recruitment process that an employer carries out, as a matter of routine, the basic disclosure search.

Organisations which are likely regularly to require standard or enhanced disclosures can apply to become a registered body or an umbrella organisation, which can act on behalf of other organisations or individuals. Such bodies must commit to high standards of performance laid down in the CRB code of practice in relation to which the CRB will undertake compliance checks from time to time to ensure that all such bodies are complying with the code.

A balance must be struck between society protecting its most vulnerable members and the right of individual citizens to be treated fairly. Accordingly, the CRB has adopted the following procedures:

- no disclosure will be issued without the consent of an individual applicant;
- the information provided on disclosures will always be provided to individual applicants, who will have the right to challenge the contents and have them reviewed;
- additional safeguards in the code of practice will ensure that for the higher-level disclosures, the information remains confidential, and the individual citizen's right to privacy is not abused.

The CRB is empowered to refuse to issue disclosures if it believes that the registered person or body has failed to comply with the code of practice.

6.14.6 Independent hospitals

Independent hospitals' staffing requirements are set out in regs 18 and 19 of the Private and Voluntary Health Care (England) Regulations 2001. Broadly, the statutory scheme follows that of the detailed provisions for care homes. However, the generic requirement for sufficiency of staff relates not only to those employed *in* the establishment, but also *for the purposes of* the establishment. It is doubtful whether this extends to external medical practitioners with practising privileges, which privileges are defined in the Regulations as 'the grant to a person who is not employed in an independent hospital of permission to practise in that hospital'. It is submitted that such a person cannot be said to be employed *for the purposes of* the hospital. This is reinforced by the registered person's obligation, in respect of those employed in or for the purposes of the establishment, to provide training opportunities for further qualifications and job descriptions, which hardly includes medical practitioners enjoying practising privileges.

Further, reg 18(3) specifically extends obligations to practitioners enjoying practising privileges. The obligation on the registered person is to ensure provision of regular and appropriate appraisal and to take steps to address aspects of clinical practice or the performance of staff who are not health care professionals where that is found to be unsatisfactory.

Classic definitions, in the medical practice context, of supervision indicate that it involves presence of the supervisor with the worker to justify the regulatory requirement. It is suggested that it would be wholly inappropriate to contemplate supervision by a registered person of medical practitioners with practising privileges. There is a distinction between working *in* the establishment and working *at* the establishment, the latter clearly embracing the medical practitioner with practising privileges and the former identifying only those directly employed in the establishment itself.

The requirement for fitness of workers as a precondition, enforceable by criminal sanction, is outlined in reg 19 in similar terms to the provisions of the Care Homes Regulations 2001.

The requirement to ensure that all workers are fit expressly extends to medical practitioners granted consulting or practising privileges. Whilst 'practising privileges' is defined, 'consulting privileges' is not so, and it is submitted that there is little distinction, possibly an oversight on the part of the draughtsman.

6.15 OPERATION OF DAY CARE CENTRES FOR CHILDREN UNDER 8 YEARS OLD, AND PROVISION OF CHILDMINDING

These operations are now governed by the Day Care and Child Minding (National Standards) (England) Regulations 2001.[1]

These Regulations were formulated by the Department for Education and Skills, formerly the Department for Education and Employment, as opposed to the Department of Health. The national minimum standards are requirements that are enforceable in relation to child care as distinct from the position in relation to other forms of care, for example care homes and independent hospitals. The national standards are defined as the standards numbered 1–14 and are set out in the national standards documents listed in Sch 1 to the Regulations. The individual standards are:

– *National Minimum Standards for Under 8's Day Care and Child Minding Full Day Care*;
– *National Minimum Standards for Under 8's Day and Child Minding Out of School*;
– *National Minimum Standards for Under 8's Day Care and Child Minding Crèches*;
– *National Minimum Standards for under 8's Day Care and Child Minding Sessional Care.*

Regulation 3 of the Regulations provides that the Chief Inspector of Schools in England shall have regard to the national standards and may take account of the duties imposed on registered persons or a failure of such a person to comply with his or her duties. A registered person who acts as a childminder or provider of day care must meet the requirements of the national standards and have regard to the supporting criteria applicable to the child care category into which he or she falls. Allegations that registered persons have failed to comply with their obligations may be taken into account in proceedings.

It remains to be seen how this will be developed in practice, but it is worrying that allegations (by definition unproved) can be taken into account in proceedings. It is difficult to see how an allegation which is no more than that can be taken to influence regulatory or criminal proceedings adversely. Surely the burden of proof required would not be discharged unless the allegation was sufficiently converted into adduced evidence which satisfied the requirements of proof.

---

1   SI 2001/1828.

6.15.1 Information

Registered persons are required to notify the chief inspector of a number of specified events and to provide any information required in relation to such notifications. The matters to be notified are as follows:

(a) in cases of childminding, the date of birth, full name and former names of any change in persons looking after children or persons living or employed at premises;

(b) in cases of day care provision, the date of birth, full names and former names and home address of any new persons engaged as persons in charge or to look after children on premises, or living at or working at premises used for day care, or changes in the chairman and/or treasurer of a committee providing day care;

(c) changes in the name or home address of registered persons;

(d) changes in the child care category applicable;

(e) changes in the address of the premises, and changes in the facilities available for the provision of day care at the registered address;

(f) changes in the hours during which day care or childminding is provided;

(g) the outbreak of infectious disease, which in the opinion of a registered medical practitioner attending a child is sufficiently serious to be notified, or a serious injury, illness or death of any child or anyone else at the premises;

(h) allegations of serious harm against a child committed by any person looking after children at the premises or anyone living, working or employed at the premises (it should be noted that the notification is of allegations not of proven material). The distinction and reliance on such material in proceedings are clear. Allegations need to be reported so that they can be investigated, and the investigations may or may not lead to a conclusion that matters have improved, and that other action is required which may result in adverse findings or criminal convictions;

(i) other events which may affect the suitability of the registered person to look after children or the suitability of persons living, working at or employed at the premises to be in regular contact with children;

(j) other significant events which are likely to affect the welfare of the children on the premises. This will cause considerable difficulties in practice. There will be considerable debate about what may or may not be significant and there is really no limit upon what may be required to be notified. Registered persons may be criticised for unnecessarily troubling the regulatory authorities and it may even be suggested that they are not fit to continue their operations because they do not know the difference between significant and insignificant events. On the other hand, those who exercise their skill and judgment may be seriously criticised for failing to notify events that others believe to be significant. In cases of difficulty, the advice must always be one of caution, and to report rather than not report.

Information is to be notified in advance of events (where practical, which may be rare) and in all other cases as soon as possible after the event, but not later than

14 days. This, it is submitted, is a relatively long period, particularly for some of the matters which are likely to be the subject of notification.

Non-notification without reasonable excuse is an offence prosecutable in the magistrates' court, punishable with a level 5 fine, which is currently £4,000 (maximum).

6.15.2   Records

Under reg 5 of the Day Care and Child Minding (National Standards) (England) Regulations 2001, certain records are required to be kept. Those records are identified in Sch 3 to the Regulations, and are as follows:

(a) name, address, and date of birth of each child;
(b) name, address and telephone number of the parent (one will suffice);
(c) name, address and telephone number of the registered person and every person living or employed at the premises;
(d) name, address and telephone number of any other person who will regularly have unsupervised contact with children;
(e) daily record of the names of children looked after, their hours of attendance and the names of the persons who looked after them;
(f) a record of accidents;
(g) a record of medicines administered including dates and circumstances of administration;
(h) in the case of day care only, the following additional information:

  (i)   a statement of the procedures to be followed in the event of fire or accident;
  (ii) a statement of the procedure to be followed in the event of a child being lost or not collected;
  (iii) a statement of the procedure to be followed when a parent has a complaint about the service;
  (iv) a statement of the arrangements in place for the protection of children, including arrangements to safeguard children from abuse or neglect.

Entries in the records of names and hours of attendance of children looked after, accidents and administration of medicines must be preserved for 2 years, and the chief inspector must be provided with copies as and when he or she requests them.

Provision is made for so-called open access schemes, where day care is provided to children who are not accompanied by parents or other responsible persons while on the premises, or children not required to be escorted by a parent or other responsible person to and from the premises. In such cases, the records required do not need to include the names, home addresses and dates of birth of the children, the name, home address and telephone number of the parent, or the daily record of the names of the children looked after on the premises. The exclusions are perhaps obvious because to keep such records would be impossible given the statutory drafting which makes provision for this individual type of scheme.

6.15.3 Enforcement

If the Chief Inspector of Schools in England considers that the registered person has failed to meet the national standards or has failed to keep appropriate records, he or she may give notice to the registered person specifying:

(a) the respect in which that person has failed;
(b) the action that is required;
(c) the period within which action should be taken, to begin with the date of the notice.

It is an absolute obligation for the registered person to comply with the notice; he or she may not object that the notice is inappropriate. This seems harsh, but objection in the form of assertion that the notice is not required would itself require no action for there will be compliance on the next inspection.

Failure to comply with the notice is an offence. The notice cannot be subject to challenge provided it is given in accordance with the provision of reg 7, ie by personal delivery, registered or recorded delivery letter service, or email.

Notices are properly addressed if addressed to the home address notified to the chief inspector as required or dispatched by email to an email address so notified to the chief inspector.

Regulation 18(4) of the Day Care and Child Minding (National Standards) England Regulations 2001 requires supervision of persons who are employed in the establishment but who are not employed by the registered person.

Previous discussion of the meaning of supervision are here in equal point.

6.16 CHILDREN'S HOMES

The requirements in relation to children's homes effectively mirror the requirements for care homes and are set out in regs 25 and 26 of the Children's Homes Regulations 2001.

Reflecting the public requirement that there be closer control of workers in children's homes, extra requirements are imposed in relation to the employment of such persons.

Regulation 26(5) and (6) of the Children's Homes Regulations 2001 make it clear that:

(a) offers of employment must be subject to supply of the appropriate statutory information, including references and criminal record checks; and
(b) persons must not commence work at the home until there has been full compliance with, and receipt of, the statutory required documentation.

An exception to this second requirement is where investigations are incomplete despite all reasonable steps having been taken by the registered person. However, employment may not commence under any circumstances unless proof of identity, criminal record certificates or enhanced criminal record certificates under the Police Act 1997 issued by the CRB and details of spent criminal convictions, and cautions, are all in place.

Employment may commence whilst awaiting the receipt of written references, verification as to the reason for termination of previous employment with children, documentary evidence in relation to qualifications and employment history. In practice, these are likely to be easier to obtain than the items required mandatorily.

In the above circumstances, the individual employed must be appropriately supervised while carrying out his or her duties.

It is submitted that in most cases arising in day-to-day practice it will be virtually impossible to justify the employment of staff pending receipt of all the statutory information required by Sch 2 to the Children's Homes Regulations 2001, and that the exceptions are for genuinely exceptional circumstances.

Chapter 7

HEALTH AND SAFETY

7.1 INTRODUCTION

To the majority of care homes the subject of health and safety is not new. There is a detailed framework of existing health and safety legislation to which care homes must adhere under the Health and Safety at Work etc Act 1974 (HSWA 1974). The regulatory regime introduced by the Care Standards Act 2000 (the 2000 Act) imposes requirements for health and safety, many of which mirror what is already required under the HSWA 1974. What is new is that health and safety has been incorporated additionally into the regulatory framework for a specific sector. This changes the emphasis of compliance and enforcement. Non-compliance with health and safety requirements and requirements under the 2000 Act give rise to criminal liabilities for the care home, with potential personal liability for its directors irrespective of the position in health and safety law. This chapter aims to provide an insight into the health and safety requirements which must be addressed by a care home.

7.2 THE HEALTH AND SAFETY REGULATORY REGIME

7.2.1 History and development

Health and safety regulation has existed in one form or another in this country for over 150 years. The present framework was introduced by the HSWA 1974. Since 1974, policy and legislation have been driven and influenced by developments of the European Union and, on an international scale, by organisations such as the World Health Organisation and the Organisation for Economic Co-operation and Development. An example of this is the explicit requirement to undertake risk assessments. The present Regulations, the Management of Health and Safety at Work Regulations 1999, replace the earlier 1992 Regulations. In turn, these Regulations are an implementation of an EU Directive (Council Directive 89/391/EEC). Much health and safety law now emanates from the European Union. This includes the 1992 'six pack', which covered work equipment, manual handling, health and safety and welfare in the workplace, personal protective equipment, control of substances hazardous to health, and display screen equipment, amongst other things.

Two organisations have responsibility for maintaining the health and safety regulatory framework in England and Wales:

(1)   The Health and Safety Commission (HSC) is a body of 10 individuals appointed by the Secretary of State for Transport, Local Government and the Regions. The role of the HSC is defined in the HSWA 1974. It proposes law and standards to government. A process of public consultation on proposals for new legislation is carried out, in which industry, business and commerce have opportunities to comment formally on the proposals. Comment can either be made through trade associations or directly by an organisation.

(2)   The Health and Safety Executive (HSE) is the principal enforcing body, providing advice to the HSC on the development of law and policy. In addition to enforcement it also has a duty to foster and improve workplace health and safety. Its enforcement role is shared with local authorities. The boundary between the HSE and the local authorities is set by the Health and Safety (Enforcing Authority) Regulations 1998.[1] Generally, the HSE looks after those businesses and sectors which involve greater workplace risks. The closer the business is to a domestic or office-type setting, the more likely the local authority will have the enforcing role. For example, local authorities were responsible for enforcing health and safety in residential homes and nursing homes, and are now so responsible in relation to care homes. HSE and local authority inspectors (typically environmental health officers) have wide but limited powers which include making inspections without warning. If they find non-compliances, they can issue improvement or prohibition notices in addition to investigating and prosecuting.

The HSE and local authorities have set up a liaison committee – the Health and Safety Executive/Local Authority Liaison Committee known as HELA. The committee produces circulars which set out guidance for environmental health officers on, *inter alia*, roles and interpretation of points of law.

7.2.2   Core obligations

The HSWA 1974 sets out, in ss 2–9, the core health and safety duties applicable to all businesses, employers and employees in all workplace or work-related situations. It is the beauty of the way in which the law is drafted that virtually all health and safety duties and obligations, including the detail in regulations, can be traced back to these core duties. However, this beauty has a sting in its tail as the enforcing authorities can choose to prosecute a failure in health and safety law either under a specific regulation – in which case the available fines in the magistrates' courts are £5000 per offence – or as a breach of one of the principle duties – where fines of up to £20,000 are available in the magistrates' courts. If a case is heard in the Crown Court, these sentencing limits do not apply, and unlimited fines can be imposed for a breach of regulations just as much as a breach of one of the general duties. The law ensures that anyone who has the capacity to create risks in work-related situations has a duty to safeguard his or her and others' health and safety. This applies to everyone, whether employers, employees or third parties, such as contractors.

---

1   SI 1998/494.

Briefly, the HSWA 1974 imposes specific duties on employers, owners and occupiers of premises and employees as follows.

Under s 2, employers must ensure, *so far as is reasonably practicable*, the health and safety at work of all their employees. This duty is deliberately widely drawn and all-embracing. The duty owed to employees is expressed so succinctly that Parliament, when passing the legislation, went on to provide specific, non-exhaustive examples of what the duty encompasses. That list includes:

– the provision and maintenance of plant and systems of work;
– arrangements for ensuring safety and absence of risk to health in connection with the use, handling, storage and transport of articles and substances;
– the provision of information, instruction, training and supervision as necessary to ensure the health and safety at work of employees;
– with regard to any place of work under the employer's control, the maintenance of it in a condition that is safe and without risk to health including the means of access to, and egress from, the workplace that are safe and without risk;
– the provision and maintenance of a working environment for employees that is safe, without risks to health and adequate as regards facilities and arrangements for their welfare at work.

In addition to the specific work-related duties, s 2 also includes four other important administrative and consultation-related duties. These are:

– the duty to prepare and revise as needs be a statement of the organisation's general policy with regard to health and safety at work. This statement of general policy has to be accompanied by the relevant organisational arrangements for giving effect to that policy, and for bringing its contents to the notice of all employees. Organisations which employ fewer than five employees are exempted from this obligation;
– the duty to consult workplace representatives with a view to making and maintaining arrangements which will enable the employer and his or her employees to co-operate effectively in promoting and developing measures to ensure health and safety at work and for checking the effectiveness of such measures;
– where employees and representatives so request, the duty to establish a safety committee with the function of keeping under review all of the measures taken to ensure health and safety, etc.

Under s 3 of the HSWA 1974, employers must conduct their undertaking in such a manner as to ensure, so far as is reasonably practicable, that persons not in their employment who may be affected are not exposed to risks to their health and safety. Such persons include service users, contractors and visitors to care homes. This duty mirrors the duty owed to employees by employers (in s 2), but protects non-employees such as residents in a care home or visitors.

Under s 4, owners and occupiers of premises, which includes employers, must take reasonable measures to ensure the health and safety of those who use the premises. The reasonableness of the measures required to be taken will depend upon the extent of control – which in turn is likely to depend on the terms of any lease or licence to occupy the premises.

Under s 7, employees, whilst at work, must take reasonable care of the health and safety of themselves and others who may be affected by their own acts or omissions, and co-operate with any person (eg their employer) regarding a duty or requirement on health and safety matters.

The standard of compliance which a person has to reach in satisfying a health and safety obligation is either absolute or qualified by the phrase 'so far as is reasonably practicable'. 'So far as is reasonably practicable' means following current standards in improving the management of the risk to the point where the taking of any further measures would be disproportionate to any residual risk. All reasonable precautions that can be taken should be taken. The size or economic situation of a company is not strictly relevant, although it may well have a bearing on what is reasonable and practicable and in determining what is disproportionate. In contrast, an absolute duty makes a person strictly liable if he or she fails to comply with that duty. Simply breaching the duty will amount to the criminal offence – although the enforcing authority must still decide whether or not to prosecute.

There are a vast number of regulations which impose specific requirements which are too detailed to consider here. That said, the obligation to perform suitable and sufficient risk assessments of health and safety risks is frequently flouted, investigated and prosecuted.[1]

In addition to the law, the HSE publishes approved codes of practice (ACOP) and other guidance which often seeks to interpret the requirements of Regulations. Failure to comply with an ACOP's guidance may be taken into account in court proceedings as evidence of a failure to comply with the provisions of the HSWA 1974 or a Regulation. However, it is always open to a person to use other, equally effective steps as an alternative to those recommended in an ACOP.

Health and safety guidance note HSG 220 is specific to the care homes sector, and is discussed at para **7.4.4**.

7.2.3   Link to the care standards regime and the National Care Standards Commission

Whilst the 2000 Act does not specifically mention health and safety matters, s 22(2) of the Act provides for regulations to be made on a number of matters of which health and safety can be said to be an element. These include, for example:

 -   the fitness of premises to be used as a care home;
 -   the management and control of operations at the care home;
 -   the management and training of staff working in the care home; and
 -   securing the welfare of persons accommodated in the home.

---

1   Management of Health and Safety at Work Regulations 1999, SI 1999/3242, reg 3.

The inclusion of health and safety requirements in the care standards regime creates the potential for dual enforcement by the local authority environmental health officer or HSE inspector and the inspector from the National Care Standards Commission (NCSC). This has been recognised by the regulators, and in April 2002 the HELA issued a circular (LAC 79/3) which reports on the discussions between local authorities and the NCSC to identify and address overlapping regulatory responsibilities. The HSE, local authorities and the NCSC have produced a memorandum of understanding which sets out the manner in which they divide their overlapping enforcement roles. The lead authority is typically the HSE or local authority in health and safety matters except where they relate to issues personal to service users where the NCSC take primacy. That said, the HSE or local authority would take primacy where serious or imminent risks to health and safety of service users arise.

LAC 79/3 proposes that the HSE and the NCSC share responsibility as follows. The NCSC will have primary responsibility for inspection regarding risks to service users. The HSE and local authorities will retain:

– an enforcement role under health and safety legislation. This implies, for example, that if an NCSC inspector notices in an inspection that a risk assessment has not been undertaken for use of lifting equipment, the inspector will notify the HSE or local authority, which may issue an improvement notice requiring risk assessments to be undertaken within a period of 28 days, or commence a criminal investigation;
– responsibility for receiving notifications for service users under the Reporting of Injuries, Diseases and Dangerous Occurrences Regulations 1995;[1]
– responsibilities for employee safety and the safety of the building and aspects of facility management.

The HSE is considering comments from various parties on the circular. We await further details regarding the apportionment of responsibilities. However, the circular confirms that care homes will have to deal with two regulators considering health and safety requirements. As the circular suggests, the NCSC will be responsible for the health and safety of users, but with the HSE/local authority having an enforcement role it is possible that a care home may be subject to enforcement action from both regulators regarding an incident or non-compliance. It is hoped that the forthcoming memorandums of understanding will clarify this issue.

7.3 ENFORCEMENT POWERS

Inspectors from the NCSC and the HSE, and local authority environmental health officers, have similar powers. The powers available to NCSC inspectors are described in Chapter 10.

---

1   SI 1995/3163.

7.3.1   Health and safety inspectors; local authority environmental health officers

An inspection may take place as part of a routine schedule, or may be unannounced. The latter is almost certain to occur after some incident, such as an accident, and following complaint by a visitor, service user or member of staff to either the NCSC, the local authority or the HSE.

(1)   *Powers*

During an inspection it is important to remember that the powers available to HSE inspectors and local authority officials are set out in s 20 of the HSWA 1974 and that these powers, whilst extensive, are limited. It is often advisable to seek legal advice either during or following an unannounced inspection. The advice may be useful in negotiations with the regulator and in building any defence which may be required. Powers of inspectors include powers to:

–   enter and search premises at any time;
–   compel individuals to answer questions (answers cannot be used to incriminate the individual or his or her spouse, but can be used in a prosecution against the individual's employer);[1]
–   seize articles and substances;
–   require the production of documents, and remove the documents or request copies;
–   take photographs, samples and measurements;
–   direct that part of the workplace be left undisturbed pending investigation;
–   dismantle equipment which caused or may cause a danger;
–   require the provision of facilities and assistance for undertaking the investigation.

Environmental health officers have similar powers. An NCSC inspector's powers are set out in ss 31 and 32 of the 2000 Act.

Whilst these powers are undoubtedly extensive, they are not unlimited. Inspectors should remain within their limitations but they do not always do that. Legal advice from specialised lawyers is advisable. Handling regulatory investigations is considered at length in para **7.6**. Health and safety prosecutions are brought predominantly against companies. However, over recent years there has been an increasing trend also to single out individuals. With society becoming increasingly risk-averse and responsibility-conscious, the enforcing authorities are making more use of ss 36 and 37 of the HSWA 1974, which provides for individuals to be prosecuted – albeit in very different circumstances.

Section 36 allows the enforcing authorities to prosecute a person – which may be either a company or an individual – in circumstances where its, his or her act or default has given rise to some other person breaking health and safety law. In circumstances where this occurs, the authorities have the choice of prosecuting either or both of the persons involved. For example where a company commits a

---

1   HSWA 1974, s 20.

breach of health and safety law, but the breach has been caused by following the erroneous advice of a consultant. Another formulation could be where one company supplies faulty equipment to another. The faulty equipment is then used in circumstances which break health and safety law. Again, s 36 could be used. Prosecutions under s 36 are rare as it is almost inevitable that other specific health and safety offences would have been committed – and the authorities often find it easier to prosecute someone directly for his or her own actions or failings, rather than base a prosecution on someone else's failure.

Under s 37 there is provision for directors, company secretaries, senior managers and others who purport to act as such to be prosecuted personally. Section 37 provides that where a company has broken health and safety law, and it can be shown that the company committed the breach through the consent, connivance or neglect of one of these officers, that individual can also be prosecuted personally. The increasing number of cases brought under s 37 concentrate more on the *neglect of* the directors and senior managers. If an enforcing authority is to succeed in a prosecution based upon neglect, it will have to show that the individual's conduct breached a duty owed by it. The HSC and HSE are actively promoting the importance of health and safety to directors and senior managers. One of the aspects of this work is to reinforce to directors the importance of taking account of health and safety in all their decisions. The HSC has published guidance which contains the following five action points:

(a) boards are to accept formally and publicly their collective role in providing health and safety leadership;
(b) each member of the board needs to accept his or her individual role in providing health and safety leadership for the organisation;
(c) the board must ensure that all board decisions reflect its health and safety intentions as articulated in the health and safety policy statement;
(d) the board must recognise its role in engaging the active participation of works in improving health and safety;
(e) the board must ensure that it is kept informed of, and alert to, relevant health and safety risk management issues.

The HSC recommends that the board appoint one of its number as health and safety director so that health and safety management has a focal point. Where these action points are put into practice together with other good risk management techniques, it is ironically the case that any health and safety failure could more easily be shown to have arisen through a director's or similar officer's neglect. It is also true that the HSE is pursuing a policy of singling out directors for prosecution *to encourage the others* to perform correctly.

Clear identification of health and safety responsibility to a director and hence the board also makes prosecuting the company and the director for corporate manslaughter and manslaughter respectively easier should a death occur through, say, gross negligence.

(2) Enforcement action

Following investigation, if an inspector or environmental health officer is not happy with the level of standards being achieved, he or she has a number of options available in order to obtain improvements. These are:

– giving informal advice;
– giving a formal warning or caution;
– issuing an improvement notice if he or she is of the opinion that there is a contravention of one or more 'relevant statutory provisions' or there has been a contravention, and there are circumstances which suggest that the contravention will continue or that a further contravention is likely. The improvement notice must state why the inspector considers that there has been a contravention, specify which statutory provision(s) is/are being contravened, give particulars of the reasons for his or her opinion, and specify a time period within which the contravention should be remedied. The time period for compliance should be at least 21 days;
– issuing a prohibition notice if he or she is of the opinion that the activities being carried on involve a risk of serious injury. A prohibition notice must state why the inspector considers that there is a risk of serious injury, specify the matters which create the risk, give reasons if the inspector believes that there is an actual or anticipatory breach, and direct that the activity cannot be carried out until the matters have been remedied. Prohibition notices take effect immediately and are usually only lifted when the enforcing authority is satisfied that the activity in question is now being controlled safely.

There is a right of appeal against service of an improvement or prohibition notice. A person has a right of appeal to an employment tribunal within 21 days of service of the notice. The operation of an improvement notice is suspended during an appeal. However, the operation of a prohibition notice is not suspended (unless the tribunal gives a direction which suspends the notice). A failure to comply with the terms of a notice is likely to give rise to criminal penalties.

The majority of health and safety offences are triable either way, which means that proceedings can be heard in the magistrates' court or the Crown Court. Penalties in the Crown Court are more severe. Penalties on conviction in a magistrates' court for breaches of the principal duties contained in ss 2–9 of the HSWA 1974 include a maximum fine of £20,000 and in some instances imprisonment of up to 6 months. Penalties on conviction in a Crown Court include unlimited fine, and in some instances up to 2 years' imprisonment. There are proposals before parliament to increase these penalties and to allow for greater use of imprisonment.

The above are examples only. Breaches of health and safety regulations will not usually incur severe penalties as, for example, a breach of one of the principal health and safety duties. For example, conviction in a magistrates' court for failure to comply with the provision of a regulation gives rise to a maximum fine of £5000, and conviction in a Crown Court, an unlimited fine.

7.3.2   The law on involuntary manslaughter

When considering personal liability of directors, regard should be had to the law of involuntary manslaughter and the proposals to reform that law. Where a fatality occurs which is due to a work activity, proceedings may be brought against individuals of the company for involuntary manslaughter where, for example, the death can be shown to have occurred through gross negligence.

The law recognises that manslaughter can arise in many different ways and circumstances. The most likely scenario relating to a care home situation is where manslaughter occurs by way of gross negligence. In determining whether a particular death does amount to manslaughter by way of gross negligence the court would first have to establish whether there was a duty of care owed to the deceased by the accused. In a care home setting, if the deceased was a service user it is highly likely that such a duty of care would be found to exist either from the employer to the service user or from a particular employee to the service user. There must be a similar duty protecting employees from the employer and fellow employees too. The death has to have occurred as a consequence of that duty of care having been breached. The breach has to be sufficiently serious as to be characterised as gross *negligence*. In other words, 'having regard to the risk of death involved was the defendant's conduct so bad in all the circumstances as to amount to criminal act or omission'?[1]

Where a death can be directly linked to a failure by a director or someone directly answerable to the Board of Directors then, in addition to prosecuting that particular individual for manslaughter, the employing company may also be liable to be prosecuted for corporate manslaughter. It is one of the peculiarities of the law that it is more difficult to convict a company of corporate manslaughter than it is an individual of manslaughter. It is generally considered that it is a prerequisite before establishing corporate manslaughter that an individual director or senior manager should be capable of being convicted of manslaughter on the facts of the case. In other words the failing or gross negligence of an individual director is required before the company itself can be convicted. This is known as the *identification principle*.

In recent years there have been several well-publicised prosecutions of corporate manslaughter. Almost inevitably these have followed various disasters. However, acquittal usually followed because of the failure to establish the *identification principle*. For example, P&O were prosecuted following the *Herald of Free Enterprise* disaster. In that case the prosecution was unable to show that a bosun's failure to close the bow doors was in some way directly attributable to failure by the Board or an individual member of the Board and, accordingly, corporate manslaughter could not be established. The outcry that has followed such well-publicised acquittals has led the Home Office to consider reforms to the law in this area. Ironically, with the pressure to make lines of accountability and responsibility clearer there may be less of a need for reform now. If, for example, one adopts the HSC's guidance of appointing a director to be in charge of health and safety, then any gross negligence on his part in

---

1   *R v Adomako* [1995] 1 AC 171.

performing his duties would make the task of establishing a case of manslaughter against him, or a case of corporate manslaughter against the company, very much easier than if responsibility for health and safety was more muddled or shared.

In the context of health and safety, and health and safety in a care home there are, or should be, several documents clearly setting out the responsibilities of individuals. Failure to adhere to those published responsibilities may well contribute to establishing a case for manslaughter or corporate manslaughter.

It is a duty of every company that employs more than five employees to have a statement of safety policy together with documents explaining the organisational arrangements for ensuring health and safety. A failure to follow those published provisions may well prove to be a clinching factor in deciding whether or not to bring manslaughter or corporate manslaughter proceedings and perhaps whether convictions are secured.

Whether the Home Office's proposals relating to corporate killing ever become law remains to be seen. The indicative proposal suggests that the offence would amount to a failure by management causing a death where that failure constitutes a failure far below what could be reasonably expected in all the circumstances.

The present law permits directors to be disqualified from acting as such when they have been convicted of an offence relating to the management of the company. The Home Office proposals look to see the use of such powers to disqualify directors extended.

7.4   HEALTH AND SAFETY REQUIREMENTS IN THE CARE STANDARDS REGIME

The Care Homes Regulations 2001 and Children's Homes Regulations 2001 contain health and safety requirements as follows.

7.4.1   Care Homes Regulations 2001

Regulations 12 (health and welfare of users) and 23 (fitness of premises) of the Care Homes Regulations 2001 include references to health and safety as follows. Regulation 12(1) states that:

> 'The registered person shall ensure the care home is conducted so as to promote and make proper provision of the health and welfare of service users ... ;'

Regulation 23(5) states that the registered person shall consult with the fire authority to:

(a)   take adequate precautions against the risk of fire, including the provision of fire prevention equipment;

(b)   provide an adequate means of escape;

(c) make adequate arrangements for:
   (i) detecting, containing and extinguishing fires;
   (ii) giving warnings of fires;
   (iii) the evacuation, in the event of fire, of all persons in the care home and safe placement of service users;
   (iv) maintenance of all fire equipment; and
   (v) reviewing fire precautions, and fire testing equipment, at suitable intervals;
(d) make arrangements for persons working at the care home to receive suitable training in fire prevention; and
(e) ensure, by means of fire drills and practices at suitable intervals, that the persons working at the care home and, so far as practicable, service users, are aware of the procedure to be followed in the case of fire, including the procedure for saving life.

The registered person must undertake appropriate consultation with the authority responsible for environmental health for the area in which the care home is situated. Schedule 1 to the Regulations sets out what should be included in the statement of purpose. Fire precautions and emergency procedures are items to be included.

7.4.2   Children's Homes Regulations 2001

The Children's Homes Regulations 2001 contain similar requirements in respect of fire precautions. In addition, regs 22 (hazards and safety) and 30 (fitness of premises) contain health and safety-related requirements as follows. Under reg 22, the registered person must ensure that:

(a) all parts of the home to which children have access are, so far as reasonably practicable, free from hazards to their health and safety;
(b) any activities in which children participate are, so far as reasonably practicable, free from avoidable risks; and
(c) unnecessary risks to the health and safety of children accommodated in the home are identified and, so far as possible, eliminated.

Under reg 30(3), the registered person must ensure that the children's home is kept free from offensive odours and make suitable arrangements for the disposal of clinical waste.

Both the above regulations refer to the need for the care home management to consult with a local environmental health officer and the fire authority in discharging its obligations under the Act and the Regulations, and in complying with the national minimum standards.

7.4.3   National minimum standards

Specific and more detailed requirements are set out in the various national minimum standards. The standards for care homes for older people and the standards for care homes for younger adults contain requirements for safe working practices. These are standard numbers 38 and 40, respectively. The main elements of these standards are as follows.

The registered manager must ensure:

(a) so far as reasonable practicable, the health, safety and welfare of service users and staff;

(b) safe working practices relating to:

    (i)   the moving and handling of people or objects;

    (ii)   fire safety;

    (iii) first aid and accident reporting;

    (iv) food hygiene and infection control;

(c) the health and safety of service users and staff, including:

    (i)   storage and disposal of hazardous substances;

    (ii)   servicing of boilers and heating systems;

    (iii)   maintenance of electrical systems;

    (iv)   regulation of water temperature;

    (v)   provision and maintenance of window restrictors;

    (vi)   maintenance of a safe environment;

    (vii) security of premises;

    (viii) security of service users;

    (ix)   compliance with legislation, including the HSWA 1974, the Management of Health and Safety at Work Regulations 1999 (note that there is a proposal to amend these Regulations to include a duty on an employer to investigate accidents), the Workplace (Health, Safety and Welfare) Regulations 1992, the Provision and Use of Equipment Regulations 1992, the Electricity at Work Regulations 1989, the Health and Safety (First Aid) Regulations 1981, the Control of Substances Hazardous to Health Regulations 1988, the Manual Handling Operations Regulations 1992, and the Reporting of Injuries, Diseases and Dangerous Occurrences Regulations 1995.

The registered manager must also provide a written statement of the policy organisation and arrangements for maintaining safe working practices. He or she must ensure that risk assessments are carried out and that significant findings are recorded, accidents, injuries and illness are recorded and reported, safety procedures are posted and explained in a format that takes account of service users' special communication needs, and all staff receive induction and foundation training and updates to meet TOPSS (the National Training Organisation for Social Care) specification on all safe working practice topics.

Standard 26, the *National Minimum Standards for Children's Homes*, is slightly different. It relates to health, safety and security, and requires:

(a) positive steps to be taken to keep children, staff and visitors safe from risk of fire and other hazards;

(b) risk assessments to be carried out, recorded and regularly reviewed, in relation to:

    (i)   the home's premises and grounds;

    (ii) children's known and likely activities;

(iii) the potential for bullying and abuse within or outside the home; and

(iv) the impact of emergency admissions to the home for the admitted child and existing children;

(c) a review of the implementation and effectiveness of action identified in risk assessments;

(d) an emergency response plan – a requirement to have planned responses to a range of foreseeable crises;

(e) recommendations from local environmental health officers regarding food hygiene, to be implemented within the stipulated timescale;

(f) children and staff to have knowledge of the emergency evacuation procedures;

(g) fire drills to take place twice in a 12-month period with regular testing of equipment;

(h) consultation with the local fire authority whenever a significant extension, change of use or alteration is made. Recommendations have to be made within the set timescale.

It should be remembered that these specific and detailed requirements *supplement* the duties and obligations under existing health and safety law; they are not alternatives.

7.4.4 Requirements of HSG 220

The Health and Safety Executive Guidance Note, HSG 220, on health and safety in care homes, sets out information on the responsibilities of employers and employees under health and safety legislation. The guidance document itself is not legally binding. However, the extent to which a care home has followed it is likely to be taken into account by regulators.

Specific requirements for care homes – HELA Circular, it has been proposed that NCSC inspectors focus on service user safety, in particular:

- control of hot water;
- burns from hot surfaces;
- falls from height;
- wandering and absconding from establishments;
- management of challenging behaviour;
- use of cot sides and lap belts;
- manual handling risks to service users;
- self-harm, including suicides.

7.5 PRACTICAL COMPLIANCE

It is possible that the enforcement approach taken by a local authority environmental health officer (EHO) concerning compliance with a health and safety requirement may be different from the approach taken by an inspector from the Care Standards Commission. The Commission inspector may regard something as a non-compliance or breach when the local authority EHO may not, and vice versa.

Penalties for non-compliance with the 2000 Act/Regulations/standards are not as stringent as those under the HSWA 1974 and its associated Regulations. Offences under the 2000 Act are triable in a magistrates' court, whereas offences under the 1974 Act are offences triable either in a magistrates' court or Crown Court. It is possible, therefore, that the Care Standards Commission inspector could notify an EHO regarding non-compliances with health and safety with a view to the EHO pursuing prosecution because the penalties available are more severe on conviction.

It is advisable for care homes to review their existing health and safety management systems against the Regulations and national minimum standards of their particular sector, and against the requirements of HSG 220. Core policies in a health and safety management system include policies concerning:

– general health and safety;
– risk assessment;
– accident investigation and reporting;
– first aid;
– training;
– manual handling;
– COSHH (Control of Substances Hazardous to Health);
– personal protective equipment;
– fire and fire precautions;
– equipment and machinery safety;
– electrical equipment;
– contractors;
– waste disposal;
– emergency evacuation;
– crises management, including managing an unannounced visit from a regulator;
– food hygiene;
– infection control;
– aggression and violence to staff and service users from other service users.

The policies must be customised and integrated into the care home's particular management system. It is now more important than ever to ensure that health and safety management is effectively integrated into the overall management system of a care home. Compliance with health and safety obligations can now impact on the ability of a care home to maintain registration. Section 14 of the 2000 Act provides for the cancellation of the registration of a care home when an offence is likely to be, or has been, committed.

In order to minimise the likelihood of non-compliance with health and safety obligations under either or both of the 2000 Act or the HSWA 1974, it is useful for operators of care homes to know the requirements in the regulations made under the national minimum standards published in accordance with the 2000 Act and those under existing health and safety legislation, and manage the expectations of the regulators.

7.6 MANAGING REGULATORY INVESTIGATIONS

Individuals and businesses when faced with investigations by a regulator whether the NCSC, HSE or, indeed, the police have to decide whether they wish to be passive during the investigatory process or whether they wish to defend themselves actively and effectively. For some reason, many businesses or individuals faced with an investigation in a business setting often opt for passivity whereas those same individuals when faced with a matter which they readily understand, such as a motoring offence, may seek to put all their 'rat like instincts for self-preservation' between them and any potential conviction. Everyone, every individual, every business is strongly advised to take an active interest in any investigation into them or their business and seek to defend themselves from those allegations from the start. The defence should not start once prosecution proceedings have commenced or at the trial itself. The best point at which to start the defence is the point at which the individual or business recognises that it is being investigated.

No matter whom the regulator or the nature of the individual officers investigating the potential offences, the process they go through is essentially the same. The regulator will have a suspicion that particular offences have been committed. They will investigate further and look to see whether their suspicions have any foundations, and where they do they will seek evidence which they can present before a court with a view to obtaining convictions. To support them in this task Parliament has granted the various regulators a sweep of powers to assist them in the task. These powers will almost inevitably include the right to enter premises, to search and seize documents, to take appropriate samples or measurements and, in certain circumstances, the right to interview individuals under compulsion.

Every power granted to a regulator has its boundaries and limitations. If an individual or business is taking an active interest in its own defence one of the strategies it may seek to adopt is to ensure that those investigating stick within their powers. It is wrong to assume that those investigating know or appreciate the limitations on their powers. The courts are littered with cases where regulators and officers have exceeded their powers. Sometimes the evidence they obtained through exceeding their powers is treated as tainted – as 'fruit from the poisoned tree'. However, there are also many occasions where the courts are prepared to accept that evidence obtained is sufficiently important that it should be admitted notwithstanding the fact that powers may have been exceeded in obtaining it in the first place. The best time and place to complain about powers being exceeded or rights abused is at the moment that it is happening – it is often too late to argue those points in court later. This often requires skilled and experienced lawyers.

The issue with relation to powers and rights is simply used as an illustration that it is wise and prudent to ensure that the investigation itself is conducted within its lawful boundaries. But dealing with an investigation goes much beyond this. Those being investigated really need to decide what they want to get out of the process.

For some individuals or businesses being convicted of particular types of offences will automatically disqualify them from being able to continue in business. For those people, and in these circumstances, if they wish to continue in business the only choice that that person has is to contest the investigation every step of the way. However, in order to do this, appropriate resources in terms of manpower, time, lawyers fees etc will need to be put aside. There is no point in adopting such a strategy if the resources are not there to support it. If an individual business considers itself, after legal advice, to be guilty of particular offences then it may be that the best course of action is to accept the consequences of what has gone wrong and seek to bring the investigation and any subsequent court case to a conclusion as rapidly as possible through timely admissions of guilt and guilty pleas even though this may mean the end of the business. To do otherwise, risks wasting money on a doomed defence and almost inevitably greater penalties on being sentenced.

Sometimes regulators will be investigating comparatively minor matters. In these circumstances and providing the company can accept, on the fact, that it has got matters wrong, it can be wise to look to end the investigation quickly and speedily. This may also involve timely admissions of guilt. However, outside these two extremes, matters are rarely clean cut. Often it is not obvious whether an individual or a business has committed the offences which are being investigated. Often the consequences can be serious, but not threatening to the business. It is here that the question of reputation necessarily arises and a judgment has to be exercised as to just how far an individual or business wishes to go in its own defence.

Irrespective of these considerations it is always right, and it is prudent to ensure that the authorities act within the law when conducting themselves. It may be that a wrong step by a regulator will give a potential suspect or defendant an opportunity to seek an acquittal. Sometimes simple delay or inactivity can confound a regulator.

Before embarking on any active defence it is essential that the business has expert legal advice. After all, no one wishes to cross the line between active management of defence and, for example, wilful obstruction of an officer in the execution of his duty. Similarly, no one wishes to be accused of, let alone convicted of, attempting to pervert the course of justice. Making sure that these lines are not crossed is an important part of the defence solicitor's role during the investigation stage.

Each investigation is inevitably different. However, certain pointers can be given in terms of sensible and prudent conduct.

7.6.1   Site visits and inspections

Where investigations are conducted on business premises, and providing that to do so will not amount to interfering with the scene of the crime, it is always wise to accompany an investigating officer during an inspection. What he or she looks at or considers should be noted together with the manner in which the investigation is carried out. The role here is simply to act as an observer to witness what is done and to record what is done. All visiting officers should be asked to produce their warrant cards.

7.6.2 Search and seizure operations

Where an investigating officer is conducting a search and seizure operation he may be acting under the terms of a warrant or under general powers granted to him by an Act of Parliament. In either case the officer should be asked to clarify from where he or she derives his or her power to conduct the search and seizure operation. If a warrant is involved the terms of the warrant should be considered in detail looking particularly at the premises authorised to be searched and any description of the materials which may be taken. Again, the individual conducting the search should be accompanied and his or her actions noted. Ideally, where documents are taken, a schedule of them should be compiled at the time. Also, if possible, duplicate sets of the documents should be created both to enable the business to continue to function without records which are being seized and also so as to see what information the regulatory authorities have obtained as part of their investigatory process.

7.6.3 Interviews with witnesses

Depending on the nature of the investigation and the regulator undertaking it, there are different powers for interviewing witnesses. For example, some witnesses can be interviewed compulsorily and under a duty to tell the truth, others can be interviewed privately. These examples come from the Health and Safety at Work etc Act 1974 and the 2000 Act respectively. Whatever the powers and limitations the decision has to be taken whether to submit to an interview voluntarily or to insist that the authorities use whatever compulsory powers they have. Sometimes that business is in a position to assist individual witnesses to make up their minds – but in the last and final resort it must always be for the individual witness to decide how he or she wishes to respond to the authorities. However, it must be right and prudent for a business facing investigation to ensure that witnesses, such as employees, which come from its own business are fully informed of their rights and the protection which the law has given them. Thus, for example, during a health and safety investigation it is always wise to insist that the individuals be interviewed compulsorily as the law protects such individuals in so far as nothing that he or she says during such an interview can be used against them in terms of a personal prosecution. They also have the right to have someone present during the interview.

7.6.4 Interviews under caution

An interview under caution is often the most difficult issue for someone being investigated to consider. Interviews under caution only take place with individuals or businesses who are suspected of having committed criminal offences. Except in circumstances where the authorities can exercise a power of arrest, such as where the police are involved, then, interviews under caution are, effectively, voluntary. Strange as it may seem, even when the police have arrested someone whom they wish to interview, as a suspect that individual still has a choice whether he or she answers the questions which are put. However, it is not just a simple matter of choice whether such questions are in fact answered. The decision whether or not to answer questions, and what information to provide at an interview under caution, very much depends upon the nature of the investigation, the assessment of exposure to the risk and prosecution of the conviction and the disclosures made by the authorities prior to the interview itself.

Interviews under caution are a complex subject necessitating careful consideration including, crucially, the meaning of the caution itself. Someone being interviewed under caution will hear the following:

> 'You are not obliged to say anything. But it may harm your defence if you fail to mention when questioned something you later rely on in court. Anything that you do say may be given in evidence.'

The meaning of the first and last sentence of the caution are clear – you have a choice whether or not to answer questions, but if you do what is said can be used as evidence in court. The meaning of the middle sentence – 'but it may harm your defence if you fail to mention when questioned something you later rely on in court' is more problematic. The essence of the caution is to advise the person being interviwed that if in court at a later stage they raise a new version of events, and it is something which they could have dealt with in the interview under caution, then in certain circumstances the court may disregard the version it hears as being a fabrication. This is called the 'adverse inference rule'. No one can have any objection to the adverse inference rule having the effect of ruling out of account false or fabricated testimony. However, it would be a correct, but harsh, application of the rule if a truthful version of events was disregarded in court simply because the version of events was not dealt with sufficiently, or at all, at the interview under caution. Thus, when faced with an interview under caution it is important to know the nature of offences under consideration and the underlying factors or issues of which the investigatory authorities are aware. This then allows the person being interviewed to consider with his or her lawyer how best to respond as well as working out what needs to be dealt with so that the adverse inference rule does not have any unfortunate consequences in court later. This takes detailed consideration and proper preparation. As a general rule of thumb, no one should ever go into an interview under caution without having considered all these issues with his or her lawyer first.

Active and proactive defence is the first and most effective line of defence.

Chapter 8

PURCHASE, SALE AND FUNDING OF CARE HOMES

8.1 INTRODUCTION

Since a registered care home is a valuable business asset, its sale or purchase should not be viewed as a simple property transaction. Whilst the underlying principal asset supporting a care home business is an interest in real property, whether it be freehold or leasehold, that real property interest may be of diminished value unless it is accompanied by the other important elements which need to be transferred to a purchaser in order that that purchaser may both inherit and exploit the business he or she has purchased.

In addition to the land transfer, all of the following will also be required:

(a) the goodwill of the business;
(b) title to fixtures, fittings and loose furniture;
(c) the full benefit and advantage of existing contracts with patients or residents;
(d) the benefit of contracts with those who sponsor such patients or residents, and local authorities purchasing community care services;
(e) contracts of employment with the staff, including key staff and, in particular, the care home manager.

These elements can be found in a wide variety of business transfers. However, with the transfer of care home businesses, the purchaser must also hold an appropriate registration certificate, without which he or she would be trading unlawfully from the moment he or she completes the purchase, which may lead to prosecution for unlawful conduct of a care home business. The purchaser has no right to expect any period of grace within which to complete registration formalities.

As the manager of a care home must now also be registered, the same considerations will apply to the purchaser's proposed manager unless he or she is already an employee who will transfer to the purchaser as part of the sale and purchase arrangements.

It is essential that a purchaser does not complete a purchase, or enter into any contract which commits him or her to complete the purchase, until he or she has received a certificate of registration. In most cases, the certificate of registration will itself not be sufficient. The conditions which limit the registration must be in terms at least identical to those which were applicable to the business prior to transfer, or in terms which the purchaser finds satisfactory. Vital issues concerning the conditions as to the numbers and categories of persons to be accommodated, and, in the case of nursing homes, the levels of nurses who must be employed as a condition of registration, will have a direct impact on the financial viability of the home.

It is beyond the scope of this book to deal in detail with general aspects arising on the conveyancing of real property or upon the transfer of a business, but some aspects in relation to general transfer issues are worthy of special attention.

8.2 PROPERTY CONSIDERATIONS

8.2.1 Restrictive covenants

Care homes are very often conversions of substantial property formerly occupied as a single mansion house residence, or possibly a conversion from a hotel, guest house or block of residential apartments. Much conversion work has been carried out on properties originally built in the latter part of the nineteenth century and the early part of the twentieth century. Where such properties were developed on substantial estates, it was common practice for the business user to be severely restricted, so as to promote the interests of the estate as a whole. Frequently, only certain professional uses, for example a solicitor's office or a doctor's surgery, were permitted.

Despite the external appearance of the property continuing to resemble a substantial private dwelling house, most care home uses will contravene standard restrictive covenants, and the issue will need to be addressed carefully.

A breach of a restrictive covenant is often discovered as part of the conveyancing process. In some cases, the issue has been overlooked in previous land transfers; in others, the proprietor may have been unaware of the existence of a covenant, for instance if he or she originally purchased the property for residential use and only converted it at a later date. Once a breach of covenant becomes an issue, a detailed investigation has to be carried out to establish whether the covenant is still enforceable and, if it is, who has the right to enforce it. There are a number of ways in which issues can be resolved. These might involve a retrospective application for consent from the beneficiary of the covenant, an application to the Lands Tribunal for removal or modification of the covenant, or, more typically, specific title insurance policies provided enough relevant information can be gathered and submitted to the insurance company so that it can assess the risk of a claim being made. An insurance policy will cover the cost of defending the claim, any damages awarded to the claimant or, ultimately, the loss in value of the care home business in the event of its closure.

8.2.2 Planning consent

Planning consent for the operation of a care home needs to be evaluated carefully. Substantial previous development by way of building works will usually have required planning consent, and if no evidence of consent is forthcoming, purchasers should exercise caution before accepting represen-tations from a vendor or a vendor's advisers that planning permission was immaterial (almost certainly never right) or not required, by reference to some statutory exemption. Although the Town and County Planning (Use Classes) Order 1987,[1] as amended, provides for change of use (between uses as a nursing home, a residential care home or a residential school) without the need for specific planning consent, care should also be given to examine existing planning consents, if any. Many planning authorities are concerned about over-development of care homes as this may have an adverse effect on property values or cause particular areas to become linked with this type of resident. In order to mitigate against the flexibility of the 1987 Order, planning authorities very often seek to limit the beneficial effect of planning consent either by imposing conditions to such consent which inhibit full flexibility to change to a different use, or by seeking to enter into planning agreements under s 106 of the Town and County Planning Act 1990, the effect of which is to severely restrict the ability of the property owner to change use or expand development. Frequently, a planning consent will contain a condition which restricts the use of the property to the particular care home use for which the proprietor applied. Over the years, the registration conditions may have changed, as may the type of home, but frequently the planning condition is overlooked and the breach comes to light only when the necessary searches are carried out as part of the conveyancing process. All such matters need to be investigated very carefully, and ultimately a purchaser may have to submit a fresh planning application for retrospective consent for an otherwise unauthorised change of use.

At the time of going to press, it is proposed that the 1987 Order will be reviewed. However, the Care Standards Act 2000 (the 2000 Act) has not made any consequential amendment to this Order, and the wording of the Act which refers simply to a 'care home' does not sit comfortably alongside the wording of the Order. It is not known how the planning authorities will seek to deal with this discrepancy, although the author suspects that the planning authorities will continue to look at the substantive use of a home, rather than its new, broader description under the 2000 Act.

A particular feature of care home development is that care homes tend to develop by slow expansion over a period of years. Small extensions, new day rooms or extra recreational or therapeutic facilities may be added, as time goes by. Unfortunately, this often occurs without approval from the local planning authority, or appropriate consents under building regulations, being obtained. These matters need to be checked carefully. A material increase in resident numbers may require planning consent, even if there is no specific restriction on the number of residents in the existing planning consent, since greater intensity of operation may be 'material development'. Registration for increased numbers does not imply planning consent. In the course of operating a home, where such increased facilities may arise as a result of internal rearrangements, many owners have overlooked the need, if there is indeed such a need, to seek consent from the local planning authority. A purchaser should obviously not purchase, nor should a mortgagee lend, unless satisfied that there is full and effective planning permission to enable the purchaser to conduct the business which he or she has agreed to purchase.

---

1   SI 1987/764.

Vendors are often surprised to learn that securing consent to an increase in registered numbers by the appropriate registration authority was not sufficient in itself to satisfy all the regulatory requirements. Some might suggest that this is, in any event, a minor technicality, but it cannot safely be regarded as such. Increases in numbers affect not merely the internal operation of a registered care home, but also impact on its locality and the amenities within that locality. Increases in numbers will mean, almost certainly, increases in staff and certainly increases in movement, in the sense that there will be a greater number of visitors for the increased number of residents.

It cannot safely be assumed that a planning authority will automatically rectify an omission on the part of a vendor, or even that the matter will be dealt with at the level of senior planning officers. It may be referred to the authority itself for a decision. Residents within a locality may perceive the potential impact as being greater than that which will actually occur. Regrettably, there still remain certain prejudices about interaction in the community with particularly vulnerable groups in care. In some cases, groups who are in care may differ so fundamentally that some concerns may have serious local repercussions. The change of use of a small residential care home from care for frail elderly ladies to the provision of care for young adults suffering from learning difficulties combined with challenging behaviour will effect a very significant change, and owners should take careful steps to ensure that all planning requirements have been fully satisfied.

8.2.3 Newly built premises

Where a care home has recently been erected, or indeed where substantial alterations have been carried out, a purchaser is well advised to review the documentation which was entered into by the vendor in connection with the construction works. This is because those persons who designed and constructed the building were employed solely by the vendor, and although the law is moving in favour of purchasers, the current position is that a purchaser has no rights against a builder, architect or other professional designer or supplier if that party's work is defective. Care homes are classed as commercial buildings and, unlike dwelling houses or flats, there is no guarantee scheme, such as that offered by the NHBC, relating to the fabric of the building. Therefore, purchasers should ensure that a full package of collateral warranties is available to them. Collateral warranties give a purchaser certain direct rights of action again the designers and builders of a property which are not currently afforded by the general law of contract and tort. This will also generally be a requirement of a purchaser's funder.

Although the construction industry has attempted to standardise the wording of collateral warranties in recent years, many of the standard forms are considered to be insufficient and deficient in a number of areas, and the warranties, together with the underlying appointments and building contract, should be reviewed carefully by the purchaser's solicitor, who will advise on their shortcomings (if any) and the ability of the benefit of the warranties to be transferred to the purchaser or its funder.

Ideally, warranties should be available in respect of any major building works carried out up to 12 years previously, but many parties will take a view if the works are more than 6 years old.

The fact that a warranty package is available does not, of course, mean that the building has been properly designed and constructed, and does not therefore take away the need for a purchaser to commission a full structural survey.

As an alternative to collateral warranties, some developers now provide a form of latent defects insurance policy, but such policies have, to date, rarely been used for care home properties.

8.2.4 National minimum standards

It need hardly be mentioned that along with the usual building surveys and valuations, an appraisal must be carried out to ensure that the home meets, and will continue to meet, the national minimum standards. Many purchasers will also be keen to ensure that the care home comfortably exceeds the current standards so as to allow for further raising of such standards in the future.

8.3 GOODWILL

8.3.1 Nature of goodwill

The goodwill of a business comprises reputation and the bond forged with customers, together with the circumstances, whether of habit or otherwise, which tend to make that bond permanent. An examination of the types of goodwill shows a distinction between goodwill that can be seen to be personally attributable to the owner, and goodwill that flows from the property and the location in which the business is situated, for example a retail shop on a prime trading site. Whilst there is an element of personal goodwill attached to the reputation of particular owners, it is submitted that, in general, the goodwill attaching to care homes is attached to the situation and property location, rather than personal goodwill. It is unlikely that existing residents will wish to leave a care home merely because there is a change of owner. Equally, it is likely that there will be a limited number of care homes within a particular area, and the needs of that area will indicate a reasonably steady flow of clients. However, a word of caution is needed, given the changes in funding of community care provision implemented on 1 April 1993.

Prior to 1 April 1993, social welfare benefit funding was directed towards individuals, who were given the opportunity to purchase care facilities of their choice. The emphasis has now changed to an increase in funds available for social welfare for purchasing local authorities, which will be the first resort for those prospectively in need of care and which, as local authorities, will purchase care for an individual, rather than funding the individual to purchase care for themselves. It therefore seems likely that greater value in the future may be attached to so-called personal goodwill, to the extent that a particular owner, through excellence in care practice, has achieved a particular relationship with a local authority. Although it is not likely that an authority, which has consented to the transfer of community care contracts to a purchaser, would seek to remove patients satisfactorily accommodated, the risk of damage to goodwill if the in-coming purchaser is unable to continue the satisfactory service to the standard and in the method expected by officers of that particular local authority is greater than circumstances where the number of purchasers are spread out among individual members of the community, rather than small numbers of large and effective purchasers.

A crucial line of enquiry for a prospective purchaser is to establish that the notional goodwill associated with the business is in reality goodwill, and not something that might be described as 'mediocre will' or 'bad will'. Accordingly, the relationship of the care home owner with the relevant local authorities, both as regulators and purchasers, must be investigated. Detailed enquiries should be made about the relationship with the local registration authority (now the local or area office of the NCSC). A purchaser should seek copies of all recent correspondence with the registration authority (and its predecessor) and should be prepared to ask searching questions about matters which appear to be less than satisfactory. At the very least, all inspection reports prepared within the last 3 years should be copied and delivered to the purchaser. If difficulties in the relationship with the registration authority are disclosed, the purchaser should meet with the authority to ascertain its attitude and whether or not its criticism is directed to the home as such and/or the particular owner.

8.3.2   Assessment of the value of goodwill

A purchaser will also wish to examine copies of the contracts with individual residents and patients accommodated within the home and, particularly, to examine contracts with purchasing local authorities, whether community care purchasers, ie social services authorities, or NHS purchasers. Since he or she will be purchasing the benefit and advantage of such agreements, the purchaser will wish to obtain disclosure of correspondence with such purchasing authorities as to the conduct of the community care contracts. The purchaser will evaluate the real extent of goodwill and the extent to which that goodwill will carry over to a new business owner, rather than evaporate once-established loyalties that no longer apply to the relationship between the purchasing authority and the particular business.

When assessing the value of goodwill, the purchaser should be aware not blindly to accept business transfer valuations prepared by so-called experts in the field. The value of goodwill will be established in relation to the true adjusted net profit of the business, and the purchaser, together with appropriate professional accountants, must examine the balance sheets and profit and loss accounts of the business carefully. If no accounts are available, the purchaser should, as a matter of good practice, insist on the preparation of accounts, or instruct his or her own accountants to construct them from available information.

Different levels of borrowing and personal drawings will have a significant effect on cashflow and profitability. Some purchasers may themselves be able to fulfil professional roles within the business, whilst others will need to employ persons with the relevant skills. All such matters need to be taken into account in adjusting a profit and loss account to show the likely profit for the purchaser.

However, certain figures will be constant, and the most important of these is the cost of staff, in terms of salaries and wages, to the business. This figure may be expected to be somewhere between 45 and 60 per cent of the turnover. Percentages at the higher end, or in excess, of this range, would suggest over-staffing, and the possibility of rationalisation. Percentages at the lower end of, or below, the range indicated would suggest under-staffing and possible difficulties with the registration authority, which may result in significantly increased staffing levels being required of or suggested to a prospective purchaser. A purchaser should take care to analyse wage and salary bills and to investigate actual staffing levels on a week-by-week basis so as to calculate the cost of staff and to check that the vendor is complying with the requirement to pay the statutory minimum wage.

Occupancy levels are a crucial factor in evaluating a care home business. Unlike many hotel businesses, care homes will expect to operate to near capacity. A prudent purchaser should ask for details of occupancy levels in respect of the home over a period of at least 2 years prior to enquiry. Sudden variations and, in particular, sudden drops in occupancy levels should be explained. A purchaser should also attempt to correlate variations in staffing levels with variations in occupancy levels.

It is also necessary to evaluate the source of referrals to the business. Following 1 April 1993, many homes will still have a combination of patients who pay their fees privately, residents and patients wholly supported by local authority community care contracts or health authority private bed contracts and, in some cases, private patients who fund their fees by continuing to draw upon social welfare benefits, supplemented by their own resources. (So-called 'preserved rights' to enhance social security benefits were abolished with effect from 1 April 2002. Any residents who were entitled to those rights should have had their contract renegotiated with the local authority.)

There can be no doubt that, for most care home businesses, the future lies in establishing and maintaining good contractual relations with the community care purchasers, ie county councils, metropolitan borough councils and London boroughs, being social services authorities and unitary authorities. A purchaser should ensure that such relations have been secured for the home, and that its continued turnover and profitability is not secured precariously on those whose rights to funding are based upon sources of benefits which have been discontinued.

All these elements will need to be drawn together to form a view about the potential value of the goodwill of a business.

8.4   FIXTURES, FITTINGS AND FURNITURE

8.4.1   Leasing agreements

A purchaser should be aware that, historically, care home owners have made extensive use of medium-term leasing facilities for a wide variety of equipment, furniture and fittings within homes. Extensive enquiries should be made about the existence of such leasing arrangements. In virtually all cases, the lessor will need to be consulted and will need to approve any transfer of the burden of leasing obligations to the purchaser. However, the purchaser should consider whether it is desirable to take on the burden of leasing obligations, rather than require the vendor to pay them off. This is frequently a requirement of funders who cannot otherwise take security over leased items. The value of the business, as specified by expert valuers, will normally be made on the basis that proper title can be made to all business assets. If, for example, nurse call systems, lifts or even carpets are not actually the property of the vendor, the value of the business may be significantly diminished.

If the purchaser decides to take on the leasing obligations, he or she should ensure that the leases do not continue for a period beyond the useful life of particular equipment. For example, carpets on lease for 7 years is a period clearly beyond the anticipated life, even of the heaviest-duty carpet, in a nursing home environment.

8.4.2   Warranties

In addition to manufacturers' or suppliers' warranties or service contracts, the purchaser should seek a warranty from the vendor that the assets transferred include all those necessary to continue the business. It will be difficult for a purchaser to check the detailed inventory supplied by the vendor, and it is not unknown for significant items to be excluded from the inventory by the vendor. It is always a wise course to allow for time to check the inventory room by room.

8.4.3   Secured/mortgaged goods

Mortgaging loose furniture items creates its own difficulties, both for the lender, who may wish to take such security, and for the purchaser, who may want to ensure that such property is free from mortgage, either to principal lenders or to hire purchase finance companies. Of course, the matter will be subject to detailed investigation by the purchaser's advisers, but they should also seek clear confirmation from any mortgagee or lender redeeming security at completion that the mortgagee or lender has no further claim or entitlement to any fixtures, fittings, furniture or items at the home.

8.5   BENEFIT OF CONTRACTS FOR CARE OF RESIDENTS

A contract for care is a personal contract. Therefore, unless it is renewed with the purchaser of the business, it is probably discharged by transfer of the business by the original care home owner. In practice, patients and residents are likely to be more concerned that a new owner may remove them from occupation, or change the material terms and conditions of their accommodation and care contracts.

This matter is usually addressed simply by the vendor notifying the residents of the transfer of ownership and the identification of the new business owner. A renewal of the contract may be inferred from this notification, as may subsequent billing and payment by the new owner and the existing patient.

8.6   BENEFIT OF CONTRACTS WITH PURCHASERS OF COMMUNITY CARE

More care needs to be taken where community care contracts have been established between the business owner and the local authority or health authority. Such contracts are likely to be lengthy compared with individual contracts, and may contain unusual terms and conditions. Purchasers should study such contracts to ensure that they understand and are prepared to deliver the level of care specified therein.

More importantly, however, is that almost all community care contracts are expressed to be personal to the care home owner, and to require the prior written consent of the authority before they are transferred. This gives the authority considerable power in relation to any proposed transfer of ownership of a registered care home. To ensure that the existing goodwill of the business has been secured, a purchaser's advisers must complete the necessary formalities in relation to the transfer of those contracts on or before completion of the main transaction. Mere written approval to transfer may be required, or a full document authorising the transfer may have to be drawn up and signed on behalf of the appropriate authority.

Vendors should therefore take particular care, in negotiating community care contracts, to ensure that their ability to transfer the business is not restricted by a local authority's unqualified power of veto over a buyer. There are limits to which an authority, as a regulator, may intervene to prevent the transfer of ownership by refusing or seeking to change conditions of registration. If the same authority, as a purchaser, has an absolute power to refuse consent to transfer the benefit of care contracts, then that authority, in effect, will have total control over the marketability of the business concerned. Those valuing or seeking to lend money against the security of such businesses must ensure that any valuation and, consequently, any loan take into account the marketability of the contracts underlying the business.

Another hidden trap awaits the unwary in relation to local authority community care contracts in nursing homes. Local authorities may enter such contracts only provided they contract within their powers and in accordance with the restrictions imposed on their contracting powers by enabling legislation. This area is governed by the National Assistance Act 1948, as amended by the National Health Service and Community Care Act 1990.

Where arrangements are made for the purchase of care in residential accommodation which provides nursing care, the premises in which such accommodation is provided must be registered under Part II of the Care Standards Act 2000 and be a care home as defined in s 3 of the Act. In cases where the establishment is not solely a 'care home', a very careful review must be conducted. No arrangements can be made by a local authority for the accommodation of any person in a nursing home without the consent of the health authority. This requirement is substantially overlooked. Arrangements made with nursing home owners for the provision of nursing care which has not been specifically approved by the health authority will be *ultra vires* the local authority. Issues may arise as to payments made under such contracts, but purchasers should ensure that approval has been granted, so that the benefit of the contract is valid and enforceable. Section 26(1D) of the National Assistance Act 1948 provides some relief for admissions to nursing homes made as a matter of urgency, but reinforces the need for health authority consent by indicating that such arrangements may be temporary only, so as to require health authority approval confirming the placement to be obtained as soon as possible.

8.7   BENEFIT OF CONTRACTS OF EMPLOYMENT

Employees in a care home will form a vital part of the assets of the home. In cases of over-staffing, a purchaser will want to reduce staff numbers; on the other hand, the vendor will want to ensure that all staff are transferred.

A purchaser may be seriously concerned to ensure that the loyalty of certain key staff, for example the manager or matron, remain loyal to the business and to the new owner.

A detailed examination of the provision of the Transfer of Undertakings (Protection of Employment) Regulations 1981 (TUPE)[1] is beyond the scope of this work. However, a number of points are worthy of comment.

(1) The transfer of the business of a care home is a transfer of an undertaking for the purpose of the Regulations.

(2) In consequence, irrespective of contractual provisions, the full benefit, advantage and burden of the contracts of employment will transfer with the transfer of the business from the vendor to the purchaser. This will include all benefits or conditions of employment, irrespective of acceptability. Therefore, the purchaser must make thorough enquiries and obtain full disclosure of the obligations he or she is undertaking. A vendor must be equally careful to ensure that all matters, no matter how trivial, which arise in relation to the contracts of employment are disclosed. Non-disclosure, to the dissatisfaction of a purchaser, may lead to a claim for breach of contract if the purchaser finds him or herself saddled with unanticipated liabilities.

---

1   SI 1981/1794.

(3) If, for any reason, any employees are not transferred to the purchaser, then such non-transfer will be regarded as unfair dismissal, leaving a potential liability in respect of such dismissal upon either the vendor or purchaser (but usually the purchaser).

If, for any reason, the vendor or purchaser does not wish particular employees to transfer, or individual employees have expressed a wish not to transfer (perhaps because their employment is relevant to other aspects of the vendor's businesses), then great care must be taken to address the issues arising under TUPE, before exchange of contracts.

8.8   AGREEMENT FOR SALE AND PURCHASE

A full review of the types and provisions of sale and purchase agreements is beyond the scope of this book. However, some common points for vendors and purchasers to consider are as follows.

8.8.1   Purchaser of assets or shares

Traditionally, most sales and purchases of care home businesses have proceeded by way of assets sale and purchase. By this route, the vendor transfers to the purchaser ownership and legal title to each of the specified business assets detailed in the sale and purchase agreement. The purchase price is apportioned between the different classes of assets and the parties also agree which contracts and liabilities are to be transferred or assumed by the purchaser and which are to be retained and discharged by the vendor. Each party indemnifies the other against the failure to perform its obligations.

Where the business has been owned and carried on by a company, the seller has the additional option of selling the shares in the company rather than the individual assets of the business. The advantage of this method is that there is continuity of ownership, and the purchaser acquires the company, and with it the business, along with all its assets and contracts in place without the need to transfer or assign those assets. The disadvantage is that the purchaser also acquires the company's liabilities, whether disclosed or undisclosed, including the liability to account for tax for the period prior to the purchase. The price paid for the shares takes into account the known liabilities.

On first sight, it would appear that a purchase of the shares in a care home business would get round many of the problems discussed above in this chapter relating to the personal nature of the majority of the contracts relating to the business and the personal nature of the registration certificate. As these are all in the name of the company, and the contracting party remains the same, there will be no need to assign or novate the trading contracts, or apply for a new registration certificate. Nor will there be any need to transfer ownership of the property at the Land Registry, or obtain new banking facilities. However, it is often discovered that most documents contain a 'change of control' clause, which effectively makes the contract personal to the vendor after all. With regard to registration under the Care Standards Act 2000, there will be no need for the purchaser to obtain a new registration certificate as there is no change in ownership of the business, although many purchasers and their funders will still wish to ensure that they have at least the tacit approval of the regulator.

The decision as to which route to take depends on numerous factors, not least the respective bargaining power of the vendor and purchaser, the financial standing of the vendor, purchaser and company and, inevitably, the taxation implications for all parties which are completely different for each of these two routes.

8.8.2   Conditional contracts

From the discussion in the previous sections of this chapter, it is obvious that there are a great number of issues which the purchaser will want to resolve prior to completing its purchase of the business, whether as an assets or shares purchase. When those issues involve the necessity to obtain the consent of a third party, the vendor and purchaser may want to enter into an agreement which is conditional upon the issues being dealt with. As part of the negotiating process, the vendor, the purchaser and their legal advisers will first identify the specific issues, and usually make the initial contact with any third parties before the agreement is entered into. The agreement itself will be drafted so as to identify the consents required, to specify which party is to obtain the consents, and what is to happen if such consents have not been obtained or can only be obtained under unsatisfactory conditions. In some circumstances (such as failure to obtain the necessary registration under the Care Standards Act 2000), the purchaser will want the right to terminate the agreement and walk away from the transaction. Other more minor issues may be dealt with by way of price adjustment.

Very often, a purchaser will not wish to commit him or herself to a purchase agreement (albeit conditional) until he or she has a very good idea that certain conditions will be satisfied, or at least dealt with on terms which meet the purchaser's expectations and allow him or her to continue to run the business in line with his or her projections. However, in probably the vast majority of transactions a purchaser will not commit to the agreement until the conditions have actually been satisfied and the parties will then proceed to an immediate simultaneous exchange and completion, perhaps entering into a simple lock-out agreement or purchaser's call option to cover the period whilst the parties are negotiating and attempting to satisfy the conditions and obtain the necessary consents.

8.8.3   Warranties

Notwithstanding the fact that the purchaser will have exercised due diligence in relation to business of the care home, he or she will expect the vendor to warrant certain issues relating to the business. This is particularly important in the case of a shares purchase where the liabilities of the business remain with the company being purchased. The purpose of warranties is twofold. First, they give the purchaser a right to sue the vendor if the purchaser discovers subsequently that things are not as they had seemed prior to his or her purchasing the care home. In some circumstances, this could give the purchaser the right to unwind the transaction and rescind the agreement. Secondly, warranties serve as a sort of checklist for the vendor in the negotiations leading up to the sale to ensure that he or she has disclosed everything which should be disclosed in connection with the sale of the business. Typically, a formal disclosure process is followed, with the vendor signing a disclosure letter setting out his or her formal disclosures, which then qualify his or her liability under the warranties.

The extent and severity of the warranties are matters which are negotiated between the parties and their legal advisers and, as is to be expected, depend on their respective bargaining powers. Usually, the vendor will seek to limit his or her liability, both in time and quantum.

8.9 VALUATIONS

Great care should be taken in placing reliance on professional valuations in relation to care home businesses. In this specialist business, more than any other, particular firms of valuers have acquired a reputation for special expertise. This has probably arisen because of the unusual nature of the business, where every business operates at or near capacity, so that it is possible to assume that similar businesses in similar areas carry readily reckoned valuations, which can circumvent the normal exercise of analysing business accounts and trading performance. This is because, given capacity trading, the potential for gross profit is present in every business, and net profit will be determined merely by reference to individual rates and expenditure in operation.

Such practices have resulted in less experienced valuers suggesting that nursing homes in particular areas have a value per bed. This is a dangerous assumption. If there were ever any justification for this proposition, it dates back to before April 1985, when every individual could claim a right to cash-limited social security benefit, and each area effectively fixed a going rate for publicly funded residential and nursing care, which rate was then payable to all applicants to the local office of the Department of Social Security.

A never-ending stream of potential customers, who were able to secure funds from a public source simply by proof of insufficiency of capital and income to meet certain limits, provided a golden opportunity for an almost risk-free business. Those days are long gone, and the final move away from social welfare benefit funding of individuals in care home placements to public authority contracting on behalf of those whom it assesses to be in need, means that it is vital that valuation, however useful as a rule of thumb, is cross-checked both against business performance and business potential, taking into account, *inter alia*, the factors which have been outlined in this chapter.

However, purchasers should note the following. Lenders, as a matter of policy, cannot undertake valuations on their own account. Lenders will want to ensure that the business proposition is sufficient to secure the repayment of the monies being advanced and, the lower the proportion of monies advanced to the purchase price, the less concerned the lender will be to ensure that the purchaser price is realistic.

Purchasers may find specialist valuations useful in order to secure the support of traditional lenders, but this should in no way be regarded as a substitute for careful analysis of the important business indicators, both past and future, before determining whether the valuation suggested represents true value or something less.

The element of change in business means that underlying business cannot truly be valued against past performance unless it is matched by performance in the community care environment. This cannot be overstated. There is no doubt that a care home business provides an opportunity for outstanding cashflow (certainly to the extent that the business is based on social welfare benefits and private individuals' own resources). Such cashflow may not be regular in the short term, with community care-based contracts payments being made against invoices issued to a local authority, but, nevertheless, local authorities will recognise that non-payment will place their sponsored patients and residents in jeopardy. Cashflow will still be good compared with many comparative businesses, particularly as occupancy levels, being near to capacity, should ensure that most well-run businesses are operating to their potential, which potential is not as affected by seasonal variations as businesses such as hotels and guest houses.

8.10   HOW SHOULD THE VENDOR PREPARE FOR SALE?

A vendor usually directs his or her attention first to the instruction of a business transfer agent. This might be the normal course in respect of other business transfer agreements, but in the case of registered care homes, this should follow only after the vendor has considered the *implications* for the registered care home business.

No transaction can be completed until a new certificate of registration in respect of the home is issued to the purchaser. Clearly, a purchaser will have to overcome the hurdle of satisfying the registration authority that he or she is not an unfit person to be concerned in the operation of the care home business. In addition, the purchaser will have to satisfy the registration authority that the premises, location, situation, staffing and method of operation of the care home business will continue to be satisfactory. At this stage, the registration authority will reconsider whether or not to refuse the purchaser registration, re-evaluating all the material that it originally considered in relation to the vendor's application. It may be that matters over which the authority was satisfied in respect of the current owner's application may give cause for concern with a less experienced or less well-funded prospective owner.

Untold damage can be done to prospective sales if purchasers make early and ill-prepared applications, or even approaches, to a registration authority. Registration authority officers may talk frankly and openly with the purchaser about their concerns to such an extent that the purchaser may be dissuaded from continuing his or her interest. Whether or not the prospective vendor has any recourse against the authority in respect of anything that has been said is a different question. In practice, the vendor may suspect that this has happened, but may not be able to get any direct evidence of the conversation, let alone its substance.

It is also important to ensure that the particulars of sale, prepared by a business transfer agency, do not misrepresent the position in regard to registration. If particulars suggest a basis of business, which then turns out to be different, a purchaser may expect a reduction in the asking price, which might not have occurred if the particulars had been drafted accurately.

8.11   REGISTRATION AUTHORITIES

Registration authorities expect (although they are not entitled as of right) to be kept informed as to developments in the operation or potential disposal of a care home business. If the vendor approaches the registration authority at an early stage, this may secure the authority as an ally, providing constructive information in support of the transfer. The registration authority's interest in relation to a home is that the transfer should proceed smoothly in the interests of vulnerable residents and patients.

It is crucial that the vendor should both clarify with the authority that it will not seek to place unnecessary objections in the path of the transfer, and ascertain any matters which the authority considers will need to be addressed before it issues a new registration certificate, for instance, compliance with the national minimum standards.

In the author's experience, early approaches to registration authorities yield dividends. Authorities are pleased to be involved and to be made aware of the process, and thus are able to deal more easily with enquiries from prospective purchasers or valuers appointed by purchasers or their prospective lenders. Establishing the matters which may be of concern to an authority and which require change will aid the vendor in negotiations, since the vendor will then be able to approach the purchaser with a view to identifying these areas of difficulty.

There may be genuine disagreement between the authority and the prospective vendor over matters that need to be addressed. A purchaser's reaction to the vendor in relation to those disagreements will be much more sympathetic if he or she has been told of the difficulty prior to discussion with the authority. A purchaser who makes enquiries of the authority, having been told that there are no difficulties, and discovers a list of problems, is likely to become difficult and demanding in relation to other details in the transaction, and is more likely to seek to reduce the price.

Issues which will be central to a purchaser, in addition to the process of registration, will be the numbers for which the home will be registered to care, the categories of patient or resident for whom the home is registered to care (if any restriction be imposed), and, in relation to nursing homes, the extent of any proposed nursing establishment conditions which the authority may seek to impose.

The Care Standards Act 2000 now requires the registration authority to impose any conditions it considers to be appropriate (subject to approval). Purchasers must take particular care, since these conditions will be binding, and breach will be a criminal offence of strict liability

An authority may use the opportunity of a transfer of ownership to seek to secure changes which it did not seek against the existing owner. This is understandable. Changes in conditions, or even the cancellation of registration, are difficult to enforce (in terms of time and expense). Every application for registration on transfer of ownership is, in effect, a new application. The authority knows that the prospective vendor's desire for sale cannot be consummated until the prospective purchaser has obtained a new certificate. The authority is thus in a stronger position to advance its case, in the knowledge that a transaction may be delayed or even frustrated by delay in effecting re-registration.

All parties must appreciate that re-registration on transfer of ownership is not a matter of right. The vendor has no right to expect the authority to register any third party, and the purchaser only has the same right to expect registration as any other applicant for registration. The matter is subject to reconsideration and, hence, the need to prepare grounds for the application for re-registration on transfer of ownership is one of paramount importance in approaching the negotiations for sale.

A registration authority may previously have accepted a situation it regarded as less than satisfactory, but not so unsatisfactory as to justify changing registration conditions or cancellation of registration, pending a possible change of ownership. In these circumstances, the vendor will know that any purchaser will face changed ground rules, and, if he or she fails to disclose this information, will only have him or herself to blame if the purchaser withdraws from negotiations or tries to negotiate a price reduction.

8.11.1   How should the authority react?

In the vast majority of cases, a registration authority will wish to assist a smooth transfer of ownership. The concern of the authority is the continued care of the frail and vulnerable residents and patients who are accommodated in the home. In the event of disruption to a seamless service of care, the authority may find itself having to re-accommodate or assist in the re-accommodation of the residents.

Nonetheless, the registration authority will recognise that each application for registration must be considered on its own merits. Registration may not have been considered fully for a number of years, and accepted standards of practice and service may have changed. The fact of re-registration operates as a statement on behalf of the registering authority that the applicant, the home and its services, facilities and staffing are all considered re-fit for registration, as is the manner in which the applicant proposes to conduct the home. An authority which registers a home out of convenience, whilst holding misgivings about particular aspects of the care service or the facilities, accommodation or location, must expect both criticism and complaint. More importantly, if it seeks to regulate the new owner in respect of matters known and material at the date of change of ownership, the authority will be met with the forceful argument that, if matters of concern were already known to it, those matters should have been brought to the attention of the purchaser at the time of re-registration. The purchaser will have a compelling argument that, if he or she had known that he or she would be required to change services and facilities at the time of change of ownership, he or she would then have had the opportunity to review the price which he or she was prepared to pay for the business.

It may be difficult for a home owner to seek to establish that the registration authority holds a duty of care in relation to information given during the course of the application for re-registration. However, in certain circumstances, and particularly if the authority takes it upon itself, through its officers, to offer guidance on registration, it is not inconceivable that such a claim could be founded if the authority seeks at, or shortly after, re-registration to suggest that facilities and services which have been acquired are inadequate or unfit for the purposes of the particular home.

Upon receipt of an application from a prospective vendor advising the authority of a proposed sale, the authority should co-operate, and seek to agree with the proposed vendor what it will require of a prospective applicant (in addition to being satisfied that the applicant is not unfit to be registered) and arrange with the prospective vendor that such matters will receive attention prior to the application, or will be the subject of agreement between the prospective vendor and the registration authority in its dealings with any prospective applicant for registration.

It has been argued that if a home is considered fit to operate in the hands of the existing owner then, subject to the establishment of fitness in any prospective applicant, it should be considered fit in the hands of such prospective new owner. Whilst there is force for such argument, it is not overwhelming.

8.12   FUNDING MODELS

8.12.1   Capital markets

Only the largest, most sophisticated care home operators have access to funding from capital markets. The majority of care home businesses are funded by traditional bank borrowing, although some of the larger operators have taken advantage of equity and mezzanine investments provided by venture capital houses.

8.12.2   Bank borrowing

The most valuable asset of a registered care home business is the property from which it trades and, initially, many care home operators were funded by simple commercial mortgage facilities made available to them by high street banks and building societies secured purely by a mortgage over the property. These facilities have usually been adequate for both the owner–operator and the lender, whose relationship has been that of the traditional owner–mortgagee. However, with the changing economic and regulatory climate, lenders have looked for more sophisticated types of facility and security, and lending to the care home sector is now regarded as business lending, carried out either by specialist health care lenders or dedicated departments of the major banks. The types of facilities now made available to care home operators are more sophisticated, and credit decisions are based not on the perceived value of bricks and mortar, but on the trading position of the business as a whole. Typically, bank facilities will encompass the following provisions.

(1) There will usually be an acquisition or term loan facility repayable by instalments over the life of the loan, with interest payable with reference to either the bank's base rate or the London Inter Bank Offered Rate (LIBOR). The bank will often also make available working capital facilities, such as overdrafts, and will hold the operator's current accounts.

(2) Loan agreements now contain the usual range of provisions for trading companies, including a full range of warranties relating to the status of the borrower, ongoing obligations relating not only to the property but the trading position of the business, and a full range of events of default which entitle the bank to demand repayment of the loan facilities in case of the operator's breach or insolvency.

(3) Financial covenants are now no longer linked purely to the value of bricks and mortar, but to performance of the business generally. For instance, it is normal for financial performance to be tested quarterly with reference to the gearing of the business (ie the ratio of its borrowings to the value of its assets), cashflow available for debt service (ie the ratio of adjusted profit to the amount required to make interest and capital payments under the loan) and interest cover (ie the ratio of profit to interest payments). In order to monitor the position, the operator must make available to the bank its monthly management accounts, as well as its annual accounts. Interestingly, although funders have traditionally regarded financial viability as their exclusive province, a care home operator must now also demonstrate to the regulator that it is 'financially viable', although the author suspects that the Care Standards Commission may be somewhat less sophisticated in its interpretation of accounting information. Funders will have to accept, however, that they are now no longer the sole judge of the financial viability of a care home business.

(4) In view of the increasing burden upon businesses to comply with the regulatory environment, including that brought about by the Care Standards Act 2000, loan agreements now contain obligations on the part of operators to comply in full with all regulations and to keep the bank informed of all correspondence, inspections and material breaches. This obligation usually extends to require compliance not just with matters of

law, but also regulatory expectations, even where those are not strictly enforced or enforceable by the regulator. This could result in the bank exerting pressure on an operator in circumstances where the regulator could not.

(5) Loans are secured by way of a full debenture containing specific charges over the whole of the assets of the operator, including goodwill, fixtures and fittings, furniture, bank accounts, and a floating charge over the whole of the operator's undertaking. Individuals (as opposed to corporate operators) are not able to enter into debentures of this type, and this is one of the reasons why there has been a move towards corporate ownership of care homes, and away from ownership by individuals.

8.12.3 Sale and leaseback

Sale and leaseback transactions became popular during the 1990s. Under such schemes, an operator of a care home does not have to incur the capital expenditure and associated borrowing in connection with the ownership of the property from which it trades. Under a typical sale and leaseback transaction, the buildings and equipment of the care home are sold to a landlord/investor (or, in the case of an acquisition, are bought directly in his or her name). The operator then leases these items from the landlord/investor for a minimum term of 25 years. The rent is fixed not by reference to the open market rental value for similar properties (for which there is little evidence), but with reference to the financial return required by the landlord/investor. Typically, this has been set to give a return of as much as 10.8 per cent on the capital invested (which could be as much as 100 per cent of the purchase price). The lease then provides that the rent will be reviewed periodically, either with reference to the tenant's turnover, or to the increase in the Retail Price Index, or a mixture of the two.

A sale and leaseback transaction of this type gives the operator several advantages, namely:

(a) the ability to raise capital for further expansion once existing facilities/ equity have been used up;
(b) off balance sheet funding more akin to retail or manufacturing businesses which do not traditionally own their property;
(c) the ability to fund further acquisitions without capital expenditure.

However, these types of transactions have fallen from favour for a number of reasons:

(1) With interest rates currently at an all-time low, the return expected by investors is a high price to pay for the additional capital facilities.

(2) A 25-year lease is seen as a very long-term commitment from the operator. Usually there is no break option, which means that the operator's only way out of an unprofitable care home is to attempt to assign the lease. Also, lease terms are generally very restrictive and take away any option for the operator to develop or expand the business without the landlord's consent.

(3) Generally, rents only increase upwards, and if the rent is index linked, it will increase by a fixed amount every review irrespective of whether the tenant is able to pay the increase. With public funding being capped or frozen, and with margins being squeezed following the introduction of the minimum wage, it is possible that the operator's profit will be reduced to the point where he or she cannot afford to continue in business.

(4) The tenant's balance sheet looks uncomfortably light without fixed assets.

At the time of writing, the major institutional landlords/investors are no longer active in this field. Nevertheless, there remain a limited number of private investors/landlords who are still willing to enter into these transactions but the yield and lease terms now reflect the more realistic approach and flexibility required by operators in the current uncertain market.

Chapter 9

RECRUITMENT

9.1 INTRODUCTION

Within the context of employment, the new legislation has a particularly significant impact upon the recruitment of staff. This legislation is already in force, and it is imperative that service providers review and assess their recruitment procedures to ensure that they comply with the appropriate regulations and national minimum standards that apply to their particular establishments in respect of the pre-employment checking of employees (including managers), agency staff and volunteers.

Key features of the new regime are:

– thorough verification of an individual's identity and qualifications;
– written references;
– physical and mental fitness for the role on offer; and
– criminal records checks (disclosure).

This chapter considers the specific legal requirements of the legislation for recruitment checking, and provides a practical approach for dealing with these checks. The chapter also focuses on disclosure, the comprehensive background-checking service offered by the newly established Criminal Records Bureau (CRB) (which has taken over the task of carrying out police checks on staff and managers) and which is a key feature of the new regulatory regime.

9.2 DISCLOSURE AND THE CRB

9.2.1 Why was the CRB established?

In the words of the CRB itself:

> 'The CRB is set up to help organisations to make safer recruitment decisions by providing wider access to criminal record information, the CRB will help employers in the public, private and voluntary sectors identify candidates who may be unsuitable for certain work, especially that involving contact with children or other vulnerable members of society.'[1]

The CRB acts as a 'one-stop shop' for background checks on potential workers (if the position that they are to take up requires such checks) which were previously only available by searching a variety of sources (such as police

---

1   See CRB website at *www.crb.gov.uk*.

records and lists of unsuitable individuals held by various government departments). The new service which simplifies this process is called disclosure.

The disclosure service enables organisations to make more thorough recruitment checks and will particularly assist organisations recruiting for positions that involve regular contact with children and vulnerable adults.

A 'vulnerable adult' for these purposes is a person aged 18 years or over who receives services of a type listed in (1) below and, in consequence of a condition of a type listed in (2) below, has a disability of a type listed at (3) below.

(1) The services are:

   (a) accommodation and nursing or personal care in a care home;
   (b) personal care or support in order to live an independent life in one's own home;
   (c) any services provided by an independent hospital, independent clinic, independent medical agency or NHS body;
   (d) social care services; or
   (e) any services provided in an establishment catering for a person with learning difficulties.

(2) The conditions are:

   (a) a learning or physical disability;
   (b) a physical or mental illness, chronic or otherwise, including an addiction to alcohol or drugs; or
   (c) a reduction of physical or mental capacity.

(3) The disabilities are:

   (a) a dependency upon others in the performance of, or a requirement for assistance in the performance of, basic physical functions;
   (b) the impairment of the ability to communicate with others; or
   (c) the impairment of one's ability to protect oneself from abuse, assault or neglect.

The CRB's disclosure service has been operational since April 2002. This service is available to employers, volunteer organisations, professional bodies and certain licensing authorities. Job applicants are requested to apply for one of three types of disclosure (basic, standard or enhanced) if the position that they are to take up requires that such a check is necessary.

The type of disclosure will depend upon the nature of the position offered, and the depth of information provided will depend upon the level of disclosure. Amendments to Part VII of the Police Act 1997 (which deals with the issue of criminal records certificates and which the CRB was set up to implement) means that the CRB will act as a central access point not only for criminal records information, but also to the Department for Education and Skills List 99 (List 99) and the Department of Health Protection of Children Act (POCA) List, each of which lists people considered unsuitable to work with children. Once Part VII of the Care Standards Act 2000 (the 2000 Act) comes into force, the Department of Health will also hold a further list, the Protection of Vulnerable Adult

(POVA) List, of those persons considered unsuitable to work with vulnerable adults. When someone is applying for a standard or enhanced disclosure to work with children or vulnerable adults, checks will also be carried out on the POCA and POVA Lists and List 99, and the disclosure will record whether the applicant is included on those Lists.

9.2.2 Rehabilitation of Offenders Act 1974

Broadly speaking, the Rehabilitation of Offenders Act 1974 (ROA 1974) provides that anyone who has been convicted of a criminal offence who receives a sentence of no more than 2½ years in prison and who is not convicted of a further indictable offence during a specified period (the 'rehabilitation period') becomes a rehabilitated person and his or her conviction becomes 'spent'. This means that the conviction does not have to be declared for most purposes, such as applying for a job. The rehabilitation period depends on the offence committed (generally, the more severe the penalty, the longer the rehabilitation period). A conviction resulting in a prison sentence of more than 30 months can never become spent.

Under the ROA 1974, a spent conviction, or failure to disclose a spent conviction or any circumstances connected with it, is not a proper ground for dismissing or excluding the person from any office, profession, occupation or employment, or for prejudicing a person in any way in any occupation or employment. However, the Rehabilitation of Offenders Act 1974 (Exceptions) Order 1975[1] (the 1975 Order) sets out those occupations and positions exempt from the provisions of the ROA 1974. These are generally positions of trust, where there is a valid need to see a person's full criminal history in order to assess his or her suitability for a position, and an employer is entitled to ask a candidate to reveal details of all convictions, whether or not spent (known as asking an 'exempt question'). Examples of such positions of trust set out in the 1975 Order include medical practitioners, any employment in connection with the provision of social services to work with people aged over 65 years, seriously ill or handicapped, employment involving the provision of services to vulnerable adults, any office or employment concerned with the provision to persons aged under 18 years of accommodation, care, leisure and recreational facilities, schooling, social services, supervision or training.

Where an exception to the ROA 1974 applies, an individual must, if asked, disclose all convictions, including spent ones. A spent conviction in these circumstances can be used as a basis for refusing employment.

Tables showing rehabilitation periods, and the exempted occupations in respect of which details of spent convictions must be disclosed if requested, can be found at the end of this chapter (see para **9.4.8**).

---

1   SI 1975/1023.

9.2.3   Three levels of disclosure

(1)   *Basic disclosure*

All employers and volunteering organisations will be entitled to ask prospective employees/volunteers to obtain a basic disclosure. The basic disclosure will be available to all members of the public and can be obtained directly from the CRB without the need to go through an employer or volunteering organisation. The basic disclosure will show all convictions held on the Police National Computer which are not 'spent' under the ROA 1974. A basic disclosure is applied for by, and issued only to, the individual concerned. It is then the individual's choice whether or not to show the disclosure to an employer. The disclosure is not job specific, and may be used more than once. The CRB was expected to make this service available by summer 2002. However, due to the unprecedented demand for the CRB's higher-level disclosures, the launch of this service has been delayed. At the time of writing, the date of the expected launch of the basic disclosure was unknown, but is now expected to be April 2004.

(2)   *Standard disclosure*

A standard disclosure will be available in respect of positions and professions within the terms of the 1975 Order. For the purposes of positions in establishments subject to the 2000 Act regulations and national minimum standards, standard disclosures are primarily for posts that involve working with children or vulnerable adults. The Police Act 1997 defines vulnerable adult for these purposes as a person aged 18 years or over who has: (i) a learning or physical disability; (ii) a physical or metal illness, chronic or otherwise, including an addiction to alcohol or drugs; or (iii) a reduction in physical or mental capacity.

Standard disclosures contain details of all convictions on record (including spent convictions) together with details of any cautions or reprimands (police records which are not criminal records but which arise from a warning about future conduct given by a senior police officer, usually in a police station after a person has admitted an offence, which is used as an alternative to charge and prosecution (for adults a caution; for youths a reprimand)).

For positions involving working with children and vulnerable adults the standard disclosure also includes information contained on government departments' lists of people considered unsuitable to work with children, and (once Part VII of the 2000 Act comes into force) vulnerable adults. The standard disclosure will also show whether, under Sch 4 to the Criminal Justice and Courts Services Act 2000, the individual is banned from working with or seeking work with young people under the age of 18 years. If the person is banned, the prospective employer/volunteering organisation should contact the police, who will take the appropriate action since it is an offence for a person banned from working with young people to apply for such work and for an employer knowingly to employ a banned person in such a capacity.

Many of the national minimum standards also make reference to checks of the UK Central Council for Nursing, Midwives and Health Visitors (UKCC – now known as the Nursing and Midwifery Council (NMC)) register, and checks on the lists held by government departments.

The authors have made enquiries of both the CRB and the NMC as to whether the NMC register will automatically be checked as part of the standard (and enhanced) disclosure service. Neither the NMC or the CRB's helpline was able to provide a definitive answer, but the CRB's helpline suggested that if the NMC's register is held on the Department of Health's website, it will be checked as part of the disclosure process. If nurses, midwives or health visitors are guilty of misconduct, they will be struck off this register by the NMC and will thus be unable to work as nurses, midwives or health visitors respectively which would be revealed as part of the disclosure process. Until a definitive answer is obtained, we would suggest that service providers carry out their own checks with the NMC in order to determine whether individuals have been struck off its register, rather than assuming that such a check will form part of the disclosure process at this stage.

(3) Enhanced disclosure

Enhanced disclosures are available for posts which involve a far greater degree of contact with children or vulnerable adults, and therefore relate to a sub-set of the positions listed in the 1975 Order. Enhanced disclosures will be available in respect of:

(a) those involved in regularly caring for, training, supervising or being in sole charge of persons aged under 18 years;

(b) those involved in regularly caring for, training, supervising or being in sole charge of vulnerable adults, ie those aged 18 years and over;

(c) certain purposes in relation to gaming and lotteries;

(d) registering for the purpose of childminding and day care under the Children Act 1989;

(e) the placing of children with foster parents in accordance with any provision of the Children Act 1989;

(f) the approval of any person as a foster carer or the placing of children with foster parents under relevant Scottish statutory provisions.

An enhanced disclosure will contain the same details as the standard disclosure but may also contain additional information since all enhanced disclosures involve an extra level of checking with local police force records, in addition to checks with the Police National Computer and government departments' lists.

Local police information can be included on both copies of the enhanced disclosure, ie the copy provided to the employer and the copy provided to the candidate (eg details of a child protection case conference). However, a chief constable can decide not to make general disclosure of all relevant information where he or she does not wish the prospective candidate to have sight of this information. This could be details of suspected criminal activity where an investigation is under way, and/or an arrest has not taken place but is anticipated. If this type of local information is available it will be indicated on the top of the enhanced disclosure that further information is being sent by the police. Such information will be sent separately to the employer/volunteering organisation only.

9.2.4 How does the disclosure process work?

Service providers can request a disclosure after a provisional offer of employment or volunteer post is made. The individual can then apply to the CRB by telephone for a disclosure. On the basis of information provided by the individual by phone, the CRB will generate a disclosure application form in respect of that individual. Alternatively, if the service provider has established a credit arrangement with the CRB (to enable it to be invoiced directly by the CRB for the disclosure fee), it will be in a position to provide the candidate with a standard CRB application form.

For standard and enhanced disclosures there is a requirement for the application to be countersigned by a registered body (ie any employer, organisation or individual who is entitled to ask exempt questions (eg for details of spent convictions) under the ROA 1974). The original standard or enhanced disclosure will then be issued to the individual and a copy sent to the registered body. In the case of basic disclosure, the individual will be able to apply directly to the CRB, and the disclosure document will be sent to the individual only.

Disclosure fees are £12 per disclosure. Standard and enhanced disclosures for volunteers will be issued free of charge.

Only organisations permitted to ask for details of spent convictions under the exceptions to the ROA 1974 can apply to the CRB to become a registered body and countersign applications made by individuals for standard and enhanced disclosures.

Each registered body is required to designate a lead countersignatory to register the organisation. The organisation is entitled to specify additional countersignatories to assist in applying for and receiving disclosures. Once the organisation is registered, the lead countersignatory and other nominated countersignatories will be responsible for the disclosure application process. In order to establish the suitability of any potential countersignatory, the CRB will carry out the equivalent of an enhanced disclosure level check on each countersignatory. Before nominating countersignatories it should be made clear that such a police record check is required by the CRB.

All countersignatories are required to:

- countersign applications and receive disclosures;
- control access to, use and security of disclosures;
- confirm the details of the documentary evidence provided by the disclosure applicant to help establish his or her identity;
- ensure compliance with the CRB's Code of Practice (see para **9.2.6**) for recipients of disclosure information; and
- ensure that the position is covered by the 1975 Order, and the disclosure requested is at the appropriate level.

In addition to his or her role as countersignatory, the lead countersignatory:

- acts as the principle point of contact with the CRB on all matters connected with disclosure and registration; and
- validates the countersignatory's application document.

A fee of £300 is charged for an organisation to become a registered body (which includes the cost of the lead countersignatory) and £5 for each additional countersignatory.

To ensure that the disclosure service is effective and accurate, the registered body and/or countersignatory must ensure that the identity and current address of each disclosure applicant are verified beyond doubt. In order to complete the relevant section of the disclosure application form, the countersignatory is requested to verify as much physical evidence of identity as the applicant is willing or able to provide. Any document offered as proof of identity must be an original: a photocopy should not be accepted. Given that many applicants may be unwilling to submit these original documents to prospective employers by post, registered bodies should make arrangements with candidates to receive completed application forms and verify supporting documents in person. The ideal opportunity to do this is at the initial interview or, where applicable, during a visit to the establishment in order to meet service users as part of the recruitment process. As a minimum, a registered body should expect to see an original of an individual's passport or driving licence (as evidence of identity) and two forms of address confirmation (such as a utility bill and a bank statement).

Registered bodies can countersign applications for disclosure at the request of other organisations or individuals who may be entitled to ask exempt questions but who do not want to register in their own right. Registered bodies who do this are known as umbrella bodies (discussed at para **9.2.8**).

9.2.5 Checks on offences committed overseas

Although the CRB will draw on data on the Police National Computer which contains details of some 70,000 offences committed overseas, a disclosure may not provide information on people convicted abroad. For this reason, registered bodies should be cautious about relying on checks on persons with little, if any, residence in the United Kingdom, and in respect of persons with gaps in their employment history. The CRB may be able to offer advice about criminal checking services overseas so that employers can ask individuals to obtain the local equivalent of a disclosure if that would be sensible in a particular case.

Some countries (including most in the European Union) have arrangements in place which allow their citizens to obtain 'certificates of good conduct' or extracts from their criminal record to show to prospective employers. The level of information varies from country to country.

9.2.6 CRB's Code of Practice

Use of the disclosure service is governed by the CRB's *Code of Practice for Registered Persons and Other Recipients of Disclosure Information* (published by the CRB in accordance with s 122 of the Police Act 1997). The Code is intended to ensure – and to provide assurance to those applying for standard and enhanced disclosures – that the information released will be used fairly, and is concerned with the use of information provided to anyone entitled to see such disclosures. A copy can be downloaded from the CRB's website at *www.crb. gov.uk*. Key points are highlighted below.

–   All recipients of disclosure information, ie registered bodies, those signing disclosure applications on behalf of registered bodies, and others receiving such information, must adhere to the Code of Practice. Whilst failure to adhere to the Code is not a specific offence under the 2000 Act or the Police Act 1997, if the CRB believes that a registered body has failed to comply with the Code, or has countersigned an application at the request of a body or individual that has failed to comply with the Code, the CRB has the power, under the Police Act 1997, s 122(3), to refuse to issue the disclosure.

–   All employers must have available a written policy on the recruitment of people who have been convicted in the past. Each applicant must be given a copy of the policy at the commencement of the recruitment process.

–   Application forms, or other recruitment documentation, must carry a statement that the provisionally selected applicant will be asked to apply for a disclosure.

–   Applicants must also be made aware of the CRB's Code of Practice and the employer's commitment to it.

–   Disclosure information must be kept securely, and only those entitled to see it in the course of their duties should have access. Service providers must have available a written security policy for handling disclosure information. Once a recruitment decision (or other relevant decision, eg for regulatory or licensing purposes) has been made, a recipient of a disclosure must not retain it, or any associated correspondence, for longer than is necessary for the particular purpose. In general (and in particular to comply with the Data Protection Act 1998), this should be for a maximum of 6 months.[1] Disclosures should be destroyed by suitably secure means, ie shredding, pulping or burning.

9.2.7   Initial practical difficulties

It was the CRB's intention to complete 95 per cent of basic and standard disclosure checks within one week, and 90 per cent of enhanced disclosure checks within 3 weeks. Within a very short time of the disclosure service becoming fully operational in April 2002, it became clear that the CRB was struggling to meet these targets due to the unprecedented volume of applications for disclosures received. Whilst the CRB has now acknowledged that checks that should take 3 weeks are in fact taking 5–6 weeks, it is the authors' experience that care providers in particular can in fact wait up to 2–3 months to receive a disclosure.

---

1   For further details on the NCSC's views on retention of disclosures, see para **9.2.11**.

The CRB has taken a number of measures to address the backlog of unprocessed applications (which, it states, fell to about 50,000 by August 2002) including sending forms to India to be processed and taking on a further 350 staff in the United Kingdom. Despite the government's announcement in late August 2002 that the CRB's resources would be focused on dealing with the backlog of disclosure applications for teachers (approximately 25,000 in mid-August 2002) in time for the start of the new school year, the situation does not seem to have improved.

Particularly in the care sector, it is already difficult to recruit and retain good staff. Care providers are understandably concerned that the delays in the time taken to carry out checks and provide disclosures will mean that staff may simply take alternative jobs elsewhere. Care providers also fear that this will lead to an overall downturn in the quality of staff, and providers being penalised by the National Care Standards Commission (NCSC) for failing to comply with their staffing obligations under the 2000 Act, Regulations and the national minimum standards. As a consequence, in September 2002 the CRB introduced 'fast track' checking of the POCA and List 99 lists for staff newly appointed to work with children since 1 April 2002, while their full disclosure results were awaited. This service is only available for staff working with children (which includes those working in any capacity in a children's home) and is designed as a short-term contingency measure intended to give care providers information from the above lists in advance of the rest of the CRB disclosure. This contingency procedure obviously does not replace the disclosure service but simply gives service providers part of the disclosure information more rapidly than the rest. Service providers must still apply to the CRB for the required enhanced or standard disclosure check on all new staff appointed to work with children. At the time of writing, this 'fast track' checking continues to be available.

Further, on 1 November 2002 the government announced changes to the requirements for CRB checks in recognition of the difficulties the CRB is continuing to face in meeting the demand for disclosure checks. The main changes can be summarised as follows.

–   A postponement of the deadline for CRB disclosure checks for the care home staff who were already in their posts on 1 April 2002. On 27 February 2003 the government confirmed that the Care Homes Regulations 2001 will shortly be amended to reflect this change and that care providers will now have until 31 October 2004 to complete the CRB checks in respect of such employees.
–   CRB checks will not be required for staff other than providers and managers of domiciliary care agencies and nurses agencies, who will instead be required to make a statement about any criminal convictions (albeit that staff from agencies will still have to have CRB checks to work in particular types of homes where the regulations for those homes require this). Indeed, this is now reflected in the final versions of the regulations in respect of these types of agencies which come into force on 1 April 2003.

- From February 2003, CRB checks will be required for providers and managers of residential family centres (who will have to register with the NCSC), for all staff already in their positions in February 2003 and for all new staff before they take up their appointments.
- From April 2003, CRB checks will be required for providers and managers of voluntary adoption agencies, for all staff already in their positions in April 2003 and for all new staff before they take up their appointments.

9.2.8 Umbrella bodies

The disclosure service is available to organisations registered with the CRB (registered bodies). It is also available to organisations which have not registered, but which use a registered body to act as their administrative intermediary to obtain disclosures. Registered bodies providing this service are known as umbrella bodies.

An organisation may prefer to use an umbrella body if: (i) it does not have the necessary additional administrative resources; (ii) it is not willing to pay the CRB registration fee; (iii) it is unable to comply with the storage and handling provisions of the CRB Code of Practice; and/or (iv) another organisation is willing to countersign applications on its behalf.

The initial registration process for an umbrella body is largely the same as for a registered body. An existing registered body can become an umbrella body at any time simply by notifying the CRB of its intention by letter, telephone, fax or email. The CRB will subsequently contact the organisation to identify the types of organisations for which it proposes to act as an umbrella body and countersign disclosure applications.

No additional fee is charged where an existing registered body becomes an umbrella body on behalf of other organisations, and it is at the discretion of each individual umbrella body to decide whether or not to make a charge for providing the disclosure service to other organisations.

An umbrella body is required to designate a lead countersignatory, and, if necessary, additional countersignatories. Those nominated undergo enhanced disclosure checks by the CRB to assess their suitability. Countersignatories undertake the same roles and responsibilities as would be expected in any other registered body. When countersigning applications for users of their services, umbrella bodies must satisfy themselves that recruiters:

- are entitled to ask exempted questions under the ROA 1974; and
- are able to comply with the relevant obligations in the CRB's Code of Practice.

It is the responsibility of the umbrella body to ensure that those who receive disclosure information comply with the CRB's Code of Practice. The account-ability of an umbrella body in respect of the use of disclosure information and any recruitment decision based on it will depend upon the arrangements it has agreed with the organisation for which it is acting. The authors recommend that an umbrella body should have a written agreement in place with each organisation for which it acts, which clearly addresses each party's roles and responsibilities.

The CRB suggest that a typical agreement might include the following:

- what disclosure information the umbrella body is to share with the organisation to whom it is providing the disclosure service;
- the role that each party plays, if any, in the recruitment decision (this may be the sole responsibility of one of the parties);
- what arrangements are kept in place for both parties for handling disclosure information and observing the CRB Code of Practice;
- with whom the responsibility lies for verifying the identity of an applicant;
- security of transmission arrangements for sharing disclosure information between the parties;
- service levels between the two parties;
- what charges, if any, the umbrella body will make for providing the service;
- what conditions apply to the withdrawal of the service.

Further, once Part VII of the 2000 Act comes into effect such an agreement could also incorporate provisions dealing with each party's liability for the obligations placed on it by Part VII of the Act as regards suspension and discipline of staff, referring staff to the Secretary of State for inclusion on the list of individuals unsuitable to care for vulnerable adults, and the sharing of information in respect of the same.

As regards sharing of information and the role each party plays in the recruitment decision, possible arrangements could include:

- that the umbrella body passes the disclosure to the relevant organisation and takes no part in the recruitment decision; or
- that the umbrella body discusses the content of the disclosure with the relevant organisation and gives advice about the recruitment decision in addition to the law regarding the correct use of disclosure information. In this instance the umbrella body may bear some liability for the recruitment decision depending on the nature of the agreement with the relevant organisation; or
- that the umbrella body does not pass the disclosure information to the relevant organisation and makes any recruitment decision in accordance with its agreement with the organisation. If the disclosure information is not shared with the relevant organisation, the umbrella body is wholly responsible for the employment decision and the security and usage of the disclosure information.

Registered bodies and umbrella bodies are required to have a written security policy to govern their handling of disclosure information, and umbrella bodies may wish to consider providing organisations on whose behalf they act with a suitable policy.

An umbrella body should not act on behalf of other organisations if it is not satisfied that it is entitled to ask an exempted question, or it believes that it may be acting illegally. In this situation, the umbrella body should contact the CRB immediately.

9.2.9   Frequency and transfer of disclosures

The Police Act 1997 provides that once a basic disclosure has been issued, the CRB may refuse to issue a further basic disclosure to the applicant within a given period. It was intended that such a period would be set out in regulations, but at the time of writing no regulations have been made. Additionally, there is no corresponding provision in the Police Act 1997 in relation to standard and enhanced disclosures.

It is intended that employers and volunteer organisations will ask successful job candidates to provide a disclosure detailing any criminal convictions only following a conditional job offer and the CRB has issued guidance on the subject of how often a disclosure might be applied for in order to reduce the necessary expense on behalf of the job seeker. Guidelines will also be issued to deter employers from using checks as a means of shortlisting candidates. At the time of writing, no such guidelines are yet available.

Where an application is made to different organisations which each require separate checks, it is possible that more than one disclosure will be required. However, the applicant will be able to share the information contained in his or her disclosure with whomever he or she chooses. Service providers should exercise extreme caution before accepting an applicant's copy of a previous disclosure. Transfer of the disclosure is legitimate only if the second appointment very closely follows the first. However, in accordance with the CRB's guidance in this regard, the following should be noted.

(1) *Standard disclosures*: if service providers wish to rely on a previously issued standard disclosure they must satisfy themselves that the correct information sources, ie the lists held by the relevant government departments, have been checked if that is necessary for the type of employment they are offering, and/or undertake such checks themselves.

(2) *Enhanced disclosures*: the same considerations apply in respect of the government departments' lists as for standard disclosures. However, non-conviction information supplied by a local police force can also be included in an enhanced disclosure. Therefore, the CRB's guidance gives two possible solutions to enable enhanced disclosure information to be passed to another potential employer. These are:

    (a) the four-questions option, where, with the consent of the candidate, the second employer contacts the first and asks:

        –   Did you employ X last week/month, etc?
        –   Did you ask X to apply for an enhanced disclosure?
        –   Did you follow CRB guidance when making the recruitment decision?

–   During the currency of his or her employment, was there any factual matter about X's behaviour which gave you cause for concern?

If the answers obtained are 'yes', 'yes', 'yes' and 'no', the second employer can be reasonably confident that a suitable level of check has recently been made and that the applicant is a safe candidate; or

(b)   the second employer can ask the first whether any non-conviction information was released in a separate letter by the police in relation to X's disclosure application. If the answer is 'yes', the second employer should ask for a further enhanced disclosure application to be made. If the answer is 'no', there will have been no inappropriate use of non-conviction information, but the second employer will know that the copy of the enhanced disclosure will tell the whole story (subject to the usual cautions relating to standard disclosures to ensure that other relevant information sources have been checked).

9.2.10   Notification of offences committed after disclosure issued

Apart from the *National Minimum Standards for Fostering Services* (Standard 15.4), neither the 2000 Act, Regulations nor national minimum standards provide any guidance on the frequency with which disclosures should be undertaken once employment has commenced. NMS 15.4 provides that police checks should be renewed every 3 years, and it is the authors' understanding from care providers that similar guidance has also been provided by the CRB's helpline. The CRB has also suggested that if a service provider has any cause for concern in the intervening period and feels that it is necessary to carry out a further disclosure, it should use its discretion and do so. Until definitive guidance on the point is available, the authors would concur with this approach.

The CRB will not inform a service provider if, after receiving a disclosure for one of its staff, that individual commits a criminal offence. However, in certain occupations, the police will inform an employer if a member of its staff commits a criminal offence. This list of occupations is currently under review, but at the date of writing the following should be noted.

(1)   All relevant convictions and cautions should be reported in relation to teachers (including former teachers and student teachers) and ancillary staff in any type of school, further education institution or independent schools, together with any other individuals who are believed to have positions giving them substantial opportunities for access to children which would render them liable to be checked prior to their employment. This includes persons employed in the care of children in community homes, children's homes, probation hospitals, social workers, and includes relevant voluntary work.

(2) All relevant convictions and cautions should also be reported in relation to registered medical practitioners (including those temporarily registered), midwives, registered nurses, enrolled nurses and student and pupil nurses. In addition (with the exception of student and pupil nurses), reports of convictions in respect of these individuals (but not cautions) should also be reported by the police to the relevant professional bodies.

9.2.11   Retention of disclosures and the NSCS's rights to review during inspections

Many care providers and suppliers to the care industry have raised concerns about the NCSC's ability to inspect disclosures obtained from the CRB. The authors raised these issues specifically with the NCSC, and have now been provided with definitive guidance from the NCSC.

Where CRB disclosures have been made to the NCSC, the following guidance applies.

(1) The registered person must be satisfied that anyone he or she employs is fit to work at the home and that the relevant information has been provided or obtained.

(2) As a consequence of this, the NCSC's inspectors should be looking for proof only that the information required to be obtained by the employer (including CRB disclosure) has been obtained.

(3) The provider can satisfy this requirement by providing for inspection the retained 'tear-off slip' attached to the top of any CRB disclosure. This slip confirms the name and address of the individual and the name and address of the umbrella body or the countersignatory, but otherwise contains no other disclosure information. It is simply a confirmation that a disclosure has been sought and provided.

(4) By retaining only the tear-off slip, the provider can prove that it has complied with its obligations to the extent that it has sought and been provided with a CRB disclosure. Unless there is a good reason to retain the actual disclosure itself on an individual's personal file, the disclosure should be destroyed by suitably secure means shortly after the recruitment decision has been made.

Where the CRB disclosures are retained, the following guidance applies.

(1) Care providers should bear in mind that if they have retained the CRB disclosure, the NCSC believes that it would have a right to see such documentation. The NCSC has statutory authority to require provision of any information relating to the establishment or agency which it considers necessary or expedient for the purposes of its function.

(2) It is the NCSC's view that employees' consent would not be required for the disclosure of the information (as would normally be the case under the Data Protection Act 1998).

Although the NCSC was unable to provide specific guidance on a service provider's liability for disclosure of this information, it is the authors' view that there is unlikely to be liability for unauthorised disclosure under the Data Protection Act 1998 since provision of the information will be in compliance with a relevant legal obligation.

Unless there is a good reason to retain the actual disclosure itself on an individual's personal file, the disclosure should be destroyed by suitably secure means shortly after the recruitment decision has been made.

9.3 RECRUITMENT CHECKS – THE PRACTICAL APPROACH

9.3.1 Introduction

A thorough and well documented recruitment procedure will be vital to ensure that the requirements of the 2000 Act, Regulations and the national minimum standards applicable to particular establishments are complied with when recruiting new staff. Full details of the relevant Regulations and the national minimum standards which apply in this context can be found at para **9.4**.

Although there are some minor variations in the Regulations dealing with fitness of staff, with more significant variations being found in the national minimum standards (further detail of which is provided below), generally all staff recruited, including managerial staff, ancillary staff, contract workers and volunteers, must be subjected to a robust recruitment procedure. Before an individual takes up any position in the establishment, the service provider should ensure the following.

(1) A candidate who is shortlisted for a particular post (from, eg, details provided by a recruitment agency or in response to an advertisement) must complete a standard application form incorporating the disclosure, data protection, health and criminal records declarations detailed below.

(2) A candidate must provide proof of his or her identity (either an original birth certificate and/or current original passport) together with a recent photograph and also evidence of his or her current address (original documentation must be inspected and verified).

(3) A written employment history or CV must be provided by the candidate which sets out his or her employment over at least the past 5 (preferably 10) years, with a written explanation of any gaps in employment. Such gaps should be explored fully at interview and particular care should be taken if an individual has spent any time abroad during those gaps, since the CRB's disclosure service will not necessarily include convictions abroad.

(4) Two written references must be obtained, one of which must be from the individual's most recent employer, which are verified by direct contact with each referee.

(5) Where the candidate had previously worked with children, he or she should also provide an explanation of why that employment ended. Similar explanations should also be sought from the candidate's relevant previous employers (eg as part of a reference request).

(6) The candidate must provide proof of his or her qualifications relevant to the post on offer (again, sight of original documentation is recommended which should be verified with the organisation from which the qualifications were obtained if there are any doubts about authenticity).

(7) Evidence that the candidate is physically and mentally fit for the purposes of the work he or she is to undertake must be obtained. The regulations and national minimum standards provide no guidance on how this evidence is to be obtained, or what form it must take. Depending upon the size of a service provider's organisation, it may be possible to have the candidate examined by an in-house doctor, who will provide a report in this regard. Alternatively, the candidate could be required to obtain a report to this effect from his or her GP, or provide a written declaration that he or she is so fit. If the service provider has any concerns at all in this regard, these must be explored further with the candidate, and a separate medical examination undertaken if necessary.

(8) The candidate must provide a statement of any criminal convictions that he or she may have, including details of any convictions which are spent within the meaning of the ROA 1974 and details of any cautions received. Although it is not necessarily the case that, in the event that a conviction that was not disclosed by the candidate in this statement comes to light through the disclosure process, it would in itself lead to withdrawal of an offer of a position, an employer may be satisfied that the lack of honesty at the outset of the recruitment process is sufficient evidence to justify the withdrawal of any offer made.

(9) A standard or enhanced disclosure in respect of the candidate as appropriate to the role on offer must be obtained, the results of which must be satisfactory and in particular demonstrate that the individual does not appear on the Government's lists of individuals unsuitable to work with children or (when Part VII of the 2000 Act comes into effect) vulnerable adults.

(10) It must be made clear to the candidate that the engagement will be subject to the satisfactory completion of a probationary period of at least 3 months.

9.3.2   Practical approach to recruitment checking

As a bare minimum, a service provider should put in place a recruitment checklist to ensure that the requirements of the regulations and national minimum standards are met for each candidate. This checklist can be kept at the front of an individual's personal file and will list the requirements that have to be satisfied before an individual can be offered employment, as detailed above. It can also record the fact that the individual has been provided with and completed the organisation's standard application form and that the organisation has had sight of original identification and qualification documentation and written references.

Further practical suggestions which can assist service providers to facilitate compliance with the regulations and national minimum standards (and the CRB's Code of Practice in relation to the use of disclosure information) and to ensure a thorough and well-documented recruitment process are as follows.

(1) Advertisements

Advertisements should state clearly that the position on offer is one in respect of which a standard or enhanced disclosure (as the case may be) will be required. Not only will this deter unsuitable applicants but it should also ensure that any issues concerning a candidate's criminal record are highlighted at the start of the recruitment process rather than when the disclosure is obtained at the provisional offer stage (which could, of course, result in the candidate withdrawing at the last moment). Such problems can be further reduced if questions about criminal records are asked at the initial application stage (eg by requiring the candidate to declare his or her convictions and cautions on an application form).

(2) Job application forms

The authors recommend that service providers put in place a standard job application form that all shortlisted candidates are required to complete. The application form should enable the candidate to provide a detailed employment history (and explain any gaps) and should state that the candidate will, if successful, be required to apply for a standard or enhanced disclosure. As an additional safeguard, and in order to flush out any potential problems with criminal records as early in the recruitment process as possible, the application form should also require the candidate to provide a declaration as to his or her criminal convictions, including any convictions which are spent, as well as details of other non-conviction information (such as cautions, reprimands and warnings) that may have a bearing on their suitability for employment. The advantage of getting candidates to disclose this information at the application stage is that it provides them with an immediate basis for deciding whether they should continue with their application for the vacancy. The obvious disadvantage is that it may deter potentially very good applicants from applying if they believe that they may be unfairly prejudiced by their convictions. Again, to help alleviate these concerns, the CRB Code of Practice requires that application forms carry a statement to the effect that a conviction will not necessarily be a bar to employment. Applicants should also be told about the existence of the Code of Practice and advised that it is available on request.

Service providers should also bear in mind the fact that information provided about a person's criminal record and other non-conviction information is sensitive personal data within the meaning of the Data Protection Act 1998. The Act requires that personal information is obtained and processed fairly and lawfully, is disclosed only in appropriate circumstances, is accurate, relevant and not held longer than necessary, and is kept securely. In order for that information to be processed fairly and lawfully, service providers should ensure that the individual gives his or her consent to the use of this information for those purposes. Again, a declaration to this effect can be included in the application form (or a separate consent form specifically completed) to ensure that these requirements of the Data Protection Act 1998 are complied with.

(3)   Interview process – identification

Proper identification of potential candidates is not only necessary to comply with the 2000 Act, regulations and national minimum standards but is also fundamental to the accuracy of the disclosure process. Where an individual's identity is verified beyond doubt, names can be matched with criminal records and, in cases where the position involves working with children, with the lists of individuals banned from working with children and (when Part VII of the 2000 Act comes into effect) vulnerable adults held by the Government. Service providers should ensure that all candidates invited to attend an interview (or, where applicable, a visit with service users as part of the recruitment process) should be requested to bring with them original copies of their passport and/or driving licence, a photograph of themselves, and original documentation showing proof of address and proof of qualifications. The service provider can then take the opportunity to examine these documents closely during the course of the interview and record on the recruitment checklist that originals of the relevant documentation have been reviewed and copies of these documents retained on the relevant individual's personal file.

As regards verification of such documentation, the CRB has published guidance for service providers in its document *Dealing with Disclosure Application Forms*. In particular, service providers should always check for signs of tampering, and documents should be queried if they display any signs of damage, especially in the area of the name and/or photograph. Service providers should generally check the quality and condition of a passport and should treat it with suspicion if it is excessively damaged. Birth certificates are not wholly reliable for confirming identities since copies are easily obtained (certificates issued at the time of birth are more reliable than recently issued duplicates). The candidate's address should be verified by the provision of at least two of the following, which confirm the applicant's current address: a recent bank, mortgage, insurance, or credit card statement, or a recent council tax or utility bill. If the candidate has moved very recently and does not yet have a statement showing his or her current address, correspondence from the solicitor who handled the purchase of the property could be accepted provided this is printed on the solicitor's headed paper and includes or mentions the current address. If the candidate is in rented accommodation, a rent book or landlord's letter may also be considered sufficient evidence.

(4)   Recruitment checks to be satisfied prior to appointment

At interview it should also be made clear to the potential candidate that his or her appointment will be strictly subject to the following:

- that the service provider has obtained two written references in respect of the candidate with which it is satisfied, one of which is from the candidate's previous employer;
- that the candidate has provided and the service provider is satisfied with details of any criminal offences of which the candidate has been convicted (including spent convictions) or in respect of which the candidate has received a caution;
- that the standard disclosure/enhanced disclosure that the service provider is required by law to obtain in respect of the candidate is satisfactory and that in particular the potential candidate does not appear on the Government's list of individuals unsuitable to care for vulnerable adults or children;
- that the candidate has provided, and the service provider is satisfied with, evidence of the candidate's qualifications relevant to the post on offer;
- the candidate's satisfactory completion of a probationary period of at least 3 months;
- that the service provider is satisfied that the candidate is physically and mentally fit for the role on offer.

Where the candidate is provisionally offered a post following interview, all of the above should be reiterated in the letter offering the post to the candidate. As a matter of good recruitment practice (and as specifically required by some national minimum standards), the authors recommend that a contemporaneous written record is made of the interview and retained on the individual's personal file.

(5) Physical and mental fitness for the post

In regard to physical and mental fitness, it is difficult to strike a balance between complying with the 2000 Act, regulations and national minimum standards, and ensuring that service providers do not discriminate against disabled candidates during recruitment, contrary to the provisions of the Disability Discrimination Act 1995 (DDA 1995). An organisation that has 15 or more employees is subject to the DDA 1995 and therefore, in terms of recruitment, it will be unlawful to discriminate against disabled job applicants in terms of:

- the arrangements for determining who gets a job – this will cover everything from application forms, tests, interviews and criteria for selection;
- the terms offered;
- refusing or deliberately omitting to offer employment.

However, such discrimination will not be unlawful if it is necessary in order to comply with a legal requirement. Such a legal requirement would be the requirement under the 2000 Act that employees are physically and mentally fit for the role that they are to undertake. In order to ensure that any potential exposure to claims under the DDA 1995 is minimised, and that this 'compliance with a legal requirement' defence can be relied upon if necessary, service providers should ensure that they have appropriate guidance in place (eg in their recruitment policy) for employees who are responsible for recruitment for dealing with disabled applicants, to ensure that such candidates are genuinely not physically and/or mentally fit for the role on offer.

Service providers may also, as a matter of good recruitment practice, wish to bring the requirements of the 2000 Act in this regard to the candidate's attention in the application form and any provisional conditional offer letter, to the effect that, subject to the legal requirement that a service provider's staff are physically and mentally fit for their specific roles (in accordance with the 2000 Act), applicants suffering from a disability will be given the same consideration as other applicants. It is also prudent to obtain as much information about an applicant's disability as possible at an early stage and, again, a section can be included in the application form for the candidate to provide this information.

(6)   Job offers

Any job offer made to an individual after interview must, in the first instance, be both provisional and conditional upon the service provider obtaining the necessary recruitment information and documentation as explained to the candidate at interview (see para (4) above).

(7)   References

References will be vital, and service providers should institute a reference policy for use by employees who may routinely receive or be asked to provide references in respect of prospective candidates or former employees/volunteers. In respect of obtaining references, service providers should utilise a standard reference request that, particularly where the individual has worked with children, asks the former employer to provide details of any concerns that it has or may have had as to the individual's suitability to work with children.

9.3.3   Summary – core recruitment documentation

By carefully scrutinising candidates at the early stages of the recruitment process, looking for inconsistencies and gaps in the information they provide, asking the right questions in interviews concerning suitability for the post on offer, and taking up and verifying references and qualifications, service providers will be in a much better position to determine whether they have a suitable person for the vacancy. In summary, therefore, the core minimum recruitment documents which a service provider should put in place to aid compliance with the requirements of the new legislation and operate a thorough recruitment practice are as follows:

–   a recruitment policy to aid those responsible for recruitment. This policy should set out the checks that must be carried out and the information and documentation that must be obtained and verified prior to an individual taking up a position, how (where relevant) visits from the potential candidate to the establishment will form part of this process and how the candidate's physical and mental health will be assessed;

–   a checklist to ensure that all the recruitment checks and information required by the regulations and national minimum standards have been carried out and obtained. This checklist should be retained on an individual's personal file and updated as necessary;

- a pro forma provisional job offer letter setting out the conditions that must be satisfied before a firm offer of employment will be made;
- a reference policy and pro forma reference request.

9.3.4   National minimum standards – specific recruitment requirements

(1) *National Minimum Standards for Care Homes for Younger Adults* (Standard 32). Standard 32 sets out the attitudes and characteristics that staff must possess, and the skills and experience necessary for the tasks they are expected to undertake. Such requirements should be set out in the recruitment policy for use in establishments to which this national minimum standard applies (both to ensure that the requirements of the standard are met by assessment of these criteria as part of the interview process, and as a means of evidencing the same to the NSCS).

(2) *Children's homes, boarding schools, residential special schools and residential family centres.* Somewhat surprisingly, the Children's Homes Regulations 2001, reg 26(6) provides that a person can start work before the relevant qualification, reference and employment history information are obtained by a service provider (although *not* before a satisfactory disclosure is obtained) if the service provider considers that the circumstances are exceptional, has made every effort to chase the checks and references and, pending receipt of the remainder of the information required by the regulations, the person is appropriately supervised. Given the potentially adverse consequences of enabling an unsuitable individual to have access to children, service providers should treat this provision with caution and consider employing individuals in the circumstances permitted by reg 26(6) only if absolutely necessary. It must be made clear to the individual that continued employment in these circumstances will be subject to satisfactory outcomes from the remaining checks. Further provisions in this regard can be found in the *National Minimum Standards for Children's Homes* (Standard 27.5), the *National Minimum Standards for Boarding Schools* (Standard 38.7), the *National Minimum Standards for Residential Schools* (Standard 34.5) and the *National Minimum Standards for Residential Family Centres* (Standard 15.4).

(3) *National Minimum Standards for Nurses Agencies* (Standard 4.2). Even more surprisingly, the *National Minimum Standards for Nurses Agencies* (Standard 4.2) provides that:

> 'If a nurse is included on the list maintained by the Secretary of State for Health of individuals who are considered unsuitable to work with vulnerable adults (when the POVA list is operational), or the list maintained by the Secretary of State for Health of individuals who are considered unsuitable to work with children, or the Sex Offenders Register, and the agency believes that there are mitigating factors (for example a person who is on the list of individuals considered unsuitable to work with children, whose duties will not bring them into contact with children), the agency seeks agreement in writing from the NCSC before engaging or supplying that person.'

Although it is far from clear, since a standard cannot override the provisions of the primary legislation in the 2000 Act (ie that individuals who appear on these lists or registers cannot work with children or vulnerable adults), it must be assumed that Standard 4.2 is meant to take effect where a nurse will not be working with children or vulnerable adults. It is difficult to imagine circumstances in which this would be the case, and given that the whole purpose of the new legislation is to promote safer recruitment in order to protect children and vulnerable adults, this standard is somewhat at odds with that purpose. Nurses agencies should think very carefully indeed before engaging a person in the circumstances envisioned by Standard 4.2 (even with the NCSC's agreement in writing).

(4) *National Minimum Standards for Independent Healthcare Establishments* (Standard 9.2). In establishments subject to the Private and Voluntary Health Care (England) Regulations 2001 and national minimum standards, a declaration should be obtained from a potential candidate (prior to making an unconditional offer) as to whether he or she is currently the subject of any investigation or proceedings by any body having regulatory functions in the health/social care professions, including such regulatory body in another country, and whether he or she has ever been disqualified from the practice of a profession or required to practice it subject to specified limitations following a fitness to practise investigation by a registered body in the United Kingdom or another country. For establishments to which these provisions apply, these requirements can be reflected in the standard application form in order to obtain this declaration at an early stage.

9.3.5 Agency staff, contract workers and other individuals not directly engaged by a service provider

Checks required for agency staff and other individuals who are not engaged by the service provider as employees or volunteers but who will, nevertheless, have access to children and vulnerable individuals in the service provider's care are also addressed in the regulations dealing with fitness of workers. Although there are minor variations between the regulations applicable to different types of establishment, on the whole the regulations provide that, where a person is employed by someone other than a registered person in a position in which, during the course of his or her normal duties, he or she will have regular contact with the service users at/of the establishment/agency then the registered person will not allow that person to work at or for the establishment/agency unless:

(a) the person is fit to work at/for the establishment/agency;
(b) the employer (generally the employment agency) has obtained the information set out in the relevant schedule to the regulations (which details the information that must be obtained in respect of all recruits to determine their fitness (see para **9.4**)) and has confirmed in writing to the registered person that he or she has done so; and

(c)   the employer is satisfied on reasonable grounds as to the authenticity of the references in respect of that person and has confirmed in writing to the registered person that he or she is so satisfied.

However, further checks which must be carried out on agency workers and which are set out in the relevant national minimum standards are not entirely consistent. Some provide (eg the *National Minimum Standards for Children's Homes* (Standard 27.3)) that a registered provider must simply ensure that individuals provided by an agency who work in a children's home have successfully passed the checks required under the Children's Homes Regulations 2001 within the previous 12 months, evidence of which is placed on an individual's file. Other standards (eg the *National Minimum Standards for Boarding Schools* (Standard 28.9), *Residential Special Schools* (Standard 27.9), *Further Education Colleges Providing Accommodation to Students Under 18* (Standard 34.7) and *Residential Family Centres* (Standard 15.8)) give the service provider several alternatives:

–   the service provider ensures that the agency has carried out the necessary recruitment checks within the previous 12 months; or
–   the service provider has a satisfactory system for carrying out CRB checks on agency staff; or
–   agency staff do not have unsupervised access to service users.

Specific reference is also made in the *National Minimum Standards for Boarding Schools* (Standard 38.10) and *Residential Special Schools* (Standard 27.9) as regards checks on taxi drivers, which are again inconsistent. Essentially, both standards require the school to take reasonably practicable steps to carry out CRB checks on taxi drivers booked by the school to drive boarders unaccompanied by staff. However, Standard 27.9 also provides that as an alternative, residential special schools can simply take steps to satisfy themselves that such checks have already been carried out on taxi drivers. Standard 38.10 therefore appears to require that boarding schools must themselves carry out checks on taxi drivers, rather than, in the case of residential special schools, giving the school the option to check with the taxi driver's provider that such checks have been carried out.

Clearly, this requirement to obtain disclosures in respect of agency and other workers not engaged directly by a service provider may cause some difficulties in practice, particularly as the final versions of the Nurses Agencies Regulations 2002 and the Domiciliary Care Agencies Regulations 2002 no longer require these agencies to have carried out a CRB check on the staff they supply (albeit that such agencies are required to obtain 'details' from such staff of their criminal convictions). The key question is whether a service provider would be entitled to ask exempt questions about individuals, and so countersign and be provided with copies of their disclosures. The ROA 1974 is far from clear on this point, but it is submitted that on a broad interpretation of the provisions of the Act, a service provider could ask individuals who are not its employees or whom it is not recruiting (such as agency staff and taxi drivers) to apply for a disclosure and so be provided with the results of that disclosure.

Clearly, agency staff will still have to have CRB checks to work in particular types of establishments where the regulations in respect of those establishments require it. One possible solution to the practical difficulties and the uncertainty surrounding a service provider's entitlement to ask exempt questions in respect of agency workers is for the service provider to act as an umbrella body for either the agency supplying the staff or the contractor whose staff will be used. How the disclosure information is handled, and the basis of any decision made as a result, can then be dealt with expressly in an agreement between the service provider and the contractor, as detailed above.

Alternatively, service providers can simply seek written confirmation from the agency that all checks have been carried out within the past 12 months. Clearly, the risks here are that the information provided by the agency may be incorrect (which the service provider has no way of confirming) or, perhaps more significantly, that a further offence has been committed since the disclosure was obtained (which, in theory, could be as much as 11 months and 30 days previously), which the service provider will have no way of knowing. If the service provider has any concerns then it should require the individual to apply for a disclosure, with either the service provider or agency as a countersignatory.

Individuals are free to provide copies of their disclosures to whomsoever they choose, and this may also be a means of satisfying the relevant regulations and standards. In such circumstances service providers should, of course, ensure that all information has been properly checked and there is no possibility of fraud on behalf of the employee (see para **9.2.9**).

9.4   RECRUITMENT CHECKS – THE LAW

9.4.1   Care homes

(1)   *Care Homes Regulations 2001*

The Care Homes Regulations 2001, together with the *National Minimum Standards for Care Homes for Younger Adults* and the *National Minimum Standards for Care Homes for Older People*, form the basis of the new regulatory framework under the 2000 Act for the conduct of care homes.

Regulation 19 of the Care Homes Regulations 2001[1] states that:

'(1)   The registered person shall not employ a person to work at the care home unless –

(a)   the person is fit to work at the care home;

(b)   subject to paragraph (6), he has obtained in respect of that person the following information and the documents specified in . . . paragraphs 1 to 7 of Schedule 2; [*unless paragraph 7 below applies in which case the documents in paragraphs 1–6 and 8 of Schedule 2*], namely:

"1   Proof of the person's identity, including a recent photograph.

2   The person's birth certificate.

3   The person's current passport (if any).

---

1   See Author's Note on p 248 re use of italics in the following provisions.

4   Documentary evidence of any relevant qualifications of the person.
5   Two written references relating to the person.
6   Evidence that the person is physically and mentally fit for the purposes of the work which he is to perform at the care home or, where it is impracticable for the person to obtain such evidence, a declaration signed by the person that he is so fit.
7   Either ... an enhanced criminal record certificate ... or ... a criminal record certificate ....
8   *Details of any criminal offences (a) of which the person has been convicted including details of any convictions which are spent within the meaning of section 1 of the Rehabilitation of Offenders Act 1974 and which may be disclosed by virtue of the Rehabilitation of Offenders Act 1974 (Exceptions) Order 1975; or (b) in respect of which he has been cautioned by a constable and which, at the time the caution was given he admitted.*"]

   (c)   he is satisfied on reasonable grounds of the authenticity of the references referred to in paragraph 5 of Schedule 2 in respect of that person.

(2) This paragraph applies to a person who is employed by a person ("the employer") other than the registered person.

(3) This paragraph applies to a position in which a person may in the course of his duties have regular contact with service users at the care home or with any other person of a description specified in section 3(2) of the Act.

(4) The registered person shall not allow a person to whom paragraph (2) applies to work at the care home in a position to which paragraph (3) applies, unless –

   (a)   the person is fit to work at the care home;
   (b)   the employer has obtained in respect of that person the information and documents specified in –

      (i)   paragraphs 1 to 7 of Schedule 2;
      (ii)   *except where paragraph (7) applies, paragraph 7 of that Schedule;*
      (iii) *where paragraph (7) applies, paragraph 8 of that Schedule*
      and has confirmed in writing to the registered person that he has done so; and

   (c)   the employer is satisfied on reasonable grounds as to the authenticity of the references referred to in paragraph 5 of Schedule 2 in respect of that person, and has confirmed in writing to the registered person that he is so satisfied.

(5) For the purposes of paragraphs (1) and (4), a person is not fit to work at a care home unless –

   (a)   he is of integrity and good character;
   (b)   he has the qualifications suitable to the work that he is to perform, and the skills and experience necessary for such work;
   (c)   he is physically and mentally fit for the purposes of work which he is to perform at the care home; and
   (d)   full and satisfactory information is available in relation to him in respect of the following matters –

      (i)   each of the matters specified in paragraphs 1 to 7 of Schedule 2;
      (ii)   *except where paragraph (7) applies, each of the matters specified in paragraph 7 of that Schedule;*

>   (iii) *where paragraph (7) applies, each of the matters specified in paragraph 8 of that Schedule.*
>
> (6) Paragraphs (1)(b) and (5)(d), insofar as they relate to paragraph 7 of Schedule 2, shall not apply until 31st October 2004 in respect of a person who immediately before 1st April 2002 is employed to work at the care home.
>
> (7) *This paragraph applies where any certificates or information on any matters referred to in paragraph 7 of Schedule 2 is not available to an individual because any provision of the Police Act 1997 has not been brought into force.*'

[**Author's Note:** Regulation 19(7) was included in the final draft of the Care Homes Regulations 2001 (and many of the other regulations detailed below) in anticipation of the fact that the CRB's disclosure service may not have been operational when this legislation was due to come into force on 1 April 2002. This did not prove to be the case, and the disclosure service is and has been provided by the CRB from April 2002 (albeit subject to considerable delays). It is therefore not the case that a CRB certificate cannot be obtained because certain sections of the Police Act 1997 have not been brought into effect, and therefore obtaining information about an individual's criminal records and/or cautions from him or her (whilst good recruitment practice) is not an alternative to obtaining a disclosure from the CRB. This provision (and the equivalent provisions of the regulations set out below) is now no longer applicable, and for ease of reference, whilst included for completeness, provisions highlighted in italics in the following and preceding regulations should be ignored.]

Regulation 9 states that:

> '(1) A person shall not manage a care home unless he is fit to do so.
>
> (2) A person is not fit to manage a care home unless –
>
>   (a) he is of integrity and good character;
>
>   (b) having regard to the size of the care home, the statement of purpose, and the number and the needs of the service users –
>
>   (i) he has the qualifications, skills and experience necessary for managing the care home; and
>
>   (ii) he is physically and mentally fit to manage the care home; and
>
>   (c) full and satisfactory information is available in relation to him in respect of the following matters –
>
>   (i) the matters specified in paragraphs 1 to 5 and 7 of Schedule 2;
>
>   (ii) *except where paragraph (3) applies, the matters specified in paragraph 7 of that Schedule;*
>
>   (iii) *where paragraph (3) applies, the matters specified in paragraph 8 of that Schedule.*
>
> (3) *This paragraph applies where any certificate or information on any matters referred to in paragraph 7 of Schedule 2 is not available to an individual because any provision of the Police Act 1997 has not been brought into force.*'

Each of the regulations set out below also includes a regulation dealing with the fitness of the registered manager. These are in largely equivalent terms and further detail is not provided in this text:

– Children's Homes Regulations 2001, reg 8;

- Fostering Services Regulations 2002, reg 7;
- Domiciliary Care Agencies Regulations 2002, reg 10;
- Private and Voluntary Healthcare (England) Regulations 2001, reg 12;
- Residential Family Centres Regulations 2002, reg 7;
- Nurses Agency Regulations 2002, reg 6.

(2) *National Minimum Standards for Care Homes for Younger Adults*

Standard 32 states that:

'32.1 Staff must have the competencies and qualities required to meet service users' needs and achieve Sector Skills Council workforce or strategy targets within the required timescales.

32.2 Staff must respect service users and have attitudes and characteristics that are important to them. They are:

(i)   accessible to, approachable by and comfortable with service users;
(ii)   good listeners and communicators;
(iii) reliable and honest; and
(iv)   interested motivated and committed.

32.3 Staff have the skills and experience necessary for the tasks they are expected to do including:

(i)   knowledge of the disabilities and specific conditions of service users;
(ii)   specialist skills to meet service users' individual needs including skills in communication and in dealing with anticipated behaviours;
(iii) understanding of physical and verbal aggression and self harm as a way of communicating needs, preferences and frustrations;
(iv)   understanding of the cultural and religious heritage of each service user;
(v)   techniques for rehabilitation including treatment and recovery programmes, the promotion of mobility, continence and self care, and outreach programs to re-establish community living;
(vi)   appreciation of and ability to balance the particular and fluctuating needs of individuals and the needs of all service users; and
(vii) professional relationships with eg GPs, social workers, nurses, psychiatrists, therapists and staff working in other care homes and community and specialist agencies.'

Standard 33 requires that:

'33.10 Staff providing intimate personal care for service users are at least 18 and staff left in charge of the home are at least age 21.'

Standard 34 (Recruitment) states:

'34.1 The registered person operates a thorough recruitment procedure based on equal opportunities and ensuring the protection of service users.

34.2 Two written references are obtained before making an appointment and any gaps in the employment record explored.

34.3 New staff are confirmed in post only following completion of a satisfactory police check, satisfactory check of the Protection of Children and Vulnerable Adults and the UKCC registers.

34.4	Service users are actively supported to be involved in staff selection and are supported throughout the processes of joining and departure of staff.
34.5	Staff are employed in accordance with and are given copies of the codes of conduct and practice set by the GSCC.
34.6	All staff receive statements of terms and conditions.
34.7	All staff appointments are subject to a minimum three month probationary period and service users are involved in their review.
34.8	The recruitment and selection of volunteers is thorough and includes police and POVA/POCA checks.'

[**Author's Note:** (1) The UKCC (the UK Central Council for Nurses, Midwives and Health Visitors) is now known as the Nursing and Midwifery Council (NMC). (2) References in the Regulations and Standards to (a) GSCC means the General Social Care Council; and (b) POVA and POCA means the lists of individuals held by the Secretary of State who are unsuitable to work with vulnerable adults and children.]

## (3)	*National Minimum Standards for Care Homes for Older People*

Standard 27 requires that:

'27.6	Staff providing personal care to service users are at least aged 18; staff left in charge of the home are at least aged 21.'

Standard 29 (Recruitment) states that:

'29.1	The registered person operates a thorough recruitment procedure based on equal opportunities and ensuring the protection of service users.
29.2	Two written references are obtained before appointing a member of staff, and any gaps in employment records are explored.
29.3	New staff are confirmed in post only following completion of a satisfactory police check and satisfactory check of the Protection of Children and Vulnerable Adults and UKCC Registers.
29.4	Staff are employed in accordance with the Code of Conduct and Practice set by the GSCC and are given copies of the Code.
29.5	All staff receive statements of terms and conditions.
29.6	The recruitment and selection process for any volunteers involved in the home is thorough and includes police checks.'

## 9.4.2	Children's homes

The Children's Homes Regulations 2001, together with the *National Minimum Standards for Children's Homes*, the *National Minimum Standards for Boarding Schools*, the *National Minimum Standards for Residential Special Schools* and the *National Minimum Standards for Accommodation of Students Under 18 by Further Education Colleges* form the basis of the new regulatory framework under the 2000 Act for the conduct of establishments in which children are accommodated.

## (1)	*Children's Homes Regulations 2001*

Regulation 26 of the Children's Homes Regulations 2001 states that:

'(1)	The registered person shall not –

(a) employ a person to work at the children's home unless that person is fit to work at a children's home; or

(b) allow a person to whom paragraph (2) applies to work at the children's home unless that person is fit to work at a children's home.

(2) This paragraph applies to any person who is employed by a person other than the registered person to work at the children's home in a position in which he may in the course of his duties have regular contact with children accommodated there.

(3) For the purposes of paragraph (1), the person is not fit to work at a children's home unless –

(a) he is of integrity and good character;

(b) he has the qualifications, skills and experience necessary for the work he is to perform;

(c) he is physically and mentally fit for the purposes of the work he is to perform; and

(d) full and satisfactory information is available in relation to him in respect of each of the matters specified in Schedule 2 [namely:

> "1 Proof of identity including a recent photograph.
>
> 2 Either ... an enhanced criminal records certificate ... or ... a criminal records certificate ....
>
> 3 Two written references, including a reference from the person's most recent employer, if any.
>
> 4 Where a person has previously worked in a position whose duties involved work with children or vulnerable adults, so far as reasonably practicable verification of the reason why the employment or position ended.
>
> 5 Documentary evidence of any relevant qualifications.
>
> 6 A full employment history together with a satisfactory written explanation of any gaps in employment.
>
> 7 *Details of any criminal offences (a) of which the person has been convicted including details of any convictions which are spent within the meaning of section 1 of the Rehabilitation of Offenders Act 1974 and which may be disclosed by virtue of the Rehabilitation of Offenders Act 1974 (Exceptions) Order 1975; or (b) in respect of which he has been cautioned by a constable and which, at the time the caution was given he admitted."]*

(4) *This paragraph applies where any certificate or information on any matters referred to in paragraph 2 of Schedule 2 is not available to an individual because any provision of the Police Act 1997 has not been brought into force.*

(5) The registered person shall ensure that –

(a) any offer of employment to a person is subject to paragraph (3)(d) being complied with in relation to that person; and

(b) unless paragraph (6) applies, no person starts work at a children's home until such time as paragraph (3)(d) has been complied with in relation to him.

(6) Where the following conditions apply, the registered person may permit a person to start work at a children's home notwithstanding paragraph (5)(b) –

   (a) the registered person has taken all reasonable steps to obtain full information in respect of each of the matters listed in Schedule 2 in respect of that person but the enquiries in relation to any of the matters listed in paragraphs 3 to 6 of Schedule 2 are incomplete;

   (b) full and satisfactory information in respect of that person has been obtained in relation to the matters specified in paragraphs 1 and 2 of Schedule 2;

   (c) the registered person considers that the circumstances are exceptional; and

   (d) pending receipt of, and satisfying himself with regard to, any outstanding information, the registered person ensures that the person is appropriately supervised whilst carrying out his duties.

(6)[1] The registered person shall take reasonable steps to ensure that any person working at the children's home who is not employed by him and to whom paragraph (2) does not apply, is appropriately supervised while carrying out his duties.'

Regulation 27 states that:

'(1) The registered person shall –

   (a) ensure that all permanent appointments are subject to the satisfactory completion of a period of probation; and

   (b) provide all employees with a job description outlining their responsibilities.'

[**Author's note:** Please refer to the Author's note in respect of reg 19(7) of the Care Homes Regulations 2001 (at para **9.4.1**) for an explanation of the provisions in italics.]

(2) National Minimum Standards for Children's Homes

Standard 27 (Vetting of Staff and Visitors) states that:

'27.1 There is a written record of the recruitment process which is followed in respect of all staff (including ancillary staff and those on a contractual/ sessional basis) and volunteers who work with children in the home including evidence that all the requirements of Schedule 2 of the Children Homes Regulations 2001 have been met in every case.

27.2 The registered person's system for recruiting staff (including ancillary staff and those on a contractual/sessional basis) and volunteers who work with children in the home includes an effective system to decide on appointment, or refusal of appointment of staff or others likely to have regular contact with children at the home, in the light of any criminal convictions or other concerns about suitability that are declared or discovered through the recruitment process.

---

1   Information: It is thought that this paragraph is incorrectly numbered owing to an error in drafting.

27.3 The registered person ensures that any staff provided through an agency who work with the children in the home have successfully passed the checks that are required in the Children's Home Regulations 2001 within the previous 12 months. There must be evidence of this, which is placed on their file. The check will be at an "enhanced level" for staff and volunteers involved in regularly caring for, supervising, training or being in sole charge of children and at that the "standard" level for all others working as paid staff or volunteers on the premises of the home or school.

27.4 The registered person has taken reasonably practicable steps to ensure that where children are driven in taxis arranged by the home, they are either accompanied by staff or other arrangements have been made to ensure that their welfare is safeguarded on the journey.

27.5 Staff members and others subject to the above checks do not normally start work at the home until all checks required in the Children's Home Regulations 2001 are completed. Exceptionally, a member of staff may be allowed to do so while the outcome of some checks are awaited but, once the Criminal Records Bureau is operational, in every case the appropriate check via the Criminal Records Bureau must have been completed before the person starts work. In such circumstances the registered person must ensure that:

- the individual is directly supervised at all times at a level that prevents them having unsupervised contact with children in the home;
- such circumstances are exceptional;
- the registered person has taken all reasonable steps to complete the recruitment process and to chase outstanding information; and
- the registered person has taken all reasonable steps to avoid such circumstances occurring.

Continued employment in such circumstances is subject to satisfactory outcomes from the checks.

27.6 The registered person provides information about the purpose of the home, consistent with its statement of purpose to all applicants for all posts in the home.

27.7 Wherever practicable, short listed applicants for appointment to any post in the home are invited for a visit to the home and to meet staff and children (subject to the children's agreement) prior to the decision on appointment being made, and observations sought from staff and children, which are taken into account in the appointment decision.'

(3) *National Minimum Standards for Boarding Schools*

Standard 22 (Educational Guardians) states that:

'22.3 Any guardians appointed by the school to look after pupils should be subject to the staff recruitment procedures set out in Standard 38 and Criminal Records Bureau checks with a satisfactory outcome before they are able to work for the school and their care of pupils should be monitored.'

Standard 38 (Staff Recruitment and Checks on Other Adults) states that:

'38.1   Recruitment of all staff (including ancillary staff and those on a contractual/ sessional basis) and volunteers who work with boarders includes checks through the Criminal Records Bureau checking system (enhanced as appropriate), with a satisfactory outcome. There is a satisfactory recruitment process recorded in writing.

38.2   The school's system for recruiting staff (including ancillary staff, contract/ sessional staff and volunteers) who will work with boarders includes all the following before appointment, which can be verified from recruitment records;

- check of identity against an official document such as a passport or birth certificate;
- Criminal Records Bureau check at highest level available for the role concerned;
- at least two written references including the most recent employer, with a reference request letter that specifically asks all referees to state any known reason why the person should not be employed to work with children and that there should be no material misstatement or omission relevant to the suitability of the applicant;
- direct contact by the school with each referee to verify the reference;
- interview, with a written record of the outcome;
- check on proof of relevant qualifications;
- requirement that applicants supply a full employment history, stating that any previous employer may be approached by the school;
- contact by the school where feasible with each previous employer involving work with children or vulnerable adults to check the reasons the employment ended; and
- explanations of any gaps in an applicant's CV, with a written record by the school that explanations for any gaps have been sought and are satisfactory.

38.3   For all adults who after April 2002 began to live on the same premises as children/students (for example adult members of staff households) but are not employed by the school there is a verifiable Criminal Records Bureau check completed at the standard level.

38.4   Appointment of "gap" student staff includes every element of the above recruitment checking system that is possible (even if the student concerned is already known to the school or to a trusted school abroad or is recruited through an agency).

38.5   Where "gap" student staff are recruited from abroad the school obtains a "certificate of good conduct" or equivalent from the relevant authorities of the student's home country where such facilities are available.

38.6   Offers of appointment to staff and others subject to recruitment checks are made subject to satisfactory completion of Criminal Records checks and satisfactory references if not all yet received.

38.7   Staff members subject to the requirements set out in 38.2 do not begin work (or residence) at the school until satisfactory completion of all checks and receipt of references. Exceptionally, a member of staff may begin work if some references/checks are outstanding, but all Criminal Records Bureau checks must have been completed. In such cases there must be evidence that every effort has been made to chase the checks and references and the person must be supervised so that they do not have substantial unsupervised access to boarders.

38.8 Criminal Records Bureau checks and references are included in the recruitment process for any Guardians arranged by the school and all adults living in lodgings arranged by the school, with a satisfactory outcome received and recorded in writing by the school before any boarder is placed.

38.9 The school either has a satisfactory system for carrying out Criminal Record Bureau checks on agency staff who have regular contact with boarders or the staff do not have unsupervised access to boarders or has evidence that the agency has carried out the necessary checks within the last twelve months.

38.10 The school has taken reasonably practicable steps to carry out Criminal Records Bureau checks on taxi drivers booked by the school to drive boarders unaccompanied by staff.'

(4) *National Minimum Standards for Residential Special Schools*

Standard 27 (Vetting of Staff and Visitors). The terms of this standard mirror standard 28 in the *National Minimum Standards for Boarding Schools* with minor differences being found in the following standards:

'27.5 Where Criminal Records Bureau checks or equivalent are not available for "gap" student staff, the school obtains a "certificate of good conduct" or equivalent from the relevant authorities of the student's home country where such facilities are available.

. . .

27.9 The school *either* has Criminal Records Bureau checks or equivalent on agency staff or has evidence that the agency has carried out the necessary checks within the last 12 months. The school has taken all reasonably practicable steps to carry out Criminal Records Bureau checks or to satisfy themselves such checks have been carried out on taxi drivers booked by the school to drive children at the school unaccompanied by staff.'

(5) *National Minimum Standards for Accommodation of Students under 18 by Further Education Colleges*

Standard 30 (Staff Job Description, Induction, Supervision and Training) states that:

'30.1 All staff with particular responsibilities for the supervision of residential students or the provision of student welfare services have job descriptions reflecting those duties, have appropriate competence, receive induction training in those responsibilities when newly appointed, and receive regular review of their supervisory and student welfare practice with opportunities for continuing training.

30.2 The college has provided job descriptions to staff with responsibilities for supervision of residential students or the provision of student welfare services which accurately and clearly reflect their current responsibilities and duties.

30.3 Staff with responsibilities for supervision of residential students or provision of student welfare services have relevant qualifications and/or experience and competence for the task and level of responsibility they undertake.

30.4 The college has clear arrangements for the supervision of ancillary and contract staff and any temporary or agency staff or volunteers working at the college.

30.5 The college has an appropriate induction training program in supervising and in safeguarding and promoting the welfare of residential students, provided for newly appointed staff with responsibilities for supervision of residential students or the provision of student welfare services.'

Standard 34 (Staff Recruitment and Checks on Other Adults) states that:

'34.1 Recruitment of all staff (including ancillary staff and those on a contract/ sessional basis) and volunteers who work with students under 18 includes checks through the Criminal Records Bureau at the standard or enhanced level as applicable to their role and with a satisfactory outcome. There is a satisfactory recruitment process recorded in writing.

34.2 The college's system for recruiting staff (including ancillary staff, contract/ sessional staff and volunteers) who will work with students under 18 includes all the following before appointment, which can be verified from recruitment records:

(i)   check of identity against an official document;

(ii)   Criminal Records Bureau checks, at the highest level available, with a written record demonstrating that these checks have been done with a satisfactory outcome;

(iii) written references, including the most recent employer, with a reference request letter that specifically asks all referees to state any known reason why the person should not be employed to work with young people and that there should be no material misstatement or omission relevant to the suitability of the applicant;

(iv)   direct contact by the college with each referee to verify the reference;

(v)   interview, with a written record of the outcome;

(vi)   check on proof of relevant qualifications, with a written record of its completion;

(vii) requirement that the applicants supply a full employment history, stating that the previous employer may be approached by the college;

(viii) contact by the college with each previous employer involving work with children, young people or vulnerable adults to check the reason the employment ended;

(ix)   explanation of any gaps in CV, with a written record by the college that an explanation for any gaps have been sought and are satisfactory;

...

34.4 Offers of appointment to staff and others subject to the above recruitment checks are made subject to satisfactory completion of Criminal Records Bureau checks and satisfactory references if not all yet received.

34.5 Staff members (and others) are subject to the requirements set out in 34.2 do not begin work (or residence) at the FE college until satisfactory completion of all checks and receipt of references. Exceptionally, a member of staff may begin work if some references/checks are outstanding, but all Criminal Records Bureau checks must have been completed. In such cases, there must be evidence that every effort has been made to chase checks and references, and the person must be supervised so that they do not have substantial unsupervised access to residential students under 18.

34.6 For all adults who after April 2002 begin to live on the same premises as children (for example adult members of staff households) who are not employed by the school, there is a verifiable Criminal Records Bureau check completed at the standard level.

34.7 The college either has a satisfactory system for carrying out Criminal Records Bureau checks on agency staff who have regular contact with young people under 18 or has satisfactory arrangements to ensure that the college does not give such staff substantial unsupervised access to students under 18 or has proof that the agency has carried out the necessary checks within the past 12 months.'

9.4.3 Fostering services

The Fostering Services Regulations 2002, together with the *National Minimum Standards for Fostering Services*, form the basis of the new regulatory framework under the 2000 Act for the conduct of fostering services.

(1) Fostering Services Regulations 2002

Regulation 20 of the Fostering Services Regulations 2002 states that:

'(1) The fostering service provider shall not –

(a) employ a person to work for the purposes of the fostering service unless that person is fit to work for the purposes of a fostering service; or

(b) allow a person to whom paragraph (2) applies, to work for the purposes of the fostering service unless that person is fit to work for the purposes of a fostering service.

(2) This paragraph applies to any person who is employed by a person other than the fostering service provider in a position in which he may in the course of his duties have regular contact with children placed by the fostering service.

(3) For the purposes of paragraph (1), a person is not fit to work for the purposes of a fostering service unless –

(a) he is of integrity and good character;

(b) he has the qualifications, skills and experience necessary for the work he is to perform;

(c) he is physically and mentally fit for the work he is to perform; and

(d) full and satisfactory information is available in relation to him in respect of each of the following matters specified in Schedule 1 [namely:

"1 Proof of identity including a recent photograph.

2 Either ... a criminal records certificate ... or ... an enhanced criminal records certificate ....

3 Two written references, including a reference from the person's most recent employment, if any.

4 Where a person has previously worked in a position whose duties involved work with children or vulnerable adults, so far as reasonably practicable verification of the reason why the employment or position ended.

5 Documentary evidence of any relevant qualifications.

6 A full employment history together with a satisfactory written explanation of any gaps in employment.

7   *Details of any criminal offences (a) of which the person has been convicted including details of any convictions which are spent within the meaning of section 1 of Rehabilitation of Offenders Act 1974 and which may be disclosed by virtue of the Rehabilitation of Offenders Act 1974 (Exceptions Order) 1975 or (b) in respect of which he has been cautioned by a constable and which, at the time the caution was given, he had admitted."]*

(4)   *This paragraph applies where any certificate or information on any matters referred to in paragraph 2 of Schedule 1 is not available to an individual because any provision of the Police Act 1997 has not been brought into force.*

(5)   The fostering service provider shall take reasonable steps to ensure that any person working for a fostering service who is not employed by him and to whom paragraph (2) does not apply, is appropriately supervised while carrying out his duties.

(6)   Subject to regulation 50(7) the fostering service provider shall not employ to work for the purposes of the fostering service in a position to which paragraph (7) applies, a person who is –

(a)   a foster parent approved by the fostering service; or
(b)   a member of the household of such a foster parent.

(7)   This paragraph applies to any management, social work or other professional position unless in the case of a position which is not a management or a social work position, the work is undertaken on an occasional basis, as a volunteer, or for no more than five hours in any week.'

Regulation 50(7) provides that reg 20(6) above shall not apply to any person to whom it would, apart from this regulation, apply if he was, on 1 April 2002, already employed by a fostering service provider in a position to which reg 20(7) applies.

Regulation 21 states that:

'(1)   The fostering service provider shall –

(a)   ensure that all permanent appointments are subject to the satisfactory completion of a period of probation; and
(b)   provide all employees with a job description outlining their responsibilities.'

[**Author's Note:** Please refer to the Author's note in respect of reg 19(7) of the Care Homes Regulations 2001 (at para **9.4.1**) for an explanation of the provisions in italics.]

(2)   *National Minimum Standards for Fostering Services*

Standard 15 (Suitability to Work with Children) states that:

'15.1   Any people working in or for the fostering service are suitable people to work with children and young people and to safeguard and promote their welfare.

15.2 There are clear written recruitment and selection procedures for appointing staff which follow good practice in safeguarding children and young people. All personnel responsible for recruitment and selection of staff are trained in, understand and operate these.

15.3 All people working in or for the fostering service are interviewed as part of the selection process and have references checked to assess suitability before taking on responsibilities. Telephone enquiries are made as well as obtaining written references.

15.4 Records are kept of checks and references that have been obtained and their outcomes. Police checks are renewed every three years.

15.5 All social work staff have an appropriate qualification, or are in the course of obtaining a suitable professional qualification, to work with children and young people, their families and foster carers, and have a good understanding of foster care. They have appropriate knowledge and skills. These include:

- understanding of the Children Act, the Children Act Regulations and Guidance, relevant current policies and procedures, Working Together and associated child protection guidance, the Framework for the Assessment of Children in Need and their Families, the regulatory requirements under the Care Standards Act 2000 and adoption law;
- knowledge of the growth and development of children and an ability to communicate with children and young people;
- understanding the importance of a complaints procedure;
- an ability to promote equality, diversity and the rights of individuals and groups;
- knowledge of the roles of other agencies, in particular health and education.

15.6 Any social work staff involved in assessment and approval of foster carers are qualified social workers, have experience of foster care and family placement work and are trained in assessment. Students and others who do not meet this requirement carry out assessments and approvals under the supervision of someone who does, who takes responsibility for the assessments and approvals.

15.7 All education lists, psychologists, therapists and other professional staff are professionally qualified and appropriately trained to work with children and young people, their families and foster carers and have a good understanding of foster care.

15.8 Where unqualified staff carry out social work functions they do so under the direct supervision of qualified social workers, who are accountable for their work.'

Standard 17 (Sufficient Staff/Carers with the Right Skills/Experience) states that:

'17.5 The fostering service has a recruitment policy and strategy aimed at recruiting a range of carers to meet the needs of children and young people for whom it aims to provide a service.'

Standard 18 (Fair and Competent Employer) requires that:

'18.1 Fostering services are fair and competent employers, with sound employment practices and good support for its staff and carers.

18.2 There are sound employment policies, in relation to both staff and carers.

...

18.6   For agencies, there is a public liability and professional indemnity insurance for all staff and carers. The insurance policy covers costs arising as a result of child abuse claims against any staff or carers.'

9.4.4   Private and voluntary health care establishments

The Private and Voluntary Healthcare (England) Regulations 2001 and the *National Minimum Standards for Independent Healthcare* form the regulatory framework for the operation of independent hospitals, clinics and medical agencies.

(1)   Private and Voluntary Healthcare (England) Regulations 2001

Regulation 19 of the Private and Voluntary Healthcare (England) Regulations 2001 states that:

'(1)   The registered person shall ensure that –

(a)   no person is employed to work in or for the purposes of the establishment or for the purposes of the agency; and

(b)   no medical practitioner is granted consulting or practising privileges,

unless that person is fit to work in or for the purposes of the establishment, or for the purposes of the agency.

(2)   a person is not fit to work in or for the purposes of an establishment, or for the purposes of an agency unless –

(a)   he is of integrity and good character;

(b)   he has the qualifications, skills and experience which are necessary for the work which he is to perform;

(c)   he is physically and mentally fit for that work; and

(d)   full and satisfactory information is available in relation to him in respect of each of the matters specified in Schedule 2 [namely:

"1   Positive proof of identity including a recent photograph.

2   Either –

(a)   where the certificate is required for a purpose relating to section 115(5)(ea) of the Police Act 1997 (registration under Part II of the Care Standards Act 2000), or the position falls within section 115(3) or (4) of that Act, an enhanced criminal record certificate issued under section 115 of that Act; or

(b)   in any other case, a criminal record certificate issued under section 113 of that Act,

including, where applicable, the matters specified in section 113(3A) or (3C) or 115(6A) or (6B) of that Act.

3   Two written references, being references from the person's most recent employers, if any.

4   Where a person had previously worked in a position which involved work with children or vulnerable adults, verification, so far as reasonably practicable, of the reason why he ceased to work in that position.

5   Documentary evidence of any relevant qualifications.
6   A full employment history, together with a satisfactory written explanation of any gaps in employment.
7   Where he is a health care professional details of his registration with the body (if any) responsible for regulation of members of the health care profession in question;
8   *Details of any criminal offences (a) of which the person had been convicted including details of any convictions which are spent within the meaning of section 1 of the Rehabilitation of Offenders Act 1974 and which may be disclosed by virtue of the Rehabilitation of Offenders (Exceptions) Order 1975; or (b) in respect of which he had been cautioned by a constable and which, at the time the caution was given, he admitted."*]

[**Author's Note:** Please refer to the Author's note in respect of reg 19(7) of the Care Homes Regulations 2001 (at para **9.4.1**) for an explanation of the provisions in italics.]

(2)   *National Minimum Standards for Independent Healthcare*

Standard C9 (Human Resources Policies and Procedures) states that:

'C9.1   There is a written human resources policy and supporting procedures, in line with current employment legislation.

C9.2   There are pre- and post-employment procedures that:

*   define the way in which advertising, selection, recruitment, induction, employment and retention of staff is managed;
*   ensure that at the short listing stage, prior to making an unconditional offer of employment, a declaration is obtained from a successful applicant as to whether he/she:

    o   is currently the subject of any police investigation and/or prosecution, in the UK or any other country;
    o   has ever been convicted of any criminal offence required by law to be disclosed, received a police caution in the UK, or a criminal conviction in any other country;
    o   is currently the subject of any investigation or proceedings by any body having regulatory functions in relation to health/social care professionals including such a regulatory body in another country;
    o   has ever been disqualified from the practice of a profession or required to practise it subject to specified limitations following a fitness to practise investigation by a regulatory body, in the UK or another country;

*   ensure that all staff are interviewed before employment, and that records of interview and written references are retained. Ensure that qualifications relevant to the post applied for are verified by validation at the interview;
*   ensure that prior to employment, the relevant regulatory/licensing body is asked to confirm whether the applicant is appropriately registered, whether that registration covers the duties to be undertaken and whether there are any restrictions in place or investigations under way;
*   ensure that employment references are sought from the two most recent employers prior to making an offer of employment;

- ensure that indemnification is checked and authenticated for healthcare professionals;
- ensure that documentary proof is maintained of the continuing registration of professional staff with their respective regulatory body;
- ensure job specifications, performance review, appraisal and line management arrangements are defined for all staff;
- ensure that the person who is being offered a post has his/her identity confirmed through the presentation of a valid birth certificate and passport or driving licence;
- ensure that there are arrangements to check that the validity of work permits are verified and their status is clarified.'

Standard C10 (Practising Privileges) states that:

'C10.1 Where healthcare professionals are granted practising privileges (ie the grant to a person who is not employed in the establishment of permission to practise in that establishment) there are written policies and procedures on allowing practising privileges.

C10.2 The following pre- and post-employment checks are carried out before a healthcare professional is granted practising privileges:

- that the practitioner is registered with the appropriate professional regulatory body;
- that the practitioner is trained and is experienced in the type of treatment he/she is given practising privileges to perform;
- that the practitioner declares whether or not he/she:

  o is currently the subject of any police investigation and/or prosecution, in the UK or any other country;
  o has ever been convicted of any criminal offence required by law to be disclosed; received a police caution in the UK, or a criminal conviction in any other country;
  o is currently the subject of any investigation or proceedings by any body having regulatory functions in relation to health/social care professionals including such a regulatory body in another country;
  o has ever been disqualified from the practice of a profession or required to practise it subject to specified limitations following a fitness to practise investigation by a regulatory body, in the UK or in another country;

- that the practitioner is interviewed before employment, and that records of interview and written references are retained;
- that qualifications relevant to the post applied for are verified by validation at the interview;
- that the practitioner is appropriately registered, whether that registration covers the duties to be undertaken and whether there are any restrictions in place or investigations under way by the relevant regulatory/licensing body;
- that employment references are sought from the two most recent employers prior to making an offer of employment;
- that indemnification is checked and authenticated;
- that documentary proof is maintained of the continuing registration with the respective professional regulatory body;
- that the procedures for practitioners to follow when gifts are offered from patients, and what may and may not be accepted, are set out;

- that the practitioner who is offered practising privileges has his/her identity confirmed through the presentation of a valid birth certificate, and passport or driving licence;
- that there are arrangements in place for insuring that the validity of work permits are verified and that their status is clarified.

C10.3 There is a written agreement with the practitioner setting out:

- details of the practising privileges, which includes a stated requirement of the practitioner's availability to attend the establishment within a certain time limit if notified of a problem with a patient;
- that he/she will comply with the organisation's policies and procedures including the complaints procedure, and which requires the practitioner to inform the appropriate person if a complaint is made directly to him/her in the first instance.

C10.5 The practitioner is made aware of the current policies and procedures in the establishment and a list of the relevant policies and procedures that he or she is expected to be familiar with is provided.'

The standards set out above are the 'core' standards that apply to all establishments subject to the *National Minimum Standards for Independent Healthcare*. There are also further national minimum standards (within the *National Minimum Standards for Independent Healthcare*) which are specific to the establishment operated. Full details are beyond the scope of this book, but the following should be noted.

- Acute hospitals: Standard A3 (*Qualification of all Medical Practitioners*) and Standard A4 (*Qualifications and Experience of Medical Practitioners Undertaking Independent Private Practice*) (ie without supervision, commonly known as 'consultants').

- Children's services: Standard 15 (*Staff Qualifications, Training and Availability to Meet the Needs of Children*).

- Child and adolescent mental services: Standard M36 (*Safeguarding Children*).

- Maternity services: Standard MC1.1 (*Human Resources*).

- Prescribed techniques and prescribed technology establishments: Standard P8 (*Staff Qualifications and Training for Type 1 and 2 Hyperbaric Chambers*) and Standard P12 (*Invitro-fertilisation Qualifications and Training of Staff*).

9.4.5 Domiciliary care agencies

The Domiciliary Care Agencies Regulations 2002 and the *National Minimum Standards for Domiciliary Care Agencies* will form the regulatory framework under the 2000 Act for the operation of domiciliary care agencies.

(1) Domiciliary Care Agencies Regulations 2002

Regulation 12 of the Domiciliary Care Agencies Regulations 2002 states that:

'The registered person shall ensure that no domiciliary care worker is supplied by the agency unless –

(a) he is of integrity and good character;
(b) he has the experience and skills necessary for the work he is to perform;
(c) he is physically and mentally fit for the purposes of the work which he is to perform; and
(d) full and satisfactory information is available in relation to him in respect of each of the matters specified in Schedule 3 [namely:

"1   Name, address, date of birth and telephone number.
2   Name, address and telephone number of next of kin.
3   Proof of identity, including a recent photograph.
4   Details of any criminal offences –

(a) of which the person has been convicted, including details of any convictions which are spent within the meaning of section 1 of the Rehabilitation of Offenders Act 1974 and which may be disclosed by virtue of the Rehabilitation of Offenders (Exceptions) Order 1975; or
(b) in respect of which he has been cautioned by a constable and which, at the time the caution was given, he admitted.

5   Two written references including a reference relating to the last period of employment of not less than three months duration which involved work with children or vulnerable adults.
6   Where the person had previously worked in a position which involved work with children or vulnerable adults, verification, so far as reasonably practicable, of the reason why he/she ceased to work in that position.
7   Evidence of a satisfactory knowledge of the English language, where the person's qualifications were obtained outside the United Kingdom.
8   Documentary evidence of any relevant qualifications and training.
9   A full employment history, together with a satisfactory written explanation of any gaps in employment and details of any current employment other than for the purposes of the agency.
10   A statement by the person as to the state of his physical and mental health.
11   A statement by the registered provider, or the registered manager, as the case may be, that the person is physical and mentally fit for the purposes of the work which he is to perform.
12   Details of any professional indemnity insurance." ']

Regulation 16 states that:

'(1) Where the agency is acting otherwise than as an employment agency, the registered person shall prepare a staff handbook and provide a copy to every member of staff.
(2) The handbook prepared in accordance with paragraph (1) shall include a statement as to –

(a) the conduct expected of members of staff, and disciplinary action which may be taken against them;

(b) the role and responsibilities of domiciliary care workers and other staff;
(c) record keeping requirements;
(d) recruitment procedures; and
(e) training and development requirements and opportunities.'

Regulation 18 states that:

'Where the agency is acting otherwise than as an employment agency, the registered person shall ensure that every domiciliary care worker supplied by the agency is instructed that, while attending on a service user for the purposes of the provision of personal care, he must present the service user with identification showing his name, the name of the agency and a recent photograph.'

(2) *National Minimum Standards for Domiciliary Care Agencies*

Standard 17 (Recruitment and Selection) states that:

'17.1 There is a rigorous recruitment and selection procedure which meets the requirements of legislation, equal opportunities and anti-discriminatory practice and ensures the protection of service users and their relatives.

17.2 Face to face selection interviews are undertaken on premises which are secure and private, for all staff (including volunteers) who are short-listed and may be engaged.

17.3 Two written references are obtained before making an appointment, one of whom should normally be the immediate past employer and are followed up by a telephone call prior to confirmation of employment. Any gaps in the employment record are explored.

17.4 New staff are confirmed in post only following completion of satisfactory checks. These checks include:

- verification of identity;
- POCA list (where the post applied for is a 'regulated position');
- work permit (if appropriate);
- driving licence (if appropriate);
- certificates of training and qualifications claimed;
- declaration of medical fitness;
- confirmation service check by the UKCC (if holding a nursing, mid-wifery or health visitor qualification);
- sex offenders register;
- General Social Care Council Register.

17.5 Checks on the suitability of temporary staff may be undertaken by an employment or recruitment agency on behalf of the provider agency, provided that those checks comply with the requirements of these standards.

17.6 New staff, including temporary workers and volunteers, are provided with a written contract specifying the terms and conditions under which they are engaged, including the need to comply with the agency's staff handbook for staff (see Standard 25).

17.7 Staff are employed in accordance with the Code of Conduct and Practice set by the General Social Care Council and are given copies of the code.

17.8 The registered person complies with any Code of Practice published by the General Social Care Council setting out the standards expected of persons employing social care workers, insofar as the Code is relevant to the management of domiciliary care.

17.9   Staff are required to provide a statement that they have no criminal convictions, or to provide a statement of any criminal convictions that they do have.'

Standard 18 (Requirements of the Job) requires that:

'18.1   All managers and staff are provided with written job descriptions person and work specification identifying their responsibilities and accountability and with copies of the organisation's staff handbook and grievance and disciplinary procedure.

18.2   The person specification includes the personal qualities required to undertake the work and the appropriate attitudes to be adopted.

...

18.5   Staff are required to notify their employer of any new criminal offence they may have committed including motoring offences.

Standard 19 (Development and Training) states that:

'19.2   There is a structured induction process, which is completed by new care and support staff which encompasses the Training Organisation for Personal Social Services induction standards.

19.3   The induction process includes a minimum of 3 days' orientation programme at the start of employment which covers the topics to be found in Appendix C and includes shadowing an experienced care or support worker prior to taking responsibility themselves for the provision of personal care services and working alone in the homes of service users.

19.4   Each new member of staff undertakes a training needs analysis on completion of induction or probationary period. This is incorporated into the staff training and development plan.'

9.4.6   Nurses agencies

The Nurses Agencies Regulations 2002[1] and the draft *National Minimum Standards for Nurses Agencies* will form the regulatory framework under the 2000 Act for the operation of nurses agencies.

(1)   *Nurses Agencies Regulations 2002*

Regulation 12 of the Nurses Agencies Regulations 2002 states that:

'(1)   The registered person shall ensure that no nurse is supplied by the agency unless –

(a)   she is of integrity and good character;
(b)   she has the qualifications, skills and experience which are necessary for the work which she is to perform;
(c)   she is physically and mentally fit for that work; and
(d)   full and satisfactory information is available in relation to her in respect of each of the matters listed in Schedule 3 [namely:

    "1   Name, address, date of birth and telephone number.
    2   Name, address and telephone number of next of kin.
    3   Proof of identity, including a recent photograph.

---

1   SI 2002/3212.

4 Details of any criminal offences –

  (a) of which the person has been convicted, including details of any convictions which are spent within the meaning of section 1 of the Rehabilitation of Offenders Act 1974 and which may be disclosed by virtue of the Rehabilitation of Offenders (Exceptions) Order 1975; or

  (b) in respect of which she has been cautioned by a constable and which, at the time the caution was given, she admitted.

5 Two written references from nurses or other health professionals, including a reference relating to the last period of employment as a nurse of not less than three months duration;

6 Where a nurse has previously worked in a position which involved work with children or vulnerable adults, verification of the reason why she ceased to work in that position, unless it is not reasonably practicable to obtain such verification.

7 Evidence of a satisfactory knowledge of the English language, where the nurse's nursing qualifications were obtained outside the United Kingdom.

8 Documentary evidence of any relevant qualifications and training.

9 A full employment history, together with a satisfactory written explanation of any gaps in employment and details of any current employment other than for the purposes of the agency.

10 Details of health record, including immunisation status;

11 Confirmation of current registration with the Nursing and Midwifery Council, including details of the part of the register in which the nurse is registered.

12 Details of any professional indemnity insurance."]

(2) The registered person shall ensure that the selection of a nurse for supply is made by or under the supervision of a nurse and that full and satisfactory information in respect of each of the matters listed in Schedule 2 is available in relation to the nurse carrying out the selection [namely:

"1 Proof of identity, including a recent photograph.

2 Either –

  (a) where the certificate is required for a purpose relating to section 115(5)(ea) of the Police Act 1977 (Registration under Part II of the Care Standards Act 2000), or the position falls within section 115(3) or (4) of that Act, an enhanced criminal record certificate issued under section 115 of that Act; or

  (b) in any other case a criminal record certificate issued under section 113 of that Act,

  including, where applicable, the matters specified in sections 113(3A) and 115(6A) of that Act and the following provisions once they are in force, namely section 113(3C)(a) and (b) and section 115(6B)(a) and (b) of that Act.

3 Two written references including a reference relating to the last period of employment of not less than three months duration.

4 Where a person has previously worked in a position which involved work with children or vulnerable adults, verification of the reason why she ceased to work in that position, unless it is not reasonably practicable to obtain such verification.

5   Documentary evidence of any relevant qualifications and training.
6   A full employment history, together with a satisfactory written expla-
     nation of any gaps in employment.
7   Details of health record.
8   In respect of a nurse to whom regulation 12(3) applies, confirmation of
     current registration with the Nursing and Midwifery Council, including
     details of the Part of the register in which the nurse is registered.
9   Details of any professional indemnity insurance." ']

Regulation 15 states that:

'(1)   Where the Agency is acting as an employment business, the registered person
       shall prepare a staff handbook and provide a copy to every member of staff.
(2)   The handbook prepared in accordance with paragraph (1) shall include a
       statement as to –

       (a)   the conduct expected of staff, and disciplinary action which may be taken
             against them;
       (b)   the role and responsibilities of nurses and other staff;
       (c)   record keeping requirements;
       (d)   recruitment procedures; and
       (e)   training and development requirements and opportunities.'

(2)   *National Minimum Standards for Nurses Agencies*

Standard 3 (*Recruitment*) states that:

'3.1   The recruitment process operates in line with equal opportunities and is
        non-discriminatory;
3.2   A person who is a registered nurse (with a current NMC registration)
        undertakes interviews for the recruitment of all grades of agency nurses. This
        registered nurse has relevant experience to enable the assessment, selection
        and placement of nurses with clients, according to their qualifications,
        competencies and skills. The nurse undertaking interviews need not be the
        same person who is responsible for the placement of nurses with particular
        clients.'

Standard 4 (*Checks on Nurses*) states that:

'4.1   All necessary and appropriate checks are undertaken on the nurse supplied or
        to be supplied, prior to commencing employment.
4.2   If a nurse is included on the list maintained by the Secretary of State for
        Health of individuals who are considered unsuitable to work with vulnerable
        adults (when the POVA list is operational), or the list maintained by the
        Secretary of State for Health of individuals who are considered unsuitable to
        work with children, or the Sex Offenders Register, and the agency believes
        that there are mitigating factors (for example, a person who is on the list of
        individuals considered unsuitable to work with children, whose duties will
        not bring them into contact with children), the agency seeks agreement in
        writing from the NCSC before engaging or supplying that person.
4.3   The applicant's health record is checked, including obtaining a copy of
        the applicant's immunisation record and current status showing that the
        necessary immunisations for practice are current – in line with the
        recommendations in the UK Health Department's publication Immunisation
        against Infectious Disease. A nurse is not engaged or supplied by the agency if

she has a history of illness that would make her unsuitable for duties to which she may be assigned. In cases of doubt the agency seeks agreement in writing from the NCSC before engaging or supplying that person.'

Standard 5 (*Identification and Qualifications*) states that:

'5.1   The agency keeps all necessary records in respect of each nurse supplied or to be supplied by the agency.

5.2   Nurses supplied by the agency have a current registration with the Nursing and Midwifery Council (NMC):

- The agency obtains a caller code from the NMC and obtains confirmation of registration of new and existing registered nurses via the NMC's Employer's Confirmation Service;
- The agency checks notifications of registered nurses who have been removed or suspended from the register;
- All nurses work within the NMC Code of Professional Conduct.

5.3   The following information is recorded:

- Record of any formal interview to a consistent and adequate procedure.
- Details of next of kin together with an emergency contact telephone number.
- A copy of the individual's immigration status, if appropriate (see Home Office Guidance on Prevention of Illegal Working).
- A copy of the driving licence, if necessary for the duties to be carried out.
- Details of other employment (if any) including current employment by other agencies.
- Details of any unspent convictions subject to the Rehabilitation of Offenders Act (1974) Exemption Order 1975.'

Standard 6 (*Competence*) states that:

'6.1   Where the agency is an employment business, there is a written formal induction process this is completed by every new nurse to be supplied. The induction process covers as fully as possible the responsibilities that the nurse supplied will have.

...

6.3   The agency shall assure itself, by confirming current registration and examining such other certificates as indicate specialist or advance knowledge and skills, that nurses supplied to service users have been trained to work in the field of practice to which they are being assigned.'

9.4.7   Residential family centres

The Residential Family Centres Regulations 2002[1] and the *National Minimum Standards for Residential Family Centres* will form the regulatory framework under the 2000 Act for the operation of residential family centres.

(1)   *Residential Family Centres Regulations 2002*

Regulation 16 of the Residential Family Centres Regulations 2002 states that:

---

1   SI 2002/3213.

'(1)   The registered person shall not:

(a)   employ a person to work at the residential family centre unless that person is fit to work at a residential family centre; or

(b)   allow a person to whom paragraph (2) applies, to work at the residential family centre unless that person is fit to work at a residential family centre.

(2)   This paragraph applies to any person who is employed by a person other than the registered person in a position in which he may in the course of his duties have regular contact with residents.

(3)   For the purposes of paragraph (1), a person is not fit to work at a residential family centre unless –

(a)   he is of integrity and good character;

(b)   he has the qualifications, skills and experience necessary for the work he is to perform;

(c)   he is physically and mentally fit for the work he is to perform; and

(d)   full and satisfactory information is available in relation to him in respect of each of the matters specified in Schedule 2[, namely:

"1   Positive proof of identity.

2   Either:

(a)   where the certificate is required for a purpose relating to section 115(5)(ea) of the Police Act 1997 (registration under Part II of the Care Standards Act 2000), or the position falls within section 115(3) or (4) of the Police Act 1997, an enhanced criminal record certificate issued under section 115 of that Act; or

(b)   in any other case, a criminal record certificate under section 113 of that Act,

including, where applicable, the matters specified in sections 113(3A) and 115(6A) of that Act and the following provisions once they are in force, namely section 113(3C)(a) and (b) and section 115(6B)(a) and (b) of that Act.

3   Two written references, including a reference from the last employer, if any.

4   Where a person has previously worked in a position whose duties involve work with children or vulnerable adults, so far as reasonably practicable verification of the reason why the employment or position ended.

5   Documentary evidence of any relevant qualification.

6   A full employment history, together with a satisfactory written explanation of any gaps in employment."]

(4)   The registered person shall ensure that –

(a)   any offer of employment to a person is subject to paragraph (3)(d) being complied with in relation to that person; and

(b)   unless paragraph (5) applies, no person starts work at a residential family centre until such time as paragraph (3)(d) has been complied with in relation to him.

(5) Where the following conditions apply, the registered person may permit a person to start work at the residential family centre notwithstanding paragraph (4)(b) –

  (a) the registered person has taken all reasonable steps to obtain full information in respect of each of the matters specified in Schedule 2 in respect of that person, but the enquiries in relation to any of the matters specified in paragraphs 3 to 6 of Schedule 2 are incomplete;
  (b) full and satisfactory information in respect of that person has been obtained in relation to the matters specified in paragraphs 1 and 2 of Schedule 2;
  (c) the registered person considers that the circumstances are exceptional; and
  (d) pending receipt of, and satisfying himself with regard to, any outstanding information, the registered person ensures that the person is appropriately supervised while carrying out his duties.

(6) The registered person shall take reasonable steps to ensure that any person working at a residential family centre who is not employed by him and to whom paragraph (2) does not apply is appropriately supervised while carrying out his duties.'

Regulation 17 states that:

'(1) The registered person shall –

  (a) ensure that all permanent appointments are subject to the satisfactory completion of a period of probation; and
  (b) provide all employees with a job description outlining their responsibilities.'

(2) *National Minimum Standards for Residential Family Centres*

Standard 15 (*Recruitment of Staff*) states that:

'15.1 There is written record of the recruitment process which is followed in respect of all staff (including ancillary staff and those on a contractual/sessional basis) and volunteers who work with families in the centre, incuding evidence that all reqirements of Schedule 2 of the Residential Family Centre Regulations 2002 have been met in every case.

15.2 The registered person's system for recruiting staff (including ancillary staff and those working on a contractual/sessional basis) and volunteers who work with families in the centre includes an effective system to decide on an appointment or refusal of appointment, of staff or others likely to have regular contact with children or vulnerable adults at the centre, in the light of any criminal convictions or other concerns about suitability that are declared or discovered through the recruitment process.

15.3 The registered person ensures that any staff provided through an agency who work with the children in the centre have successfully passed the checks that are required in the Residential Family Centre Regulations 2002 within the previous twelve months. There must be evidence of this which is placed on their file. The check will be at an enhanced level for staff and volunteers involved in regularly caring for, supervising, training or being in sole charge of children, and at the "standard" level for all other working as paid staff or volunteers on the premises of the centre.

15.4 Staff members and others subject to the above checks do not normally start work at the centre until all the checks required in the Residential Family Centre Regulations 2002 are completed. Exceptionally, a member of staff may be allowed to do so while the outcome of some checks are awaited but in every case the appropriate check via the Criminal Records Bureau must have been completed before that person starts work. In such circumstances the registered person must ensure that:

- the individual is directly supervised at all times at a level that prevents them having unsupervised contact with children in the centre;
- the registered person has taken all reasonable steps to complete the recruitment process and to "chase" outstanding information;
- such circumstances are exceptional; and
- the registered person has taken all reasonable steps to avoid such circumstances occurring.

15.5 Continued employment, in such circumstances, is subject to satisfactory outcomes from the checks.

15.6 Staff are employed in accordance with the code of conduct and practice set out by the General Social Care Counsel (GSCC) and are given copies of the code.

15.7 The registered person provides information about the purpose of the centre consistent with its statement of purpose, to all applicants for all posts in the centre.

15.8 Wherever practicable, shortlisted applicants for appointment to any post in the centre are invited for a vist to the centre and to meet staff and families (subject to the family's agreement) prior to the decision on appointment being made, and observations sought from staff and families which are taken into account in the appointment decision. In such circumstances, candidates are not given unsupervised access to families or to children.

15.9 Any employment reference provided by the registered person on any existing or past staff member for work with children clearly state where there are any concerns regarding the suitability of the person to work with children and, if so, explain what those are.

15.10 Adults living in households on the premises of the centre who are not members of staff at the centre are checked through the Criminal Records Bureau at the "standard" level of checking.

15.11 Any visitor to the centre who has not been satisfactorily checked through the Criminal Records Bureau is not allowed unsupervised access to the centre.

15.12 There is a clear policy, with procedures, implemented in practice, for monitoring all such people. There is a system in place to record all visits to the centre. Staff take responsibility for the monitoring and management of such visitors, in consultations with families, in the interests of the safety and welfare of all resident families and children. Families are given clear written and verbal guidance on receiving their own visitors into the centre. Visiting relatives are not given unsupervised access to other children in the centre.'

Standard 16 (*Adequacy of Staffing*) states that:

'16.2 Care staff are at least 18 years old and staff who are given sole responsibility for the unit or management role are at least 21 years old.'

Standard 18 (*Staff Training and Development*) states that:

'18.2 Staff who are new to the service (including any agency, volunteer and student staff) receive induction which continues throughout their probationary period and training appropriate to the purpose and function of the service and their work. New staff are supervised and are informed about account-ability and reporting lines and procedures to be followed in relation to emergencies, health and safety, child protection and notification of incidents.'

9.4.8 Rehabilitation periods and exempted occupations under the ROA 1974

Sentence	Rehabilitation period
Imprisonment or corrective training or youth custody or detention in a young offenders' institution or corrective custody for:	
• between 6 and 30 months	10 years
• less than 6 months	7 years
Fine or community service order	5 years
Conditional discharge, probation, care or supervision order	1 year (or duration of order if longer)
Absolute discharge	6 months
Disqualification (eg from driving)	Period of disqualification
A remand home, approved school or attendance centre order	The period of the order plus + 1 year

NB For terms of imprisonment or fines, the rehabilitation period is halved for those under 17 at the date of conviction.

Exempted occupations

Professions
• Medical practitioner
• Barrister (in England and Wales), advocate (in Scotland), solicitor, legal executive or registered foreign lawyer
• Chartered accountant, certified accountant
• Actuary
• Receiver appointed by the Court of Protection
• Chartered psychologist
• Dentist, dental hygienist, dental auxiliary
• Veterinary surgeon
• Nurse, midwife
• Ophthalmic optician, dispensing optician
• Pharmaceutical chemist
• Registered teacher (in Scotland)
• Any profession to which the Professions Supplementary to Medicine Act 1960 applies

Offices and employments:
- Judicial appointments
- The Director of Public Prosecutions and any employment in his office
- Crown Prosecution Service
- Procurators Fiscal and District Court Prosecutors, and any employment in their offices
- Justices' chief executives, clerks and their assistants
- Clerks and officers of the High Court, the Court of Session and the district court
- Constables, police cadets, special constabulary and armed forces force police
- Serious Fraud Office
- National Crime Squad
- National Criminal Intelligence Service
- Any employment in a prison
- Customs and Excise
- Traffic wardens and Probation officers
- The RSPCA involving work requiring killing of animals
- Any employment in connection with the provisions of social services to work with people over 65, those seriously ill and those handicapped
- Employment involving the provision of services to vulnerable adults
- Any employment which is concerned with the provision of health services and where the job holder has access to those being treated
- Any office or employment concerned with the provision to persons aged under 18 of accommodation, care, leisure and recreational facilities, schooling, social services, supervision or training
- Those who apply to become registered day care providers
- Building society employees convicted for a 'relevant offence', such as fraud
- Work concerned with the monitoring of internet communications for the purpose of child protection

Regulated occupations
- Taxi driver
- Firearms dealer
- Any occupation in respect of which an application is required to the Gaming Board
- Director, controller, or manager of an insurance company
- Any occupation which is concerned with managing an abortion clinic, carrying on a nursing home, social services and keeping explosives

Chapter 10

INSPECTION OF REGISTERED ESTABLISHMENTS AND AGENCIES

10.1 INTRODUCTION

The power of inspection lies at the very centre of the regulatory process. Without effective and robust penetrative inspection many of the powers vested in the registration authority would be meaningless.

The question of inspection is sensitive. There is a difficult interface between the duty of registration authorities to take effective action to protect vulnerable service users, and the rights of providers, managers and their staff – and indeed service users – not to be subjected to unwelcome, intrusive and in some cases damaging invasions which are often the result of inspection. Those who observe inspections may draw conclusions about the adequacy of the provision of facilities and services in a particular establishment or agency.

The law gives firm precedence to the need to have full and complete access without limitation for inspectors to give effect to the powers of registration.

Some have suggested that the powers of inspection do not give sufficient respect to the rights of providers, managers and their staff, and in some cases the rights of service users as enshrined in the Human Rights Act 1998. The authors do not believe that a challenge to these powers under the 1998 Act would be successful. Albeit decided before the implementation of the 1998 Act, the decision of the House of Lords in *Green Environmental Industries*[1] established very clearly that powers provided, in the public interest, for inspectors to question people conducting various businesses in a way in which those persons are required to answer and in circumstances in which answers may be expected to form the basis of adverse regulatory action do not contravene reasonable expectations of protection of the rights of the individual. That case was concerned with civil regulatory proceedings, not with criminal sanctions. As suggested in the House of Lords, the question of whether admissions made in the course of such investigations could be properly relied upon in criminal proceedings may be another matter. In exceptional circumstances, the prosecution of criminal proceedings may be significantly less important than ascertaining material to be used in civil regulatory proceedings to ensure that poor practice ceases or that poor practitioners are taken out of the business cycle. Whilst important, the subsequent prosecution for criminal infringement is a different priority,

---

1   *R v Hertfordshire County Council ex parte Green Environmental Industries* [2000] 2 WLR 373, HL.

concerned with punishment of the individual for wrongdoing rather than protection of innocent and vulnerable service users, which is the purpose of civil regulatory action.

The core principle is that operators of registrable care establishments and agencies have become used to intrusive inspection. Detailed provision for such intrusion was found in the Registered Homes Act 1984 in relation to residential care homes and nursing homes. That legislation is now repealed and entirely replaced by the code set out, for all registrable establishments and agencies, in ss 31 and 32 of the Care Standards Act 2000.

The powers of inspectors and the registration authority have been redefined and extended. It is no exaggeration to say that the powers of the registration authority and of properly authorised inspectors are effectively without limit, and include powers to require complete co-operation from any persons concerned with the premises, establishments or businesses subject to inspection to ensure that it can be carried out robustly.

The inspection process is an important part of the history of registration of any establishment or agency. The inspector, the provider and the manager must all appreciate this importance. Material observed or gathered during the course of the inspection will crucially form part of the operation of registered establishments, and agencies will inevitably form the core for evidence adduced against an establishment or agency in any regulatory action. Thus, it is vital that all concerned ensure that they are able to establish at a later date exactly:

–   what was observed;
–   what was heard;
–   what was said; and
–   what circumstances were discerned.

Inspectors who do not record information in a manner that can be represented will find their cases weakened and regulatory action frustrated. Providers and managers who do not take steps to monitor the course of inspection so that they are able to give precise first-hand evidence of proceedings will be less able to challenge evidence led on behalf of the registration authority.

There is a difference between a provider or manager managing the inspection process to achieve that purpose so as to be able to recollect and retell what has happened, and obstruction of the process. There is no reason why providers, managers and their staff should be excluded from the activities of inspectors and indeed it is desirable that they should accompany them. Such accompaniment is to assist rather than obstruct the inspector.

10.1.1   National minimum standards

The inspections of care establishments and agencies will be conducted against the benchmark of the national minimum standards for the establishment or agency concerned. Background material may be supplemented by directions and guidance from the Secretary of State either informally or pursuant to s 6 of the 2000 Act.

Inspectors, providers and managers should be well informed about the detail of the national minimum standards and relevant directions and guidance. Providers and managers should be particularly briefed so that where there are divergences from national minimum standards they are in a position to advance explanations at an early stage.

Inspectors will no doubt make use of the practice of pre-inspection question-naires in order to establish the framework for the context of inspection. Section 23 of the 2000 Act requires the national minimum standards to be taken into account in relation to regulatory decisions. Those standards cannot conceivably be taken into account unless the inspection is conducted so as to gather factual evidence as to compliance with the standards. The conclusions that are drawn from the factual evidence, and the decisions which are then made, will be different from the balancing of the decision as to whether or not regulatory action should follow. None of those steps can be effectively taken (or indeed challenged by owners and managers) unless there is core evidential material from which the facts can be judged.

Inspectors should avoid muddling their reports with opinions or subjective views. The purpose of inspection is to establish facts from which inspectors (or more likely others) will take decisions. Inspectors must understand that their senior offices at area and regional office level will take decisions based upon the facts they report. Inevitably, senior managers will support the inspector's finding, and may be unhappy if those findings are effectively challenged.

Acts should be investigated coolly and reported in minimalist language. To overstate is to risk disappointment and damage the real thrust of a case.

The introduction to every set of national minimum standards first published states that:

> 'These standards (*national minimum standards*) will form the basis for judgments made by the NCSC regarding registration and the imposition of conditions for registration, variation of any conditions and enforcements of compliance with the 2000 Act and associated regulations, including proceedings for cancellation of registration or prosecution.
>
> The Commission will therefore consider the degree to which a regulated service complies with the standards when determining whether or not a service should be registered or have its registration cancelled or whether to take any action for breach of regulations.
>
> While the standards are qualitative – they provide a tool for judging the quality of life of service users – they are also measurable. Regulators will look for evidence that the requirements are being met and a good quality of life enjoyed by service users through:
>
> * discussions with service users, families and friends, staff and managers and others;
> * observation of daily life in the home;
> * scrutiny of written policies, procedures and records.
>
> The involvement of lay assessors in inspections will help ensure a focus on outcomes for and quality of life of, service users.'

This places in context the purpose for which the standards will be used in the inspection process.

It is disappointing to note the confusion between standards and requirements in the text. Indeed, the standards are qualitative, and the regulators will be looking for evidence that the requirements are met. However, the introduction fails to draw the reader's attention to the fact that the requirements are not the standards, but merely that the standards will assist the regulator in determining whether the requirements have been met. Requirements are the 'must dos' for the provider or manager.

By contrast the introduction to the NMS for Care Homes for Older Persons now provides (following the review published in March 2003):

> 'Under the Care Standards Act 2000 the Secretary of State has powers to publish statements of National Minimum Standards. In determining whether a care home conforms to the Care Homes Regulations 2001, which are mandatory, the National Care Standards Commission *must* take the standards into account. However, the Commission *may* also take into account any other factors it considers reasonable or relevant to do so [*sic*].

> Compliance with national minimum standards is not itself enforceable but compliance with regulations is enforceable subject to national standards [*sic*] being taken into account.

> The Commission may conclude that a care home has been in breach of the regulations even though the home largely meets the standards. The Commission also has discretion to conclude that the regulations have been complied with by means other than those set out in the national minimum standards.'

[The authors would say that failure to comply with the national minimum standards is not in and of itself evidence of breach of regulations; it rather depends in scientific terms on whether one views the glass as half empty or half full.]

10.1.2 Statute

Sections 31 and 32 of the 2000 Act set out the powers of inspection and, to some extent, the duties of providers and managers. Section 31 sets out the rules in relation to inspections by persons authorised by the registration authority, whilst s 32 provides supplementary provisions, although, in essence, it deals to a large extent with additional powers for those authorised to inspect.

The powers of inspectors comprehensively exceed those of almost any other statutory agency. Both those exercising and those subject to the powers must understand that the core principle is that the Act takes away the basic common law principle that the owner or lawful occupier of premises is entitled to exclude unwanted guests, who can remain only with the consent of the property owner.

Correct understanding of the limit (if any) of the powers and of preconditions to exercise the power is essential. If the preconditions are not followed, and the inspector manages to exceed the powers, he or she will be acting as a trespasser, and his or her actions will be unlawful.

The permission for the inspection (extensive as it is) is dependent wholly upon following the legal preconditions to exercise of the power, as one would expect.

10.1.3 Regulations

Given the importance of the powers of inspection and their intrusion upon rights of the individual, it is not surprising that Parliament has decided to reflect those powers within primary legislation and not to delegate detailed regulation-making power to the Secretary of State.

Regulations which can be made by the Secretary of State on behalf of central government are limited by s 31(7) of the 2000 Act to regulation requiring the Commission to arrange for premises which are used as establishments or for the purposes of an agency to be inspected on occasions at such intervals as may be prescribed, set out in the National Care Standards Commission (Fees and Frequency of Inspection) Regulations 2001.

10.2 CONTEMPORARY EVIDENCE

Section 31(8) of the 2000 Act provides that a person who proposes to exercise a power of entry or inspection must, if so required, produce a duly authenticated document.

Providers and managers should ensure that their staff know of this requirement and should insist upon compliance. The right to demand production of the authority exists at the commencement of the inspection. A later demand may be legitimately resisted. It will not be sufficient for staff to wait until providers or managers arrive. Senior staff on duty should be advised always to ask that the appropriate documentation to prove the authority for the exercise of the power be produced, even in cases where the inspector is known to them. That is not to say that every visit or enquiry from inspectors should be resisted, but, if in doubt, it is appropriate to issue the challenge, since the inspector will know, if he or she is unable to comply, that the whole power to proceed is lost until the authenticated document can be produced.

There are sometimes visits by other public officials. Unless authorised under the 2000 Act, such officials do not possess the powers of inspection and may have little or no right to be present save with the status of invited guest.

10.3 POLICE AND CRIMINAL EVIDENCE ACT 1984

Inspecting officers under regulatory legislation, including the predecessors to the 2000 Act, are broadly treated as police officers for the purpose of the Police and Criminal Evidence Act 1984. Therefore, if the inspectors are investigating with a view to commencing criminal proceedings based upon the evidence they find, they must conduct themselves in accordance with the limitations, restrictions and codes of practice set out in the Police and Criminal Evidence Act 1984.

There is an important distinction between visits by police officers or even searches of suspects' premises under warrants, and the activities of inspectors under the 2000 Act. In the absence of a search warrant, and subject to its limitations, investigating police officers are not permitted to enter and inspect premises or seize documents or assets. Inspectors, on the other hand, have full and extensive powers to do all such things.

The quality of evidence obtained during the course of an inspection is adducible freely in civil regulatory or criminal proceedings. The one exception will clearly be the confessions of a prospective defendant as to admissions of criminal offences or admissions of facts and circumstances which lead objectively to the conclusion that a criminal offence has been committed.

In accordance with the requirements of the Police and Criminal Evidence Act 1984, inspecting officers should follow the appropriate codes of practice. If they wish to rely in criminal proceedings upon confessions or admissions, they should ensure that the appropriate statutory caution is administered as soon as they have reasonable grounds to suspect that a criminal offence has been committed.

Prior to the implementation of the 2000 Act it was well settled that upon administration of the caution the suspect was entitled not to respond. There will now be a tension between that principle, and the inspector's right to demand an interview, and the registered person's obligation to participate in the interview. The problem, as argued above, is probably solved by the submission that confessions and admissions obtained after cautioning, whether extracted by demand after the suspect has declined to answer, will be admissible in civil regulatory action but almost certainly will be non-admissible in criminal proceedings. Inspectors should consider that matter when considering how to conduct questions.

There would be clear infringement of the Human Rights Act 1998 if in criminal proceedings persons were convicted as a result of confessions extracted perforce under regulatory requirements. However, administration of the caution means that a criminal offence is suspected. The power to demand an interview after such caution is in direct conflict with the suspect's right to protection from self-incrimination. The caution cannot be withdrawn. The administration of a caution may well negate the duty to co-operate in interview. An inspecting officer should consider carefully in such circumstances whether it is valuable to proceed with questions the answers to which tend to incriminate in such circumstances.

The Police and Criminal Evidence Act 1984 code of practice in relation to inspection of premises requires a police officer to give notice of reasonable grounds of a suspected criminal offence at the point in the inspection when such information is discovered. The person whose premises are being inspected is entitled to decline permission for the inspection to proceed, and the police officer will be required to withdraw and seek a search warrant, otherwise a second police officer (or perhaps a trading standards officer under the Trade Descriptions Act 1968) may not be able to return at all. However, under the 2000 Act inspectors have an absolute right to inspect, and thus the requirement to notify of reasonable grounds of suspicion of criminal offence is somewhat nugatory. The notification must be given, but the inspector can continue.

10.4   INSPECTION REPORTS

The law relating to inspection reports has been entirely reformed by the 2000 Act. Section 32(5) provides that where premises are used as an establishment or for the purpose of an agency and those premises have been inspected, the registration authority:

(a)   must prepare a report on the matters inspected; and
(b)   must, without delay, send a copy of the report to each person who is registered in respect of the establishment or agency.

There was no previous obligation either to write a report or to send a copy of the report to the person registered.

Good practice and common sense suggest that this has been done in the vast majority of cases. However, the authors are aware of many cases where there has been a failure on either or both counts.

The clear obligation to prepare the report means that inspectors must look to their laurels after inspection. The requirement to send a copy of the report without delay means, it is suggested, that the report must be prepared without delay. Registered persons will gear the preparation of their own reports with that in mind. Reports which are not prepared and delivered in a timely fashion will be less impressive, and under certain circumstances courts and tribunals will not allow witnesses to rely upon the contents of such reports if there has been non-compliance with s 32(5). The evidence will not be inadmissible, but in an appropriate case a judge or tribunal might decline to receive the information if he, she or it considers that it is inherently unreliable because of delay, particularly where that delay is in breach of the registration authority's obligations. Delay will also colour the gravity with which the registration authority reports criticisms found during the course of the inspection.

Open reporting has been codified and simplified. Reports must be available to everybody on request at any reasonable time at the registration authority's offices (which will be the regional or area office of the National Care Standards Commission or the head offices of the Assembly for Wales). The registration authority is entitled to take any other steps it considers appropriate for publicising the report. It is clear therefore that any arguments that might restrict publication of the report by reference to confidentiality are overridden by statute.

The registration authority is subject to all general laws (including the law of defamation) in relation to the contents of material published. It is unlikely that defamation would succeed (given the defences of qualified privilege) in relation to publication to registered persons and other persons closely connected with the home, but similar considerations cannot be said of wider publication, and care must be taken.

In the openness and transparency of inspection reports, and the clear obligation for reports, registered persons should request delivery of reports in a timely fashion and be more careful than hitherto in challenging material which is not agreed. If the report states something which is not true (particularly where that can be demonstrated by reference to the registered person's own inspection report), it is essential that a challenge be made. A challenge made late will not carry sufficient weight. Even if the material has been gathered, it is important from a reputational point of view that challenges are incorporated in background papers circulated with the report, so that those who read the report know of the existence of the challenge.

10.5   NATIONAL CARE STANDARDS COMMISSION (FEES AND FREQUENCY OF INSPECTIONS) REGULATIONS 2001

Regulation 6 of the National Care Standards Commission (Fees and Frequency of Inspections) Regulations 2001 sets out the requirement for inspections to be carried out at particular intervals. The power in s 31(7) of the 2000 Act, and the drafting of reg 6, make it clear that the Regulations are imposing upon the registration authority requirements that they inspect on a minimum number of occasions within certain time frames. Nothing in the Regulations restricts the registration authority from inspecting as often or as infrequently as it sees fit subject to the minimum inspections required.

In essence, inspection is required of every establishment or agency at least once a year. A year is taken to run from 1 April to 31 March except in relation to residential family centre, nurses agencies and domiciliary care agencies, when the year commences on 1 April 2003 for the first year of inspection. Inspections of care homes and children's homes must be conducted twice in every 12-month period.

Where a care home or children's home is first registered, the requirement to inspect is limited to once between 1 April and 30 September and not at all between 1 October and 31 March.

Nonetheless, it is worth emphasising that there is no restriction on the number of inspections. Repeated inspections may, however, call for justification from the registration authority. If a complaint is made that an inspection was intrusive, disproportionate and vindictive, the registration authority, if it had been inspecting more frequently than the statutory minimum, might have to justify its position. In the authors' experience, however, the number of cases of genuine over-inspection through vindictive purposes is very small. Providers and managers should not anticipate that there will be any reasonable prospect of success in challenging over-inspection, and should appreciate that frequency of inspection will often be used as an opening gambit in regulatory proceedings and so as to justify regulatory action including prosecution.

10.6   POWERS OF THE REGISTRATION AUTHORITY

In a sense, all powers are powers of the registration authority, but a distinction can be drawn between powers which are expressed to be powers of the registration authority, and powers which are expressed to be powers of persons authorised by the registration authority.

A person authorised will be acting on behalf of the authority, and the majority of powers are applied to such a person. However, s 31(1) of the 2000 Act sets out a distinct power for the registration authority:

> 'At any time to require a person who carries on or manages an establishment or agency to provide it with any information relating to the establishment or agency which the registration authority considers it necessary or expedient to have for the purpose of its functions under this part.'

'Functions under this part' are, of course, the processes of registration and regulatory enforcement. Thus, the power does not extend to powers to gather information for the purposes of informing the Secretary of State about the availability or quality of provision. The reasons for requesting information which is 'necessary or expedient' effectively destroys any reasonable expectation that an objection to a request can be raised.

Previous legislation limited the right to require information in relation to nursing homes to that deemed 'necessary for the purpose of inspection', and residential care home proprietors under the Registered Homes Act 1984 were only required to provide information which was required by the Regulations. The new law goes much further.

Nonetheless, 'necessary or expedient' as opposed to 'at whim' or 'out of curiosity' will have to be justified if a challenge is made.

The requirement may be made of both provider and manager, but not other staff. Importantly, the requirement must be made by the registration authority, ie by a duly authorised officer for and on behalf of the National Care Standards Commission. The requirement should come in written form clearly associated with the Commission and should not arise (as an addition to other powers of inspecting officers) during the course of or after inspection unless specifically authorised by an appropriate senior officer within the Commission. Parliament must have intended to distinguish between powers of the authority as opposed to powers of the person authorised by the authority.

10.7   POWERS OF THE INSPECTOR

Powers of the inspector are set out in s 31(2)–(6), and may be summarised as follows.

(1)   At any time to enter and inspect premises which are used or which the inspector has reasonable cause to believe to be used as an establishment or for the purposes of agency.

(2)   To make any examination into the state and management of the premises and treatment of the patients or persons accommodated or cared for there which the inspector thinks appropriate.

(3) To inspect and take copies of any documents or records (other than medical records) required to be kept under statutory regulation.

(4) To interview in private a manager or the person carrying on the establishment or agency.

(5) To interview in private any person employed there.

(6) To interview in private any patient or person accommodated or cared for there who consents to be interviewed.

(7) To require the manager or person carrying on the establishment or agency to produce any document or records wherever kept for inspection.

(8) To require records kept on a computer to be produced in a form which is legible and which can be taken away to examine the patient or person accommodated in respect of whom there is reasonable cause to believe that proper care is not being provided in private and to inspect any medical records relating to the treatment, provided the inspector is a medical practitioner or a registered nurse and the patient consents to the examination or inspection.

Where the patient is incapable of giving consent, the powers of examination and inspection of medical records can be carried out without the patient's consent.

10.7.1 Enter and inspect premises

This provision negates the normal right of an owner or occupier to exclude unwanted visitors from entering or remaining upon premises. The power includes the right to inspect the premises.

In most cases, premises will be known to be used if they are so registered. The 'reasonable cause to believe' will arise where premises are not registered but evidence available to the registration authorities suggests that registrable activities in the form of a registrable establishment or agency are being conducted. Inspectors should note that they will have to demonstrate reasonable cause for their belief (and a similar provision may apply where registered premises have ceased to be used). If the registered person has indicated that the premises have ceased use, inspection can continue or commence only if there is reasonable cause to believe that such a statement is incorrect.

The reasonable cause for belief is the necessary precondition to the right to override the property and occupational rights of owners and users. If there is no reasonable cause for the belief, the entry will be as a trespasser, and consequences will follow. The inspector may be liable for damage to the premises, but that is unlikely. More importantly, in such circumstances the restrictions on obstructing the inspector will cease to have effect, and the provider or manager or the person who happens to be on the premises will have a defence to obstructing the inspection.

A reasonable cause for belief is clearly related to the mind of the inspector and thus, it is suggested, will be judged subjectively, assessing what conclusions a reasonable inspector might have drawn from the information available to him or her. In such a context the test will be that of a reasonable inspector having the reasonable knowledge and competence of an inspector engaged to inspect establishments or agencies of the type concerned.

10.7.2 Inspect and take copies of documents and records

There were doubts under previous legislation as to whether the power of inspection itself generated an implied power to take copies of documents inspected. This issue is now resolved, but the power is limited to records required to be kept in accordance with regulations made under Part II of the 2000 Act and certain other regulatory legislation. The power does not extend to any documents and records. That power, if required, is exercisable by the registration authority rather than the person authorised to enter in to inspect, who generates his or her power of inspection and copying from his or her authority to inspect. Hence, a distinction is drawn between documents which the inspector can demand and copy and other documents which require the sanction of the registration authority itself. However, the inspector is entitled to call for the production of any documents or records to be inspected on the premises.

Power to require legible forms of records kept on computer is interesting because it requires the person subject to regulatory action to take positive action during the course of the inspection rather than to be passive. This provision thus guarantees protection for the provider or manager in that there is no power for the inspector to interfere with the computer, and the provider or manager must necessarily know what information has been taken.

The inspection of medical records is limited to inspectors who are qualified medical practitioners or registered nurses.

10.7.3 Interview in private

The power to demand interviews in private is new. It remains to be seen how this will be adopted in practice.

The concept of an interview involves a degree of invitation and acceptance leading to consent. The context of the requirement for the interview is the antithesis of a consensual situation.

An application of the principles which arose in the House of Lords in *R v Hertfordshire County Council ex parte Green Environmental Industries Ltd*[1] suggest that the statutory requirement for an interview in private does not offend against the principles of the European Convention on Human Rights, but it may be questionable whether the contents of such an interview could be relied upon in the course of criminal proceedings. The right to require an interview also raises interesting questions as to what happens if the prospective interviewee declines, or if the interviewee's employer or manager seeks to prevent the interview.

Two separate points are worthy of consideration.

---

1   (2000) 2 WLR 373.

(1) A request for interview is a clear interference with the business affairs of the establishment or agency. The Human Rights Act 1998 requires legislation to be construed so as to be compatible with the European Convention on Human Rights. It would be a matter of concern if an inspector could demand interviews from managers or staff, thus reducing the numbers of staff available to care below those required for the establishment or agency. It is submitted that this power should be interpreted so that the powers of interview are exercised at places and times that do not interfere with the appropriate operation of the establishment or agency unless there is good cause in particular circumstances. An inspector should also have in mind the risk to service users of the premises by having staff numbers depleted.

(2) Section 31(9) states that it is a criminal offence punishable by fine for anyone to intentionally obstruct the exercise of the powers or fail without reasonable excuse to comply with requirements made in accordance with ss 31 and 32. Failing to collaborate in the interview would plainly constitute a failure to comply with the requirement for the requested interview by the inspector. In an appropriate case it could be seen as intentional obstruction of the registration process. How far this can be extrapolated so as to fix with a criminal liability those who answer questions in a less-than-co-operative or forceful way is difficult to judge. It is unlikely, for the reasons advanced, that the request for the interview will be seen as contravening established rights under the Human Rights Act 1998, but in appropriate circumstances a prosecution for obstruction or failing to co-operate might fail if it is considered that the manner, style and circumstances of the interview were inappropriate. This would not adversely impact upon the registration authority's ability to rely upon the facts and circumstances of the interview in civil regulatory proceedings concerning the potential variation of conditions or cancellation of registration.

10.7.4   Consent

The consent of persons carrying on or managing the home, or their staff, to the interview is not required under s 31(3)(c) and (d) of the 2002 Act. However, interviews with patients or persons accommodated are subject to consent.

Consent is also required for the examination and inspection of medical records of a patient or service user where the inspector has formed a reasonable belief that that service user or patient is not receiving proper care.

Clearly, the inspector must be able to demonstrate that he or she has good reason to doubt the care, and that reason must be justified by professional judgment unless the circumstances are so obvious, for example beds or clothing soaked with urine, open bed sores or frail appearance. A particular difficulty is caused by lack of capacity to consent. Section 31(3)(e) does not provide for permission to conduct an interview where a service user is incapable of consent, but the lack of capacity can be overridden in relation to the examination and inspection of medical records. This is clearly a sensitive area since it is concerned with the rights of vulnerable service users. Inspectors must exercise these powers with great care. In any event, they will be qualified medical practitioners or registered nurses and in the conduct of their examinations and inspections of records they will be accountable to their professional bodies (General Medical Council and Nursing and Midwifery Council) in the same way as they are accountable in relation to any activities concerning the care or treatment of patients within their trust.

It may be that the provisions of the legislation add little to the general common law principle. These issues have been canvassed recently in a number of cases (see *Airedale NHS Trust v Bland;*[1] *R v Bournewood Community and Mental Health NHS Trust ex parte L.*[2] Where the service user is incapable of consent, the normal common law principle is that the medical or nursing practitioner responsible should proceed with the course of action in relation to the individual's body and/or care only if, in the judgment of that professional, the intervention will be to the benefit of the patient. In the overwhelming majority of cases concerning the enforced examination and medical record inspection of incapable patients in care establishments and agencies, it will be self-evident that the practitioner concerned believes that examination and inspection are in the interests of the patient.

Notwithstanding the wide statutory wording, it is suggested that inspectors would do well to stick to the common law principles as justifying the action. This will concentrate the inspector's mind on the real issue as to whether improper care is being provided.

10.7.5   Seizure and removal of documents and material

The power of seizure is new under the provisions of the 2000 Act. This power involves the physical removal of the property of others. If no reasonable grounds for seizure exist, resistance to the seizure by the provider or manager will not constitute obstruction. The seizure is legalised only by the presence of reasonable grounds. Thus, it is fair to assume that the reasonable grounds for seizure will be considered more strictly than in some other examples of exercise of power.

The inspector and the registered persons should note that the power of seizure relates only to documents which can establish failure to comply with conditions of registration or requirements of registration. Documents which establish non-compliance with the national minimum standards do not fall within this power, since the standards are not themselves requirements. Inspectors, in seizing documents, would have to be able to demonstrate a reasonable belief that the document demonstrated failure to comply with regulations, possibly amplified in understanding by the application of particular national minimum standards. The grounds for belief must relate to the Regulations and not the standards alone.

Furthermore, other reasons for seizing documents are clearly inadmissible and unlawful. Indeed, the authors suggest that a degree of proportionality must be

---

1   [1993] AC 789.
2   [1998] 3 WLR 107.

addressed to balance the competing rights to take copies or seize originals (where such would have other damaging consequences, eg make the business uncontrollable) should only occur where demonstrably the originals are required.

10.7.6   Assistance

Extraordinarily, inspectors may require anyone (not just registered persons/ providers/managers) to afford them with facilities and assistance in exercising the power of inspection. There appears to be no limit to persons who may be called upon to assist. It will be recollected that anyone who fails without reasonable excuse to comply with a requirement may commit a criminal offence. Therefore, in an extreme case, a stranger to the proceedings who failed to assist could be guilty of a criminal offence under the 2000 Act. Certainly the power extends to staff members and is not a power simply to be required of persons registered or those who may be directly concerned in the inspection.

The inspector also has authority to have access to and check the operations of computers. As opposed to requiring legible forms for computer-held information, this gives the inspector the right actually to use the computer. Since access to the computer could damage it, the inspector could be at risk of civil liability if he or she fails to take appropriate steps to ensure that he or she is exercising the powers correctly and in accordance with the correct legal preconditions.

10.7.7   Evidence gathering

It has long been the practice for inspectors to take measurements, photographs and make recordings to capture the evidence discovered during the course of an inspection. No serious challenge has been made to any of these activities under the Registered Homes Act 1984 or the Children Act 1989. However, this is now beyond doubt under the 2000 Act. The power to take steps permanently to record matters that are discovered does not mean that that material will itself be impressive evidence. Persons taking measurements and photographs or making recordings should take the usual protective steps to ensure that it can be demonstrated that such evidence is genuine and was obtained at the time and place stated: digital cameras, timing of recordings and countersigning of measurements are some examples of how this can be assisted. This is no different from taking steps to ensure that photocopies are legible and correctly identified.

10.8   CONDUCT OF THE INSPECTION

It will be clear from the above that it is vital for inspectors to conduct inspections in a manner which takes full advantage of the powers granted. Inspectors must ensure that they are properly authorised. They must ensure that they have fulfilled all the preconditions to inspection and to the exercise of particular powers of inspection. Failure to do so will mean that the inspector and registration authority may be:

(a) liable to complaints and actions for damages in relation to damage caused;
(b) failing to succeed on a prosecution for obstruction;
(c) failing to be able to rely upon material obtained, at least in criminal proceedings.

The inspection is equally important for registered persons, ie providers and managers, and indeed for their senior staff. The risk of regulatory breach or criminal contravention of the regulations exists for anyone who is present, however directly or indirectly concerned, during the course of an inspection. An accurate recapturing of the events of inspection is as essential for the registered persons as it is for the inspector and the registration authority.

There have been few actual prosecutions for obstruction and no case-law exists to identify what constitutes obstruction and what does not. However, clearly taking steps to monitor, observe and capture evidence during the course of an inspection for use of the registered person cannot conceivably be cause for obstruction. Indeed, the registered person and his or her staff may need to be present to respond to the lawful requests for assistance which inspectors may make.

It should be noted that 'obstruction' is now only an offence if 'intentional', ie mens rea is a constituent requirement of the offence. Previously the offence was one of strict liability (see s 31(9) of the 2000 Act).

Registered persons should note the following guidelines.

(1) Appropriately experienced staff should be deployed to monitor the course of the inspection.

(2) Such staff should make notes and prepare detailed inspection reports.

(3) Senior staff at the establishment or agency should always seek a verbal debrief at the end of inspections.

(4) Where written debrief is offered by inspecting officers, staff should absolutely decline to sign any documents other than simple documents of receipt of the written debrief. There is no obligation to accept the findings of the inspector at any time, let alone at a time when due consideration has not been given.

(5) Staff should note any documents copied, documents seized, photographs taken or recordings made, and should request copies at the earliest possible time.

(6) Particularly in cases where no adverse circumstances are reported in the verbal or written debriefs at the time of the inspection, registered persons should seek to make their own report of the inspection and supply that to the registration authority promptly.

(7) Where appropriate, the registered person or his or her staff should seek to take photographs and make recordings (openly) or take extra copies of material copied by inspectors at the time. In this way, a comparable dossier will be built up.

(8) The registered person should keep detailed records of inspection and should attempt to share the debrief of inspection from the registered person's point of view, perhaps in advance of receipt of the registration and inspection authority's report.

Unless steps are taken to recapture the evidence of the inspection, registered persons will be in no position to challenge the findings of officers. Challenges many months after the event are seldom successful.

Chapter 11

SERVICE AND ACCOMMODATION CONTRACTS FOR CARE HOMES

11.1 INTRODUCTION

For every business to survive it requires a reliable stream of income to meet its expenditure. If it is a charity, any surplus enables it to pursue its charitable objectives. If it is a private venture, it produces profit.

Care homes are no different from any other business. They must attract clients who in consideration of their serviced accommodation pay fees of a sufficient amount regularly to exceed expenditure. The services supporting the accommodation will be tailored to meet the client's need. However, care homes are unique in that many of their clients are unable to pay the fees sufficient to meet the expenditure of the provider. Such clients are largely dependent upon public funding to support their needs and care.

This feature of the client's funding does not alter the basic premise that accommodation and service provided in a care home are agreed by contract. The relationship between the client and public agencies or others who may financially support the client is a different relationship.

In this chapter we will consider the nature of the contract between care home and client, the expectations of the parties to or associated with that contract and how the contract is affected by the source and availability of resources to meet the client's needs. Thereafter, we shall examine the system of public funding of care homes in its current application.

11.2 ELEMENTS OF A CONTRACT

A contract is a legally enforceable agreement giving rise to obligations on the parties who enter into it. A contract is formed when three basic elements are satisfied:

(1) an offer;
(2) an acceptance of the offer; and
(3) consideration.

11.3   PARTIES TO A CONTRACT

A contract for care in a care home is a contract by which the client secures the provision of serviced facilities from the care home owner to meet his or her needs. As referred to above, the contractual relationship between the parties is more complicated where the client is (partially) financed by another person or body.

Those parties may be identified as:

(a) the client;
(b) the client's sponsor (where applicable);
(c) the care home owner.

11.3.1   Client

The client will seek to secure certainty as to:

(a) the amount payable and times at which payment should be made;
(b) the scope and quality of the service to be provided, so that he or she is able to judge any failure in the service, which will entitle him or her to withhold payment or leave the home.

The specification in the contract should be sufficiently flexible and broadly drafted to meet the changes of everyday life, and adapt (possibly with consequent changes in price) to rises and falls in levels of dependency and the care needs of the client.

11.3.2   Sponsor

The sponsor may be either the local authority, a family member of the client, or another who is willing to accept the financial responsibility of the client. The sponsor's aims will be similar to the client's but, since the sponsor is responsible for payment, he or she may wish to ensure that he or she is able to control and supervise the delivery of care as circumstances demand.

The sponsor, in consideration of rights of consultation and intervention, may be expected to be contracted as a primary party rather than as, for example, a guarantor. This will make it easier to identify who is responsible for payment and against whom a judgment can be enforced in the event of failure to pay. Further, the client him or herself may be incapable, due to lack of capacity, to understand or intervene in the contractual relationship and may depend upon the sponsor for advocacy and support. It is always advisable to have only two parties to the contract, rather than three.

11.3.3   Care home owner

The care home owner must know:

(a) to whom he or she must look for payment;
(b) with whom he or she must negotiate changes in payment levels or services;
(c) the scope and quality of service he or she must provide;

(d) how he or she can change service specification to meet changing client needs.

A care home owner has a restricted business. He or she has a limited number of sales opportunities, ie a finite availability of beds. Commercial markets suggest that, in order for his or her business to be viable, homes should be filled to capacity most of the time. The only alternative to increasing bed numbers in a home in order to increase income is to increase fees. The care home owner requires certainty of income flow and sufficient time to manage potential changes caused, for example, by a client choosing to go elsewhere, a client's increase in dependency or the death of a client.

11.4   GENERAL

In the interest of all parties to the contract, there is the need for certainty of contractual terms. The contract draftsman should anticipate the likely changing circumstances during what may, in many cases, be a long-term relationship, and seek to ensure simply and clearly that those circumstances are documented in advance and are understood.

Those concerned with handling such contractual negotiations need to appreciate the inequality of bargaining power. The client and private sponsor are not well placed to negotiate unless there is a surplus of accommodation available in their local market. The care home owner should not seek to take advantage of this. The public authority sponsor (a common participant in the form of the local authority in such negotiations since the introduction of the 'Care in the Community' scheme in 1993) is a dominant purchaser. However, in purchasing, the local authority is performing a public service. It is charged with ensuring the proper delivery of social welfare care both in residential and non-residential settings. The authority must strike a proper balance between the needs of clients and the needs of other social services users. It is important that care home owners in a particular locality be recognised by the dominant purchaser, which should ensure, by open and fair contractual negotiation, that a choice of facilities remains available for those in need. Overly zealous negotiation by local authorities may lead to significant numbers of care home owners being forced out of business. The local authority should ensure value for money combined with adequate facilities to ensure that those who rely upon that authority for protection receive adequate care at all times.

That authority should:

(a) act only within its powers;
(b) not constrain or fetter its activities by preordained policy;
(c) act in accordance with proper procedures;
(d) not act irrationally.[1]

---

1   See discussion below but, in particular, *Associated Provincial Picture Houses Ltd v Wednesbury Corporation* [1947] 2 All ER 680; *Council of Civil Service Unions v Minister for the Civil Service* [1984] 3 All ER 935; and *Bromley London Borough Council v Greater London Council* [1982] 1 All ER 129.

11.5   FUNDING SCHEMES

There are three funded schemes which are outlined below.

11.5.1   Entirely self-funded

Self-funding is self-explanatory. The client has sufficient means to purchase his or her own care needs and enters into a contract with the care home owner for services which are funded from the client's own resources.

11.5.2   Client-supported scheme

In a client-supported scheme the client has insufficient personal resources to fund the care and relies upon the financial support of a sponsor. Here, the care home owner, client and third party (the sponsor) must consider carefully the contractual arrangement with the sponsor. Within such schemes fall those administered by the Benefits Agency of the Department of Social Security by which the client receives funds to enable him or her to meet his or her contractual obligations. That support may ultimately be provided by the safety net of income support but will include other means-tested and non-means-tested benefits, including State pension entitlements.

The Health and Social Care Act 2001, ss 50–52 require that local authorities are now responsible for arranging and meeting the care needs of people who used to have their long-term care funded through preserved rights to income support and job seeker's allowance.

Other sponsors may include relatives and/or appropriate charities.

The principles of the scheme are the same as direct contract with service user. The care home owner is entitled to contract with its client for payment of appropriate charges to receive services. The resources of the client or the client's sponsors are entirely available to meet the contractual obligation. The contract should include provisions for extras if the care needs of the client change, otherwise there may be a restriction in the contract on charging extra for additional services. Clients must be aware of potential extras.

11.5.3   Public authority-funded scheme

The public authority, whether a health authority or local authority, contracts with the care home owner to provide care within a particular specification. The client may not be a party to the contract. The client may seek to have rights to enforce the contract, but this will not be the usual practice. Health authorities, acting under delegated power from the Secretary of State, may enter into contracts for the purchase of long-term care for certain periods and at appropriate rates.[1] Those patients are and remain patients of the National Health Service (NHS) and may not be charged any extra by the care home owner or provider. NHS patients are entitled to be treated free of charge.

---

1   See National Health Service Act 1977, s 23.

Similarly, if a local authority undertakes responsibility, following an assessment of need, it is responsible for making arrangements for the provision of residential accommodation and for paying for each in full.[1] Local authorities are rightly astute to negotiate detailed specifications for services. Care home owners need to be sure that they are content to provide full services, as identified in the specification, for the fee contracted.

Recent legislative changes have ensured that the needs of the client (through his or her care plan) will dictate the terms of the contract. Thereby, a standard fee is agreed to provide care for the client based upon his or her individual needs. If the client requires extra services or items based upon his or her care assessment plan, these can be paid for by the funding party. However, the service and accommodation contract must include this provision in the contract.

11.6 STATE OF MIND FOR ACCEPTANCE

Having established who the potential parties will be in a service and accommodation contract it is necessary to consider elements which are unique to contracts dealing with older persons, and to understand how these elements apply to the ability of the elderly freely to consent to the terms of the agreement.

11.6.1 Undue influence

For care home owners whose clients are frail, elderly or who suffer from mental illness, the doctrine of undue influence must be considered in the contractual context.

Parties to a contract should give their consent to contract fully and freely. The doctrine of undue influence provides that an agreement, where consent to the terms of the contract has been obtained by undue persuasion or influence, is unenforceable. This situation may arise when an older person who is self-funded agrees to sign his or her service and accommodation contract. A claim of undue influence undermining the validity of the contract is likely to arise where there is a relationship of trust and confidence between the parties of such a nature that it can be presumed that there has been an abuse of that relationship to the benefit of the wrongdoer. It is necessary only to prove that a confidential relationship existed between the parties. It is then the burden of the wrongdoer to show that the contract was entered into freely by the injured party. It is possible that such claims will be made by family members.

A care home owner should take steps to protect him or herself from such claims. These are:

(a) to put in place a standardised set of protocols and procedures which apply to all new clients and which will demonstrate that all clients are treated equally and that no undue influence has been exercised;

---

1   See National Assistance Act 1948, s 21.

(b) to encourage an older client to consult a solicitor to review the terms and conditions of the service and accommodation contract before he or she signs it;

(c) if possible, to include the family members at an early stage, to discuss with them the terms of the contract and explain the responsibilities the older client will undertake in signing the agreement.

11.6.2   Incapacity

The law presumes that everyone has the capacity to enter into a contract. Therefore, any lack of capacity must be strictly demonstrated by the person who claims the exemption. The rule is that a mentally disordered person is not bound by a contract when it can be demonstrated that: (a) as a result of his or her mental incapacity, he or she was unable to understand; and (b) that the other party was unaware of his or her incapacity. If these two elements are satisfied, the contract will be voidable.

Presumably, the service provider will have knowledge of whether the client lacks capacity (ie demonstrated by the care plan).

11.7   TERMS OF CONTRACT

The following are standard terms which should be considered in negotiations.

11.7.1   Scope of services

It is vital for the contract to define the service that will be provided in sufficient detail for the parties to know:

(a) whether the service has objectively failed;
(b) whether a service sought is additional to the contractual service and additional payment is required;
(c) whether the actual service is a reduction or enhancement of that contracted for, by reference to a predetermined base.

The scope of the service should be defined by reference to the requirements of the client (ie the client's care plan).

11.7.2   Trial period

The contract should include a provision which allows for the client and the care home owner to determine whether the home is suitable and whether the client is settling into his or her new accommodation. If it is decided by either party that the client is not properly placed, the contractual relationship should be capable of being terminated by either party. The client will be placed in an alternative care home and other alternative arrangements will be made. Pursuant to the Care Homes Regulations 2001, a care home owner must be very clear as to the type of clients he or she can care for, and be able to meet the needs of those clients.

11.7.3   Payment/deposit

The contract must provide clearly for the amount and timing of payment, and whether payment is made in advance or in arrears. It should also provide a mechanism for adjusting the payment (an increase as well as a decrease) as a consequence of a change in service specification and increases in the home's costs. Service and accommodation contracts are usually long term, and care home owners are unlikely to be able to retain original contractual prices for longer than one year.

Where possible, items which may form the subject of an additional charge separate from the weekly fee should be identified.

The contract should provide a procedure for withholding payment if a client has justifiable dissatisfaction with the service.

It is financially prudent for the care home owner to request a deposit from the funding party. This will create a financial buffer for the care home owner in relation to any monies due or delays in the income stream (eg because a vacated room needs redecorating for the next client, or administrative bureaucracy has caused a delay in payment by the local authority, etc).

11.7.4   Occupation of the premises

The contract must address the basis upon which the client occupies the accommodation. In most cases, the care home owner will require continuing exclusive control over the premises. Tenancies providing any degree of security of occupation for the client are inappropriate in long-term care establishments (unlike, eg, sheltered housing).

The needs of the business operation and the need to change accommodation to meet client dependency requirements will require that most care home owners retain control of accommodation so that occupants occupy on a non-exclusive licence basis. Further, to grant a client greater rights than a non-exclusive licence will mean that the care home owner must seek greater legal remedies to preserve his or her control over the premises.

11.7.5   Personal belongings

In a long-term contract for care, the care home owner needs to make the client feel welcome into what will become the client's new home. Therefore, it is expected that the client will bring with him or her personal belongings, money, and perhaps furniture, books or other items of varying value.

The care home owner is expected to provide and accommodate the client's request in bringing his or her personal items into the home. If the owner excludes in the service and accommodation contract the ability of a client to bring any items into the home or states that he or she will not provide safekeeping for the client's personal items, the contract could be considered unfair and the provision struck out.[1]

However, it is important that a balance is struck between granting the client's wishes and the ability of the care home owner to run his or her business without interference. The contract should provide for any limitations or restrictions on personal belongings, rather than their complete exclusion, by setting out the items that are excluded and the responsibility for insuring such belongings under particular circumstances.

Regulatory law provides that records are kept as to money and valuables held in safe custody. The contract should take that matter further and make it clear how such items will be protected. It is good practice for the care home owner to keep a detailed list specifying the value of the personal items which the client brings into the care home. This is to ensure that if an item goes missing and/or a dispute arises, the matter can be resolved in part by reference to the detailed list.

11.7.6   Gifts and gratuities

The offer and acceptance of unsolicited gifts is a problem in the operation of care homes and should be covered in the agreement. It is not unheard of for an older client to want to thank a particular employee or staff member who has been particularly kind during the client's stay. However, it should be made clear to clients that they should not make gifts to the owner or owner's staff under any circumstances. This will also be regulated by the employment contract between the owner and his or her staff.

There should also be a provision in the contract which prohibits staff from witnessing wills.

11.7.7   Confidentiality

The contract should include a provision which addresses confidentiality of a client's records. Until the coming into force of the Access to Health Records Act 1990, patients had no statutory right of access to their own health records. The concern is that often a third party (ie a family member) will wish to have access to the client's records. The simple and safe answer is that the confidentiality of the medical record should lie with the client unless there are special circum-stances where the client lacks legal capacity to exercise his or her right. The right of a third party is very limited, and at the moment the law under the Data Protection Act 1998 is not particularly clear.[2] Therefore, if in doubt, the care home owner should decline the request of a third party to access to the client's records.

11.7.8   Free nursing care

As from 1 October 2001 the NHS has made available nursing care to privately funded patients outside the hospital setting. Nursing care provided by the

---

1   Unfair Terms in Consumer Contracts Regulations 1999, SI 1999/2083 regs 5(1), 6(1).
2   The Data Protection Act 1998 failed to include the mechanical provision for a third party to request information on behalf of a person who lacks capacity.

Government is limited to include services which may *only* be provided by a *registered nurse*, ie a person with accredited nursing qualifications.

The contract should include a provision whereby registered nursing care is distinguished as a separate service. This is important because failure to make this distinction could lead to refund claims on the basis that the provider is charging for an NHS service.

The contract should specify a set fixed fee for all services including registered nursing care but the individual elements of the service should be identified separately. Once the fee is paid, the service user should receive a credit for the money actually paid for the free nursing care. In this way the integrity of the whole fee is preserved and the service user receives credit for that which the NHS pays. It is important to ensure that if the registered nursing care reduces, the integrity of the fee is maintained albeit by a commensurate increase in the remainder of the fee. The fee for total care remains the same but the service/sponsor is only entitled to credit for whatever the NHS pays.

Similar provision could cover situations where other elements of the service are paid by third parties in due course, for example housing. This situation will become more acute with the implementation of the scheme for local authority funded patients with effect from 1 April 2003. It may be more difficult to persuade local authorities to increase personal care and accommodation charges where registered nursing care costs reduce. There is a real risk of loss to the care provider.

EXAMPLE	Total care and accommodation cost	£450.00 per week
	less registered nursing care contribution	£120.00
	local authority commitment	£330.00

What if registered nursing care contribution reduces to £45 per week? Unless protected by contract the care provider will lose £75 per week (in a 50-bedded care home this could be as much as £3,750 per week).

A Consultation Paper issued by the Department of Health in December 2002 addressed the difficulties. This is likely to be in the form of formal guidance by the time this book is published.[1]

Two contracting propositions are suggested.

(1) Where there is a partnership between a local authority and a primary care trust under the Health Act 1999, s 31 and the NHS Bodies and Local Authorities Partnership Arrangements Regulations 2000.

  In essence the care home continues to contract with the local authority for the full care package but the provider must ensure that there is in place both a partnership agreement and a pooled funding agreement between the local authority and a Primary Care Trust. Without this the agreement may be unlawful on the part of the local authority. With correct attention to detail this model avoids the revenue loss predicament outlined above.

---

1   Guidance available at *www.doh.gov.uk*.

(2) Where there is no partnership arrangement the care provider should contract with the Primary Care Trust direct for registered nursing care. This is exactly the situation of concern – not with the Primary Care Trust but if the local authority contract does not provide for equal increases where registered nursing care contribution fails.

The Government is intending to amend reg 5 of the Care Homes Regulations 2001 so that a registered person will have to provide residents with a breakdown of the care home's fee with respect to accommodation, nursing and personal care. This will give residents a better understanding of what they are paying for and what they are receiving for that fee. Further, the registered person will also need to provide a statement of payments made by a health authority in respect of nursing provided to the resident by the care home. However, care homes usually charge inclusive fees. The presumption will be, in such a case, that unless expressly excluded everything will be included in the fee.

11.7.9   Disputes

The drafting of every contract must take into account that there may be disputes between the contracting parties. Where one of the parties is old, sick or vulnerable the efficiency of dispute-resolution must be considered carefully. The contract should provide for a clearly transparent complaints procedure. The contract should also provide identification of those who will resolve disputes on behalf of clients who cannot speak or act for themselves.

11.7.10   Choice of care home

Clearly, in the first two schemes for funding care, ie self-funding or sponsor funding, the capacity to move from one home to another is both transparent and paramount. The position is less clear with the third scheme, ie those who are funded by a public authority, since they may feel that they should follow the suggestions and advice or even 'so-called' requirements of the local authority in selecting a particular home. The local authority may consider that if it is paying the fee(s), it should make the selection.

To deal with the situation, the Secretary of State issued the National Assistance Act 1948 (Choice of Accommodation) Direction 1992 (as amended), para 2 of which provides that if a resident for whom accommodation is to be provided has indicated a wish for 'preferred accommodation', then he or she should be accommodated in the place of his or her choice. Clients and care home owners should note that this obligation arises only if a preferred choice has been indicated.

Paragraph 2 of the Direction limits the requirement of the local authority to accede to the client's choice. The accommodation must appear to be suitable to the client's needs as assessed. The cost of making the arrangements must not require the authority to pay more than it would usually expect to pay having regard to those needs. If there is no care home available at that price, the local authority will have to pay a higher price, if necessary.

The owners of the preferred accommodation must provide the accommodation upon the authority's usual terms and conditions.

As a matter of fulfilling its public duty, the authority should not seek to impose 'usual terms and conditions which constrain choices', being terms and conditions which providers in the locality would not normally or usually accept. Such a provision might be regarded as an unlawful fetter upon the authority's power to provide accommodation and an unlawful constraint upon the individual's right of choice.

Under para 4 of the Direction, if the charge for the preferred accommodation exceeds that which the authority would normally expect to pay, it may still be required to fund a placement in the preferred accommodation if a third party makes a contribution sufficient to make up the difference between:[1]

(a) the cost which the local authority would usually expect to pay; and
(b) the full cost of the accommodation.

The local authority is entitled to make arrangements for the provision of accommodation anywhere, even at a cost which is above that usually paid, but it cannot be compelled to purchase such accommodation.

The third-party contribution must be shown to be available for the duration of the arrangements, in which case third parties may have to disclose evidence of their long-term means if they are to assist clients in choosing accommodation beyond an authority's normal budget.

Care should be taken to ensure that contracts with the third-party contributor are properly negotiated. Owners must be careful not to request payment in two parts. Failure of one paying party could leave the owner obliged to continue the service for less than the full charge. The third party must consider carefully his or her long-term commitment.

The better course is for the third party to contract with the client and the local authority to make the contribution by way of payment to the local authority as part of the client's contribution under s 22 of the National Assistance Act 1948 so that client and owner know that they may look to the authority to meet the whole of the cost of residential care. The third party will then face an enforceable obligation at the suit of the local authority, but the client's interest will be protected. The local authority will always be responsible for the whole fee. It is not lawful for the local authority to contract to pay part of the cost. The only exception would be identifiable extras.

11.8 TERMINATION OF CONTRACT

Most contracts will be long term. Short-term respite care contracts can be predetermined by reference to a fixed period. In such cases, agreements to extend the period or an absolute requirement to depart at the conclusion of the contract period must be clearly specified.

---

1   National Assistance Act 1948 (Choice of Accommodation) Direction 1992, para 4.

In longer-term contracts, each party should know the circumstances in which the contract may be terminated, ie on death or failure of payment. Owners should ensure that they can terminate the contract if the dependency needs of the client increase to such an extent that the home is no longer able to provide the care required.

Clients should have rights to terminate the contract should they wish to leave the home either because of dissatisfaction with the service or because their families or friends have moved elsewhere, or for any reason that may occur.

Both parties will, of course, be mindful of the effect on the contract of the client's death. The client and the client's sponsor will wish the contract to terminate immediately. The owner, however, may be faced with an unforeseeable vacancy and, without protection, a gap in the income flow. A balance should be struck which identifies a reasonable period for the owner to seek a new client on the one hand, and certainty as to determination of obligation of the client or the client's sponsor, on the other.

Local authorities rarely agree to continue payment beyond death. It must also be noted that in respect of clients who are dependent upon public funding, social security benefit ceases with death. Therefore, it is advisable to include a provision in the contract that addresses the responsibility of the local authority to continue payment for a limited time (ie 2 weeks) after the client has died.

Alternatively, owners may wish to take a deposit, if possible, from such clients. Unpaid care home liabilities are merely liabilities of the deceased's estate, and come second to preferential claims, for example funeral expenses.

11.9   CONTRACTING WITH THE LOCAL AUTHORITY

Section 21(1) of the National Assistance Act 1948 provides as follows:

> '(1) Subject to and in accordance with the provisions of this part of this Act, a local authority may with the approval of the Secretary of State, and to such extent as he may direct shall, make arrangements for providing:
> (a) Residential accommodation for persons aged 18 or over who by reason of age, illness, disability or any other circumstances are in need of care and attention which is not otherwise available to them ...'

This section has recently been much litigated. A little-used section, it has become the focus of public attention since it has translated into the vehicle for operation of the 'Care in the Community' scheme for funding care home placements through local authorities since 1 April 1993.

The section has been amended to extend provision of accommodation by local authorities for the sick and the disabled, who were previously considered to be clients of the NHS. For patients of the NHS, significantly, care is free, whereas under the National Assistance Act 1948, care is subject to repayment to the local authority of the costs of accommodation for care, subject to means.

Such accommodation may be provided by the local authority from its own accommodation or by purchase from voluntary organisations or private contractors pursuant to the provisions of s 26 of the 1948 Act. Section 26 is produced in full as follows.

'**26. Provision of accommodation in premises maintained by voluntary organisations**

[(1) Subject to subsections (1A) and [(1C)] below, arrangements under section 21 of this Act may include arrangements made with a voluntary organisation or with any other person who is not a local authority where –

(a) that organisation or person manages premises which provided for reward accommodation falling within subsection (1)(a) or (aa) of that section, and

(b) the arrangements are for the provision of such accommodation in those premises.

[(1A) Arrangements must not be made by virtue of this section for the provision of accommodation together with nursing or personal care for persons such as are mentioned in section 3(2) of the Care Standards Act 2000 (care homes) unless –

(a) the accommodation is to be provided, under the arrangements, in a care home (within the meaning of that Act) which is managed by the organisation or person in question; and

(b) that organisation or person is registered under Part II of that Act in respect of the home.]

(1C) Subject to subsection (1D) below, [no arrangements may be made by virtue of this section for the provision of accommodation together with nursing] without the consent of such [Primary Care Trust or] [Health Authority] as may be determined in accordance with regulations.

(1D) Subsection (1C) above does not apply to the making by an authority of temporary arrangements for the accommodation of any person as a matter of urgency; but, as soon as practicable after any such temporary arrangements have been made, the authority shall seek the consent required by subsection (1C) above to the making of appropriate arrangements for the accommodation of the person concerned.

(1E) ...]

(2) Any [arrangements made by virtue of ... this section] shall provide for the making by the local authority to [the other party thereto] of payments in respect of the accommodation provided at such rates as may be determined by or under the arrangements [and subject to subsection (3A) below the local authority shall recover from each person for whom accommodation is provided under the arrangements the amount of the refund which he is liable to make in accordance with the following provisions of this section].

(3) [Subject to subsection (3A) below] a person for whom accommodation is provided under any such arrangements shall, in lieu of being liable to make payment therefor in accordance with section twenty-two of this Act, refund to the local authority any payments made in respect of him under the last foregoing subsection:

Provided that where a person for whom accommodation is provided, or proposed to be provided, under any such arrangements satisfies the local authority that he is unable to make a refund at the full rate determined under that subsection, subsections (3) to (5) of section twenty-two of this Act shall, with the necessary modifications, apply as they apply where a person satisfies the local authority of his inability to pay at the standard rate as mentioned in the said subsection (3).

[(3A) Where accommodation in any premises is provided for any person under arrangements made by virtue of this section and the local authority, the person concerned and the voluntary organisation or other person managing the premises (in this subsection referred to as "the provider") agree that this subsection shall apply –

   (a) so long as the person concerned makes the payments for which he is liable under paragraph (b) below, he shall not be liable to make any refund under subsection (3) above and the local authority shall not be liable to make any payment under subsection (2) above in respect of the accommodation provided for him;

   (b) the person concerned shall be liable to pay to the provider such sums as he would otherwise (under subsection (3) above) be liable to pay by way of refund to the local authority; and

   (c) the local authority shall be liable to pay to the provider the difference between the sums paid by virtue of paragraph (b) above and the payments which, but for paragraph (a) above, the authority would be liable to pay under subsection (2) above.]

(4) Subsections [(5A)] ... (7) and (9) of the said section twenty-two shall, with the necessary modifications, apply for the purposes of the last foregoing subsection as they apply for the purposes of the said section twenty-two.

[(4AA) Subsections (2) to (4) shall have effect subject to any regulations under section 15 of the Community Care (Delayed Discharges etc) Act 2003 (power to require certain community care services and services for carers to be free of charge).]

[(4A) Section 21(5) of this Act shall have effect as respects accommodation provided under arrangements made by virtue of this section with the substitution for the reference to the authority managing the premises of a reference to the authority making the arrangements.]

(5) Where in any premises accommodation is being provided under ... this section in accordance with arrangements made by any local authority, any person authorised in that behalf by the authority may at all reasonable times enter and inspect the premises.

(6) ...

(7) In this section the expression "voluntary organisation" includes any association which is a housing association for the purposes of the Housing Act 1936 ... [... and "exempt body" means an authority or body constituted by an Act of Parliament or incorporated by Royal Charter].'

11.10 CONSTRAINTS ON CONTRACTING

It is necessary for the care home provider to be registered as a care home pursuant to s 3 of the Care Standards Act 2000. Therefore, a prerequisite to contracting with the local authority requires the establishment to be registered, since public money is used to purchase care. In other difficult cases the Local Government Act 2000 may provide assistance.

11.11 CLIENT'S CONTRIBUTION

Pursuant to s 22 of the 1948 Act, clients accommodated in premises provided or purchased by the local authority are required to contribute to the costs of care either to cover the whole of that cost or to such extent as may be limited by their means assessed in accordance with the National Assistance (Assessment of Resources) Regulations 1992.[1]

Clients accommodated in accommodation operated by the private sector are obliged to refund the whole or part of the authority's cost in the same way as they are obliged to pay to the authority the cost of provision of service in directly managed units.

Section 26(3A) provides that the owner, local authority and client may make a tripartite agreement so that the client's contribution is paid directly to the owner, and to the extent that that payment is made, the local authority is relieved of liability.

It must be emphasised that it is *the fact of payment* that relieves the local authority of liability. If no payment is made, the local authority remains liable and retains its obligation to recover that payment from the client. The owner is not expected to look to two sources for payment.

The prerequisite that such an arrangement should be by agreement suggests that it would be unlawful for an authority to require such an agreement as a condition of providing accommodation unless the price of the accommodation was above that which the authority would normally expect to pay.

The authority has a separate right of inspection of premises, where accommodation has been purchased by it or a client, in addition to its regulatory powers of inspection under the 1948 Act, ie sponsoring local authorities have a separate right of inspection of homes which they would not normally enjoy.

---

1   SI 1992/2977.

Chapter 12

FUNDING CARE HOMES

12.1 INTRODUCTION

This chapter should be seen as a natural extension of Chapter 11 which deals with the formation of the contract.

Funding a care home or other care establishment or agency is critical to its success. Funding, put simplistically, arises out of the revenue generated by those who are accommodated and cared for within the care home. Revenue is generated only as a result of contracts made between the care home and its customers. Those contracts must define and manage both the service specification and the price payable for the service in order to be sure that a sustainable revenue stream is generated.

The issue of funding has been obscured by the developments of the care home industry. Over the last 20 years, major purchasers of care (mainly local authorities) have determined maximum prices that will be paid for generic packages of care in standard care homes and other establishments and agencies. Similar practices have not been seen in specialist care establishments and agencies, or even in care homes which provide for specialist need. Dangers can lurk even there for the generation of fees which are higher than those generated by care homes for older persons which may lead to the assumption that margins and profitability will be higher. The correct position is that the fees must be generated by reference to the principle of making a margin upon the operating cost base. Higher turnover, in itself, does not make for a more profitable business.

The financial management of such situations is considered in much greater detail in Chapter 15.

It is essential that providers and managers of care establishments and agencies focus on the preparation of sensible contracts which will deliver financial objectives and secure financial viability. Endeavouring to cram expanding costs and overheads into inadequate contracts determined by dominant purchasers is fatally flawed.

No revenue is generated by a care establishment or agency which does not flow through a contract. It is well established that in contracting for arrangements for residential accommodation under the National Assistance Act 1948, local authorities are performing a private law, and not a public law, function. The normal rules of supply and demand and negotiating principles in the market-place apply to such arrangements.

12.2   PRICE AS PART OF THE CONTRACT

All too frequently, contracts for the provision of accommodation and care within a care establishment or agency are unduly complex and, in fact, fail to address the most important issue, namely price. Price cannot be determined unless there is specific definition of the care services to be delivered.

Specialist care homes, establishments and agencies have historically identified service level specifications and priced accordingly. Additional services thus attract extra fees, or the service user is required to vacate and make room for another service user who will either pay the additional fees or whose needs will not generate the services which require the additional fees.

The financial directorate of the care establishment or agency must be efficient in pricing the care services available. The contract must specify the care in as much detail as is possible. The obligation to pay the nominated price in the contract is a simple provision. The price should be negotiated prior to admission.

The provisions of the Care Standards Act 2000 (the 2000 Act) and the various Regulations make this easier. It will be a criminal offence not to have in place a detailed assessment of service user needs before a service user is admitted to a care establishment or agency and particularly to a care home.[1] It will also be a criminal offence not to have in place and regularly to review a care plan for every service user within a care establishment or agency.[2] Thus, as a fundamental obligation of the new regulatory regime under the 2000 Act there is a requirement to put in place and review assessments and care plans for all service users.

A reasonably competent professional within the care establishment or agency should be able effectively to price the cost of care within an appropriate margin armed with the assessment and care plan. Indeed, service users are likely to fall into a limited number of broad bands, save in very specialised units. Therefore, the ability to nominate the price in the contract should be simple.

All care establishments and agencies are required to be carried on in a manner which is likely to ensure that they will be financially viable for the purpose of achieving the aims and objectives set out in the statement of purpose.[3] Therefore, effective pricing is an absolute requirement of fulfilling the obligation to achieve financial viability, enforceable by criminal sanction, and the gathering of information which feeds the ability to price is also required as a matter of absolute obligation enforceable by criminal sanction.

If these steps are followed, the contract will need to provide robust provisions for adjustment (up or down) of the price under certain circumstances. The most

---

1   See, eg Care Homes Regulations 2001, reg 14.
2   see, eg ibid, reg 15.
3   See, eg ibid, reg 25.

obvious reason for adjustment is where the assessed and reviewed care needs of the service user change. In an appropriate case it may be appropriate to terminate the contract if the service user's needs have diminished to such an extent that the price falls to be reduced by a substantial margin, since there will be price levels below which the operation of the care home will not be viable.

The proper establishment of price with an appropriate review mechanism to maintain a margin notwithstanding fluctuations in need is essential to a contract which properly supports the funding of the care establishment or agency.

12.3 RESPONSIBILITY FOR PAYMENT

Identification of the contractual party responsible to pay the fees should be obvious. However, in the development of commercial practice in relation to care establishments and agencies, considerable confusion has made this matter more difficult, and has often led to a blurring of the realities of obligation.

In simple terms, obligations are undertaken either by:

(a) the service user; or
(b) a sponsor for the service user.

The provider and manager must ensure that one or both of the above are responsible individually, or jointly and severally, for the payment of the whole of the fee. The interrelation between them, whereby one may be obliged to contribute more or less than the other, should not be a matter of concern to the service provider.

Less damage than might have been done has occurred because care homes on the whole manage to recover the fees (albeit inadequately) almost certainly without recourse to enforcement. Thus, the true liability for fees is often not considered properly.

In principle, there is no difference between a third party undertaking responsibility for the service user's accommodation and care where that third party is:

(a) a relative;
(b) a supporting voluntary organisation or charity;
(c) a local authority;
(d) the NHS.

All these are examples of third parties who, by reason of obligation, commitment or ethics, undertake responsibility for meeting the fees which will secure the accommodation and care of the service user.

The contract must make clear who is responsible for paying (and this may be more than one person). Where possible, the service provider should ensure that there is clear responsibility for payment of the whole of the fees by all responsible parties.

12.4   PRINCIPAL AND GUARANTEE LIABILITY

It is not the purpose of this book to examine in detail the legal niceties as to the differences between primary and secondary responsibility for contractual debt. It is, however, important to draw attention to those differences.

A paying party who accepts responsibility for liability for payment of fees undertakes a primary responsibility. A guarantor whose obligation is called upon to meet the obligations of another has a secondary liability. A party with a secondary liability will not be called upon to honour that obligation save in circumstances where the primary party has failed. Accordingly, it is essential to ensure in simple service provision contracts that all those responsible to pay are undertaking primary responsibilities.

Sponsors (from whatever source) should never be invited or encouraged to sign guarantee liabilities since enforcement will be difficult. If sponsors undertake the responsibility for payment of fees, they should accept as a primary responsibility (this may be jointly and severally, ie one or both may be sued for the full amount due) payment of those fees.

In drafting terms, this is simple. The contract will provide that the identified parties will be responsible for paying the fee, and the service provider will be responsible for providing services to the service user as a direct contractual commitment to the paying party.

Providers may wish to ensure that in contractual terms, service users who are either not responsible for payment or, in realistic terms, cannot be expected to be responsible for payment should not be parties to the contract, which avoids possible allegations by the sponsor of failure to meet the service by the service provider in order to avoid payment. The sponsor may still avoid liability if there is a breach in the service provision, but it is simpler to exclude from the contract those who are not realistic parties for enforcement.

Under those circumstances, it is appropriate for the contract to exclude the provisions of the Contracts (Rights of Third Parties) Act 1999. This is not to diminish the professional and care obligations of the service provider towards the service user, but merely to define obligations. It may advantage the service user since he or she will not have direct responsibility. It may also be nothing more than a realistic recognition that the service user is not in a position to face enforcement proceedings. If a sponsor fails to pay, the service user may be required to vacate. However, the service provider should note that there are legal preconditions to enforcing vacation, as follows:

(a)   the contract giving a right to occupy must be terminated (in accordance with its terms, or on reasonable notice if there are no terms);

(b)   in any event, termination cannot be enforced without notice (probably 'reasonable' notice) under reg 40 of the Care Homes Regulations 2001;

(c)   the home is the service user's home and thus eviction cannot be enforced without a court order (Protection from Eviction Act 1977).

12.5   LOCAL AUTHORITIES

The principles advanced above also apply to contracts with local authorities. Local authorities have historically exploited their dominating purchasing position. Often this amounts almost to a monopsony. Recent developments, for example service users recognising their right to enforce a duty to make arrangements for accommodation with care against local authorities, and the shrinking care home market, have dramatically improved the ability of providers to negotiate robustly with local authority purchasers.

Local authorities have a genuine interest in endeavouring to fix fees for standard price service specifications so as to be able to manage their own fixed financial budgets. Local authorities adopt a number of tactics which should be resisted. These are:

(a)   demanding agreement to increasingly complex forms of agreement which are in place wholly to protect the local authority without providing any mutual obligation for the service provider;
(b)   seeking to fix prices for broad bands of service specification for long periods of time;
(c)   avoiding service user care specifications;
(d)   avoiding any clause which allows for the review of price by reference to changes in service user need, or which permits termination of individual service user contracts (the natural response of the service provider faced with a loss-making contract).

There is no reason for service providers to accept any such postures from local authorities. Whether or not such terms are required to be accepted will be entirely determined by the state of the demand for, and supply of, residential accommodation with care in the particular area. Under s 21 of the National Assistance Act 1948, local authorities are entitled and in most cases (involving disabled or older persons) obliged to provide residential accommodation and care for those in need where such facilities are not otherwise available to them. Under s 26, local authorities may provide such accommodation and care from their own resources or purchase it from private or voluntary providers (s 26 of the National Assistance Act 1948).

Where local authorities, as is often the case, have reduced or extinguished their own stock of community care establishments, they will have no alternative but to deliver their obligations to the individual by purchase from the private and/or voluntary sector.

Failure to meet the demand following an assessment of need under s 47 of the National Health Service and Community Care Act 1990, or even significant delay in meeting the demand, is unlawful.[1] Under the National Assistance Act (Choice of Accommodation) Direction 1992, service users entitled to the right to have arrangements for residential accommodation with care made are also entitled to have their preferred choice of accommodation honoured. Provided

---

1   See eg *R v Islington London Borough ex parte Betantu* (2001) 33 HLR 76, QBD.

the choice of preferred accommodation is made on first contact with the authority, the local authority must honour the choice irrespective of location and even where that location is outside its own geographical jurisdiction. The only limits to honouring the preferred choice are that the establishment must provide or be able to provide for the needs of the service user, and that provision should be at a price which is not more than the local authority would usually expect to pay. In the current circumstances, local authorities regularly argue that they would expect to pay a price which is lower than the proper price for the delivery of the services.

Local authorities are public bodies and are required to act reasonably and rationally. It is submitted that a local authority cannot refuse to honour the choice of preferred accommodation on the basis that the price is too high unless it can show that the particular service can be delivered properly in accordance with the requirements of the care specification and the relevant regulatory legislation (ie the 2000 Act and associated Regulations) for a price which is lower than that demanded. The proposition that authorities expect to pay less than the proper cost for services, and also expect the proper and effective provision of those services, appears to be untenable.

Of course, if there is evidence in the marketplace which shows that other establishments are able and willing to provide the service effectively and in accordance with legal requirements at a lower price, then the local authority will be able to choose such units of accommodation rather than the preferred accommodation of the service user.

A provider who has entered into a contract which fixes the price irrespective of service specification will not be able to take advantage of fluctuations in the market or even increases in the service user's needs.

12.6 NATIONAL HEALTH SERVICE

The purpose of the National Health Service (NHS) is to provide a comprehensive health care system for citizens in the United Kingdom, free of charge. The responsibility of the Secretary of State is to promote the provision of the NHS. NHS bodies (which constantly change) have always had the capacity to purchase NHS-required services from external agencies and, in particular, private and voluntary sector providers.

No service user has the right to demand particular accommodation or particular NHS services, but service users do have the right to expect that needs will be met in accordance with local priorities established by local NHS bodies, and that if NHS-managed resources are unavailable for any particular purpose, such services and facilities will be purchased from external agencies.

In the autumn of 2001 the government and representatives of the private and voluntary healthcare providers struck what was described as an historic 'concordat' whereby it was argued that the NHS would make greater use of private and voluntary services to meet NHS requirements. This was supplemented a year or so later by the government paper *Joint Working*

Towards a Partnership in Care, the theme of which was to reinforce the Concordat and back the Concordat with extra financial resources to enable hard-pressed NHS bodies to enjoy the true flexibility to purchase private and voluntary services and facilities. The theme of the policy was that high quality and true costs were the current criteria in making resourcing decisions as opposed to stigmatising the source of services, ie in either the public or private sector.

In legal terms there was no change – existing powers remained as before, but government encouragement to use alternative sources was more positive.

It is also interesting to note that the clear identification of patient cohorts as groups for whose benefit Primary Care Trusts must perform their functions, may well encourage the proposition that individuals within these groups are sufficiently well identified to seek personal redress in an appropriate case.[1]

12.7   WHOLE PAYMENT FOR SERVICE

This issue is developed in greater detail in Chapter 2 and will be developed later in this chapter.

A local authority makes arrangements to purchase accommodation in care to meet the needs of a citizen who would not otherwise have resources available to meet those needs. The NHS determines to provide a national health service which is tailored for a service user.

In either case, it is evident that the public authority must pay for the whole of the cost of the service which it is bound to supply or which it has elected to supply in accordance with the performance of its duties.

Public authorities cannot demand that part of their obligation be discharged by third parties or by the service users themselves, even where they are obliged to honour the service user's preferred choice of accommodation. Where a third party has agreed to underwrite the difference between the price of the service and the price which the authority would normally expect to pay, the local authority still has underlying primary responsibility to pay the whole of the fee, with the right subsequently to recover the contribution from the third party (in the same way as it is required to recover the contribution from the service user).

The contributions, whether by third party or service user, are made to the local authority and not by way of separate contract to the service provider.

12.8   MANAGING CARE HOME REVENUE

Care home revenue can only be effectively managed if the contracts for service provision and cash generation are drafted so as to allow the care home sufficient

---

1   See in particular para 3(1) of the NHS Administration Regulations which should be considered in light of both its promulgation and potential implementation in the context of the Human Rights Act 1998.

flexibility to meet rising costs associated with the provision of accommodation or increase in need.

Contracts must clearly and transparently allow for adjustments in fee income, or where such adjustments cannot be made or do not work, allow for contracts to be terminated so that placements are vacated by service users and are available to be taken up by others who (or whose sponsors) are able to meet increased fees. Any failure to follow this course may mean that the care home provider and manager are subject to challenge, both by civil regulatory action and prosecution, in one or more of the following ways:

(a) on the basis that the home is not being conducted so as to be financially viable;
(b) on the basis that the home is not properly meeting the needs of the service user as identified in the care plan (ie because the revenue is insufficient to establish and maintain resources to meet care needs);
(c) on the basis that the care provider is not meeting the needs of the service user as assessed prior to admission (similar provisions arise as those in relation to non-compliance with the care plan).

This could restrict or terminate the care establishment or agency business, or, in the worst-case scenario, lead to the principals being prosecuted before or after termination of the business.

12.9   NEW CARE BENEFIT AND LOCAL AUTHORITY FUNDING

Until the mid-1500s, relief of poverty was largely a matter for the church, and there was little systematic provision. More formal provision was made by the Elizabethan Poor Law with responsibility being placed firmly on local (parish) authorities. Poor houses were built, maintained, controlled and funded by local authorities.

A major change in 1948 meant that funding was moved from local to central government. From 1948, all housing costs for assisted persons were met under the National Assistance scheme, and later under the Supplementary Benefits Act 1976, under which claimants were divided into a number of groups: non-householders, who were not liable for housing costs; householder tenants, who were responsible for rent; householder owners, who were responsible for mortgage interest; and boarders, who paid an inclusive charge for board and lodging. Residents of both public and private care homes fell into this latter category, and the Supplementary Benefits Commission was content to pay the whole of the charges, including any 'care' element.

The Social Security Act 1980, which fundamentally reorganised supplementary benefit, began a process of differentiation between housing and other costs. In 1985, the housing costs of tenants became the responsibility of local authorities whilst boarders and owner–occupiers remained the responsibility of the Department of Health and Social Security. Responsibility for funding the whole of private care home fees remained with central government. There were, however, special arrangements with local authorities as to the funding of persons in National Assistance Act 1948 (Part III) accommodation, ie public care homes, whereby the local authority became responsible for the 'housing' and 'personal care' elements, leaving central government with responsibility for food, clothing, personal expenses, etc.

In 1986, supplementary benefit was replaced by income support and the whole benefit structure was 'simplified' by the Social Security Act 1986. It is in the Regulations made under this Act that the first distinction was made between 'boarders' and residents of residential care homes.

After a number of scandals in the early to mid-1980s involving 'young spongers' spending the summer as 'boarders' in holiday resorts, benefit for boarders was split into income support at the ordinary scale rates for day-to-day needs, and housing benefit, which was paid by the local authority with standard deductions for the food and utilities supplied as part of the board and lodging package.

Residents of private residential care homes, however, remained as part of the income support scheme as one of the 'special cases', and it was not until the coming into force of the National Health Service and Community Care Act 1990 (the 1990 Act) in April 1993 that responsibility for the 'care element' of new entrants to private residential care and nursing home fees passed from the Department of Social Security (now the Department for Work and Pensions (DWP)) to local social services authorities.

One of the driving forces behind the 1990 Act was that central government had woken up to the fact that, by a series of historical accidents, it had created a position whereby elderly persons with little or no means could place themselves in a private residential care home and income support would be provided to pay the whole of the (substantial) weekly bills. The independent sector, and accordingly the income support budget, were rapidly running out of control. It was not until the commencement of the 1990 Act in 1993 that there was an attempt to control these costs by the twin strategies of transferring responsibility for the 'care element' of new entrants to private residential care and nursing homes from the DSS (now DWP) to local social services authorities; and controlling who could and could not benefit from assisted accommodation in private residential care homes by way of an assessment of need conducted by the local authority. 'Self-placement' was ended except in relation to those who were able to pay the full cost themselves without recourse to a means-tested benefit. Those who had been funded under the pre-1993 scheme with their full costs paid by the DSS remained within that scheme as residents with preserved rights.

With the introduction of s 52 of the Health and Social Care Act 2001, and the Social Security (Amendment) (Residential Care and Nursing Homes) Regulations 2001 on 8 April 2002, central government finally relinquished direct responsibility for the funding of any part of residential care in independent homes save for day-to-day needs by way of the income support ordinary scale rates such as it would pay to elderly persons in the community. Preserved rights were abolished, and save for a limited transitional scheme, local authorities were left to pay for the 'housing' and 'care' elements of private care home charges.

12.10   ENTERING A CARE HOME

The Government's intention was that people who needed (or wanted) to live in a private care home after the introduction of the 1990 Act should fall into one of two groups. Those who can manage to pay the fees can simply find a home, place themselves in it, make a contract with the owner and pay the fees until they die. Those who cannot afford to pay the fees can request assistance from the local authority, which carries out an assessment of need. If the assessment shows that a person needs to be in a care home, he or she will be offered a choice of home (within financial limits). Some homes are local authority run, whilst others are privately run. The authority makes all the arrangements, agreeing a contract with the home, paying the fees, and recovering from the resident as much as he or she can statutorily afford to pay. The resident, meanwhile, is able to claim pension credit at ordinary rates to cover day-to-day needs and personal expenses.

12.11   LOCAL AUTHORITY ASSESSMENT[1]

Income support is replaced by pension credit from 6 October 2003. For simplicity, although it is called a credit it is not a tax credit and is not administered by the Inland Revenue but is in fact a benefit administered by the DWP.

It has two separate elements – very broadly, a guarantee element which applies to all claimants aged 60 or over and a savings element which applies to claimants aged 65 and over. In fact, entitlement to the guarantee element is linked to the minimum qualifying age at which a woman can receive State pension which is currently 60 but will rise steadily to 65 between 2010 and 2020.

12.11.1   Pension credit – how it works

Guarantee credit

1.   Calculate minimum guarantee. This is:
     (a)   £102.10 for a single person
     (b)   £155.80 for a couple
     (c)   £53.70 for each additional spouse in a polygamous marriage
     (d)   £42.95 single disability element
     (e)   £85.90 couple disability element
     (f)   £25.10 carer element
     (g)   Housing costs (mortgages and rents for Crown tenants)
     (h)   Transitional element to cover the change from income support.

---

1   The following text and accompanying example state the position as from 6 October 2003 at which date income support for the over 60s is replaced by pension credit which removes the upper capital limit, revises tariff income to £1 for each unit of £500 instead of £250 and introduces a savings credit. The formula used in *Registered Homes* (Jordans, 1998), the predecessor to this book, stated the position up until 5 October 2003, save that the specific figures have been amended annually.

Add together all the applicable elements to get the minimum guarantee credit.

2. Calculate total income – this is very much what is included for present awards of income support except the capital limit is abolished and tariff income becomes £1 for each unit of £500 or part thereof.

3. If income including tariff income is greater than or equal to minimum guarantee credit then guarantee credit is zero. Otherwise, it is the difference between the minimum guarantee credit and the total income to bring income up to the minimum guarantee level.

If the claimant is under 65 STOP HERE.

For 65s and over – savings credit

The savings thresholds are:

Single person   £77.45
Couple   £123.80

First do steps 1 and 2 above.

4. Now reduce the total income at step 2 by any working tax credit; incapacity benefit; contribution based job seeker's allowance; severe disability allowance; maternity allowance and maintenance payments.

5. If this new income figure is greater than the minimum guarantee figure from step 1 reduce it to the minimum guarantee figure.

6. From the figure obtained in step 5 above deduct the savings credit threshold. The result is the qualifying income figure.

7. Calculate 60 per cent of the qualifying income figure.

8. Compare the total income with the minimum guarantee figure (steps 1 and 2). If total income is less than minimum guarantee figure then your savings credit is the answer at step 7.

9. Total income is more than or equal to minimum guarantee figure. Deduct minimum guarantee figure from total income. Calculate 40 per cent of this figure.

10. Deduct the figure in 9 above from the figure in 7 above and the answer is your savings credit.

Example:
Mrs Jones is an 81-year-old woman who lives alone in a council house. She has no capital but lives on her old age pension and a small private pension from her late husband's employment of £15 per week. She gets retirement pension of £75.70 per week. She is not disabled.

Her pension credit then is as follows:

Single minimum guarantee	£102.10
Total income	£90.70
Guarantee credit	£11.40

Qualifying income (difference between savings threshold
£77.45 and total income £90.70)   £13.25
Total income less than minimum guarantee so savings
credit 60% of £13.25   £7.95

Total credit £11.40 + £7.95   £19.35

She also gets approximately £40 per week help with her rent and council tax
from the local authority. She has no children or other family, but manages well
with the help of neighbours, a home help and meals on wheels.

She then has a stroke which paralyses her left side but leaves her mind as sharp as
ever. She is admitted to hospital and, whilst the treatment gives her some use in
her left side, it is clear that she cannot go home and live as she used to. The
hospital therefore arranges a visit from the social worker. The social worker
shows her brochures for various homes in the area and arranges for her to visit
some of these. At one home, Sunnyside, she meets Mrs Smith, whom she has
known for years, and decides that this is the home for her. She gives up her
tenancy, sells or gives away her furniture, and moves into the home
permanently.

The local authority contracts with the owner of Sunnyside for Mrs Jones'
accommodation there, and agrees to pay £210 per week. Had Mrs Jones been
able to go home she would have got attendance allowance of about £57.20, a
small amount of pension credit each week, and all her rent and council tax paid.
Since she cannot go home, there is no rent or council tax to pay, but she is not
allowed to have attendance allowance after the first 28 days in Sunnyside
because that is a 'care'-type benefit from central government and the local
authority is responsible for 'care' for people in homes. The local authority must
therefore decide how much she can pay. It advises Mrs Jones to claim pension
credit, which she does. The DWP assesses Mrs Jones for pension credit in exactly
the same way as it assessed her when she was at home.

Single minimum guarantee   £102.10
Total income   £90.70
Guarantee credit   £11.40
Qualifying income (difference between savings
threshold £77.45 and total income £90.70)   £13.25
Total income is less than minimum guarantee so
savings credit 60% of £13.25   £7.95

Total credit £11.40 + £7.95   £19.35

So Mrs Jones' income is £75.70 retirement pension +
£15.00 private pension + £19.35 pension credit
TOTAL   £110.05

However, the local authority then sends her a bill for £93.25 per week (see
below). Since £16.80 is the amount fixed by law which residents must be left

with in their pockets or handbags each week, this is what Mrs Jones is left with for her personal expenses:

Applicable amount		*Resources*	
Personal allowance	£16.80	Retirement pension	£75.70
		Private pension	£15.00
		Pension credit	£19.35
TOTAL	£16.80	TOTAL	£110.05

The amount payable by Mrs Jones is £110.05 less £16.80, which amounts to £93.25. Thus, the local authority is paying out £210 for Mrs Jones, and recovering £93.25 in respect of day-to-day needs, which amount is paid by Mrs Jones and central government between them. The local authority is therefore left to pay the outstanding £116.75 in respect of Mrs Jones' housing and care.

12.12 CAPITAL

What would happen if Mrs Jones had capital? Capital is the main bone of contention in the process of moving into residential care and the answer depends on how much and what it is.

12.12.1 What is 'capital'?

Capital includes any sort of assets or savings which belong to the applicant. It is sometimes difficult to decide whether money should be treated as capital or income. In most cases, capital resources arise out of income resources. They represent savings out of past income. However, before they undergo the change from income to capital, all relevant debts, including, in particular, tax liabilities, are first deducted.

12.12.1A What is 'tariff income'?

Because benefit law ignores the income from capital it assumes a certain weekly income from part of the capital. For pension credit, the first £6,000 of capital or £10,000 if you are in a care home is ignored. You are then assumed to have a weekly income of £1 for each £500 unit or part of such a unit. So if you have £19,000.01 capital in a care home, £10,000 is ignored, £9,000 is 18 units of £500, 0.01p is part of a £500 unit so your tariff income is £19 per week. For local authority assessment purposes the rules are different; they ignore the first £11,750 and then assume an income of £1 per week for each whole or part unit of £250. So if you have £15,000.01 they will ignore £11,750 leaving £3,250.01, that is 13 full units and one part unit of £14 per week.

12.12.2 Capital over £19,000

This used to be very simple. Now it is not so simple. A person who has capital over £19,000, even 1p, is billed by the local authority for the whole of the amount of care – £210 per week in Mrs Jones' case. However, pension credit has removed the upper capital limit (but only for pension credit) so people can claim pension credit no matter how much capital they have. In fact, a single person in Mrs Jones position can have up to £34,000 and still get some pension credit. For as long as she can get pension credit she is funded partly by public funds and cannot get attendance allowance. As soon as she runs out of pension credit and becomes completely self-funding she will again be able to claim attendance allowance.

It would be extremely difficult to calculate the basic pension credit sums without a computer. Perhaps a small prize should be offered for the first person to calculate the point when they become better off by abandoning the pension credit claim and claiming attendance allowance instead.

For most badly disabled people with at least a basic retirement pension and capital greater than £19,000, a claim for attendance allowance will serve them better than a claim for pension credit. Perhaps the wisest advice is to claim both and then abandon one as soon as it is clear which is higher.

For the purposes of this example, let us assume that Mrs Jones has £19,000.01. Her pension credit would be:

Weekly income		£90.70
Tariff income		£19.00
Total income		£109.70
MIG – income = guarantee credit		£00.00
Qualifying income	£24.65	
Potential savings credit	£14.79	
Savings credit		£11.75
Total credit		£11.75

So her income would be

Retirement pension	£75.70
Private pension	£15.00
Pension credit	£11.75
TOTAL	£102.45

With lower rate attendance allowance it would be:

Retirement pension	£75.70
Private pension	£15.00
Lower rate attendance allowance	£38.30
TOTAL	£129.00

With higher rate attendance allowance it would be:

Retirement pension	£75.70
Private pension	£15.00
Higher rate attendance allowance	£57.20
TOTAL	£147.90

In these cases the net cost of her weekly care to her, the figure by which her saving would be reduced each week, is £226.80 (£210 + £16.80 for personal expenses) minus £102.45 with pension credit = £124.35

£226.80 – £129.00 with lower rate attendance allowance = £97.80

£226.80 – £147.90 with higher rate attendance allowance = £78.90

12.12.3   Capital under £10,000

If Mrs Jones has less than £10,000 then there is no effect on the amounts either paid by pension credit or taken by the local authority, but she must make sure that she spends the income from the capital as she gets it. If she does not, this becomes capital itself, and is added to the original sum. If this process takes her over the limit, the next-level rules apply.

If capital is between £10,000 and £19,000 then two versions of the single set of tariff income rules apply. One for the pension credit paid to Mrs Jones and one for the contribution collected from Mrs Jones.

12.12.4   Capital between £10,000.01 and £11,750

At one time, 'tariff income' used to have the same meaning for both income support and local authority assessment. In more recent times the limits at which 'tariff income' was applied were varied as between income support and local authority assessment. Now with the introduction of pension credit not only do the limits vary but also the amount.

For pension credit there is no upper limit. The lower limit for people in care homes is £10,000. Pension credit assumes an income of £1 per week for each unit of £500 or part thereof in excess of the lower capital limit. Therefore, on capital of £11,690, the first £10,000 is ignored, the balance of £1,690 produces three whole units of £500 and one unit of £190 – four units in all.

Therefore, Mrs Jones is assumed to have an additional weekly income of £4, and her pension credit now looks like this:

Weekly income	£90.70	
Tariff income	£4.00	
Total income	£94.70	
MIG – income = guarantee credit		£7.40
Qualifying income	£17.25	
Potential savings credit	£10.35	
Savings credit		£10.35
Total credit		£17.75

If Mrs Jones has more than £10,000 but up to £11,750 then there is no direct effect on the amounts taken by the local authority because it ignores capital up to £11,750. However, in calculating pension credit, capital between £10,000 and £11,750 is taken into account. Mrs Jones gets less pension credit and, because of this, pays less to the local authority.

So now pension credit only gives Mrs Jones an extra £17.75p per week. However, the local authority reduces her bill to £91.65 per week, leaving her with the same £16.80 per week for her personal expenses such as clothes, hairdressing, newspapers, etc. The local authority assessment now looks like this:

Applicable amount		*Resources*	
Personal allowance	£16.80	Retirement pension	£75.70
		Private pension	£15.00
		Pension credit	£17.75
TOTAL	£16.80	TOTAL	£108.45

The amount payable is £108.45 less £16.80, which amounts to £91.65. The local authority will now pay out £210 for Mrs Jones and recover £91.65 in respect of day-to-day needs, which is paid by Mrs Jones and central government between them. The local authority must therefore pay the other £118.35 in respect of Mrs Jones' housing and care.

This is a saving for central government, but the local authority sends a bill for slightly less and Mrs Jones finishes up with the same £16.80 per week.

12.12.5   Capital between £11,750.01 and £16,000

If Mrs Jones has more than £11,750, but less than £16,000, tariff income is applied to both the pension credit payment and the amounts taken by the local authority and, of course, it is applied differently.

Assume that Mrs Jones has £14,690. It is first necessary to calculate the pension credit. The DWP ignores the first £10,000; the balance of £4,690 produces nine whole units of £500 and one unit of £190 – 10 units in all. Mrs Jones is assumed to have an additional weekly income of £10 and her pension credit calculation now looks like this:

Weekly income	£90.70
Tariff income	£10.00
Total income	£100.70

MIG – income = guarantee credit		£1.40
Qualifying income	£23.25	
Potential savings credit	£13.95	

Savings credit	£13.95
Total credit	£15.35

NB   The local authority tariff income unit is still £250 *not* £500 which is the pension credit unit.

The local authority now proceeds as follows. It ignores the first £11,750; the balance of £2,940 produces 11 whole units of £250 and one unit of £190 – 12 units in all. Thus, Mrs Jones is assumed to have an additional weekly income of £12.

However, the local authority changes her bill to £101.25 per week, technically leaving her with the same £16.80 per week for her personal expenses. The local authority assessment now looks like this:

Applicable amount		Resources	
Personal allowance	£16.80	Retirement pension	£75.70
		Private pension	£15.00
		Pension credit	£15.35
		Local authority tariff income	£12.00
TOTAL	£16.80	TOTAL	£118.05

The amount payable is £118.05 less £16.80, which amounts to £101.25. The local authority will now pay out £210 for Mrs Jones and recover £101.25 in respect of day-to-day needs, which is paid by Mrs Jones and central government. The local authority is left to pay the outstanding £108.75 in respect of her housing and care.

The astute reader may have noticed that Mrs Jones' actual weekly income is only £106.05, but that her weekly bill is £101.25 and of course she still has her weekly personal expenses, so she will have to dip into her capital each week to provide for her own personal expenses. The drain on her capital will be about £12 per week.

12.12.6   Capital between £16,000.01 and £19,000

If Mrs Jones has more than £16,000, but less than £19,000, she would not have been entitled to any income support because of the statutory capital limit but now she can still get pension credit because the upper capital limit is gone. Different versions of tariff income are applied to the pension credit and to amounts taken by the local authority.

Assume that Mrs Jones has £16,690. The pension credit calculation looks like this.

For this calculation, if Mrs Jones has £16,690, the DWP ignores the first £10,000, the balance of £6,690 produces 13 whole units of £500 and one unit of £190 – 14 units in all. Thus, Mrs Jones is assumed to have an additional weekly income of £14.

Weekly income	£90.70
Tariff income	£14.00
Total income	£104.70
MIG – income = guarantee credit	£00.00
Qualifying income	£24.65
Potential savings credit	£14.79
Savings credit	£13.75
Total credit	£13.75

For this calculation, if Mrs Jones has £16,690, the local authority ignores the first £11,750, the balance of £4,940 produces 19 whole units of £250 and one unit of £190 – 20 units in all. Thus, Mrs Jones is assumed to have an additional weekly income of £20.

The local authority puts up her bill to £107.65 per week, technically leaving her with the same £16.80 per week for her personal expenses such as clothes, hairdressing, newspapers, etc. The local authority assessment now looks like this:

Applicable amount		Resources	
Personal allowance	£16.80	Retirement pension	£ 75.70
		Private pension	£15.00
		Pension credit	£13.75
		Local authority tariff income	£20.00
TOTAL	£16.80	TOTAL	£124.45

The amount payable is £124.45 – £16.80, which amounts to £107.65. The local authority will now pay £210 for Mrs Jones and recover £107.65 in respect of day-to-day needs, which is paid by Mrs Jones with central government still making a contribution. The authority is left to pay the other £102.35 in respect of her housing and care. Mrs Jones will of course have to dig in to her capital to pay her personal expenses and part of her bill because her real income is only £104.45 and her local authority bill is £107.65.

12.12.7   Summary

Capital

	Income	Tariff income (pension credit)	Tariff income (local authority)	Pension credit	Total income	Local authority	Mrs Jones	Weekly capital drain
<£10,000	£90.70	£0.00	£0.00	19.35	£110.05	£116.75	£93.25	£0.00
£11,690	£90.70	£4.00	£0.00	£17.75	£108.45	£118.35	£91.65	£0.00
£14,690	£90.70	£10.00	£12.00	£15.35	£106.05	£108.75	£101.25	£12.00
£16,690	£90.70	£14.00	£20.00	£13.75	£104.45	£102.35	£107.65	£20.00
£19,000.01	£90.70	£19.00	£0.00	£11.75	£102.45	£0.00	£210.00	£124.35
£19,000.01	£90.70	£0.00	(LR AA)[1]	£38.30	£129.00	£0.00	£210.00	£97.80
>£19,000.01	£90.70	£0.00	(HR AA)[1]	£57.20	£147.90	£0.00	£210.00	£78.90

One of the things that frequently goes wrong for people in this group is that pension credit (and technically the local authority charge) needs to be reassessed frequently. Mrs Jones, in five out of seven of the above examples, would be spending part of her capital on her local authority bill and/or her personal expenses each week, so every now and again her capital will drop by a £250 unit and/or a £500 unit and her pension credit should increase by £1 per week if she is entitled to it or she might become entitled if she was not entitled before. Since she is unlikely to know the ins and outs of the tariff income rules herself, and has no relatives to keep an eye on this, the DWP will not take any action unless instructed to do so and they are moving towards 5 or 7-year assessment periods for people of Mrs Jones' age. It makes little difference to the local authority and no difference to the owner of Sunnyside, who are paid the same amount no matter what happens. It should be in the local authority's interest to keep her pension credit up as high as it will go because it will then be able to recover more

---

1   LR AA = lower rate attendance allowance; HR AA = higher rate attendance allowance.

from her, although by the same token its tariff income take will fall. It seems unlikely in the present climate that authorities will have sufficiently intelligent systems to pursue the most appropriate tariff income calculations which will give them and Mrs Jones the best and most accurate deal. It is likely therefore that in such circumstances Mrs Jones will lose track of her savings and lose benefit.

12.12.8 Capital and *R v Sefton Metropolitan Borough Council ex parte Help the Aged*[1]

In 1997, Sefton Metropolitan Borough Council claimed that it was desperately short of money and had more than its fair share of elderly people (Sefton takes in Southport in Lancashire – a favourite seaside resort for elderly people in the north). The council decided to refuse to accommodate anyone until he or she was down to his or her last £1,500 (the price of a decent funeral). The High Court upheld this decision. The Court of Appeal overturned the High Court and held that authorities are not entitled, because of their own finances, to defer performance of their duty to accommodate certain persons in need of care and attention not otherwise available to them, under s 21 of the National Assistance Act 1948, pending their own resources falling below a financial threshold set by the particular authority. Although it was anticipated that this case would go to the House of Lords, it did not in fact do so, and the Court of Appeal judgment is the final word on the subject. Anyone assessed as in need of accommodation by a local authority must be accommodated if he or she has less than £19,000 (as it now is) in capital and, of course, meets the income criteria.

12.12.9 Ignored capital

Some capital will be ignored, such as:

–   the cash or surrender value of an annuity;
–   the value of the right to receive any income under a life interest, a life rent or an occupational or private pension, or any rent or most reversionary interests;
–   the right to receive a capital sum by instalments;
–   the sale value of the right to an income in another country which cannot be transferred to this country;
–   money from social work departments for children, unless the claimant is on strike;
–   money from the Social Fund, the Macfarlane Trust, the Macfarlane (Special Payments) Trust or the Independent Living Fund, or its successors;
–   the assets of any business, but only for 26 weeks or longer than that if reasonable where the applicant is ill, unable to work in the business because of the illness, and intends to return to it;
–   any NHS travelling expenses, welfare foods payments, prison visiting payments, or any arrears of special war widow's payments, but only for up to 52 weeks.

---

1   [1997] 4 All ER 532, CA.

12.12.10   Income treated as capital

Although few of the following items will apply to residents in care homes, they are treated as capital, although they would otherwise be regarded as income:

- annual bounty from the fire brigade, coastguard, lifeboat, territorial or reserve forces;
- holiday pay payable more than 4 weeks after the end of the employment;
- most income derived from capital;
- advances of earnings or loans from employers or income tax refunds (except to strikers);
- prisoners' discharge grants;
- arrears of custodian's payments from a local authority.

12.12.11   How to value capital

Capital is valued at its current market or surrender value, after deducting any debt or mortgage secured on it and 10 per cent for the expenses of the sale, if there will be such expenses.

Capital abroad which cannot be brought to this country is valued at the price it could be sold for in the United Kingdom. In cases of dispute it must be first established that the applicant owns an asset which is saleable. Assets should not be valued at a figure higher than anything a person could realise on them.

Where an applicant owns something jointly with one or more other persons, they are treated as if each of them were entitled to equal shares. The cost of converting money into sterling is deducted from the value of capital paid in any other currency.

Personal possessions will not be counted as part of capital unless it is thought that they have been acquired in order to reduce capital and increase benefit. There is no clear definition of 'personal possessions', but items in regular use would presumably count, even if they were valuable, such as an expensive car. It is less clear, for example, how stamp collections or valuable paintings would be treated.

Capital paid to a third party on behalf of any member of the applicant's family is treated as capital of the applicant if the money is derived from social security, or if it is used for food, ordinary clothing or footwear (not school uniform or sports kit), household fuel, rent or rates which qualify for housing benefit, or other housing costs to the extent that they are met by pension credit.

12.12.12   Capital other than property

Money paid to the applicant in consequence of damage or loss to the home or any personal possession is ignored for 26 weeks or longer if it is to be used for repair or replacement.

The surrender value of an endowment policy is completely ignored, but not the money when the policy matures.

Money in trust must be valued just as any other capital or income. Money put in trust for a child after a personal injury will be ignored until the child leaves school. Payments actually made by these or other personal injury trusts will normally be treated as capital or income.

Payments of income from a discretionary trust will normally be treated as voluntary or charitable payments.

The value of a trust derived from a personal injury to the applicant is wholly ignored (but the income from it is not). However, the compensator of a personal injury victim is required to recover all benefits paid to a victim from the final settlement, then return them to the DWP.

The assets of a business wholly or partly owned by the applicant will be ignored provided he or she is engaged in the business, or for long enough to allow for the sale of the business if it ceases trading. Business assets have been defined as part of the fund employed and risked in the business. If the applicant owns a business in the form of a company either alone or with partners, the capital of the business is treated as belonging to him or her and the value of the shares is ignored.

All social security payments are taken into account first as income, and then as capital (if not spent immediately) except arrears of DLA and attendance allowance, and of any means-tested benefit, all of which are ignored for 52 weeks.

Social fund payments are completely ignored.

12.12.13 Valuation of property

Valuation of property is not the legal interest in the house, but the beneficial interest. Where a house is solely beneficially owned by the resident, it is valued in the ordinary way, ie its market value minus 10 per cent for the costs of sale. Where a house is jointly beneficially owned together with someone who is not a relative who would cause the property to be disregarded (see below), the valuation is markedly different. What is to be valued is not a fraction of the market value of the property, but the market value of the resident's individual interest.

The following is an example: Mr Smith is the sole legal owner of a house with a market value of £120,000. An agreement signed at the time of the purchase makes it clear that the house is beneficially owned as a tenancy in common between Mr and Mrs Smith and their daughter, Sally. Sally owns one-half and Mr and Mrs Smith own one-quarter each. Mr Smith becomes a resident at Sunnyside home. The temptation is to say either: 'The house is in his sole name – we will treat him as having £120,000'; or 'Mr Smith is beneficially entitled to one-quarter of the house – we will treat him as having £30,000'. Both approaches are wrong. What is for sale is his interest, that is, his rights in the house which are:

(a) the right to occupy the whole of the house but with Mrs Smith and Sally having the same right; and

(b) 25 per cent of the equity should the house be sold; and
(c) power to sell or will his interest to someone else.

Anyone who purchased or inherited Mrs Smith's interest who would receive exactly what he had. That is the right to occupy the whole of the house but with Mrs Smith and Sally having the same right at the same time and 25 per cent of the equity should the house be sold. Usually the value of such interests is nil or not much above.

12.12.14   Capital value of the home

The dwelling occupied as the home is ignored for capital purposes, as are any parts of the premises which it would be impracticable to sell separately, and croft land in Scotland. The home includes the dwelling, together with any garage, garden and outbuildings. Of course, people who move permanently into residential care no longer live in what were their homes, so they do not come under this category.

(a)   *Capital value of premises other than the home for pension credit purposes only*

Any premises occupied by a partner or close relative, who is over 60 years old or incapacitated, 'as his home' are ignored completely for capital purposes. The value of the following premises is disregarded for a period of 6 months, or longer if it is thought reasonable:

–   premises acquired for occupation;
–   premises which the claimant is taking steps to dispose of;
–   premises in respect of which the claimant has commenced legal proceedings with a view to occupation;
–   premises which are being repaired or altered before occupation.

The following amounts are disregarded for a period of 6 months, or longer if it is thought reasonable:

–   the value of capital connected with property;
–   the proceeds of the sale of a former home, if they are to be used to buy another home;
–   compensation for damage to, or loss of, a home;
–   money acquired for essential repairs or improvements;
–   money deposited with a housing association as a condition of occupation of a former matrimonial home.

Of course, the key provision is 'premises which the claimant is taking steps to dispose of'. The DWP will ignore the value of the former home if it is on the market for a reasonable sum for 6 months, or longer if it is thought reasonable.

(b) Capital value of premises other than the home for local authority purposes only

The value of the home must be disregarded in three circumstances:

(1) if it is the dwelling of a temporary resident in circumstances where:
- he intends to return to occupy that dwelling as his home and which is still available to him; or
- he is taking reasonable steps to dispose of the property in order to acquire another more suitable property to return to; or
(2) if it is occupied by a partner, former partner or a relative (defined in the regulations and guidance), provided the partner or relative is aged 60 or over, or is incapacitated or is a child whom the resident is liable to maintain. (NOTE: Incapacitated is not defined but would probably be accepted without question if the person received or qualified for incapacity benefit, severe disablement allowance, disability living allowance, attendance allowance, constant attendance allowance, or a similar benefit.); or
(3) throughout the first 12 weeks of a permanent stay. (NOTE: This stay need not be the first permanent admission to permanent residential care. It is not unheard of for people to become 'permanent' residents and then improve sufficiently to return home. If they then are readmitted after more than a year they will qualify for the disregard again. Where someone leaves residential care where they have been living on permanent basis before the end of the 12 weeks and then re-enters on a permanent basis within 52 weeks they will be entitled to the remaining balance of the 12-week disregard.)

The local authority has a discretion to disregard property which is property occupied by someone else, for example an ex-carer or a companion who has given up his or her own home to care for the resident before admission. Any decision to disregard a property under this provision is reviewable at any time.

A situation could thus arise where the Department for Work and Pensions (DWP) will pay a resident pension credit because his or her house is on the market for less than 26 weeks, or for some other reasonable purpose, and ignore its value, but after 12 weeks the local authority can bill the resident for the whole amount of his or her care because it does not ignore the value of the house.

The circumstances of Mrs Jones can be changed as an example. She has a house worth £50,000 which she puts on the market immediately upon going into the home, and 12 weeks go by. Her pension credit assessment still looks like this:

		Total income
Single minimum guarantee	£102.10	
Total income	£ 90.70	
Guarantee credit	£ 11.40	£ 11.40
Qualifying income	£ 13.25	
Savings credit		£ 7.95
Retirement pension		£ 75.70
Private pension		£ 15.00
		£110.05

Mrs Jones' real income is £110.05 per week because the DWP ignores the value of the house. The local authority considers that Mrs Jones has capital assets of £45,000, so she must pay the full cost, and bills her for £210 per week. She cannot pay this. What can she do? The local authority is bound to pay for her care in these circumstances and cannot stop paying, so the whole burden falls on the authority. However, it always had and still has the discretionary power to take a 'charge' on the house through an administrative procedure. A 'charge' is a legally imposed mortgage, and when the house is eventually sold, the local authority can recover everything that it is owed by Mrs Jones from the proceeds of the sale. There are, however, three important points to note:

(1) The power to charge is discretionary, the local authority does not have to do it, and it can be petitioned all the way through its formal procedures not to do so.

(2) A charge is a real mortgage and the local authority can apply to the courts at any time for an order to sell the property no matter who is living in it. Such an application can, of course, be defended.

(3) A charge can be registered under these provisions only if the land is the sole property of the resident. If it is jointly owned, the best the authority can do is to register a caution.

A new scheme introduced in 2001 allows people who are unable or unwilling to sell their homes to defer payment of part of their fees to the local authority for an agreed fixed period. This scheme requires the authority and the resident to make such an agreement in writing, and the resident to consent to a legal charge being placed on the home. The obvious advantage of this scheme is that it enables people to leave the family home to whomever they desire, and for the beneficiary to be able to settle the resident's debt at a later date, possibly after his or her death, by releasing the equity in the house. An additional advantage is that the resident is still treated as a 'self-funder', and is able to claim attendance allowance of up to £56.25 per week to help him or her pay the local authority's bills, if the time comes when he or she is not entitled to income support.

12.12.15   Notional capital

Let us assume that Mrs Jones decides to give the house to a kindly neighbour who has helped to look after her for some years.

If a person spends or gives away a large sum of money shortly before or after going into residential care, it will be assumed that the money has been spent or given away to take advantage of the system:

> 'A claimant shall be treated as possessing capital of which he has deprived himself for the purpose of securing entitlement to income support or increasing the amount of that benefit (or reducing liability to the local authority for residential care costs).'

A person deprives him or herself of capital if he or she ceases to possess it, even if he or she receives some other resource in return. The crucial question is the intention of the claimant. Obtaining benefit must be a reasonably foreseeable purpose of the transaction. If it can be shown that the money has been spent on something a prudent person would have spent it on if he or she had no intention of claiming any benefit, the rule should not be applied.

Thus, in Mrs Jones' situation, the local authority could continue to bill her, make her bankrupt and reverse the gift of the house under the provisions of the Insolvency Act 1986.

Gifts of capital are horribly complicated and gifts into trust are even more complicated. The rule of thumb is that any gift made once it is reasonably foreseeable that entitlement to income support and/or admission to a care home will arise will be ineffective in so far as it seeks to enhance entitlement to benefit or reduce liability to local authority charges. Furthermore, any gift which does not relinquish complete control of the asset, such as the gift of a house with a lease back or licence to continue to occupy, will also be ineffective for those purposes.

There are, however, some precautions which can and should be taken. For example, Mr Kennedy and his wife are aged 67 and have no capital or income except for the usual State pensions. They live in a house which, because of the quirks of the property market, is now worth £200,000 and which they own jointly. Neither of them is in particularly good health, but Mrs Kennedy needs so much care that she has had to move into a care home. For pension credit and Care in the Community purposes, they are no longer a couple, and Mrs Kennedy gets pension credit to pay for her care home fees, with the council finding the rest. If Mr Kennedy dies, Mrs Kennedy would have to sell the house, and either keep the money, or be treated by the DWP and the local authority as having the money, so that her pension credit would stop, and she would become liable for the whole of the care home fees. There is, however, nothing to prevent them giving the house away now and retaining a beneficial life tenancy for Mr Kennedy, since this is disregarded, and to sell the house would not establish or increase entitlement to income support, or reduce Mrs Kennedy's fees.

Of course, Mr Kennedy would have to beware of other pitfalls associated with giving away assets. Such gifts can also disrupt the donee's entitlement to benefit by putting them over the capital limit for things like working tax credit. However close and trusted they are, donees can go bankrupt or die, removing the donated asset completely from the donor's sphere of influence.

Capital which is available on application will be treated as the claimant's notional capital unless it is either part of a discretionary trust, a trust derived from a personal injury, or a loan which would be secured on disregarded capital.

Chapter 13

REGULATION AND REGULATORY ACTION

13.1   OVERVIEW AND APPROACH TO REGULATION

As was described in Chapter 1, the thrust and purpose of regulation are to ensure that registrable premises, the activities carried on there and the paper audit trail (ie the full array of business and service user-specific documentation) are maintained in such a way as to comply with the requirements of legislation and regulations issued by the Department of Health and others empowered to issue regulations which impact upon the sector, for example the Department for Education and Skills, in the case of residential special schools. The intention is to ensure, so far as is possible, that minimum standards are applied and maintained consistently across the health care sector's diverse specialties. Readers will be aware that Scotland and Wales have slightly different regulatory environments from England, and from each other. However, whilst this book is written with regulation in England in mind, the contents of this chapter are of relevance to each of the three different jurisdictions.

This chapter addresses the regulatory action that may be taken to correct any misconduct in relation to care homes, whether this amounts to mere oversight, or more serious inadequacies embedded within systems and procedures.

Inspection is the single most obvious aspect of regulation.[1] However, regulation embraces every aspect of the operation of a care home. Accordingly, it is necessary to ensure that all the relevant legislation and regulations are adhered to, and that the national minimum standards are followed. It is important to emphasise that whilst legislation has force of law, the national minimum standards[2] do not. These must, however, be taken into account by regulators, courts and the Care Standards Tribunal, and breach of which could provide sufficient reason to reject any application for registration, or to qualify or cancel a registration.

The standards, in the way in which they apply to, and affect, the conduct of care homes, are in many ways similar in status to the Highway Code and the way in which it applies to and affects the conduct of road users, particularly drivers.

Regulatory action is the prerogative of the regulatory authority. The aim of regulation should be to protect the frail, vulnerable, sick and needy. Regulation

---

1   See Chapter 7.
2   These will be referred to hereafter as 'standards'.

should not be undertaken punitively or capriciously. In exercising their regulatory powers, regulators should always have in mind the needs and interests of the service users accommodated in the regulated care home. The question to be considered by the regulatory authority ought to be:

> 'Will the action that we propose better serve the interests of the service users in care than some other action or no action?'

Preparation for regulatory action will be time-consuming. Save in sudden and unexpected applications for urgent cancellation of registration, there will be opportunity for discussion, the taking of advice from lawyers and the convening of case conferences to ensure that the correct course of action is followed.

The National Care Standards Council (NCSC) may take many courses of action which fall short of formal action. It can for example:

– record matters of concern arising at inspection and which require rectification;
– write to care home owners with the results of investigations into complaints that require improvement of standards;
– issue informal notices requiring improvements in standards, failing which regulatory action may be taken.

Warnings are always sensible. It does not need statutory regulation to suggest to the NCSC that it should give warning indications when standards are falling or when rectification may be required.

Provided care is taken in preparing any regulatory action, and this action is preceded by correspondence or, if necessary, visits to the home or contact by telephone, and is documented by detailed and witnessed attendance notes, it should be relatively easy to persuade courts and the Care Standards Tribunal to endorse and sustain the action.

Regulatory action should be flexible. If the shortcomings which led to regulatory action have been corrected, the NCSC should not be slow to withdraw its action; indeed, in these increasingly cost-conscious times it would be irresponsible to do otherwise.

Clear strategic aims, effectively controlled and implemented, will impress both the courts and Care Standards Tribunal, and shorten the regulatory process, if such becomes necessary.

## 13.2	TYPES OF REGULATORY ACTION

There are three types of regulatory action:

(a)	to vary condition(s) of registration or impose new conditions;
(b)	to cancel registration; and
(c)	to prosecute those responsible for an offence committed in the operation of a regulated care home.

13.2.1 Variation of condition/imposition of new conditions

There is now power for an owner to seek the removal or variation of a condition of registration or seek the imposition of a new condition.[1] Similarly, the registered person may apply for cancellation of a registration,[2] but not if the registration authority has given him or her notice of its proposal to cancel the registration,[3] unless the registration authority subsequently decides not to take that step.[4]

The NCSC, as the registration authority, may, as one would expect, vary or remove any condition of registration or seek to impose a new condition in relation to the registration.[5] However, with the exception of situations requiring the application of the urgent procedure for cancellation of registration, removal or variation of any condition of registration, or imposition of a new 'additional condition'[6] of registration,[7] notice of such proposed variation must be given to the registered person.[8] Such notice must give the reasons for the NCSC's decision.[9]

13.2.2 Cancellation

Power to effect cancellation of the registration of a registered care home is contained in s 14 of the Care Standards Act 2000 (the 2000 Act), which states that:

'(1) The registration authority may at any time cancel the registration of a person in respect of an establishment or agency –

(a) on the ground that that person has been convicted of a relevant offence;

(b) on the ground that any other person has been convicted of such an offence in relation to the establishment or agency;

(c) on the ground that the establishment or agency is being, or has at any time been, carried on otherwise than in accordance with the relevant requirements;

(d) on any ground specified by regulations.

(2) For the purposes of this section the following are relevant offences –

(a) an offence under this Part or regulations made under it;

(b) an offence under the Registered Homes Act 1984 or regulations made under it;

(c) an offence under the 1989 Act or regulations made under it;

(d) ...

(3) In this section "relevant requirements" means –

---

1   Care Standards Act 2000, s 15(1).
2   Ibid, s 15(1)(b).
3   Ibid, s 17(4)(a).
4   Ibid, s 15(2)(a).
5   Ibid, s 17(4).
6   Ibid, s 20(i), (ii).
7   See generally ibid, s 20.
8   Ibid, s 17(4).
9   Ibid, s 17(6).

(a)   any requirements or conditions imposed by or under this Part; and
(b)   the requirements of any other enactment which appear to the registration
        authority to be relevant.'

It can be seen that the grounds extend to any offences committed by the
registered person generally in relation to several different categories of regulated
home. Further, offences committed by others in relation to the regulations can
also result in the cancellation process being initiated. The most likely offence for
which others might be responsible is obstruction of the process of inspection.[1]
Any evidence of instruction by the registered person to so obstruct would, it is
submitted, amount to evidence of unfitness of that person to own or manage the
home.

Breach of a condition of registration is clearly good reason to consider
cancellation of registration. Curiously, as was the case under previous
legislation,[2] the breach probably does not have to have been proven by a
successful prosecution to conviction, but simply established as a fact by the
NCSC before the tribunal.

The only grounds for cancellation under s 14(1)(d) as set out in the National
Care Standards Commission (Registration) Regulations 2001 are:

(a)   non-payment of annual fee;
(b)   a false statement on a registration application; and
(c)   lack of financial viability.

For cancellation at the request of the registered person, and the effect of
cancellation, see para **13.5**.

13.2.3   Prosecution

The 2000 Act provides that certain acts and omissions in contravention of the
provisions of the Act and/or Regulations amount to an offence. Such acts or
omissions are, perhaps, better described as statutory offences rather than
criminal offences. Nevertheless, the consequence of committing such offences
may be criminal prosecution and, if convicted, may lead to cancellation of
registration.[3]

(a)   Notice of prosecution

The practice previously found in reg 20 of the Residential Care Homes
Regulations 1984[4] and reg 15 of the Nursing Homes and Mental Nursing
Homes Regulations 1984[5] of serving notice on the person registered, who is
believed to have acted in such a way as to amount to contravention of
regulations, has been adopted in each set of regulations made in England under
the 2000 Act. However, no such advance notice is required in relation to an
offence created by the 2000 Act.

---

1   Care Standards Act 2000, s 31(9)(a).
2   Registered Homes Act 1984, s 28.
3   See para **13.2.2**.
4   SI 1984/1345.
5   SI 1984/1578.

(b)   How will the decision 'to prosecute or not' be arrived at?

The decision to prosecute comes about, for the most part, only once the responsible individual has been given notice. It should be borne in mind that the decision is made by a senior officer within the NCSC. The decision is discretionary and, for the most part, exercisable only after certain preliminary steps have been observed.

In the overwhelming majority of cases the NCSC must have observed the prescribed process identified in the relevant Regulations. The process is, in effect, identical in each set of Regulations, and is as follows:

'(1)   A contravention or failure to comply with any of the provisions of regulations x to y shall be an offence.

(2)   The Commission shall not bring proceedings against a person in respect of any contravention or failure to comply with those regulations unless –

(a)   subject to paragraph (4) he is a registered person;
(b)   notice has been given to him in accordance with paragraph (3);
(c)   the period specified in the notice has expired; and
(d)   the person contravenes or fails to comply with any of the provisions of the regulations mentioned in the notice.

(3)   Where the Commission considers that the registered person has contravened or failed to comply with any of the provisions of the regulations mentioned in paragraph ... it may serve a notice on the registered person specifying –

(a)   in what respect in its opinion the registered person has contravened or is contravening any of the regulations, or has failed or is failing to comply with the requirements of any of the regulations;
(b)   what action, in the opinion of the Commission, the registered person should take so as to comply with any of those regulations; and
(c)   the period, not exceeding three months, within which the registered person should take action.

(4)   The Commission may bring proceedings against a person who was once, but no longer is, a registered person, in respect of a failure to comply with regulation ... [record keeping] ... and for this purpose, references in paragraphs (2) and (3) to a registered person shall be taken to include such a person.'

It is important to remember that proceedings in relation to an offence under the 2000 Act itself can be brought immediately and without advance notice. However, the same is not true for proceedings in respect of contravention, or failure to comply with regulations. Further, the NCSC must identify in the notice what steps must be taken so as to ensure compliance, and the period within which those steps should be taken, which must not exceed 3 months.

The Regulations do not state that the remedial action must have been *completed* within 3 months. At present, it is not clear whether the Regulations will be interpreted restrictively, ie that all remedial steps will need to have been completed within the period specified, or interpreted more liberally, so that taking all reasonable steps to comply will itself be sufficient. For example, if a requirement entails a change to the physical environment of a care home necessitating planning consent, it is inconceivable that the planning process, once initiated, would complete within 3 months, less still the building work. The view of the NCSC will probably turn on the specific circumstances of each case.

Offences created by regulation can only be prosecutable provided the prosecuting authority complies with the detailed procedure prescribed in the relevant Regulations.

(c)   Who may commence a prosecution?

As under previous legislation, it is not possible for a regulated care home owner or a prospective care home owner to initiate the regulatory process. Accordingly, it is not possible to know in advance, whether a proposed individual, care home or facility will meet with the relevant requirements of the 2000 Act, Regulations or standards.

The power to initiate the process of proceedings concerning the regulation of aspects of a care home rests, in England, with the NCSC, in Wales with the National Assembly for Wales, the Care Standards Inspectorate for Wales and in Scotland with the Scottish Commission for the Regulation of Care.

It should be remembered, however, that in relation to children's homes the local authority for the area within which the home is situated will retain its duty to protect young people[1] including, for example, making an emergency application to the magistrates' court for an order removing a child to a place of safety.

If anyone other than the NCSC[2] wishes to initiate proceedings in relation to the 2000 Act or any of the regulations made under it, the written consent of the Attorney-General must first be secured.[3]

13.3   AGAINST WHOM MAY REGULATORY ACTION BE TAKEN?

Regulatory action will be taken against the registered person being the owner, or, where a body corporate, the responsible individual and/or manager of the registered care home. Prosecutions of persons who are carrying on or managing an 'establishment' without being registered will be brought against those persons. It is the simple fact of the absence of registration which leads to prosecution in these cases.

In offences of obstruction of an inspection under ss 31 and 32 of the 2000 Act, the proceedings will be against those individuals who intentionally obstruct the inspection or, without reasonable excuse, fail to comply with any requirement of s 31 or s 32.

Under previous legislation there had been some instances where proceedings, for example, against a company, were thought to have been frustrated where no

---

1   Child protection powers are contained in ss 43–52 of the Children Act 1989.
2   With limited exceptions: see s 113 of the 2000 Act.
3   Ibid, s 29.

identifiable person could be held to account. To address this, a care home manager and responsible person must be registered.

Proceedings may be brought against a former registered person in relation to any failure to ensure that comprehensive and contemporaneous medical records were compiled and retained for not less than 3 years (from the date of the last entry).[1]

In respect of children's homes, records must be retained for not less than 75 years from the date of birth of the child; alternatively, where the child dies before the age of 18 years, records must be retained for 15 years from the date of death.[2]

Where any offence is committed by a body corporate[3] and the offence is proved to have been committed with the consent or connivance of, or due to the neglect of any director, manager, company secretary or anyone purporting to act in such a capacity, that person will also be guilty of an offence and be liable to be punished accordingly.[4]

13.4 COMMENCEMENT OF PROCEEDINGS

Proceedings for an offence under Part II of the 2000 Act or under regulations must be brought within a period of 6 months from the date on which the evidence giving rise to the prosecution came to the NCSC's attention.[5] This will, in all probability, be self-evident from any contravention notice which may have been served and will usually arise from an inspection in any event. Proceedings cannot be commenced where the commission of an offence occurred 3 years or more previously, no matter when the circumstances actually came to the attention of the prosecutor.

13.5 URGENT SITUATIONS

Where the mechanism of prior notice to the registered person is too cumbersome and slow to address an immediate and serious risk to service users, the urgent cancellation of a registration has been retained in the 2000 Act.[6] The decision to cancel a registration rests with the magistrates' court, to which an application for urgent cancellation must be made. The NCSC can only decide whether or not to *initiate* the cancellation process.

In order to be able to grant an application, the magistrates' court must believe that unless an order is made there will be a serious risk to a person's life, health or well-being,[7] which includes members of staff, visitors, etc, as well as service users.

---

1   Private and Voluntary Health Care (England) Regulations 2001, reg 21.
2   Children's Homes Regulations 2001, reg 28.
3   Principally companies and local authority social services departments.
4   2000 Act, s 30(2).
5   Ibid, s 29(2).
6   Ibid, s 20(1)(b).
7   Ibid.

The NCSC's decision to make application for urgent cancellation must be reasonable, rational and not taken capriciously or for improper purpose.[1]

Where circumstances arose under the previous regulatory regime[2] which warranted an application for urgent cancellation, it was usually the case that such application was made within 24–48 hours of the regulator becoming aware of the situation precipitating the application. It is to be anticipated that a similar approach will be adopted by the NCSC since to allow any longer period to elapse without the making of an application suggests that urgency does not exist.

Further, because applications can be made to a court without notice,[3] the NCSC will have standing orders regulating who can initiate the process, and in what circumstances they have such authority. Standing orders, and verification that the decision-making process followed these orders, must be produced at the request of the registered person.

This urgent procedure, in addition to seeking a magistrate's order cancelling a registration, may also be used to vary or remove existing conditions, and imposing new conditions.[4]

Any order must be in writing[5] and served on the registered person and the 'appropriate authorities' as soon as practicable after the making of an application.[6]

An appropriate authority is, undoubtedly, a reference to placing authorities, ie those public bodies with financial responsibility for meeting the cost associated with a particular service user.

An appeal against a decision of the magistrates' court to cancel registration pursuant to s 20 of the 2000 Act shall be to the Care Standards Tribunal.[7] The appeal must be made within 28 days after service of the order.[8] The tribunal may either confirm the order made or direct that it ceases to have effect.[9]

13.5.1   Judicial review of magistrates' decision to cancel

The magistrates' decision is subject to judicial review to suspend the order of the magistrates pending either a full hearing of the judicial review or the tribunal appeal. The application for judicial review may be a device to keep the home in business, and may be no more than a stalling tactic. However, it illustrates that the magistrates' order is not absolutely final. Judicial review applications are now a more frequent event.

---

1   In such circumstances individual officers of the NCSC may become personally liable for the consequences of the decision.
2   For example, the Residential Homes Act 1984.
3   2000 Act, s 20(2).
4   Ibid, s 20(1)(a).
5   Ibid, s 20(4).
6   Ibid, s 20(3).
7   Ibid, s 21(1)(a).
8   Ibid, s 21(2).
9   Ibid, s 21(4).

In *R v Ealing, Hammersmith and Hounslow Health Authority ex parte Wilson*,[1] in relation to which orders to suspend the operation of the magistrates' order were made on an interim basis, the harsh words with which Laws J rejected the application on a full hearing have caused subsequent judges to take a less accommodating view of judicial review applications. Laws J suggested that the court should intervene only where such orders were clearly perverse. The court should not allow itself to be manipulated to stall orders made for the protection of the frail and vulnerable. However, a number of judges have been persuaded to intervene in such circumstances. This is a poor reflection on the integrity of public authorities which made the applications, and may be regarded as a reflection of the inadequacy of the statutory appeal process.

Grounds for applying for judicial review might include:

(a)   the reasons given for the order cannot sustain an assertion of 'serious risk';
(b)   the NCSC did not make a full disclosure of material facts which might have influenced the magistrates;
(c)   the NCSC was less than full and frank;
(d)   the delay between the discovery of the circumstances and the action taken was so long as to negate the proposition of serious risk;
(e)   the allegations are well known and the subject of dispute, rather than arising as a sudden emergency;
(f)   the magistrate was misled as to his or her discretion and the law by the material placed before him or her.

Applications for judicial review must be made quickly. Any delay may be fatal to the application.

13.5.2   Consequences of cancellation

Cancelling registration does not entitle the NCSC, without the owner's co-operation, to close a regulated care home. The order will have been obtained in the interests of the service users, and this must be remembered at all times. The movement of service users to other accommodation should be effected as quickly, painlessly and in as low a profile as possible.

The NCSC has no right or power in relation to the premises in addition to the power of inspection. There will be a right to enter and inspect premises reasonably believed to be conducted as a regulated care home, but not to remove anyone, save with their consent.

Authorities must appreciate that adults not subject to a custodial prison sentence or to a secure detention order pursuant to the Mental Health Act 1983 cannot be compelled to vacate premises. Service users themselves commit no offence by remaining in place. However, in extreme circumstances, local authorities may consider seeking to have service users detained under the provisions of the Mental Health Act 1983 on the basis that they are a danger to themselves or others.

---

1   (1996) 30 BML 92.

Section 47 of the National Assistance Act 1948 provides for a local authority to make application to detain, in secure accommodation, persons who are certified to be:

(a) suffering from grave chronic disease or, being aged, are infirm or physically incapacitated and are living in unsanitary conditions; and

(b) are unable to care for themselves and are not receiving proper care and attention.

The difficulty will undoubtedly be in establishing unsanitary conditions. Many reasons may have given rise to the order cancelling a care home registration, but it is extremely unlikely to be the case that the premises can be shown to be unsanitary.

Under Part III of the National Assistance Act 1948, a local authority is under a public duty to service users to provide accommodation. A health authority is under a similar duty to provide for the health care needs of persons resident within its jurisdiction, free of charge. If, as a result of cancellation of registration, service users are abandoned, health care professionals may consider themselves professionally obliged to provide appropriate care, perhaps in the existing establishment. If that occurs, it cannot be said that the service users are not receiving proper care and attention.

The NCSC must consider carefully the risk of lack of co-operation from service users and the availability of appropriate alternative accommodation before initiating the cancellation process. Obtaining the magistrate's order is relatively easy. Dealing with the consequences that flow, in an area not well covered by legal provision, may prove more difficult.

It is submitted that such action should be taken only when circumstances are truly grave, ie in the words of the Act, 'there will be a serious risk to a person's life, health or well being' unless the order is made.

13.6   FAILURE TO COMPLY WITH THE NATIONAL MINIMUM STANDARDS

Failure to comply with the national minimum standards does not amount to an offence. The standards are intended to be used to achieve a minimum standard of service delivery and physical environment in regulated care homes across the country. However, whilst the standards are to be taken into account by the NCSC, the courts and tribunal, offending against any one or more of the standards will not, of itself, result in prosecution, or the issue of notice for failure to comply.

In addition, as is the case under the Highway Code, in any proceedings for an offence under the Regulations, the standards will be taken into account.

13.7 OFFENCES

Carrying on or managing an establishment[1] without being registered is an offence[2] punishable by a fine not exceeding level 5. If the person convicted was registered, but the registration was cancelled before the commission of the offence, or the conviction is a second or subsequent conviction for an offence in relation to an establishment or agency of the same description, then that person may be sentenced to up to 6 months' imprisonment or subject to a fine not exceeding level 5 or to both.[3]

Any materially false or misleading statement[4] made knowingly in relation to an application for registration will constitute an offence,[5] punishable by a fine not exceeding level 4.

Failure to display, in a conspicuous place at the establishment, the certificate of registration constitutes an offence, punishable by a fine not exceeding level 2.[6]

Deceiving another into believing that the care home is registered is an offence. Section 26(1) of the 2000 Act states that:

'A person who, with intent to deceive any person –

(a) applies any name to premises in England or Wales; or
(b) in any way describes such premises or holds such premises out,

so as to indicate, or reasonably be understood to indicate, that the premises are an establishment, or an agency, of a particular description shall be liable on summary conviction to a fine not exceeding LEVEL 5 on the standard scale unless registration has been effected under this Part in respect of the premises as an establishment or agency of that description.'

'A person' clearly envisages that anyone might commit this offence, and may include a person conducting a care home which is not registered for the provision of particular types of care, but which is held out as such, for example a home that advertises itself as providing nursing care. An offence can also be committed by somebody unconnected with the operation of an establishment who holds out to others that the establishment is a care home of a particular type, even if those responsible for the conduct of the establishment are innocent or ignorant of the circumstances.

Holding out to no particular purpose, possibly by way of gossip or rumour, does not create an offence. The intention must be to deceive, but the person deceived may be anyone. Persons likely to be deceived are:

---

1   Children's home, independent hospital, independent clinic, care home, etc (2000 Act, ss 1–4).
2   Ibid, s 11(1).
3   Children's home, independent hospital, independent clinic, care home, etc (2000 Act, s 11(5)(b), (6)).
4   A statement is likely to be material if it would have affected the outcome of the application for registration.
5   2000 Act, s 27(1).
6   Ibid, s 28.

(a)	service users in the establishment;
(b)	persons who are encouraged to become service users of the establishment;
(c)	sponsors of persons who are or may become service users in the establishment, for example relatives, charities or sponsoring local authorities;
(d)	the Department of Social Security or a local authority, which may be encouraged to pay benefit for persons resident in an establishment or make arrangements for accommodation of persons within the establishment without checking the registration;
(e)	potential purchasers.

The term 'describes ... or holds ... out' amounts, in the simplest case, to actually using the term 'care home' in relation to the premises. However, suggesting that the premises provide the services of nursing care, which require registration as a care home with nursing, is as much 'holding out' as attributing a particular name, type or style to the premises. Accordingly, individuals have been prosecuted successfully under the old law where they have issued advertisements for homes, indicating that those homes were:

(a)	under the control of a qualified nurse;
(b)	providing 24-hour nursing care;
(c)	providing full nursing cover.

Any use of the words 'nurse' or 'nursing' in a commercial context, in connection with the operation of an establishment which is not registered as a care home with nursing, must place the issuer of such words at risk of prosecution. Certainly, there is a proviso that the words must be published or used with intent to deceive, but a plea of ignorance of the Act, or ignorance of the likely effect of the words, is highly unlikely to succeed.

It is a principle of the common law that a person is to be taken as intending the natural consequences of his or her action. If the conduct of a person in relation to an unregistered establishment is such that ordinary people would expect others to infer from that conduct that the premises were registered as a care home, then such a person must expect to be convicted. At the very least, during the course of the trial, the burden of proof will, effectively, shift from the prosecution onto the defence to adduce evidence that no deceit was intended, but only where the prosecution has raised a prima facie case of 'deception'.

The words 'indicate, or reasonably be understood ...' are carefully drafted to cover arguments over the construction of particular advertisements, publications, sign boards or hoardings. It is submitted that no amount of fancy footwork on the part of prospective defendants will avoid the consequences of their actions.

Any description applied to premises intending to deceive others into believing that those premises are an establishment or agency of a particular description will be an offence unless those premises are so registered,[1] and is punishable by a fine not exceeding level 5.

1	2000 Act, s 26.

Failure, without reasonable excuse, to comply with a condition which is in force is also subject to a fine not exceeding level 5.[1] This aspect of the provision comprises two elements: first, there must exist an excuse, and, secondly, that excuse must be reasonable. Clearly, what is reasonable will depend on the nature of the condition breached. However, one of the more common conditions is staffing levels. There have, in the past, been many successful prosecutions for breach of staffing conditions. An excuse to breach of this condition would arise, for example, if an epidemic of influenza broke out amongst the staff. Clearly, it would be inappropriate to expose service users, particularly those who are frail to risks of contracting the illness, to the illness. Thus, there exists a reasonable excuse in breaching the staffing conditions for probably the first 24 or 48 hours. Any longer period and it would be expected that contracted agency staff would be put in place to replace the absent employees.

The obstruction of a person properly authorised to enter and inspect premises (where such obstruction is made knowingly) to exercise powers under s 32 of the 2000 Act is an offence, as is a failure, without reasonable excuse, to comply with the requirements of ss 31 and 32 of the 2000 Act.

In common with criminal law principles, it is submitted that it is for the prosecution to prove beyond reasonable doubt that the offence has been committed without reasonable excuse. That burden will lie upon the prosecution whether or not the defence profers an excuse; however, if no excuse is proferred, the prosecution's task may be made easier.

An offence is committed where any application made for registration or for variation of any condition of registration contains any statement which is false or misleading in a material respect. What is 'material' in these circumstances is undoubtedly something which, by its inclusion, would induce the NCSC to register an application, or which, conversely, if omitted, would adversely affect, or is likely to have adversely affected, the outcome of an application if that material had been included.

Failure to return to the NCSC the certification of registration once registration has been cancelled will amount to an offence.[2]

There are currently approximately 12 sets of regulations issued by the Minister pursuant to the powers created by the Act.[3] We will examine one, the Care Homes Regulations 2001, in detail.

13.8 CARE HOMES REGULATIONS 2001

Offences are contained in each of the several parts of the Care Homes Regulations 2001, as follows:

---

1   2000 Act, s 24.
2   National Care Standards Commission (Registration) Regulations 2001, reg 11(1).
3   2000 Act, s 22.

- Part I relates to the statement of purpose and service user's guide;
- Part II relates to the qualities of the registered persons;
- Part III concerns the records, administration and running of care homes, including staff and staffing;
- Part IV concerns fitness of the premises;
- Part V deals with management aspects of running a care home, including financial management;
- Part VII concerns notification of prescribed events.

13.8.1   Statement of purpose[1]

Regulation 4 of the Care Homes Regulations 2001 states that:

'(1)   The registered person shall compile in relation to the care home a written statement (in these Regulations referred to as "the statement of purpose") which shall consist of –

   (a)   a statement of the aims and objectives of the care home;
   (b)   a statement as to the facilities and services which are to be provided by the registered person for service users; and
   (c)   a statement as to the matters listed in Schedule 1.

(2)   The registered person shall supply a copy of the statement of purpose to the Commission and shall make a copy of it available on request for inspection by every service user and any representative of a service user.

(3)   Nothing in regulation 16(1) or 23(1) shall require or authorise the registered person to contravene, or not to comply with –

   (a)   any other provision of these Regulations; or
   (b)   the conditions for the time being in force in relation to the registration of the registered person under Part II of the Act.'

The creation of a statement of purpose is clearly obligatory since failure to have one, or to have one which fails to address all of the very detailed matters listed in Sch 1 to the Regulations, may result in a prosecution and, if convicted, exposes the registered person to a penalty not exceeding level 4.[2]

There are, of course, risks in drafting the statement of purpose. If there is a failure to comply with and meet its stated aims that will, of itself, amount to an offence in respect of which the registered person can be prosecuted. It should be emphasised that failure to comply with one's own documentation may become the sole basis upon which one is prosecuted.

13.8.2   Service user's guide

Regulation 5 of the Care Homes Regualtions 2001 states that:

'(1)   The registered person shall produce a written guide to the care home (in these Regulations referred to as "the service user's guide") which shall include –

   (a)   a summary of the statement of purpose;

---

1   See discussion of statements of purpose in Chapter 6.
2   By virtue of the 2000 Act, s 25(2).

(b)   the terms and conditions in respect of accommodation to be provided for service users, including as to the amount and method of payment of fees;
(c)   a standard form of contract for the provision of services and facilities by the registered provider to service users;
(d)   the most recent inspection report;
(e)   a summary of the complaints procedure established under regulation 22;
(f)   the address and telephone number of the Commission.

(2)   The registered person shall supply a copy of the service user's guide to the Commission and each service user.
(3)   Where a local authority has made arrangements for the provision of accommodation, nursing or personal care to the service user at the care home, the registered person shall supply to the service user a copy of the agreement specifying the arrangements made.'

It is clearly mandatory to produce a service user's guide. Failure to comply, if that failure results in conviction, will expose the registered person to a fine not exceeding level 4. The intention, which is clearly laudable, is to have what, in modern parlance, is called 'transparency', ie that every party to the overall bargain, even different aspects of the overall bargain which may well be separate, individual contracts between third parties, is fully informed of the rights and obligations of every other party to the overall transaction. Every service user must be supplied with his or her own copy of the complete collection, not just have access to one.

It is likely that documents will evolve and be amended from time to time. Such documents, if they are to bind pre-existing service users, must be provided well in advance of any proposed change becoming effective. Failure to do so may place the care home owner in breach of contract with the service user and any third-party funder. Careful thought and planning are necessary before changes affecting contractual arrangements with pre-existing service users are introduced.

An identical set of documents must be filed with the NCSC. The NCSC will probably have a 'core' bundle of the required documents, but with variations being supplied from time to time as they affect service users. It is conceivable that several different contracts will be in force for a particular home at any one time.

13.8.3   Notification of offences

Regulation 11 of the Care Homes Regulations 2001 states that:

'Where the registered person or the responsible individual is convicted of any criminal offence, whether in England and Wales or elsewhere, he shall forthwith give notice in writing to the Commission of –

(a)   the date and place of the conviction;
(b)   the offence of which he was convicted; and
(c)   the penalty imposed on him in respect of the offence.'

This provision is clear: if the registered person is convicted of any offence, whether or not directly relevant to the provision of care, the fact of the conviction, and the details as specified, must be reported to the NCSC.

However, there may be some difficulty policing this requirement. National police forces in the United Kingdom share intelligence on a range of illegal activity, but not on everything. Thus, for example, whilst it is probable that a conviction in the sheriff court in Aberdeen will find its way onto the Police National Computer and then to the Criminal Records Bureau, convictions in, say, Spain are less likely to do so.

Notwithstanding, there is still a duty to report the conviction to the NCSC.

13.8.4   Health and welfare of service users

Regulation 12 of the Care Homes Regulations 2001 states:

'(1)   The registered person shall ensure that the care home is conducted so as –

   (a)   to promote and make proper provision for the health and welfare of service users;
   (b)   to make proper provision for the care and, where appropriate, treatment, education and supervision of service users.

(2)   The registered person shall so far as practicable enable service users to make decisions with respect to the care they are to receive and their health and welfare.

(3)   The registered person shall, for the purpose of providing care to service users, and making proper provision for their health and welfare, so far as practicable ascertain and take into account their wishes and feelings.

(4)   The registered person shall make suitable arrangements to ensure that the care home is conducted –

   (a)   in a manner which respects the privacy and dignity of service users;
   (b)   with due regard to the sex, religious persuasion, racial origin, and cultural and linguistic background and any disability of service users.'

The promotion of health and welfare will, clearly, depend upon issues such as the ready availability to the registered person of necessary finances, although it is clear that the proper provision of health and welfare is an essential minimum. What is 'proper provision' will no doubt become a contentious issue. However, if the registered person acts in accordance with the recommendations and guidance of appropriately qualified professionals, for example a GP, the NCSC is unlikely to complain unless the advice being followed is unarguably wrong.

Service users should be encouraged to become involved in the process of making decisions relating to their own health, care, treatment and so on. The extent to which this will be possible will vary with the capability and inclination of the individual.

13.8.5   Further requirements as to health and welfare

Regulation 13 of the Care Homes Regulations 2001 states:

'(1)   The registered person shall make arrangements for service users –

   (a)   to be registered with a general practitioner of their choice; and
   (b)   to receive where necessary, treatment, advice and other services from any health care professional.

(2)   The registered person shall make arrangements for the recording, handling, safekeeping, safe administration and disposal of medicines received into the care home.

(3)   The registered person shall make suitable arrangements to prevent infection, toxic conditions and the spread of infection at the care home.

(4)   The registered person shall ensure that –

(a)   all parts of the home to which service users have access are so far as reasonably practicable free from hazards to their safety;

(b)   any activities in which service users participate are so far as reasonably practicable free from any avoidable risks; and

(c)   unnecessary risks to the health of safety of service users are identified and so far as possible eliminated,

and shall make suitable arrangements for the training of staff in first aid.

(5)   The registered person shall make suitable arrangements to provide a safe system for moving and handling service users.

(6)   The registered person shall make arrangements, by training staff or by other measures, to prevent service users being harmed or suffering abuse or being placed at risk of harm or abuse.

(7)   The registered person shall ensure that no service user is subject to physical restraint unless restraint of the kind employed is the only practicable means of securing the welfare of that or any other service user and there are exceptional circumstances.

(8)   On any occasion on which a service user is subject to physical restraint, the registered person shall record the circumstances, including the nature of the restraint.'

That the registered person must make arrangements for service users to be registered with a GP of their choice and must ensure that the service user visits or is visited by the GP as and when necessary, is non-controversial. However, what if the GP refuses to register a service user? The authors are aware of a number of instances where GPs have wrongly demanded and are paid a retainer to attend upon service users of a care home when, under the National Assistance Act 1948, there is an obligation to provide such services free of charge.

Further, the registered person is obliged to arrange for advice and treatment where *necessary* by other 'healthcare professionals'. What is 'necessary' in this context is not clear, but the NCSC will probably define the word flexibly and widely. The registered person will undoubtedly recognise what is 'necessary' when the situation arises.

The term 'health care professionals' is not defined in the Regulations or the 2000 Act. However, the Professions Supplementary to Medicine Act 1960[1] lists a number of professions additional to doctors, nurses, opticians and so on.

Regulation 13(4)(b) states that activities must be free from any avoidable risks. In an attempt to increase a service user's independence there will almost always be an element of risk. However, consideration of such risks in advance, and, where possible, controlling or reducing those risks will be critical.

---

1   The list includes chiropodists, dieticians, medical laboratory technicians, occupational therapists, physiotherapists, radiographers and remedial gymnasts.

Regulation 13(5) is in many ways a repetition of the duties the registered person has to employees under the Health and Safety at Work etc Act 1974, namely providing a safe system of work.

Regulation 13(6) seems to be aimed at something more than having a rigorous recruitment policy, and suggests an extension of the responsibilities of the registered person to deliver training and raise levels of awareness amongst those charged with the day-to-day care of service users.

13.8.6   Assessment of service users

Regulation 14(1) of the Care Homes Regulations 2001 states that:

> 'The registered person shall not provide accommodation to a service user at the care home unless, so far as it shall have been practicable to do so –
>
> (a)   needs of the service user have been assessed by a suitably qualified or suitably trained person;
>
> (b)   the registered person has obtained a copy of the assessment;
>
> (c)   there has been appropriate consultation regarding the assessment with the service user or a representative of the service user;
>
> (d)   the registered person has confirmed in writing to the service user that having regard to the assessment the care home is suitable for the purpose of meeting the service user's needs in respect of his health and welfare.'

Assessments should be carried out by someone who is suitably qualified or trained.

As part of the Government's initiative to accelerate the discharge from hospital of elderly patients otherwise fit for discharge but for the lack of availability of suitable accommodation, the assessment will probably be carried out by the NHS and social services in partnership, according to agreed protocols.[1]

Adherence to the detailed procedure will be required in relation to every admission to the care home, save in situations regarded as urgent. However, it is submitted that the fact that there is an urgency for a third party, for example the local authority, which may be surcharged by a health authority in relation to the delayed discharge of an elderly patient, should not be regarded as an urgency by the registered person, although, undoubtedly, he or she will be encouraged to regard it in that way by the placing authority.

Regulation 14(2) states that:

> 'The registered person shall ensure that the assessment of the service user's needs is –
>
> (a)   kept under review; and
>
> (b)   revised at any time when it is necessary to do so having regard to any change of circumstances.'

If a service user's needs change, they must be reassessed and, where appropriate, adjustment must be made to the care plan and other documentation.

---

1   Consultation paper, *Implementing Reimbursement Around Discharge from Hospital* (2002).

13.8.7   Service user's plan

Regulation 15 of the Care Homes Regulations 2001 states that:

'(1)   Unless it is impracticable to carry out such consultation, the registered person shall, after consultation with the service user, or a representative of his, prepare a written plan ("Service User's Plan") as to how the service user's needs in respect of his health and welfare are to be met.

(2)   The registered person shall:

(a)   make the service user's plan available to the service user;
(b)   keep the service user's plan under review;
(c)   where appropriate and, unless it is impracticable to carry out such consultation, after consultation with the service or a representative of his, revise the service user's plan; and
(d)   notify the service user of any such revision.'

It seems self-evident that the preparation of the service user's plan will take place at the time of, or very shortly after, his or her assessment.

The plan must be a 'living' document, reviewed and refreshed regularly and its contents shared with the service user or his or her representative.

13.8.8   Facilities and services

Regulation 16 of the Care Homes Regulations 2001 states that:

'(1)   Subject to regulation 4(3), the registered person shall provide facilities and services to service users in accordance with the statement required by regulation 4(1)(b) in respect of the care home.

(2)   The registered person shall having regard to the size of the care home and the number and needs of service users –

(a)   provide, so far as is necessary for the purpose of managing the care home –

(i)   appropriate telephone facilities;
(ii)   appropriate facilities for communication by facsimile transmission;

(b)   provide telephone facilities which are suitable for the needs of service users, and make arrangements to enable service users to use such facilities in private;
(c)   provide in rooms occupied by service users adequate furniture, bedding and other furnishings, including curtains and floor coverings and equipment suitable to the needs of service users and screens where necessary;
(d)   permit service users, so far as it is practicable to do so, to bring their own furniture and furnishings into the rooms they occupy;
(e)   arrange for the regular laundering of linen and clothing;
(f)   so far as it is practicable to do so, provide adequate facilities for service users to wash, dry and iron their own clothes if they so wish and, for that purpose, to make arrangements for their clothes to be sorted and kept separately;
(g)   provide sufficient and suitable kitchen equipment, crockery, cutlery and utensils, and adequate facilities for the preparation and storage of food;

(h) provide adequate facilities for service users to prepare their own food and ensure that such facilities are safe for use by service users;

(i) provide, in adequate quantities, suitable, wholesome and nutritious food which is varied and properly prepared and available at such time as may reasonably be required by service users;

(j) after consultation with the environmental health authority, make suitable arrangements for maintaining satisfactory standards of hygiene in the care home;

(k) keep the care home free from offensive odours and make suitable arrangements for the disposal of general and clinical waste, not an offence under these regulations if contravened;

(l) provide a place where the money and valuables of service users may be deposited for safe keeping and make arrangements for service users to acknowledge in writing the return to them of any money or valuables so deposited;

(m) consult service users about their social interests, and make arrangements to enable them to engage in local, social and community activities and to visit, or maintain contact or communicate with, their families and friends;

(n) consult service users about the programme of activities arranged by or on behalf of the care home, and provide facilities for recreation including, having regard to the needs of service users, activities in relation to recreation, fitness and training.

(3) The registered person shall ensure that so far as practicable service users have the opportunity to attend religious services of their choice.

(4) In this regulation "food" includes drink.'

This list is broad and all-encompassing and, it is submitted, the meaning is sufficiently clear not to be in need of any further explanation here.

13.8.9 Records

Regulation 17 of the Care Homes Regulations 2001 states that:

'(1) The registered person shall:

(a) maintain in respect of each service user a record which includes the information, documents and other records specified in Schedule 3 relating to the service user;

(b) ensure that the record referred to in sub-paragraph (a) is kept securely in the care home.

(2) The registered person shall maintain in the care homes the records specified in Schedule 4.

(3) The registered person shall ensure that the records referred to in paragraphs (1) and (2) –

(a) are kept up to date; and

(b) are at all times available for inspection in the care home by any person authorised by the Commission to enter and inspect the care home.

(4) The records referred to in paragraphs (1) and (2) shall be retained for not less than three years from the date of the last entry.'

These provisions are clear as to their meaning and, again, no further explanation is thought by the authors to be helpful.

13.8.10 Staffing

Regulation 18 of the Care Homes Regulations 2001 states that:

'(1) The registered person shall, having regard to the size of the care home, the statement of purpose and the number and needs of service users –

   (a) ensure that at all times suitably qualified, competent and experienced persons are working at the care home in such numbers as are appropriate for the health and welfare of service users;

   (b) ensure that the employment of any persons on a temporary basis at the care home will not prevent service users from receiving such continuity of care as is reasonable to meet their needs;

   (c) ensure that the persons employed by the registered person to work at the care home receive –

      (i) training appropriate to the work they are to perform; and

      (ii) suitable assistance, including time off, for the purpose of obtaining further qualifications appropriate to such work.

(2) The registered person shall ensure that persons working at the care home are appropriately supervised.

(3) Where the care home –

   (a) provides nursing to service users; and

   (b) provides, whether or not in connection with nursing, medicines or medical treatment to service users;

   the registered person shall ensure that at all times a suitably qualified registered nurse is working at the care home.

(4) The registered person shall make arrangements for providing persons who work at the care home with appropriate information about any code of practice published under section 62 of the Act.'

The issue of staffing levels has been a significant battleground in the past, with authorities purporting to impose staffing levels in circumstances where they frequently had no entitlement, at law, to act. The issue of staffing levels has continued to be a matter of some contention under the new regulatory system. However, it is right to give credit where it is due, and, in the experience of the authors, those issues have been more readily resolved by the NCSC than previously under the former law and regulations.

13.8.11 Fitness of workers

Regulation 19 of the Care Homes Regulations 2001 states that:

'(1) The registered person shall not employ a person to work at the care home unless –

   (a) the person is fit to work at the care home;

   (b) subject to paragraph (6), he has obtained in respect of that person the information and documents specified in –

> (i)   paragraphs 1 to 6 of Schedule 2;
> (ii)   except when paragraph (7) applies, paragraph 7 of that Schedule;
> (iii) where paragraph (7) applies, paragraph 8 of that Schedule; and
>
> (c)   he is satisfied on reasonable grounds as to the authenticity of the references referred to in paragraph 5 of Schedule 2 in respect of that person.

(2)   This paragraph applies to a person who is employed by a person ("the employer") other than the registered person.

(3)   This paragraph applies to a position in which a person may in the course of his duties have regular contact with service users at the care home or with any other person of a description specified in section 3(2) of the Act.

(4)   The registered person shall not allow a person to whom paragraph (2) applies to work at the care home in a position to which paragraph (3) applies, unless –

> (a)   the person is fit to work at the care home;
> (b)   the employer has obtained in respect of that person the information and documents specified in –
>
> (i)   paragraphs 1 to 6 of Schedule 2;
> (ii)   except where paragraph (7) applies, paragraph 7 of that Schedule;
> (iii) where paragraph (7) applies, paragraph 8 of that Schedule;
>
> and has confirmed in writing to the registered person that he has done so; and
>
> (c)   the employer is satisfied on reasonable grounds as to the authenticity of the references referred to in paragraph 5 of Schedule 2 in respect of that person, and has confirmed in writing to the registered person that he is so satisfied.

(5)   For the purposes of paragraph (1) and (4), a person is not fit to work at a care home unless –

> (a)   he is of integrity and good character;
> (b)   he has qualifications suitable to the work that he is to perform, and the skills and experience necessary for such work;
> (c)   he is physically and mentally fit for the purposes of the work which he is to perform at the care home; and
> (d)   full and satisfactory information is available in relation to him in respect of the following matters:
>
> (i)   each of the matters specified in paragraphs 1 to 6 of Schedule 2;
> (ii)   except where paragraph (7) applies, each of the matters specified in paragraph 7 of that Schedule;
> (iii) where paragraph (7) applies, each of the matters specified in paragraph 8 of that Schedule.

(6)   Paragraphs (1)(b) and (5)(d) in so far as they relate to paragraph 7 of Schedule 2, shall not apply until 1 April 2003 in respect of a person who immediately before 1st April 2002 is employed to work at the care home.

(7)   This paragraph applies where any certificate or information on any matters referred to in paragraph 7 of Schedule 2 is not available to an individual because any provision of the Police Act 1997 has not been brought into force.'

All staff at a care home who have 'regular' (note that the provision of reg 19(3) does not say 'frequent') contact with service users must be 'fit'. 'Fit' is defined by reference to when a person is not fit.

Very careful attention will need to be given by the registered person to reg 19 since, if things go wrong, NCSC inspectors will inevitably investigate circumstances relating to staff, and whether they were appropriately qualified, properly trained, and subject to a rigid recruitment process of checking, confirmation, etc. Only where the registered person has adequately answered these enquiries can he or she expect the NCSC to conclude that something was an 'accident', not the inevitable outcome of bad practice.

13.8.12 Restrictions on acting for service user

Regulation 20 of the Care Homes Regulations 2001 states that:

'(1) Subject to paragraph (2), the registered person shall not pay money belonging to any service user into a bank account unless –

(a) the account is in the name of the service user, or any of the service users, to which the money belongs; and

(b) the account is not used by the registered person in connection with the carrying on or management of the care home.

(2) Paragraph (1) does not apply to money which is paid to the registered person in respect of charges payable by a service user for accommodation or other services provided by the registered person at the care home.

(3) The registered person shall ensure so far as practicable that persons working at the care home do not act as the agent of a service user.'

This Regulation is largely self-explanatory. The authors recommend, however, that employers incorporate, within the employment contract, a prohibition on staff members acting as agents of service users.

13.8.13 Staff views as to conduct of care home

Regulation 21 of the Care Homes Regulations 2001 states that:

'(1) This regulation applies to any matter relating to the conduct of the care home so far as it may affect the health or welfare of service users.

(2) The registered person shall make arrangements to enable staff to inform the registered person and the Commission of their views about any matter to which this regulation applies.'

This mirrors the arrangements for service users to express their views. Forums in which staff can express their views will, it is hoped, be run in a positive way to promote best practice and reinforce the concept of excellence, rather than merely as opportunities to complain.

Clearly, as part of the process, complaints can be raised, and the opportunity to rectify unsatisfactory situations should be seized before an event or set of circumstances becomes a 'conflict'.

13.8.14 Complaints

Regulation 22 of the Care Homes Regulations 2001 states that:

'(1) The registered person shall establish a procedure ("Complaints Procedure") for considering complaints made to the registered person by a service user or person acting on the service user's behalf.

(2) The complaints procedure shall be appropriate to the needs of service users.

(3) The registered person shall ensure that any complaint made under the complaints procedure is fully investigated.

(4) The registered person shall, within 28 days after the date on which the complaint is made, or such shorter period as may be reasonable in the circumstances, inform the person who made the complaint of the action (if any) that is to be taken.

(5) The registered person shall supply a written copy of the complaints procedure to every service user and to any person acting on behalf of a service user if that person so requests.

(6) Where a written copy of the complaints procedure is to be supplied in accordance with paragraph (5) to a person who is blind or whose vision is impaired, the registered person shall so far as it is practicable to do so supply, in addition to the written copy, a copy of the complaints procedure in a form which is suitable for that person.

(7) The copy of the complaints procedure to be supplied in accordance with paragraphs (5) and (6) shall include –

(a) the name, address and telephone number of the Commission; and

(b) the procedure (if any) that has been notified by the Commission to the registered person for the making of complaints to the Commission relating to the care home.

(8) The registered person shall supply to the Commission at its request a statement containing a summary of the complaints made during the preceding twelve months and the action that was taken in response.'

Regulation 22(3) states that a complaint made under the complaints procedure must be 'fully investigated'. The vast majority of matters raised by way of complaint will, undoubtedly, be addressed by minor changes to the running of the care home by or on behalf of the registered person, thereby having a positive impact on the life of the service user whose home, in the true sense of the word, it is. Unfortunately, there will be occasions where matters complained about are so serious that lawyers may need to be employed to investigate, rather than the service provider or manager investigating the circumstances him or herself. In such circumstances it may be necessary also to consider passing information to the proper authorities to investigate.

Under reg 22(7), unless the NCSC local or regional office has notified the responsible person that the local/regional office details are to be provided to service users, details of the headquarters at Newcastle should be provided instead.

Regulation 22(8) relieves the registered person of providing an annual report to the NCSC summarising complaints and action taken in relation to each. However, complete records should be compiled and retained since the NCSC may request such records at any time.

13.8.15   Fitness of premises

Regulation 23 of the Care Homes Regulations 2001 states that:

'(1)   Subject to regulation 4(3), the registered person shall not use premises for the purposes of a care home unless:

(a)   the premises are suitable for the purpose of achieving the aims and objectives set out in the statement of purpose; and

(b)   the location of the premises is appropriate to the needs of service users.

(2)   The registered person shall having regard to the number and needs of the service users ensure that –

(a)   the physical design and layout of the premises to be used as the care home meet the needs of the service users;

(b)   the premises to be used at the care home are of sound construction and kept in a good state of repair externally and internally;

(c)   equipment provided at the care home for use by service users or persons who work at the care home are maintained in good working order;

(d)   all parts of the care home are kept clean and reasonably decorated;

(e)   adequate private and communal accommodation is provided for service users;

(f)   the size and layout of rooms occupied or used by service users are suitable for their needs;

(g)   there is adequate sitting, recreational and dining space provided separately from the service user's private accommodation;

(h)   the communal space provided for service users is suitable for the provision of social, cultural and religious activities appropriate to the circumstances of service users;

(i)   suitable facilities are provided for service users to meet visitors in communal accommodation, and in private accommodation which is separate from the service users' own private rooms;

(j)   there are provided at appropriate places in the premises sufficient numbers of lavatories, and of wash-basins, baths and showers fitted with a hot and cold water supply;

(k)   any necessary sluicing facilities are provided;

(l)   suitable provision is made for the storage for the purposes of the care home;

(m)   suitable storage facilities are provided for the use of service users;

(n)   suitable adaptations are made, and such support, equipment and facilities, including passenger lifts, as may be required are provided, for service users who are old, infirm or physically disabled;

(o)   external grounds which are suitable for, and safe for use by, service users are provided and appropriately maintained;

(p)   ventilation, heating and lighting suitable for service users is provided in all parts of the care home which are used by service users.'

A vast amount of detail concerning fitness of premises is set out in various national minimum standards, for example standard 15 of Care Homes for Older People on meals and mealtimes. It would be misleading to summarise any of the standards since there can be no substitute for familiarising oneself with the detail of those standards relevant to particular care provision in a specific establishment.

Regulation 23 continues:

'(3)   The registered person shall provide for staff –

(a)   suitable facilities and accommodation, other than sleeping accommodation, including:

(i)   facilities for the purpose of changing;
(ii)   storage facilities;

(b)   sleeping accommodation where the provision of such accommodation
is needed by staff in connection with their work at the care home.'

The effect of reg 23(3)(a) and (b) is that the 'staff room' and changing facilities
cannot also be used for staff sleeping or storage.

Regulation 23 continues:

'(4)   The registered person shall after consultation with the fire authority –

(a)   take adequate precautions against the risk of fire, including the
provision of suitable fire equipment;
(b)   provide adequate means of escape;
(c)   make adequate arrangements –

(i)   for detecting, containing and extinguishing fires;
(ii)   for giving warnings of fires;
(iii)   for the evacuation, in the event of fire, of all persons in the care
home and safe placement of service users;
(iv)   for reviewing fire precautions, and testing fire equipment, at
suitable intervals;

(d)   make arrangements for persons working at the care home to receive
suitable training in fire prevention; and
(e)   to ensure, by means of fire drills and practices at suitable intervals, that
the persons working at the care home and, so far as practicable, service
users, are aware of the procedure to be followed in case of fire, including
the procedure for saving life.

(5)   The registered person shall undertake appropriate consultation with the
authority responsible for environmental health for the area in which the care
home is situated.'

Fire prevention, alarms and fire-fighting are areas on which the registered
person, and his or her architect, must take advice from the relevant fire
authority. It is inconceivable that such advice would not be followed, save
through inadvertence. Once installation has taken place, or a modification
carried out, an inspection of the premises should be carried out by the fire
prevention officer of the relevant fire authority.

There are recognised risks involved in the handling and storage of food. The very
young and the elderly are particularly vulnerable to the effects of food
poisoning. Since care homes typically cater for numbers significantly greater
than in a domestic setting there is a responsibility to exercise even greater care.
Professional catering staff should be trained in appropriate food handling and

storage practices, and a good working relationship with the local authority environmental health officer should be established.

13.8.16 Review of quality of care

Regulation 24 of the Care Homes Regulations 2001 states that:

'(1) The registered person shall establish and maintain a system for –

    (a) reviewing at appropriate intervals; and
    (b) improving

    the quality of care provided at the care home, including the quality of nursing where nursing is provided at the care home.

(2) The registered person shall supply to the Commission a report in respect of any review conducted by him for the purposes of paragraph (1), and make a copy of the report available to service users.

(3) The system referred to in paragraph (1) shall provide for consultation with service users and their representatives.'

It may come as no surprise to readers that such extensive regulations devote only three short paragraphs to the issue of care and nursing.

13.8.17 Financial position

Regulation 25 of the Care Homes Regulations 2001 states that –

'(1) The registered provider shall carry on the care home in such manner as is likely to ensure that the care home will be financially viable for the purpose of achieving the aims and objectives set out in the statement of purpose.

(2) The registered person shall, if the Commission so requests, provide the Commission with such information and documents as it may require for the purpose of considering the financial viability of the care home, including –

    (a) the annual accounts of the care home certified by an accountant;
    (b) a reference from a bank expressing an opinion as to the registered provider's financial standing;
    (c) information as to the financing and financial resources of the care home;
    (d) where the registered provider is a company, information as to any of its associated companies;
    (e) a certificate of insurance for the registered provider in respect of liability which may be incurred by him in relation to the care home in respect of death, injury, public liability, damage or other loss.

(3) The registered person shall –

    (a) ensure that adequate accounts are maintained in respect of the care home and kept up to date;
    (b) ensure that the accounts give details of the running costs of the care home, including rent, payments under a mortgage and expenditure on food, heating and salaries and wages of staff; and
    (c) supply a copy of the accounts to the Commission at its request.

(4) In this regulation a company is an associated company of another if one of them has control of the other or both are under the control of the same person.'

A definition of 'financial viability' would have been of great assistance to those owning and operating care homes. However, no such definition has been provided, nor has one emerged from the Department of Health or the NCSC. In the view of the authors, financial viability must be something more than merely 'breaking even', and should embrace the concept of paying owner/manager and executive directors (where relevant) a proper remuneration together with a proper return on the capital employed in the business.

Whilst the registered person is required to maintain 'adequate accounts', these do not have to be submitted to the NCSC as a matter of course, only upon request by the NCSC.

What will amount to 'adequate accounts'? Accounts will probably have to identify the amount of income received and expenditure. In relation to expenditure, omnibus amounts relating to each of the categories of expenditure identified in reg 25(3)(b) must be provided as a minimum. Much more detail will inevitably be required in relation to handling/managing funds of a service user.

13.8.18   Visits by registered provider

Regulation 26 of the Care Homes Regulations 2001 states that:

'(1)   Where the registered provider is an individual, but not in day to day charge of the care home, he shall visit the care home in accordance with this regulation.

(2)   Where the registered provider is an organisation or partnership, the care home shall be visited in accordance with this regulation by –

   (a)   the responsible individual or one of the partners, as the case may be;
   (b)   another of the directors or other persons responsible for the management of the organisation or partnership; or
   (c)   an employee of the organisation or the partnership who is not directly concerned with the conduct of the care home.

(3)   Visits under paragraph (1) or (2) shall take place at least once a month and shall be unannounced.

(4)   The person carrying out the visit shall –

   (a)   interview, with their consent and in private, such of the service users and their representatives and persons working at the care home as appears necessary in order to form an opinion of the standard of care provided in the care home;
   (b)   inspect the premises of the care home, its record of events and records of any complaints; and
   (c)   prepare a written report on the conduct of the care home.

(5)   The registered provider shall supply a copy of the report required to be made under paragraph (4)(c) to –

   (a)   the Commission;
   (b)   the registered manager; and
   (c)   in the case of a visit under paragraph (2) –

      (i)   where the registered provider is an organisation, to each of the directors or other persons responsible for the management of the organisation; and

  (ii) where the registered provider is a partnership, to each of the
    partners.'

As stipulated, a registered provider, not in day-to-day charge of the home, or a partnership or company, must make arrangements for someone other than a person who works at the care home to monitor, by regular unannounced visits, the activities at the care home.

A report must be prepared and sent to, amongst others, the NCSC. It has become apparent to the author that the NCSC use the information provided by such reports to inform them in advance of unannounced inspections and particular areas/issues they will focus their inspection upon.

13.8.19 Notification of death, illness and other events

Regulation 37 of the Care Homes Regulations 2001 states that:

'(1) The registered person shall give notice to the Commission without delay of
   the occurrence of:

  (a) the death of any service user, including the circumstances of his death;
  (b) the outbreak in the care home of any infectious disease which in the
    opinion of any registered medical practitioner attending persons in the
    care home is sufficiently serious to be so notified;
  (c) any serious injury to a service user;
  (d) serious illness of a service user at a care home at which nursing is not
    provided;
  (e) any event in the care home which adversely affects the well-being or
    safety of any service user;
  (f) any theft, burglary or accident in the care home;
  (g) any allegation of misconduct by the registered person or any person
    who works at the care home.

(2) Any notification made in accordance with this regulation which is given
   orally shall be confirmed in writing.'

Much of this regulation will be familiar to the care home community. In relation to the requirement in reg 37(1)(b), it is submitted that on every such occasion a registered medical practitioner, for example a GP, should attend any service user who is suffering from an infectious disease. The GP should be formally asked whether the outbreak is sufficiently serious to warrant notification to the NCSC, and his or her response noted and retained.

In light of reg 37(1)(e), it is clear that adverse effect to the well-being of a service user does not have to be 'serious' to trigger the requirement to report the event to the NCSC. An example might be the departure of a key worker of whom the service user has become very fond.

Any allegation of misconduct must be reported to the NCSC. A report is clearly required no matter how outrageous or unlikely the complaint; and similarly a report to the NCSC must be made even if a service user is known to have delusions and habitually makes the same complaint.

As mentioned earlier, these requirements are intended to ensure transparency.

13.8.20   Notice of absence

Regulation 38 of the Care Homes Regulations 2000 states that:

'(1)   Where:

    (a)   the registered provider, if he is an individual; or
    (b)   the registered manager

proposes to be absent from the care home for a continuous period of 28 days or more, the registered person shall give notice in writing to the Commission of the proposed absence.

(2)   Except in the case of an emergency, the notice referred to in paragraph (1) above shall be given no later than one month before the proposed absence commences or within such shorter period as may be agreed with the Commission and the notice shall specify –

    (a)   the length or expected length of the absence;
    (b)   the reason for the absence;
    (c)   the arrangements which have been made for the running of the care home during that absence;
    (d)   the name, address and qualifications of the person who will be responsible for the care home during that absence; and
    (e)   in the case of the absence of the registered manager, the arrangements that have been, or are proposed to be, made for appointing another person to manage the care home during that absence, including the proposed date by which the appointment is to be made.

(3)   Where the absence arises as a result of an emergency, the registered person shall give notice of the absence within one week of its occurrence specifying the matters mentioned in sub-paragraph (a) to (e) of paragraph (2).

(4)   Where –

    (a)   the registered provider, if he is an individual; or
    (b)   the registered manager,

has been absent from the care home for a continuous period of 28 days or more, and the Commission has not been given notice of the absence, the registered person shall without delay give notice in writing to the Commission of the absence, specifying the matters mentioned in sub-paragraphs (a) to (e) of paragraph (2).

(5)   The registered person shall notify the Commission of the return to duty of the registered provider or (as the case may be) the registered manager not later than 7 days after the date of his return.'

The authors recommend that each care home prepares a checklist of emergency situations so that the correct procedure is adopted. The careful drafting of reg 38 means that all 'prolonged' absences whether planned or otherwise are 'caught' and must be addressed. In the case of injury or illness, reports to the NCSC must be made within 7 days of the commencement of the absence.

13.8.21   Notice of changes

Regulation 39 of the Care Homes Regulations 2000 states that:

> 'The registered person shall give notice in writing to the Commission as soon as it is practicable to do so if any of the following events takes place or is proposed to take place –
>
> (a)   a person other than the registered person carries on or manages the care home;
>
> (b)   a person ceases to carry on or manage the care home;
>
> (c)   where the registered provider is an individual, he changes his name;
>
> (d)   where the registered provider is a partnership, there is any change in the membership of the partnership;
>
> (e)   where the registered provider is an organisation –
>
> > (i)   the name or address of the organisation is changed;
> >
> > (ii)   there is any change of director, manager, secretary or other similar officer of the organisation;
> >
> > (iii)   there is to be any change of responsible individual;
>
> (f)   where the registered provider is an individual, a trustee in bankruptcy is appointed;
>
> (g)   where the registered provider is a company or partnership, a receiver, manager, liquidator or provisional liquidator is appointed; or
>
> (h)   the premises of the care home are significantly altered or extended, or additional premises are acquired.'

Notice must be served 'as soon as it is practicable to do so'. Such period will be very shortly after the occurrence giving rise to the obligation to report the matter. In some instances the obligation to notify will arise in anticipation of an event, ie before it occurs. For example, following a decision to change the name of a company, notice must be served after the decision has been approved by the members, but before notice of change is provided to the Registrar of Companies. Similarly, in relation to changes to premises, notice must be served after planning consent and/or building regulations are approved, but before commencement of the works.

13.8.22   Notice of termination of accommodation

Regulation 40 of the Care Homes Regulations 2000 states that:

> '(1)   Subject to paragraph (2), the registered person shall not terminate the arrangements for the accommodation of a service user unless he has given reasonable notice of his intention to do so to –
>
> (a)   the service user;
>
> (b)   the person who appears to be the service user's next of kin; and
>
> (c)   where a local authority has made arrangements for the provision of accommodation, nursing or personal care to the service user at the care home, that authority.
>
> (2)   If it is impracticable for the registered person to comply with the requirement in paragraph (1) –

(a) he shall do so as soon as it is practicable to do so; and

(b) he shall provide to the Commission a statement as to the circumstances which made it impracticable for him to comply with the requirement.'

It is interesting to note that whereas reg 39 requires that notice to the NCSC be in writing, there is no such requirement in reg 40. It seems therefore that oral notice will be adequate to ensure compliance with the obligations which arise upon termination. Notwithstanding, the authors would recommend that notices ought always to be given in writing to ensure adequate evidence should this ever be needed.

13.9 PENALTIES

The penalties which can be imposed for breach of any duty under the 2000 Act or Regulations vary and are predominantly prescribed by the 2000 Act and Regulations themselves. By far the most common penalty will be a fine in respect of each offence proved.

Fines are subject to various maxima defined by reference to a 'level' of penalty. There are five levels of penalty prescribed by the Standard Scale.[1] The Standard Scale maximum fines which can be imposed on an adult on conviction for a summary offence[2] are:

- Level 1	£200;
- Level 2	£500;
- Level 3	£1000;
- Level 4	£2500;
- Level 5	£5000.

Payment of a fine will normally be required within 28 days.[3] Any default in payment of a fine may result in a period of imprisonment, as follows:[4]

Magistrates' court

An amount not exceeding £200	7 days
An amount exceeding £200 but not exceeding £500	14 days
An amount exceeding £500 but not exceeding £1,000	28 days
An amount exceeding £1,000 but not exceeding £2,500	45 days
An amount exceeding £2,500 but not exceeding £5,000	3 months
An amount exceeding £5,000 but not exceeding £10,000	6 months
An amount exceeding £10,000	12 months

A conviction may lead to the cancellation of registration[5] which, whilst not strictly a 'penalty' in the sense intended here (ie punishment), will be regarded in

---

1   Criminal Justice Act 1982, s 37(2).
2   Summary offences are triable in the magistrates' court only.
3   At the time the fine is imposed or, by consent, the date for payment specified.
4   Magistrates' Courts Act 1980, Sch 4 as amended.
5   2000 Act, s 14(1).

this way by the registered person. Offences which may be relevant include offences under:[1]

(a) Part II of the 2000 Act or Regulations made under it; or

(b) the Registered Homes Act 1984 or Regulations made under it; and

(c) the Children Act 1989 or Regulations made under it.

---

1   2000 Act, s 14(2).

Chapter 14

CARE STANDARDS TRIBUNAL

14.1 INTRODUCTION

The Care Standards Tribunal (the tribunal) has been established by the Secretary of State to hear and determine appeals in relation to certain regulatory decisions incuding those of the National Care Standards Commission (NCSC) and the National Assembly for Wales. It was originally established under the Protection of Children Act 1999 to consider appeals from those officially listed as being unsuitable to work with children. The tribunal's functions were later extended by the 2000 Act and other legislation to preside over a wider range of appeals emanating from the care sector. It is available to all those who operate or are concerned with any establishment or agency regulated under the Care Standards Act 2000 (the 2000 Act).

The tribunal replaced the old Registered Homes Tribunal and came into existence by virtue of the Protection of Children and Vulnerable Adults and Care Standards Tribunal Regulations 2002 (the Tribunal Regulations).

The tribunal is an entirely new body, governed by a new constitution and set of rules, as set out in the Regulations. The decisions of the tribunal will be reported, published and publicly available, as was the case with the Registered Homes Tribunal. It is anticipated that the tribunal will hear a larger number of appeals than the Registered Homes Tribunal. This is due to the greater numbers and varieties of care establishments and agencies which are now regulated under the 2000 Act, together with other factors brought about by the introduction of the Act, including greater scope for the imposition of registration conditions.

The tribunal will inevitably be faced with a variety of diverse and challenging questions which will build up a body of case-law. It is anticipated that this case law will provide guidance and context for many typical questions and problems faced by providers under the new regulatory regime. It remains to be seen whether the decisions of the tribunal over time will provide consistency of approach in relation to the typical day-to-day regulatory issues arising between provider and regulator.

The following sections of this chapter will focus on:

–   the constitution and powers of the new tribunal;
–   the grounds and basis of the right of appeal and jurisdiction of the tribunal;
–   the procedure for appeal;

- the evidence and preparation for a hearing;
- the conduct of proceedings;
- the costs.

14.2   CONSTITUTION OF THE TRIBUNAL

14.2.1   President, chairperson and lay members

The Lord Chancellor's Department (LCD) has the power to appoint a president, who presides over all the administration and functions of the tribunal and also sits as chairperson in tribunal hearings. In addition to the president there are a number of other tribunal chairpersons eligible to sit on tribunal panels. The president is a member of the judiciary. Chairpersons are also legally qualified.

Every tribunal case will be heard by a panel of three tribunal members, including the legally qualified chairperson. In addition, there will be two 'lay' members. Lay members are selected from a broad range of individuals who must satisfy certain criteria laid down in Part II of the Tribunal Regulations selected by the LCD after consultation with the Secretary of State. The typical qualifying criteria for lay members are:

- experience in relevant social work;
- experience in the provision of services by a health authority, special health authority, National Health Service trust or a primary care trust;
- experience in the provision of education;
- experience of formal child protection proceedings;
- experience in carrying out inspections of care homes and other care establishments or agencies;
- experience of managing a care home or other care establishment or agency;
- that the person is a registered nurse or registered medical practitioner with experience of provision of health care services.

A variety of other criteria are laid down fully in reg 3 of the Tribunal Regulations.

The president has responsibility for selecting the three tribunal members when an appeal is being listed for final hearing. The president will endeavour to select lay members whose experience is relevant to the issues in the case. However, the president is not *obliged* to do so, since other factors in determining the make-up of the tribunal panel include the availability of panel members at the required time. In the authors' experience, the president will rarely delay the listing of a case simply to secure a lay member whose experience and knowledge most closely match the issues in the case. All lay members are selected on the basis of their broad experience and expertise, and on the basis that they are persons of integrity and impartiality.

14.2.2   Secretary

In addition to the president, numerous chairpersons and lay members, the president must appoint a secretary to run the administration of the tribunal. Any appellant in tribunal proceedings will be in regular contact with the secretary to the tribunal. The secretary is a valuable source of assistance and information in conducting the appeal process. Under reg 2 of the Tribunal Regulations the secretary may authorise members of the Tribunal staff (appointed by the Secretary of State) to carry out certain of the tribunal's powers and functions where appropriate.

14.3 GROUNDS OF APPEAL

A typical appeal to the Care Standards Tribunal would follow the issue of a notice of proposal to cancel registration, or to vary, remove or impose a condition of registration under the 2000 Act.

Other factors giving rise to a right of appeal to the tribunal include: cancellation of registration under s 20 of the 2000 Act, ie the emergency closure procedure involving an urgent application to the magistrates' court or a refusal to cancel registration upon application of the registered person (s 15 of the 2000 Act); and refusal by the NCSC to register a person, for example the manager, in respect of an establishment or agency. A right of appeal also exists in relation to the 'transitional provisions', the mechanics by which registration under the Registered Homes Act 1984 was transferred to the NCSC on the 2000 Act coming into force. Numerous appeals to the tribunal were launched, in circumstances where providers considered that the details of registration under the new regime had been misstated by the regulator in the transfer of registration form.

Therefore, almost any official regulatory decision affecting registration will be capable of an appeal to the tribunal. The right of appeal will be notified to the service provider by the Commission, and any official notice will specify the time-limit in which to commence an appeal.

14.4 COMMENCEMENT OF AN APPEAL

Once the right of appeal to the Tribunal has been established, the procedure will depend upon the nature of the decision being appealed. In the majority of typical cases, the appeal will be pursuant to s 21 of the 2000 Act, being an appeal against:

(a) a decision of the registration authority; or
(b) an order made by a justice of the peace for emergency closure under s 20 of the Act.

The procedure for commencing an appeal in these circumstances is found in Sch 1 to the Tribunal Regulations and it is on this procedure that the following discussion will concentrate. Certain aspects of the procedure are slightly different where the appeal arises out of the Children Act 1989 or from decisions concerning the protection of children and protection of vulnerable adults lists (POCA and POVA lists). Schedules 2–8 to the Tribunal Regulations deal with these alternative procedures which, whilst following a common theme, have their own distinct features. Two more schedules (9 and 10) are due to be added shortly.

14.5 APPLICATION ON BEHALF OF A PERSON UNDER A DISABILITY

Under reg 30 of the Tribunal Regulations a person can write to the secretary requesting authorisation to bring an appeal on behalf of a person who is prevented from acting on his or her own behalf by reason of mental or physical infirmity. If authorisation is granted by the president under reg 30, the person appointed may take all necessary procedural steps under the Tribunal Regulations on behalf of the incapacitated person as though he or she were bringing the appeal on his or her own behalf.

14.6 WHO MAY APPEAL?

Generally, any registered person who wishes to contest a final decision of the registration authority may appeal. On the question of an individual's right to bring an appeal, there will be instances where a provider has received a notice of proposal from the NCSC to cancel registration, for example on the grounds of unfitness, and at the same time the bank has taken possession of and sold the premises or the provider has decided to close the business. The same situation would arise where there has been an emergency closure order and the business is no longer trading. This gives rise to the unusual situation where there is no longer a care home in operation and yet the provider's registration still exists in law. Provided an appeal is commenced within the proper time-limits, the notice of proposal will not formally take effect unless and until there is a finding in favour of the proposal to cancel by the tribunal.

This point was considered in relation to the old Registered Homes Act 1984 by the Court of Appeal in the case of *R v Suffolk Health Authority ex parte Kowlessur*.[1] In this case, a notice of proposal to cancel registration was served on Mr and Mrs Kowlessur, who subsequently gave notice of closure of all their nursing beds. The appellants asserted that as they were no longer operating as a nursing home, the notice of proposal could not proceed as the registration had already ceased to exist. The Court of Appeal disagreed. Lord Justice Jonathan Parker commented that there was no statutory provision allowing for registration to 'expire'. It could only come to an end by formal cancellation.

However, he also commented:

> 'The registration is necessarily limited to in effect in so far as it must relate to the premises where the nursing home is, or is intended to be, carried on otherwise the person carrying on the nursing home at those premises will be guilty of an offence under section 23; but there is no provision in the Act which has the effect of terminating the registration under Pt II if the registered person ceases to carry on a nursing home at the premises specified in the registration. It would appear that in such circumstances, and subject to cancellation for non-payment of the annual registration fee, the registration continues to exist but is simply otiose (unless and until it is revived by the registered person once again to carry on a nursing home at the premises in question). In short, registration is only of practical relevance in circumstances where its absence would render a person guilty of an offence.'

---

1   (2000) *The Independent*, December 15.

Therefore, even if a care home business is no longer in operation, a provider's registration will still exist unless and until it is cancelled by the proper methods laid down in the 2000 Act. In these circumstances, it is permissible for the provider to launch or continue with an appeal to seek to clear their name of any unfitness or wrong doing despite there no longer being an 'establishment' to which the registration attaches.

As outlined in earlier chapters there is some question as to whether appeals do lie in the case of referrals to grant variations of conditions of registration or applications for voluntary cancellation of registration. The statutory jurisdiction of the Tribunal must be studied. No doubt the Tribunal will make decisions in due course.

14.7 TYPICAL APPEAL PROCEDURE (SCHEDULE 1)

Section 21 of the 2000 Act makes it clear that an appeal can only be brought within 28 days after service of the notice of the decision or order. The notice of proposal or order will itself highlight the fact that the right of appeal lies to the tribunal, and that the appeal must be brought within 28 days. This is a strict time-limit, and the Act makes no provision for any discretionary extension of this time. The Tribunal Regulations make provision for the president to extend time-limits in relation to procedural deadlines, but only once an appeal has been commenced. The president can extend such a deadline if it is unreasonable to expect a party to comply with an original deadline and if it would be unfair not to extend it. (See reg 35 of the Tribunal Regulations.)

To initiate an appeal, the applicant must make the application in writing to the secretary of the tribunal. The tribunal has devised its own set of application forms for the appeal process in accordance with the procedure laid down in the Tribunal Regulations. An appeal is commenced by completing form B1, which is available from the secretary. It is also available from the tribunal's website at www.carestandardstribunal.gov.uk.

Form B1 is self-explanatory, requiring the applicant's full name and address, date of birth (in the case of an individual) or registered office (in the case of a company). The form can be completed and submitted by a legal representative. In addition, the applicant must state in form B1 with reasonable particularity the nature of the decision being appealed, and must give a short statement of the grounds upon which the appeal is being brought. Form B1 must be signed and dated by the applicant, and sent to the secretary within the deadline.

Once form B1 has been submitted, the Tribunal Regulations require the Secretary to acknowledge receipt to the applicant immediately and send a copy of form B1, together with any documents in support, to the respondent, ie (in a care homes case) the Commission. The secretary also has powers to correct any obvious errors in the application form, but must notify the applicant of any such amendment.

Upon receipt of the papers from the secretary, the respondent has 20 working days from receipt to respond to the application. If the respondent fails to respond, it is not permitted to take any further part in the proceedings. This means that the tribunal can refuse to receive any late response, or to consider any evidence on the part of the respondent. The hearing will then proceed on the basis of the documents and evidence from the applicant alone.

In its response, the respondent must indicate whether it opposes the appeal and, if it does so oppose, the reasons why, and must provide any supporting documents to illustrate its reasons. Once this information and documentation have been returned to the secretary by the respondent, the secretary must send copies to the appellant without delay.

Further procedures for the exchange of evidence and listing of a final appeal hearing are set out below.

The president or nominated chairperson has the power to strike out an appeal on the basis, for example, that the wrong procedure has been used or if the appeal is considered to be 'frivolous or vexatious'. This terminology is taken from general civil court procedure where a claim can be struck out if it is considered to be without substance and amounts to a time-wasting tactic. However, to strike out an appeal is not a decision that the president may take lightly. Before striking out an appeal, the president or nominated chairperson must invite representations from the parties within such period as he or she may direct. The president or chairperson must then provide an opportunity for the parties to make oral representations at a hearing if so requested, and to consider such representations before making any final decision on strike out.

Once the secretary has received the respondent's response, he or she must write to each party requesting certain information, including:

- the names and addresses of any witnesses required and the nature of their evidence;
- whether any other directions should be made by the president under the tribunal's 'case management' powers (set out below), for example whether the respondent considers the appeal to be misconceived, in which case the tribunal should set a hearing to consider whether the appeal should be struck out;
- whether there needs to be a preliminary hearing for the tribunal properly to consider which further directions might be necessary for the preparation of evidence or to deal with any preliminary issues before the main hearing;
- a time estimate for the hearing, and the earliest date by which the party considers that the case will be prepared and ready for hearing; and
- whether the appeal should be determined without an oral hearing (on the basis of the papers submitted and without the attendance of the parties).

In practice, the tribunal will use forms B5 and B6 to gather this information from the parties. These are like the 'allocation questionnaires' used in civil proceedings to assist the judge in understanding the nature of the case, and enabling appropriate directions to be made. Form B5 is sent to the applicant, and form B6 is sent to the respondent. Each form is slightly different, but they are both designed to extract the same categories of information. This process is generally to enable the president to consider what further directions need to be made for the preparation and exchange of documentary and witness evidence before the case is listed for final hearing.

14.7.1   Preparation for the hearing – directions

As stated above, the president can consider whether a preliminary hearing will be necessary for the purpose of setting further directions for preparation of the case, and the parties have an opportunity to request a preliminary hearing in forms B5 or B6. Regardless of the parties' wishes, the president or nominated chairperson can set a preliminary hearing if he or she considers that this would assist him or her in making directions for the conduct of the case. If the president determines that a preliminary hearing is necessary, the secretary will notify the parties as soon as possible of the date fixed for the hearing.

If no preliminary hearing is necessary, the president can consider the responses of the parties in forms B5 and B6 and determine appropriate directions on the basis of that information. Written directions will then be sent out to the parties. The president may also use this opportunity to nominate a chairperson and two lay members to hear and determine the case. The president will issue written directions as to the dates by which any document, witness statement or other material upon which a party is intending to rely must be sent to the tribunal and, if appropriate, to the other party. In most cases, the tribunal will direct that witness statements and documentary evidence be submitted to the other party as well as to the tribunal since this facilitates the proper and thorough understanding of an opposing party's case. This ensures that each party has a full opportunity to answer any point raised by the other party and to prepare its case properly. In line with general civil court procedure, the tribunal will not tolerate any tactics to 'ambush' the opposing party or to produce surprise documents late in the day, thus depriving a party of the opportunity to respond and prepare its case. The days of such tactics in civil courts and in tribunal procedures are well and truly over.

If there is to be no oral hearing, the president will set a date by which the parties must send written representations regarding their appeal to the secretary and to the other party. This will be following submission of documents and witness evidence, and must be not less than 10 working days after the last piece of evidence has been submitted.

The secretary must fix a date for the appeal hearing in consultation with the president, which must be the earliest practicable date allowing for all directions made in the case to be complied with. Under reg 7 of the Tribunal Regulations this date should be no sooner than 15 working days after the last date for filing or exchange of evidence. Notification of the hearing date, time and venue must be notified to the parties by the secretary in writing, not less than 20 working days before the date fixed for the hearing. This may be altered as necessary, but the secretary must notify the parties without delay. The president will entertain requests for an adjournment but proper grounds must be submitted by the party seeking the adjournment. The president must not adjourn the hearing unless satisfied that refusing the adjournment would prevent just disposal of the case.

However, if the hearing is adjourned, the secretary must inform the parties of a new hearing date without delay.

14.7.2　Multiple appeals

Under reg 8 of the Tribunal Regulations, the president has the power to link two or more cases together where they relate to the same person, establishment or agency. This means that in circumstances where an appeal is brought in relation to two separate establishments in common ownership, the cases can be heard together and the directions in the case can be the same. The hearing of multiple appeals can be directed on the president's own initiative, or upon application of either party. Again, this can be indicated in form B5/B6.

Appeals against inclusion in the POCA and POVA lists can also be heard as multiple appeals where necessary. In these circumstances an appeal against inclusion in the POCA list will be heard first. Inclusion in the lists effectively prevents the listed individual from working with children (POCA) or vulnerable adults (POVA), so an appeal with be necessary if the individual believes their inclusion is wrong.

Before making a decision to hear multiple appeals, the president will give the parties an opportunity to make representations. The president must also consider any cost or delay implications of hearing the cases either together or separately. Therefore, any decision made by the president under reg 8 should be in the interests of dealing with the matter speedily and cost effectively.

The president also has powers to vary any directions or to impose new directions on his or her own initiative or upon application of either party, but again must give the parties an opportunity to make written representations.

The president also has the power under reg 10 to make an 'unless order' requiring a party to take a specific step, for example to file a certain document or statement. Breach of an unless order entitles the president to determine the case in favour of the other party. Unless orders have been used in civil court procedure for many years and are a powerful control mechanism to ensure that parties comply with directions made by the president.

14.7.3　Documentary evidence

Forms B5 and B6 will ask whether a party considers it necessary to submit documents in support of its case. These documents will be referred to during the final hearing and must therefore be disclosed to the other party and to the tribunal in advance. The president may also give directions requiring one party to send to the secretary and to the other party any document or other material which may assist in determining the case. The president will make the appropriate directions for disclosure of such documents and the provision of copies. Regulation 12 refers to documents 'which [the party] considers may assist the tribunal in determining the case and which that party is able to send'. This falls far short of the very strict disclosure requirement in ordinary civil court procedure which requires parties to make 'full and frank' disclosure of all documents relevant to the issues in the case, whether or not they intend to rely on those documents. However, it is open for either party to request the president to make a direction for 'specific disclosure' from the other party if it is considered that particular documents or classes of documents should be disclosed by that party for the proper determination of the case. Therefore, the more stringent obligation of disclosure will apply only upon a specific direction from the president following an application by one party.

The president also has wide powers to make a 'third party disclosure order' requiring a person who is not a party to the proceedings to disclose any document or other material. This direction can be made upon application by either party. The president must be satisfied that the documents or material sought are likely to support the applicant's case or adversely affect the case of the other party. An order may attach to a third party only if the documents sought are within the power, possession and control of that person. Further, disclosure will be ordered only if it is necessary for the fair determination of the case. The parties should consider very carefully before attempting to use this provision as a 'fishing expedition' for documents which may or may not be relevant. An application in such circumstances is unlikely to be successful.

In relation to disclosure, reg 12 establishes a strict requirement that documents, once disclosed, can be used only for the purpose of the proceedings. There is therefore an implied obligation of confidentiality outside the proceedings. Disclosure will only apply to documents which can be the subject of disclosure in general county court proceedings, which means that documents attracting 'privilege' cannot be the subject of a disclosure order. Examples of privileged documents include communications between a solicitor and his or her client, or documents prepared solely in contemplation of proceedings.

Before making any direction under reg 12, the president must take into account issues of confidentiality and commercial sensitivity, so that representations can be made to the effect that disclosure could adversely affect a party in some way not connected to the proceedings. In most cases, documents required to be disclosed will not have particular commercial sensitivity, and it is submitted that this provision will rarely be invoked, and only in the most unusual of circumstances.

The president will make a direction about the preparation of tribunal 'bundles', including who shall prepare them and the date by which copies are to be lodged with the secretary. The bundles should be in logical order with an index and sections where appropriate. They should contain all the documents (including witness statements) upon which both parties intend to rely at the hearing so both parties should cooperate to agree the content of the bundle.

14.7.4 Witness evidence

Forms B5 and B6 will request details of any witnesses on whose evidence a party intends to rely. At the directions stage, the president may direct the parties to exchange (either simultaneously or sequentially) a witness statement on whose evidence a party wishes to rely. The statement must contain a 'statement of truth' at the end, worded 'I believe that the facts stated in this witness statement are true'. The statement must be signed by the person who makes it.

Witness statements should be clear and concise. They should introduce the witness by stating his or her position and role and, if relevant, some of his or her personal or career history, and qualifications. The statement should then set out the witness's factual evidence, concentrating on the issues, and the arguments being advanced, in the case.

The president has the power to exclude a witness's evidence if he or she considers that it will be unfair in all the circumstances to consider it, or it would not assist the tribunal in determining the case. Further, the evidence can be excluded if the party wishing to rely on it has failed to submit the statement in compliance with the tribunal's direction. Parties should therefore pay careful attention to the deadlines set by the president in his or her directions. Failure to adhere to such directions can result in an unless order (described above), or a direction excluding the evidence from the procedings.

The president also has the power to direct that a witness shall not give oral evidence at the hearing, which means that the tribunal can consider the witness statement without the witness being present. In practical terms, in most circumstances it is preferable to ensure that the witness is present to give oral evidence since this can be more persuasive than simply a written statement. Issues of witness credibility may need to be considered. However, it may be time and costs saving to avoid having a witness present to oral evidence if that evidence can be agreed with the other party or is uncontroversial.

14.7.5   Expert evidence

In addition to witness evidence, the president can direct the involvement of an expert if he or she considers that it would be of assistance to the tribunal in determining the case. For example, the tribunal may decide that a qualified accountant be appointed to report on the financial viability of an establishment or agency in an appeal against a notice of proposal to cancel registration for a failure to demonstrate financial viability in accordance with the 2000 Act. It should be noted that the onus is upon the tribunal to appoint the expert, not the parties themselves, and reg 13 of the Tribunal Regulations requires the tribunal to pay such reasonable expert fees as the president may determine. When an expert report is obtained, the secretary must supply the parties with copies in advance of the hearing, or determination of the appeal on the papers if there is to be no oral hearing. Further, the president can direct that the expert attend the hearing to give evidence.

14.7.6   Witness summonses

As in civil court proceedings the president has power to make an order requiring a person to attend as a witness at the date, time and place set out in the summons, and to answer any questions or produce documents or other material in his or her possession, power or control relating to any issue in the case. Failure to attend in accordance with the summons constitutes an offence. The recipient of the summons, can, however, apply in writing to the secretary for the summons to be varied or set aside.

A summons will be valid only if the witness has been given at least 5 working days' notice of the hearing, and necessary expenses of his or her attendance have been paid to him or her.

14.7.7 Children and vulnerable adult witnesses

Regulation 17 of the Tribunal Regulations set out special rules in relation to the giving of evidence by children and vulnerable adults. The president must give a direction before a child can give evidence in person, and such direction will be made only if the president considers that the welfare of the child will not be prejudiced in giving evidence.

The president must take necessary steps to safeguard the welfare of the child, including arranging for use of a video link where possible and appointment of a person with appropriate skills to facilitate the giving of evidence by the child.

In the case of vulnerable adults, the rules are slightly different. A vulnerable adult can be required to give evidence unless the president directs that it would not be in the best interests of the vulnerable adult to do so. The parties have an opportunity to make written representations and, again, the president should consider arrangements to safeguard the welfare of the vulnerable adult, including the use of video link and appointment of an appropriately qualified person to facilitate the giving of evidence.

14.7.8 Other miscellaneous case management powers

Care Standards Tribunal hearings are public proceedings. However, the president can make a restricted reporting order prohibiting the publication of any matter in the proceedings likely to identify the applicant, or any child or vulnerable adult witness to the public. Further, the president can make a direction excluding the press and/or the public from the hearing to the effect that the hearing is conducted in private. The president may exercise such power where he or she considers it necessary to safeguard the welfare of a child or vulnerable adult, protect a person's privacy, or avoid the risk of injustice in any other legal proceedings.

14.8 WITHDRAWAL OF APPEAL

Once an appeal process has been commenced, an applicant can notify the secretary in writing that he or she no longer wishes to pursue the proceedings. In these circumstances, the president must dismiss the proceedings and can consider whether to make a costs order against the applicant. Thus, where the appeal is being withdrawn following a negotiated settlement or resolution of the issues with the respondent, the applicant must make this clear to the secretary and explain why a costs order should not be made.

Similarly, the respondent can notify the secretary in writing that he or she no longer opposes the proceedings, and in these circumstances the president must determine the case in favour of the applicant, and may make a costs order. However, where the respondent withdraws his or her opposition to the proceedings, the president must consider making a costs order.

14.9   THE APPEAL HEARING

The tribunal has the power to regulate its own procedure as appropriate in accordance with the requirements of the particular case. Further, the president may direct that the case be heard in any location convenient to the parties. In many instances, the secretary will make every effort when listing the hearing at directions stage to find a venue close to the location of the applicant's establishment or agency. Alternatively, the appeal will be held at the tribunal's offices in London. In practice, the tribunal will be convened at the London offices if principal witnesses can reach Pocock Street within 90 minutes by commuting to a London main travel arrival centre. Video-link has been and will be extensively used to assist out-of-area witnesses.

At the commencement of the hearing, the chairperson must explain the order of proceedings the tribunal proposes to adopt. Either party can, of course, have legal representation, or conduct the proceedings on its own behalf. If either party fails to attend, the tribunal may still hear and determine the case.

The chairperson will determine which party will present its case first. In most cases this will be the respondent as it is the respondent which has the 'burden' of proving its decision giving rise to the appeal was justified, who or which will be entitled to make an opening speech, and will then be expected to introduce the evidence including witness evidence in support of its case. The president may direct in advance of the hearing that a witness statement is to be the evidence-in-chief, which means that the statement will simply be read over by the tribunal and accepted as that witness's evidence. The opposing party will then have an opportunity to cross-examine the witness and there may be re-examination by the applicant as the tribunal shall direct.

The applicant will then make its opening speech and lead its evidence, with an opportunity for cross-examination and re-examination in the same way.

Both parties will have an opportunity to make their final submissions at such stage as the tribunal shall direct.

It is open to the tribunal to require that any witness give evidence on oath or by affirmation as in civil court proceedings. However, this requirement may be dispensed with, particularly if there is no issue concerning witness credibility, which is more likely to be the case where the issues turn on legal points rather than disputed facts.

14.10   TRIBUNAL'S DECISION

Since there are three members of every tribunal, the decision can be a majority of 2:1. The written decision must record whether the decision was unanimous, or taken by the majority.

The tribunal may be in a position to hand down its decision at the conclusion of the hearing, but in some circumstances this may be reserved to a later date. When the decision is made, it must be recorded without delay in a document signed and dated by the chairperson.

The written decision must state the reason for the decision and what order the tribunal has made as a result of its decision. The secretary must send a copy of the written decision to each party as soon as reasonably possible, together with a notice explaining the parties' rights of review or any further appeal (see below). There may be a right of further appeal to the High Court and from the High Court to the Court of Appeal and the House of Lords depending on the nature of the case before the tribunal.

Where the appeal was against a magistrates' court order for emergency closure under s 20 of the 2000 Act, the secretary must also send a copy of the written decision to the magistrate who made the order, as soon as reasonably practicable.

The tribunal's decision will be entered in its records and posted on the tribunal's website, and a formal tribunal report can be obtained from the secretary upon payment of a fee. However, it is understood that the tribunal does not in fact charge. The tribunal's reported decisions are available for public inspection and may be published in electronic form. Tribunal decisions are likely to be available from the tribunal website (see above).[1]

14.11 COSTS

The tribunal has power to make a costs order for payment of a party's legal costs or other expenses under reg 24 of the Tribunal Regulations. However, the power to make a costs order will be exercised only if a party has acted unreasonably in bringing or conducting the proceedings. In such circumstances, the tribunal may order that one party make a payment to the other party to cover costs incurred by that party. There is no automatic right to a costs award in the event of a successful outcome, and costs will be awarded only where the conduct or behaviour of the paying party is considered to have been unreasonable. The test has been described by Judge Pearl as a high one.[2]

In causes of withdrawal of an appeal, the tribunal will not take into account untested allegations. The tribunal will be impressed by an early withdrawal of an appeal.[3]

Where the tribunal is invited to make a costs order, the party seeking costs must provide a schedule of costs incurred in respect of the proceedings. The opposing party can make representations and the tribunal must consider whether that party would be able to comply with a costs order.

---

1   Some cases may have been subject to a restricted reporting order so will not be generally available for public inspection.
2   *Dr RA Fairburn v NCSC* (2002) 76 NC.
3   *Fun Camps Ltd and Others v OFSTED* (2002) 124 EY.

Once a costs order has been made it can be enforced in the same way as a judgment or order of the county court.

14.12 REVIEW OF DECISION

Under reg 25 of the Tribunal Regulations a party can apply to the president for the tribunal's decision to be reviewed if it is considered that:

(a) the decision was wrongly made as a result of an error on the part of the tribunal;
(b) a party who failed to appear at the hearing or to be represented had good and sufficient reason for failing to appear; or
(c) there was an obvious error in the decision.

An application to the president under reg 25 must be made no later than 10 working days after the date on which the decision was sent to the party. The application must be made in writing, stating the grounds for the review in full.

The president can refuse the application if he or she believes that it has no reasonable prospects of success. The party seeking the review must ensure therefore that his or her grounds are fully set out in the application.

An application for review will be determined after the parties have had an opportunity to be heard by the tribunal which decided the case, or another tribunal panel appointed by the president.

On review, the tribunal can confirm or vary the decision, or substitute such other decision as it thinks fit. Alternatively, the tribunal can order a complete rehearing before the same or a differently constituted tribunal, as appropriate.

Chapter 15

FINANCE AND FINANCING

15.1 INTRODUCTION

Among the many areas the Care Standards Act 2000 (the 2000 Act) brings under the scrutiny of external inspections for the first time is the financial management of registered enterprises. Prior to this legislation, persons seeking registration for a new care home were often required to make submissions to show that the home would be financially viable, but, once registered, finances were not a matter the registration authority would usually take account of. This all changed with the introduction of the 2000 Act, and the National Care Standards Commission (NCSC) will have wide-ranging powers to inspect accounts, accounting records and business plans. The registered enterprise will have an ongoing duty to demonstrate its financial viability.

The obligations of registered enterprises are set out in the various Regulations and national minimum standards. These vary in their wording between the different registration categories and there are certain requirements specific to only certain registration categories. However, some broad requirements which apply to most or all of the registration categories are discussed below.

(1) Suitable accounting and financial procedures must be adopted to demonstrate current financial viability and to ensure that there is effective and efficient management of the business.
(2) Adequate insurance cover must be put in place.
(3) Adequate systems must be set up to record transactions.
(4) Certified accounts must be prepared at least annually.
(5) A business and financial plan must be created, which is open to inspection and reviewed at least annually.
(6) Certain requirements must be met in circumstances where the registered establishment becomes subject to formal insolvency proceedings.
(7) Funds belonging to service users should be managed by service users wherever possible and, where management on behalf of the service user is required, that funds be kept separate, and are properly accounted for and managed.

Most of the above simply represent good accounting and business practice, and many registered enterprises will already have systems in place that need little, if any, change to achieve compliance with the new legislation. However, some smaller operators that have been used to controlling enterprises through the cash book/bank account, combined with their particular knowledge of the enterprises, and with accounts prepared once a year for tax return purposes, may need to make substantial changes to their systems. That said, the appropriate level of system will vary with the size and complexity of the enterprise itself. If the enterprise is small and relatively straightforward, the accounting systems required will similarly be simple.

Although the Regulations and national minimum standards impose requirements on registered persons, they also indicate that the NCSC 'may' request information from registered persons. It is under no obligation to do so. Whilst the NCSC will be expected to examine financial plans in detail at the time of an initial registration, it is not clear what its role will be in looking at financial matters thereafter. It may be that for the majority of registered enterprises, the NCSC will merely request a copy of the annual accounts and the annual business plan, provided these indicate no concern over the viability of the registered enterprise. For established enterprises, the NCSC has indicated that it may only examine annual accounts on a sample basis. However, the NCSC is likely to be more robust in the use of its powers if it has other grounds for believing that a registered enterprise is unviable or is failing to deliver effective and efficient management, for example where there have been consistent breaches of other standards or where improvements required to meet standards have not been carried out due to lack of funds.

15.2 FINANCIAL VIABILITY

Financial viability is not defined anywhere in the Regulations or national minimum standards. It is not a matter that has previously been considered in the context of an ongoing registration requirement. The definition of what constitutes financial viability will vary with the circumstances of the registered enterprise. It is logical to suppose that the overriding context which will be used by the NCSC will be the ability for the registered enterprise to continue to deliver the service to service users (as set out, where appropriate, in the enterprise's statement of purpose).

It is important to distinguish 'non-viability' from 'insolvency'. 'Insolvency' is usually defined as either an excess of liabilities over assets (the balance sheet test) or an inability to pay debts as and when they fall due (the cash flow test). Neither of these is an adequate test of financial viability on its own. For instance, the application of certain accounting standards used to produce formal accounts can operate to produce a balance sheet showing net liabilities even though the underlying enterprise is profitable and generating cash. In such a case the registered enterprise would usually be considered to be financially viable.

The cash flow test is more reliable: over the longer term, an enterprise will need to generate sufficient cash to enable it to meet the costs and investment necessary to provide service users with an acceptable level of service. In commercial enterprises the funds will be generated mainly from trading, loan capital and investment through shares or owner's capital. However, in relation to not-for-profit organisations, significant other income may be generated from donations, endowments or grants that are used to subsidise trading losses and produce a level or type of service which would not otherwise be possible. Other situations may exist whereby a commercial enterprise effectively subsidises a registered part of its operations because this enhances the income in the organisation's main business. An example of this in the past was where care homes operated a small domiciliary care agency at a loss in the belief that this acted as a good source of marketing for the main care home business.

It is worth considering some of the potential threats to financial viability faced by a registered enterprise. Examples are set out below, dealing first with circumstances that could lead to the short-term or immediate threat to financial viability, and secondly with those that could threaten the viability of the enterprise over the longer term.

15.2.1 Short-term threats

Short-term threats to the viability of a registered enterprise include:

– The registered enterprise is insolvent and is unable to pay its creditors. This would probably be as a result of trading losses or possibly because drawings exceed available profits, but it could also be a result of cashflow problems, for example where the payment of fees is delayed by the legal process being completed prior to the distribution of a deceased's estate, or where a privately funded resident is dependent on selling a property to meet his or her fee commitments. In such circumstances the enterprise may therefore be unable to pay staff or obtain supplies to carry on its business, but can continue to operate under the protection and control afforded by a formal insolvency procedure, as discussed further below.
– A sudden event causes a financial disaster for the enterprise. Examples of such financial disaster could include: a substantial liability arising from the loss of a court case; an uninsured loss; a natural disaster such as flooding; loss of income due to the loss of a contract or a reduction in occupancy due to a flu epidemic; grant income being withdrawn; or the write-off of a significant debtor when a key customer becomes insolvent.
– A loss of funding occurs because of the withdrawal of facilities by a bank, parent company or other investor.
– Circumstances mean that the registered enterprise is unable to continue to provide the registered service, for example because of a lack of trained staff or a strike.

15.2.2 Longer-term threats

Longer-term threats to the viability of a registered enterprise include:

– Profits generated by the registered enterprise are insufficient to fund the level of capital investment required in the business to meet increasing national or industry standards.
– Profits are insufficient to meet the requirements of drawings by the owner or to meet funding constraints imposed by funders.
– Wage inflation outstrips the ability to raise fees.

- Trading costs are not properly controlled.
- Interest rate rises take the cost of borrowing to an unsustainable level.
- There is a downturn in the market, for example due to a change in government policy or competition from a new operator.
- Fee income decreases due to an inability to charge higher fees or declining occupancy. The impact of this may be exacerbated if a previous high period of fee income has resulted in an increase in a turnover-related rent on leasehold premises.
- There is no successor management or owner for the enterprise as the return on capital capable of being generated by the business is too low.

15.2.3   Proof of financial viability

The registered enterprise should consider how it will demonstrate its financial viability to the NCSC should it be called upon to do so. For most viable enterprises this will be a case of providing a copy of annual accounts which show net assets on the balance sheet and profitable trading, and a copy of the annual business plan, showing that this situation is anticipated to continue. The various regulations give the NCSC the power to be provided with such information and documents as it may require for the purpose of considering the financial viability of the registered enterprise. Listed below are ways in which financial viability could be demonstrated. None of these on their own, or even collectively, is proof of financial viability, but provides evidence to support such viability.

- The enterprise has up-to-date accounting records that can provide current information on the state of the enterprise's finances. Annual accounts are audited or certified by an independent accountant and produced within a reasonable period after the year end.
- The accounts show that the enterprise is profitable after taking account of depreciation, interest and financing charges, loan capital payments, and drawings or dividends.
- The balance sheet shows that the enterprise has net assets, after taking account of any off-balance sheet financing (but, as noted above, a balance sheet with net liabilities will not necessarily indicate non-viability).
- A guarantor of substance is in place to guarantee the enterprise's liabilities or make good any operating loss.
- Budgets or forecasts show that the enterprise will trade profitably. The evidence from these will be enhanced if the enterprise has previously always been accurate in its forecasting. This should include a cashflow forecast which ties in with the trading forecasts and includes non-profit matters such as capital expenditure, loan repayments, payment of tax liability, etc.
- If the cashflow forecast shows there is a funding requirement, then evidence should show that this is available, for example through a bank overdraft facility. The NCSC has the power to require a banker's reference, but banks are becoming increasingly wary of giving general references and those that are given are heavily caveated. However, such references may show that there are adequate facilities in place to meet a stated level of forecast funding requirements, and when those facilities fall due for renewal.

– In certain circumstances, other businesses under the same ownership or companies associated with the enterprise may have an effect on the financial viability of the registered enterprise, for example when they have guaranteed each other's liabilities. Where the registered enterprise is a company, the NCSC has the power to require information to be given to it as to its associated companies.

In addition to the national minimum standards requiring registered enterprises to have suitable accounting systems and procedures to be able to demonstrate financial viability, reg 13 of the National Care Standards Commission (Registration) Regulations 2001 states:

> 'If it appears to the registered person that the establishment or agency is likely to cease to be financially viable at any time within the following six months, the registered person should give a report to the Commission of the relevant circumstances.'

This does not mean that 6 months' notice must have been given to the NCSC before the registered enterprise becomes non-viable. Rather, it means that the NCSC must be informed of circumstances of impending or current non-viability immediately the registered person becomes aware of these, unless the circumstances will not arise for a period of more than 6 months. It is difficult to envisage that there will be many circumstances where the registered enterprise will have more than 6 months' notice of its financial non-viability.

Possible circumstances where the NCSC would be more likely to take action against a registered person for breach of reg 13 would be if it was already taking action against the registered person on other grounds, or if there was little or no notice given to the NCSC prior to a formal insolvency or cessation of the service. In these circumstances, the NCSC would have to consider whether the registered person knew or ought reasonably to have known that the registered enterprise was financially non-viable at an earlier stage than when notice was actually given.

The nature of the report given to the NCSC of the relevant circumstances will vary with those circumstances and how the registered person intends to proceed. The NCSC will wish to know whether the financial circumstances will have an adverse effect on the service given to service users and, if so, what this is likely to be and when it is likely to happen. If the registered person has a plan for a turnaround or rescue of the enterprise, it will be important to bring this to the attention of the NCSC at the earliest opportunity. The NCSC may require evidence that the rescue or turnaround plan has a realistic chance of success. Such a plan may incorporate a formal insolvency appointment (examined in more detail below). As with breaches of other standards, the NCSC will expect a recovery plan to be put in place to correct the breach. It will also be important to ensure that the matter is dealt with by persons at the NCSC with the financial training to understand the proposals being put forward, and that the details of the financial position are kept confidential, so as not to worsen the enterprise's position further. The NCSC has indicated that comments on the financial position of registered enterprises will only be included in inspection reports in exceptional circumstances and only after approval by a regional director.

It is important to realise that many registered enterprises will go through periods of poor trading or financial uncertainty, but will be able to survive these because of reserves built up, funding obtained from a bank or investor, or a successful turnaround strategy put in place. The decision of whether or not there is a requirement to inform the NCSC of the financial situation under reg 13 will therefore depend on the registered person's reasonable assessment as to certainty of the survival plans succeeding and the degree to which these are within his or her control.

15.3 INSURANCE

Part of ensuring the financial viability of a registered enterprise is that adequate insurance is in place to cover any contingencies that may befall the enterprise.

The Regulations state that the NCSC may require the registered person to provide it with a certificate of insurance in respect of liability for death, injury, public liability, damage or other loss. The national minimum standards provide more detail. The exact wording varies in each of the categories, but generally includes:

–   cover at full replacement value on buildings, fixtures, fittings and equipment;
–   business interruption cover; and
–   cover for liabilities to employees, service users and third parties at a level appropriate to the extent of activities undertaken but with a minimum value of £5 million.

This should not prove to be too difficult for the majority of registered enterprises. At the time of writing, the minimum level of employee liability offered by most insurance covers is £10 million, but the level of public liability cover offered can be as low as £2 million.

The majority of care homes are now insured on specialist packages designed specifically for the industry and these should have no difficulty in complying with the legislation at a competitive premium. However, if cover is arranged through a non-specialist insurer, checks should be made to ensure that the cover is compliant. Care should be taken to ensure that the insurance covers all the registration categories, particularly where an additional category is added to the registration. Certain categories are regarded as high risk and may be difficult to cover or require much higher premiums to be paid.

The national minimum standards state that nurses agencies must ensure that nurses have professional indemnity cover of not less than £5 million in respect of their own actions in private practice.

15.4 FINANCIAL MANAGEMENT

The national minimum standards state that suitable financial and accounting systems must be put in place to ensure 'efficient and effective management', as well as financial viability. What such systems will entail will depend on the size and complexity of the business. It is important to note that these systems should be a tool of the management in carrying out its duties, rather than a paper trail put in place to satisfy regulators. Over-complicated systems may simply detract management from its functions, but proper systems will give management the information it requires in a timely manner. Most enterprises will already have adequate systems in place, if only to meet their audit/tax requirements and the existing needs of management.

Most enterprises will use some form of computerised package for maintaining their accounts. Some will use an outside contractor to carry out all or part of the accounting functions, and this is most common in the use of payroll bureaux or where a factoring company undertakes the management of the sales ledger.

For the majority of enterprises, the systems will include the following:

–   a cash book showing receipts and payments reconciled to bank account statements on a regular (usually monthly) basis;
–   a sales ledger showing invoices raised, when these are due for payment and when payment is overdue, which should be in such a form that late payments can be chased and effective credit control operated;
–   a purchase ledger showing the details of all purchase and expense invoices received and accepted for payment and when these are paid, which should be capable of showing at any point in time what the business owes to its creditors and what payments are overdue;
–   payroll systems and personnel records;
–   a fixed asset register (unless the level of fixed assets is not material);
–   a nominal ledger;
–   regular production of management accounts or business information;
–   where the business information is maintained on computer, systems to ensure that it is kept secure and that back-up copies are maintained at a separate location;
–   clear lines of responsibility for financial affairs, including who has the authority to order goods, enter contracts, or employ staff for the enterprise;
–   where funds are held on behalf of service users (eg pocket money or personal allowances), a separate record of these monies.

This is not a comprehensive list, and individual enterprises will need to decide what other information is required by management. Accounts and business plans will have to be prepared (both of which are considered below) and the accounting system must be capable of providing information on these plans. The system must be capable of recording every transaction entered into by the enterprise, and separating these into their relevant categories. Certain regulations (including those for care homes) specify that the enterprise's accounts must identify separately rent, mortgage payments, food costs, heating costs and wages and salaries.

National minimum standard 13.2 also states that 'Receipts are issued in respect of every payment to the agency'. This requirement does not appear in any of the other national minimum standards and it is not clear what specific purpose it serves here. With payments increasingly made by BACs or electronically and rarely by cash, this is not a practice with which many nurse agencies will currently comply. It may be that a monthly statement showing payments received during the month will suffice as a form of receipt for this purpose.

The regulations for Domiciliary Care Agencies and Nurses Agencies specify that the following financial records must be maintained for inspection. These must be kept separately from any other business which shares the same premises as the agency, and must be maintained securely, in good order and retained for a period of at least 3 years:

- a record of all business transacted by the company;
- counterfoils or copies of all receipts issued;
- details of the charges payable by each service user in respect of the supply of a nurse/personal care;
- records of tax and National Insurance contributions relating to each person who works for the purpose of the agency.

The Nurses Agencies Regulations 2002 also state that where the agency is an employment business, it must ensure that nurses are paid within 10 days of submitting a valid timesheet or other proof that payment is due.

The Domiciliary Care Agencies Regulations 2002 also require that the registered person maintain a register of interests in which he or she must declare any financial interest in, or connection with, any other agency. The registered manager must make a similar declaration in respect of him or herself and his or her relatives.

15.5   ACCOUNTS

15.5.1   Annual accounts

The NCSC has a right to request a copy of the registered enterprise's accounts. Where accounts are not audited, they must be certified by an accountant. This is a new requirement for individuals, partnerships and companies which are currently below the thresholds for an audit to be required. However, in practice, many enterprises will already employ an accountant to prepare accounts or present them to the Inland Revenue for tax purposes, who will usually be able to certify the accounts to the NCSC.

Annual accounts should be drawn up using UK accounting standards on a full accrual basis, with full account taken of any material accruals, prepayments, provisions and including a provision for depreciation on fixed assets. The accounts should include a balance sheet showing the assets and liabilities of the enterprise at the year or period end. The balance sheet should distinguish between fixed and current assets and between creditors falling due for payment within one year and those falling due after more than one year.

The regulations for Care Homes, Domiciliary Care Agencies and Nurses Agencies specify that the accounts should show the following costs: rent; payments under a mortgage; and expenditure on food, heating, salaries and wages.

The notes to the accounts should disclose the accounting policies adopted in drawing up the accounts. These should also provide details of any contingent liabilities the enterprise may have (such as guarantees given to associated companies). Where assets have been revalued, this should be explained, together with the basis of the revaluation.

Given that annual accounts may be used by the NCSC in assessing the viability of a registered enterprise, care should be taken in ensuring that the accounts are straightforward. Context and explanations should be added where necessary, particularly if there are any figures that might seem to be indicators of poor profitability or viability. Examples of when explanations could be useful are:

–   where trading has suffered in the short term due to planned changes in the business;
–   where the business is being supported by its owner or a third party of substance;
–   where a substantial part of the liabilities represent long-term loans from the owner/shareholder;
–   where there has been a write-down of the value of the assets as a result of their revaluation, which has no impact on the operating performance of the enterprise.

15.5.2   Management accounts

As well as annual accounts, management should consider what information it requires on a more regular basis to help it run the business. In small, owner-managed businesses, this need will be less, since management will be aware of many of the factors governing the enterprise's performance from its day-to-day involvement in it. In this context, management accounts will merely represent a check on the owner's own knowledge. In many cases, registered enterprises will already be producing management accounts for their banks, which will be adequate. Management accounts should be produced on at least a quarterly basis, but it may be appropriate to produce these on a monthly basis.

In larger enterprises, more complex management accounting will be required, particularly where the information is the main check for monitoring the performance of local management. Monthly management accounts would be usual, and management may require individual registered enterprises to report even more frequently on certain data, such as occupancy of care home beds, or staff hours.

Management accounts should usually be prepared on an accruals basis, but it is rarely necessary to perform a full calculation of accruals and prepayments unless they are substantial. Consideration should be given to whether a simple trading account is sufficient, or whether cashflow or balance sheet information is also necessary.

Management accounts should be produced in a format where results can be compared to budgets for the period, and explanations given for any variances. This may include expressing the information not simply in a normal accounting form, but also using ratios that are more useful to management in monitoring the performance of the enterprise, particularly compared with what may be run by the same enterprise. This analysis can help management identify the cause of poor or good performance. Examples of such ratios might include: percentage of beds occupied; average fee per service user; costs of food per service user per day; and staff costs as a proportion of fees.

15.6   BUSINESS PLANNING

The national minimum standards for care homes, younger adults, domiciliary care, residential family centres and nurses agencies all require that registered enterprises have a 'business and financial plan open to inspection and reviewed annually'. The *National Minimum Standards for Domiciliary Care Agencies* also specifies that business plans should cover:

– information about the business;
– financial planning and projections;
– human resource implications; and
– plans for the development of the service.

This gives a good indication of what the NCSC will expect to see in the business plans of other registration categories. In assessing what to include in the plan, management will need to consider who it will be used by and for what reasons (discussed further below).

Business plans are open to inspection by the NCSC and can therefore be commented on in its open inspection reports. Nothing in the national minimum standards indicates that business plans themselves are open to inspection by persons other than the NCSC or the registered enterprise's management. However, this will be a matter for the management to consider, since parts of the document may well be of benefit to service users and staff, particularly with regard to changes or developments in the service. Sections of the plan that are disclosed to staff and service users may need to be edited or adapted in their presentation so as to be clear and appropriate to those parties.

However, it is likely that the key use of business plans will be as a tool for efficient management of the enterprise. In many cases this will consist of bringing together budgets and plans that may have been prepared informally in the past into one formal document. Financial matters within business plans may be highly confidential and this should be made clear to all parties to whom the document is given, including the NCSC.

Where appropriate, a registered enterprise may wish to involve service users in its planning process and in developing the business plan, for example in discussing the spending priorities or the development of the service. This is a requirement of standard 43.6 of the *National Minimum Standards for Care Homes for Younger Adults*.

Financial projections should, at minimum, include a trading projection and cashflow projection, together with some notes on the key assumptions made in compiling these projections. An integrated set of trading, cashflow and balance sheet projections will make the projections more robust.

As noted above, an enterprise's cashflow is a key indicator of its viability and success over the short term. Cashflow projections should therefore include, where appropriate:

– reasonable payment periods for both creditors and debtors;
– capital expenditure;
– repayment of loans and hire purchase contracts;
– funds introduced through investment or borrowings;
– funds paid out as owner's drawings or dividends;
– taxes payable;
– funds generated or paid out in the sale or purchase of fixed assets or parts of the enterprise.

As a minimum, financial projections should be prepared showing the year ahead as a whole. For management purposes, it will be useful to split this down into the same periods as used for the management accounts (usually monthly or quarterly) so that the actual results shown in the management accounts can be compared easily with the projections or budgets. Where the management accounts include key performance indicators such as the ratios noted above, it would be useful to set these out in the projections for ease of comparison.

Business plans should address any outstanding requirements or recommendations identified at previous inspections. Where appropriate, there should also be included details of how the enterprise intends to become compliant with the national minimum standards by the relevant deadlines.

It is important to note that each registered enterprise should have its own business plan. Where a number of different registered enterprises are owned and run as a single business, it will be necessary to separate figures that relate to a particular registered enterprise, and those that are relevant to central or head office.

Where unknown material contingencies or variances exist at the time of preparing the financial projections (eg it is unsure whether a key contract will be renewed), the enterprise may wish to prepare its projections on both bases. Alternatively, if a material assumption made in the projections is found to be wrong, it may be necessary to revise the projections part way through the financial year.

In addition to the plans for the immediate year ahead, the enterprise should consider its longer-term plans. This would include plans for expansion or contraction, new services, or infrequent but substantial expenditure, such as roof repairs.

15.7 REACTION TO FINANCIAL DOWNTURN

When a registered enterprise suffers a financial downturn, its management should consider the issues raised in the discussion on financial viability above. In particular, it will need to consider whether there is a threat to the viability of the enterprise and whether the NCSC needs to be informed of the circumstances under reg 13 of the National Care Standards Commission (Registration) Regulations 2001.

The management will need to understand the reasons underlying the downturn. Are they long term or only temporary? Are they structural or something more easily addressed such as management personnel changes? It is likely that the enterprise will need to revisit its business plan, and possibly resubmit or discuss it with the NCSC.

Management must take account of whether the enterprise has sufficient reserves to survive whilst action is taken to respond to any downturn. Very often, cash will be the key indicator, and management should concentrate on controlling this tightly. Are debtors collected promptly enough and can longer credit arrangements be obtained from suppliers? Are there any assets that are non-essential to the enterprise which could be disposed of to raise cash, or could funds be raised through sale and leaseback of certain assets? If funding is insufficient, can funds be borrowed or raised from an investor?

All the services offered by the enterprise should be examined to see whether they are making a profitable or cash-generative contribution to the enterprise. Unprofitable contracts may need to be dropped or renegotiated. There may be scope for offering additional services or increasing fees to generate further income. However, changes in services subject to registration may have to be agreed with the NCSC, and may require a change in registration.

The costs of the enterprise should be examined carefully to see whether savings could be made. Purchasing arrangements could be renegotiated or put out to competitive tender. There may be scope for reducing staff hours or changing the conditions or working arrangements. However, any such changes may again need to be agreed with the NCSC, so as to reassure it that the appropriate level of service to service users is maintained.

If it appears that the enterprise will not be viable in the longer term, then more radical planning may be necessary. Management may need to consider closing, selling or changing the business of the enterprise. An insolvency arrangement could free the enterprise from the burden of creditors, and this may be an option if the underlying business would then become viable. However, existing management runs the risk of losing control of the enterprise under most forms of insolvency procedure.

In considering options that result in a material change to the enterprise, such as closure, disposal, restructuring or changing the business, it is important to take account of the costs that will be associated with such changes. For instance, if a decision is made to close a care home for the elderly, it will be necessary to involve the NCSC fully, and to take the time to communicate with the residents and give them sufficient notice to be able to arrange alternative accommodation (there may be a minimum notice period in the resident's contract). During the closure period, income will drop rapidly as residents leave, but staff and other costs may be fairly static, leading to large losses. Redundancy costs for staff may be substantial, particularly if they have been employed by that enterprise for many years. The taxation effect of any restructuring plan should also be considered.

If there is a change in the registered person or manager as a result of the restructuring, a re-registration requirement will arise, and the newly registered person will have to submit plans and financial projections to prove that the enterprise will be financially viable in its new form.

15.8   INSOLVENCY

Regulations governing the insolvency of a registered enterprise provide that:

– the registered person must inform the NCSC when an insolvency prac- titioner is appointed or when it is proposed that an insolvency practitioner be appointed;
– the appointed insolvency practitioner must inform the NCSC of his appointment forthwith;
– the insolvency practitioner must appoint a manager to take day-to-day charge of the registered enterprise in any case where there is no registered manager; and
– within 28 days of his appointment, the insolvency practitioner must inform the NCSC of his or her intentions regarding the future operation of the registered enterprise.

These conditions apply where:

– the registered person is an individual, and a trustee in bankruptcy is appointed, or the registered person makes a composition or arrangement with his other creditors;
– the registered person is a partnership, and a receiver or manager is appointed to its property; and
– the registered person is a company, and a receiver or manager, liquidator or provisional liquidator is appointed to the company.

It is clear from the above that the legislation contemplates registered enterprises trading and operating under the protection of formal insolvency proceedings. This will give the opportunity to save a registered enterprise, either through a financial restructuring (eg via a company voluntary arrangement) or through the sale of the enterprise to a third party.

The main difference between the new regime and the practices that existed under previous registration is that insolvency practitioners must provide a report to the NCSC within 28 days on his or her intentions in relation to the registered enterprise's future. The report should cover the following matters:

– whether it is intended that the registered enterprise will continue to trade and, if so, for how long;
– if applicable, what plans exist for an orderly cessation of business so as to protect vulnerable service users;

- if a going concern sale, whether of the business is anticipated and the likely timescales;
- if there is to be a restructuring of the business, whether to allow it to continue;
- how the business will be funded to ensure that services continue to be provided to service users; and
- how it is intended that any concerns raised by the NCSC will be dealt with (eg any outstanding requirements from previous inspection reports).

Whilst the regulations do not specify all the types of insolvency arrangement that could apply to registered enterprises (eg the appointment of an administrator to a company or partnership, or the appointment of a receiver to the property of an individual), it will most likely be appropriate for the registered person and insolvency practitioner to comply with the above conditions in any event.

15.9   FUNDS BELONGING TO SERVICE USERS

The basic rule is that service users, wherever possible, should look after their own financial affairs, maintain their own bank and building society accounts and carry their immediate cash needs in a purse or wallet. Support, training and assistance should be provided to the service user to do this where necessary. In a residential setting, there needs to be somewhere accessible for residents to keep their cash, account books and other valuables safe and secure.

If the service user is unable to look after his or her own financial affairs, it is usual for someone with power of attorney on behalf of the service user, or a close relative, to manage the service user's finances on his or her behalf. However, in certain circumstances it may fall to the registered manager to look after the financial affairs of a resident, provided this is agreed with the resident (if possible), and with the resident's relatives and social worker.

Funds belonging to service users must be kept and accounted for separately from the registered enterprise's own funds and records. Unless it is a purely nominal amount (eg pocket money for school children), money should not be held as cash, but should be paid into separate interest-bearing accounts in the name of the service user. If the service user has need of cash to meet small purchases, a small amount may be held by the registered manager to meet such expenditure.

An individual ledger account should be maintained for each service user for whom funds are kept. This should detail receipts and payments out of the account, whether paid out of a bank account or from cash held. It should include sufficient detail to fully identify every transaction. Payments out should be authorised, and a copy of the receipt for the goods or services purchased attached. Wherever possible, the service user should countersign for the money or goods received.

Subject to the service user's stated wishes, funds received for the service user should be paid directly into his or her bank account immediately on receipt. Where funds are mixed with other monies, such as payment of fees, a system should be put in place to identify these and separate them as soon as possible after receipt. This may involve the payment of the entire amount into the service user's bank account and then the payment out of that account of the funds relating to fees. Funds that belong to the service user should never be paid into a general bank account belonging to the service provider.

INDEX

References are to paragraph numbers.